LIVING OUT LOUD WITH GRACE, GRIT, AND GRATITUDE

LIVING OUT LOUD WITH GRACE, GRIT, AND GRATITUDE
(with over three hundred mini-stories)

By Michael John McArthur

COPYRIGHT 2022

ALL RIGHTS RESERVED. No portion of this publication may be reproduced or transmitted in any form or fashion, or by any means, including but not limited to electronic or mechanical. This prohibition includes photocopying, recording, or any information storage and / or retrieval system whatsoever without permission in writing from the copyright owner, except for brief quotations for review, for authorized promotional opportunities, or where permitted by law.

The author and the publisher have made every effort to ensure the accuracy and completeness of information contained herein, though acknowledging that some of it may be partially or totally inaccurate. They assume no responsibility for errors, inaccuracies, omissions, or any inconsistencies herein. Any slights of people, places, or organizations are purely and solely unintentional. Please do not participate in or encourage piracy.

ISBN: 979-8-9850177-6-2

JEBWizard Publishing

First Edition 2022

Printed in the United States of America by Ingramspark

Back photo Credit Anna Bunch

DEDICATION

In all of my life, I have tried to do the right thing, for the right reason, the first time. Without the help of my beautiful and loving wife, Becky I could neither have succeeded nor survived.

"I am authorized to tell you that!"

She and my whole family continue to give me the moral compass upon which to set my sights, and to lead rather than follow. I am forever thankful for every tender drop of sometimes force multiplied guidance that they continue to provide.

Table of Contents

Acknowledgment i
Forward ii
Opening Letter to Becky, Jenny, John, Pat, and Kathy 1
    Open Invitation to Read, Learn, Laugh, and Cry 1
    Wilson County Motor Speedway 2
    Wilson County Fair 2
    "Hawkshaw Hawkins" 4
    "Lucky Me" 5
    "Stay Out of the Road" 6
    The Shriners Arrive 9
    The Ku Klux Klan 10
    What Does "Ill Repute" Mean, Anyway? 11
    Cherry Bombs, Silver Tips, Black Cats, and M-80s 11
    "The Goat Man" 13
The Tobacco Trail Motel 16
    (June of 1947 through September of 1983) 16
    Wilson, North Carolina 16
    A Southern Belle and a Merchant Marine 17
    Contract Bridge 21
    "Shots Fired!" 23
    "Here Comes the Goat Man" 26
    Motel Duty 28
    Croppin' Tobacco 28
    The Fishing Hole 31
    "Sea food" and Tobacco Gum 34
    Liberty Tobacco Warehouse 37
    Waiting Tables at Parker's Barbecue Restaurant 1963 -1971 38
    Tip Thief 40
    Henry's Tenderloin Breakfast 41

Donkey Ray's Antics 43

Rowdies and Two Half Benjamins 44

Friends, the Beach, Ducks, and More 46

Warren Dixon Barnes 46

Emerald Isle 47

The Marines Have Landed 48

The Embers Club at Atlantic Beach 50

Then Came Purple Jesus 52

Junior-Senior Weekend 1967 53

Pranks and Martha Reeves and the Vandellas 54

Muscle Cars and Chaperones 56

Snooker and Other Games of Chance 57

The Nags Head Casino 59

Movin' On 62

"Leave 'em Lay…" 64

Taxpaid Bootleg and Homemade Hooch 65

"Sneak" 66

Texas Gulf Sulfur Company Aurora, North Carolina 67

Warren's Plunge 70

The Onslaught 71

"Pass the Pepper, Please" 73

Dr. Stotesbury's Goose Lodge — Heaven on Earth 74

The Peeping Tom 78

"Won't Nothing Come of It!" 87

Bloodhounds and Flashlights 90

Wilson County Fair Exposure 93

Hard Work and Other Blessings 96

The North Carolina State Highway Patrol — North Carolina's Finest —
Get Ready Michael John McArthur 96

State Fair Stories 96
Polished Chrome Wire Wheels and the Commotion They Wrought 101
Patrol Car Wrecks and other Calamities 103
   "The Good, the Bad, and the Ugly" 103
Bean Counters 107
Wreck Reports and Those Who Can Read Them 108
Joel Never Had a Wreck From Which He Didn't Learn Something 110
Princess Anne Visits Manteo 114
That Breathtaking Moment Oven the Croatan Sound 116
Agona Rules! 116
Westbound and Hammer Down 118
My Friend, Trooper Lin Godfrey 120
Kudzu Closeup 123
The Shootout 125
   Firefight on Governor Ehringhaus Road 125
Senior Resident Superior Court Judge Thomas S. Watts, and Judgment Day 134
Post-Traumatic Stress Disorder and a Brighter Future 135
Smokey Bear Hats 136
   "Don't Touch 'em" 136
"Just Too Drunk" 137
Speed Timing Devices 146
   The Other "STD" 146
Smokey Blackouts 148
Death Notifications 149
Midway Fiasco 149
   School Teacher: Billie Gray Womack and her Father, Bill Womack, Jr. 149
Joby Johnson's Five Lives 151
   Pedestrian: Joe Boy (Joby) Johnson 151

- Deputy James Walter Peal, Jr. 154
- Suffering Alongside Death 159
  - Chatham County Oil Tanker Drowning 159
- Mrs. Constance Goodwin 161
- I Feel "Eel" 162
- A Dark Cloud? 163

The North Carolina State Agricultural Fair 168
- Calling the Cavalry 168
- A Sheepdog, Fireworks, and a Torn Tunic 169
- Wolfpack Placard, and "You Can't Get There From Here" 171
- Mrs. Louisburg and the Magic of the S H P Helicopters 172
- "Country Come To Town" 174
- D-Cells and "HAPPY MOTORING" 176
- One "SLIM JIM" Is Just Not Enough 176

Gilchrist Bank Robbery Exercise SHP Hostages 179
- You'd a Really Had ta' Been There 179
  - "Do Fewer Things Better" 179
- The Future Colonel 181
- 40 Miles of "Git Back" 181

People's Bank Robbery and Billy Spruill Shooting 184
- The Bank Robbery 184
- The Cavalry Arrives 187
- GSR – Gun Shot Residue 192
- The "Porcupined" Patrol Car and Three Self-Inflicted Fatal Wounds .. 193

Building a Better World at $6.00 Per Hour 195
- NCSU and the Angel Farm 195
- Out of the "Field" and into the "Office" 198
- Those with Whom We Work 198
- Learning Things the Hard Way 199

Grinding Steel and the Co-eds 201

The Angel Farm and the .22 Caliber Rifle Gunfights 202

Bill Ellis's Barbecue, "Miss Wilson," and Gunfire 205

Roof Jobs, Bad Brakes, and a Slipping Clutch 207

Crabtree Valley Mall and "Juaquin" 210

The Methodist Orphanage and "The Car with No Top" 213

    Great Kids and Great Fun 213

Next Stop: The North Carolina Highway Patrol 214

Benjamin Franklin Chappell Rides Again as Only He Could 216

  From Harley Davidson Choppers to Black and Silvers to Piper Aircraft to The Pearly Gates 216

  The State Fair Rebel 216

  Ben's Bi-monthly Inspections, Dejections, Injections, And Rejections ... 218

  Language a Child Can Understand, Part One 219

  What Cassette Recorder 220

  Language a Child Can Understand, Part Two 222

  The Checking Station 223

  The Sunday Matinees 224

  Ben Chappell's Harley Davidson 227

  Trooper Chappell's Colt "Trooper" 228

  Factory Defects Galore 229

  The Infamous "Machine-Gun Search" of the Micro Minibus 230

  Warning Shots and Face Plants 231

  Paradise Road and All Its Glory 232

  Fruit Loops and Looney Toons 235

  Bless His Heart, Ben Goes Home 235

The Peerless, Fearless Sidekick Extraordinaire 238

Highway Patrolman Michael John McArthur Meets Julian Robert Hendrix 241

  Back to MY Sidekick, J. Robert Hendrix 242

"Is That a Bullet Hole in Your Car?" 244
"Wolfpacking" 246
Getting "Rolled" at Choke's Grill 247
Tonto and his Hook Truck 249
Mr. and Mrs. Do No Wrong 250
"Marine! Ten-Hut!" 251
Sheriff "Little Man" Broughton Invades the Bear's Den 253
"I Stobbed Him to Death!" 254
"Talkin'" 256
Hootie to the Rescue 258
Location, Location, Location 260
    Location #1, The Plane Crash 260
    Location #2, The Floater 261
    Location #3, Fishing/Driving Drunk 262
Don't Rob Your Neighbor in the Snow 263
Sneaky Snakes X 9 265
    #1. "The Flying Black Snake" 265
    #2. Who Put That Snake In The Telephone Booth? 266
    #3. Snakes in General 268
    #4 Snake Mail 269
    #5. Whose road is this, anyway? 271
Fire in the Hole, Almost 272
Puzzletown 274
"Leave It Go, Mama, Leave It Go" 276
Bessie's Bottom 278
The Good Life 281
    "Trash Ducks" to Treasure Trove 281
        "The Best Day Ever" 281
    Scrambled Eggs and Spanish Moss Sausage 286

Grandmother's House 288

Mayhem on the Millpond: Another History Making Hunt 289

One Shot = Five Ducks 290

"Sneak" on Wiggins Millpond Wilson, North Carolina 292

Mourning and White-winged Dove Hunt... 294

Opening Day 2019.. 294

Game On... 297

Hardison's Carolina Barbecue in Jamesville, N.C. 300

Watermen are Survivors 303

"Listen Close" 303

The Real Issues in Life 303

Life's Lessons 307

Chowan County's Bounty... 309

   A 5:00am FISHING OPPORTUNITY 309

William "Dossey" Pruden, V "The Salt of the Earth" Mathew 5:13 311

"Crabbing is an Acquired Skill" 313

H L and Sharon Bond, Vintage Americana 313

   Defying the Odds and Cheating the Grim Reaper 313

What a Benevolent Soul 317

Bambi, Buck, and H L 318

"I'll Stop Twice Next Time" 319

Returning a Favor... 320

H L to the Rescue 321

Big Snakes, Little Snakes, Live Snakes, Dead Snakes 323

   Good Snakes, Bad Snakes 323

Lucky, Lucky 324

"Watch 'Em Get Up" and a Remington .30-06 Rifle............................. 326

Four Units of Blood and a Remington .30-06 Rifle............................... 328

Fishing and Funning the Old-Fashioned Way.. 332

The Early Years... 332

- Our Cape Fear River Caper 335
- Jenny, Would You Please Sit Down! 336
- Moonshiners and Trotliners 337
- Raven Rock State Park 338
- Chatty Kathy "Loose Lips Sink Ships 340
- Fishing Poles, Fishing Holes, Fishing Frenzy and "Jump over Grandmother" 342
- Fish and Chips 344

An Elected Clerk of Superior Court in Chowan County, NC 346
- "The Perfect Clerk" 347
- Just What Does It Take To Be An Elected Clerk of the Superior Court? 348
- North Carolina Administrative Office of the Courts 351
  - Legal Quagmire! 351

Honor and Cherish Them, For They are the Wings Beneath our Wings ... 353
- The Raucous Caucus Pushes Its Luck 354
  - You Ready? 354
- Liar's Poker 358
- Slap the Table 359
- "Odd Man Out" 360
- "Is It Ten O'clock Yet?" 361

Dove Hunt Opening Day 2020, and other Trivia 364
- The Wary Woodcock and the Sly Sleuth 368
- Poachers and Bootleggers 369
- Shooting Doves in Self Defense 370
- Pungo County Store and the Memories 372
- Concealed Carry Handgun (CCH) Permit 373

BONUS! 377
- January 15, 2022 377
  - The Benevolence of an Eight-Year-Old: 377

- Swan Hunting– 101 377
- Preaching 379
- The Decoy Set 379
- The Ditch 380

Youth Tundra Swan Hunt - 2022 385
- February 12, 2022 385
- About the Author 392
- Index and Page References 394

Acknowledgment

A heart felt, "THANK YOU," to all who helped transform a poor ol' country boy into a full grown, halfway interesting man. While many times I thought I was on my own, little did I know that my backpack was full of wisdom and upbringing from two parents who could NOT have loved me more.

To my Mother who instilled in me pride and kindness, to my father who taught me how to work and how to be a respectable man; I miss you.

To my brother and sister who never gave up on me, thank you both for your incredible fortitude; I know it wasn't easy.

To my many taskmasters, guess what: while defying the odds, Ol' Mike's still here!

Looking ahead brings great challenge to an aging old man, but with the bounty of life's lessons safely tucked under my Sam Brown Belt, I am prepared. Thanks to all who lifted me up and spurred me on!

Forward

These stories allow all who read them to know the life and understand some of the motivations that inspire those with inquiring minds. Occasionally you may wonder "Why did he do that?" or "How did he do that?" or even, "How COULD he have done that?" I have often, to no avail wondered the very same things, usually during the dark of night when I should be sleeping. It is sorta like the acrid sting of battery acid: there is no mistaking it, you know you've gotten into it, but where, how, and to what extent. There is no getting away from it.

As I relate these anecdotes, they are true to the extent that my memory serves me. Some parts I remember clearly, while other parts blend together to accommodate seamless retelling. My remarkable childhood and bounteous upbringing transformed an unbelievably scrawny dirt-poor Southern boy into a self-made man.

My formal educational shortcomings were bolstered by my school of hard knocks. I have the scars and mended broken bones (8) to prove it. Fire always burned when I touched it, and my incredibly hard head was forged by those very flames.

But here I am, having weathered the storms, having survived the encounters, and pressed on to the greater achievements of the future.

My recollections sometimes needed rethinking and correction by those who had been present and brought more clear interpretation. That only means that I was occasionally mistaken, not prevaricating. Every story in this book is true, nearly true, or based upon another teller's integrity and fortitude. While many names have been changed to protect the privacy of those implicated, with permission some names are factual.

As I wrote, I learned that a good story must flow: more often than not, mine gushed! I would be remiss if I failed to acknowledge the significance of my Ralph L. Fike Senior High School English teacher, Mrs. Loretta Parker who sparked the fires of the passions contained herein. To all of you who are embarking on this thrill ride, I welcome your enthusiasm, and envy your experience, because for the most part, I wish I could do it all over again. Albeit with some minor modifications. My caveat is that had I had different surroundings and circumstances, the outcomes may have been altered.

The only Latin that I really understood read something like,

"*In omnia paratus.*" Ready for all things!

By conjuring up and writing my memoirs, and then rewriting them, I have lived, relived, and will live again the HUGELY rewarding events that have defined me for over seven decades. If no one else will have enjoyed reading this book, I HAVE! And I WILL!

Climb aboard and buckle up!

PROLOGUE

Growing up poor in a small southern town demanded that I become innovative. Helping others became my mantra. By always "being there" and lending a hand, I became a participant. The more I participated, the better I became at being, "One of the guys." Isn't that what we all want? To be accepted?

Well, by not limiting myself to a certain class of "cohorts," I became well rounded. I had rich friends, and I had poor friends. I had white friends, and I had black friends. I had smart friends, and I had incredibly stupid friends. I had young friends, and I had old friends. As you read this book, you will meet them all. I hope you will learn to love them, just as I did then, AND STILL DO NOW!

My parents were the hardest working people I ever knew, and it didn't kill them: cigarettes did. Spuds. They taught me that the ability to work is a blessing from God, and that I had better not let them, or HIM down. They also taught me how to work, how to plan my work, how to set attainable goals, and how to accomplish those goals.

To sum it up: "The harder I worked, the luckier I got!"

I am the luckiest man alive!

Opening Letter to Becky, Jenny, John, Pat, and Kathy

Open Invitation to Read, Learn, Laugh, and Cry

This letter was written in 1998 and is but a snapshot of the details contained throughout the following collection of mini stories.

Dear Becky, Pat, Kathy, Jenny, John, Nakayla, Jay, Leela, and Nolan,

Do you remember what it was like to grow up while living at Tobacco Trail Motel (in business from 1947 through 1983), right on the highway? "Tobacco Road" was a hotbed of 24-hour activity, and many times Tobacco Trail Motel, "two miles south of Wilson, NC on US-301," was right in the middle of all that happened.

I can remember lying in my twin bed with just one holey US Army blanket on it in the dead of winter, under the front window on those cold nights when rippled ice formed on the outside, and condensation froze to ice on the inside. Remember we could scratch our names on the frosty panes with our fingernails. In the summer, the windows were cranked open wide so Granddaddy could hit his head on them. The nights would get so stifling hot that sweat would collect in my GI sideburns, and trickle down into a puddle in my ears or on the pillowcase. There was no air conditioning in any of our rooms, and the single unit in the living room was like a small chest of drawers that we pulled open to get the cool air (angel breath).

Lying in bed we could hear the heavily loaded tractor trailer trucks pulling out of the NCDMV Weigh Station up the other side of Parker's Barbecue Restaurant, and heading south. As they "barreled down the highway," we listened as their eighteen wheels "clip-clopped" over the tar striped expansion joints on the divided four lane concrete super slab. The suicide jockeys were usually in 12th or 13th gear as they accelerated past the motel. Sometimes the biggest trucks were still shifting through 19, 20, and twenty-one as they rounded the curve down at Wiggins's Mill, bouncing across the narrow bridge over Contentnea Creek by The Wilson Country Club.

Wilson County Motor Speedway

On Saturdays and Sundays during the Summer, there were always souped-up stock car races on the oval, half-mile dirt track up at the Wilson County Motor Speedway on the fairgrounds beside The American Legion. When those 427s and 396s cranked up, the earsplitting roar was unbearable as they powered and careened around the track.

When the thunder merchants came by where I was standing barefooted, both my kneecaps would uncontrollably jump up and down! Standing next to the chicken wire fence at the edge of the commotion was a challenge for lots of reasons. Grease and dirt mixed with fiberglass and chunks of tire rubber were always coming over, under, and through the fence.

One afternoon, following a crash, a whole tire and wheel assembly busted through the fence into the grandstand packed with farm families. White coated medics carried the most severely injured on stretchers through the crowd, and out to the ambulance parked beside the main gate. The red clay dust was enough to choke a mule, but I stood strong. It settled onto all the cars and hats, and anything else that was horizontal, all the way down to the motel. Yankee customers would complain about the noise and the dust, but we would admonish them, "This is The South. Enjoy it!"

Wilson County Fair

In September when the American Legion Post 13, Regional Fair took Wilson County by storm, the night air crackled with excitement. The aroma of Parker's fried chicken, and Food Truck vendors' Polish Sausages wafted the half-mile down to Tobacco Trail and stirred enthusiasm. We didn't have to listen too closely to hear the crack of the .22 rifles at the shooting gallery, and the grind of the merry-go-round. Children's squeals and laughter could be heard all the way down to the millpond while I was shooting Wood Ducks. The orchestra inside the grandstand cranked out that old familiar beat and brought thrills and excitement to the outdoor stage. The wicked growls of the hoochie-coochie barkers made chills run up and down the spines of 'most everybody there. The hucksters running "the games of chance" beckoned all of us to, "Come on over, and try your luck."

Every night, when the fireworks started lighting the sky, it seemed that everything else stopped. I can remember being at the top of the Ferris Wheel and wondering would the sparks fall on me. Oh yeah, the bright explosions of color seemed to be much brighter and lots louder back then, as a little boy.

The County Fair and its "Can-Can Follies" always brought its own brand of novelty and intrigue. "Daddy's Girls" would arrive at Tobacco Trail Motel on Sunday afternoon, and "check-in" to numbers 1, 2, 3, and four. He was their own personal bouncer, cooler, chaperone, guidance counselor, information center, petty-cash banker, and car mechanic. These young women, ages 16 to 50 performed nightly on the outdoor stage in front of the Grandstand on the edge of the racetrack. The troupe invariably brought a certain mystique to the good ol' farm boys and drove some of them "slam-damn crazy."

It never failed: by about Tuesday night one or more of the girls would sneak up to the house and cry about being overworked, picked on, scorned, pregnant, or just plain homesick. Mother and Daddy would commiserate with them for hours and hours, and make long-distance expensive telephone calls from 0243, not 237-0243, and certainly not from (252) 237-0243, back to New York for them. They would ultimately slip on back down to their room, not wanting any of the others or their chaperones to know that they had had a weak moment. The letters of gratitude that came later were always endearing. They and their families loved us, and we loved them.

Michael J. McArthur

"Hawkshaw Hawkins"

"Hawkshaw Hawkins," (December 22, 1921 – March 3, 1963) at six feet five inches was the most amazing man that I had ever had the privilege to be around. He wore a cowboy hat, too! He could do more tricks with a ten-foot leather bullwhip than a crazy monkey could do on a ten-foot flagpole. With that whip, he could knock apple sized chunks of bark off that Sweetgum Tree in front of number 4 where our basketball goal was mounted. He could cut individual or clumps of leaves out of Mother's Red Maple trees, much to her chagrin! Those little skinny cigars clenched in his teeth made him look tantalizingly evil, while he drank his bootleg liquor out of a Mason jar that he kept hidden in the trunk of his red over white '60 Ford Convertible. He was quite a formidable entertainer, and everybody gave him plenty of room.

One Saturday night he snuck me into the grandstand, right down on the racetrack at showtime. I wasn't much bigger than some of those monkeys I was talking about. Mother had let him show me how to light the twirling fireworks that he would shoot out with his Remington, Nylon 66, .22 caliber, semi-automatic rifle. One of his gimmicks was to put on a sharp shooting exhibition, and all of us boys would be tremendously impressed. During part of his act, he coiled his whip over his head and under his left arm. He then took his Marlin lever action .22 rifle and stood before a 7-foot wooden female mannequin with large red balloons for breasts. Her wooden arms held a double - bladed lumberjack ax out in front of those balloons. Supposedly the blade was razor sharp, and ol' Hawkshaw's trick was to shoot the blade of the ax, split the bullet in two, and bust the balloons on each side, beside the blade.

I learned a valuable lesson from this adventure: "All is not always what it appears." This huckster was shooting "shotshell" cartridges with #12 shot in them like miniature shotgun shells. He couldn't miss, AND HE NEVER DID.

The hawkers at the side shows wanted us to pay $3.00 to watch a so called, human being eat a chicken <u>alive</u>. Yeah, I did. Also there was a "blood-sweating hippopotamus" in a big cage/truck that we could pay

$1.00 to see. Turned out that the "zoo-zoo flies" were biting him and making small trickles of blood run down the sides of his hide. These raunchy fair people were the most astounding spectacles that I had ever encountered. They elicited way more attention than they deserved, but coming from a home like ours, I could not believe my eyes. Mother always warned us to, "BE CAREFUL," when we went up there. If you will remember, though, she told us that every time we went anywhere, Right?

"Lucky Me"

As the week wore on, the gambling games became bigger attractions and bigger money was seen flashing back and forth. I remember one of the gambling games allowed the winner to rake in "half the pot." When a bouncing red ball landed in a gridded square with the number corresponding with your number, you won. A leather "pill bottle" held numbered wooden marbles that were doled out for $2.00 apiece, and that was your number. After each round, the "pills" were collected from each of the eight to ten gamblers, the winner raked in his 6 or 8 dollars, and new "pills" were rolled out. Somehow, I ended up with two "pills," one clenched in each fist. I rested both my forearms on the edge of the table, and when the ball settled onto a number, I would present whichever "pill" that won the money. As it turned out, Mike McArthur's "pill" was winning twice as fast as the other cheater thought it should be. He haughtily dumped out all the "pills" onto the table to take an inventory. I was so glad that I happened to still be standing there when he decided that something was awry. As you know, he found where one "pill" was missing, and I knew exactly which "pill" that was: the one clenched tightly inside my left fist. Welp, it was time to move on.

I still have that #8 "pill," and have found that to be my life's "lucky number." 1969 was the first of four years that the Military Draft Lottery was conducted by Congressional order. Of the 366 dates in that leap year, the administrator drew 195 dates of those 366 possibilities. November 19, 1949, my date of birth, was lottery number 203, missed me by "8." Needless to say, our Mother was elated. HOWEVER, I have always regretted not having enlisted, served my country, and been shipped straight to Viet Nam and the melee following the Viet Cong, Tet Offensive.

The cacophony of shows always escalated in trashiness as the Fair's last day approached: so did the risks to fairgoers. Remember one of our school bus drivers, Yancey Cole? He was the "cool guy" who would rest a lit cigarette in the crevice of his forearm pressed up against someone else's forearm until one idiot or the other would pull away. Whoever pulled away first got a line branded (cauterized) onto his forearm by the "winner." They used a steak knife from The Heart of Wilson Steak House.

Being that there were no winners, who was the biggest loser? The one with the most cauterized hash marks. Yancey also could jab a hat pin straight into his thigh, or through his cheek. He would bite it with his teeth and let us try to pull it out! He also was the one who got "stobbed" by the security officer guarding the perimeter of the fairgrounds over by the Ladies' Rest Rooms. Seems that as Yancey went over the fence behind the Grandstand, the security guard punched him with a switchblade knife, causing him to fall onto the hood and bleed all over Mrs. Walston's, our seventh-grade teacher's brand-new Oldsmobile.

Monday mornings after the fair left town, the kids in the hall and in the lunchroom at Ralph L. Fike Senior High School would whisper and laugh about who got turned away at the hoochie-coochie (yeah he did), and who had done what inside that sinful tent. The absolute truth was absolutely indescribable!

"Stay Out of the Road"

As you can imagine, Highway 301 was never without interest. Do you remember when Pan Am Flight 101 brought Beatlemania to New York's Kennedy Airport? It was Friday, February 7, 1964, and I wanted to watch the arrival of George, Paul, John, and Ringo on Channel 5, WRAL in Raleigh. I played hooky, feigning an upset stomach, but Mother knew better! It was foggy that morning, and when Wilson County School Bus #22-I came to a halt in front of the motel, Pat and Kathy were running for the open door. I was watching out my bedroom window when all of a sudden, a big white Cadillac swerved and plowed into the left rear of the bus, hit the concrete curbing, and flew airborne over the northbound lane, hitting no one. Nosediving into the roadside ditch, do you remember how many folks crawled out of the Cadi? Thirteen, and they all ran through the fog over to Daddy's Esso Station.

Do you remember when two drunken soldiers pulled out of the Service Distributors gas station southbound, and floorboarded it? They swerved into the grass median, hit the concrete culvert at the "cut-through," and went airborne in front of the motel's Smokey Joe billboard. The entire front bumper crashed through the windshield of a northbound station wagon loaded with eleven family members returning from a Camden, South Carolina funeral. The only survivor was a ten-month old baby found in the floor under the dashboard. The Highway Patrol pulled thirty-eight Pabst Blue Ribbon beer cans out of the wreckage and stacked most of them on top of the soldiers' car.

Remember when the farmer on his Massey Ferguson tractor on 301 was hit from behind and killed up in front of The Coral Room Restaurant across the road at the Huntington Motel? Traffic was backed up in the northbound lanes until after dark. That restaurant was a favorite hangout with free coffee for law enforcement officers. Highway Patrolman Charlie Lee was in there one afternoon when he spotted a southbound car in the northbound lanes running about 100 miles per hour. He tripped twice trying to get outside to his Black and Silver Patrol Car.

Do you remember one of the other Highway Patrolmen putting the make on our Mother, and following her around. He got too close to her once up at the Five-Points Laundromat while she was doing the motel laundry. When Daddy finally got the First Sergeant to send the Patrolman around to the motel, it was a fearsome and fearful sight. We three kids were in tears. The Patrolman stood by his gasoline fill cap, and Daddy stood in his open patrol car door. With his left hand, Daddy beat a dent in the top of the Patrol Car while yelling at him. Daddy called him everything BUT a child of God. Daddy threatened to beat his ass, right then and there. We were crouched down beside Mother's red vinyl chair by that little square end table, below the front windowsill, and could hear and see it all as we peered through the open window. Even our dog, Silly (Silhouette) was riled up. Somehow it got resolved, but it was such a traumatic event that I can't remember much more.

Furthermore, there was a midnight break-in silent alarm at Wilson Hardware Store on Nash Street, right across from the Wilson County Courthouse. When the Wilson Police arrived, they found a uniformed Highway Patrolman placing a twenty-inch color television into the trunk of his marked Black and Silver.

No wonder that our Daddy was not too thrilled that yours truly, Mike McArthur was later to become a sworn North Carolina State Highway Patrolman some eight years later. Not to mention the fact that Daddy's father had succumbed to alleged injuries suffered in an automobile accident at the hands of the Indiana State Police some thirty years earlier.

It seems that our Grandfather had suffered a stroke while driving and glided into the ditch. Upon arrival of the Patrolman, he placed the driver (Grandfather) under arrest for driving drunk and handcuffed him to a stretcher on the side of the road. Great-Grandfather Bill died handcuffed, moments later from the cerebral hemorrhage.

Can you imagine the chaos that erupted inside that Roadmaster Buick when it hit Tony Langston's mule up in front of Tommy Matthews Motor Court about 8:00 one Friday night? The whole mule ended up inside the car in the laps of the occupants. It was still very much alive!

It seemed that things were always falling off the trucks on the highway. There was a case of spare .22 bullets that my friend Donnie Murray (Don Murray's Barbecue, Raleigh, NC) found. There was a Bowie knife that Jimmy Williamson found. There were bales of hay that fell onto the pavement and busted. Since we had two Guinea Pigs, Leo and Cleo that needed hay in their pen, we went to pick up that hay after it was pushed into the field beside the Esso Station. While we were doing that, the complete wheel assembly from a tractor trailer "18 wheeler" flew off a northbound big rig, bounced into the Esso lot beside the gas pumps, and then bounced into the field right beside where we were bundling the hay into our Radio Fliers. That was one of many "close calls' that we all endured.

Not long before that nearly catastrophic event, we had built a campfire in that same field with branches from the Maple Trees at the motel. Ronnie and Donnie Williamson had taken their mother's empty Duke's Mayonnaise gallon jar and filled it with gasoline from Earl's tank in the yard at Williamson's Plumbing Company. They built a tripod over the fire and suspended that "bomb" right over the foot-high flames. We got behind the fence at the Esso Station and shot the jar with our Daisy, long-pump BB guns. Black smoke plumed hundreds of feet over the gas pumps. Needless to say, that "brought on more talk."

Remember when the U. S. Army used to send their convoys of trucks, jeeps, personnel carriers, and tanks by the front of the motel on US-301? We would get those rickety red and white and yellow metal chairs from in front of the house, and take them out to the roadside, sit beside the bushes, and count the vehicles. One hundred-and-forty-two seems to be the most we ever counted, but it seemed like it took hours for them to parade past. It was hard to imagine that all those waving soldiers were old enough to go and fight for our country, as they headed for Fort Bragg in Fayetteville, NC.

The Shriners Arrive

Remember when the Shriners and the Knights of the Sudan Temple stormed into Wilson and immediately took over every motel, hotel, restaurant, and parking lot? There were more big, red, shiny Cadillacs around town than there were acres of tobacco in the Barfield's allotment. Motorcycles the size of Corvair Monzas came in hooked behind motor homes and converged on the fairgrounds for their four-day convention. One year, when the upcoming year's model cars had not been marketed, the local dealerships had rented part of the fairgrounds to hide the new models until the official unveiling. Those conventioneers descended on those new hot wheels like ducks on a June Bug. With cold, hard cash, they bought every one of those prized cars before they ever made their debut at Corbett Buick, Kenly Ford, or Wilson Chevrolet.

Michael J. McArthur

The Ku Klux Klan

Remember when The Royal Knights of the Ku Klux Klan would hold cross-burning "convocations" down the other side of Lamm's Store by the dam at Wiggins's Mill on Contentnea Creek? They took over that big field right behind Ray's Bargain House where I bought that 36-inch barrel, 12-gauge goose gun. With their white Cadillac deVilles ringing the perimeter, the hooded, so called, "Race Soldiers" wore holstered handguns and brandished white painted, Louisville Slugger baseball bats. They would guard the entrances while they stood beside their own individual six-foot-tall propane fired burning crosses. A bunch of us (Johnny Bailey, Polly Newton, Raymond Lucas) were swimming in the pool at Tobacco Trail when we saw the glow, "down south." We loaded up into Johnny's red hot, Hot Red Chevelle, and went down there to see what was happening. We got in line to buy black market, Star .25 caliber automatic pistols, still in wrapped in Cosmoline.

We stood in awe of the sight of the gigantic 50-foot burning wooden cross in the center of the field, surrounded by flying sparks and frenzied Klansmen. Every now and then a single megaphoned voice would rise above the crowd and would be followed by lots of pistol and shotgun blasts.

Kerosene-soaked rags continually fell from the crossarms of the spectacle, and smoke filled the air. One lone black man was being cursed as he knelt at the black booted feet of the "Grand Dragon," or whoever seemed to be in charge of the hellions. Gunfire broke out near where Johnny, Polly, Raymond, and I were standing, and we knew it was time to get the H out of there, back to the car parked out on the shoulder of the highway. Such a ranting and raving, scared bunch of rednecks I had never before seen, and hoped to never see again, BUT I HAVE!

What Does "Ill Repute" Mean, Anyway?

The outlaw faction seemed to roam at large, up and down US-301. Remember The Forest Inn Motor Court, and the six rooms of prostitutes that worked there? Some of the older guys supposedly went up there and got kicked out for not having enough money. On Sunday mornings, Brother Pat and I waited on the tables full of working girls inside Clubroom #1 at Parker's Barbecue. They were all cleaned up and looked presentable. "But they weren't," as our Mother said.

They seemed relaxed while comparing notes from the night before, and we never heard them speak above a whisper. The Gridleys, who drove that little black Studebaker, were Mother's and Daddy's friends who had built The Forest Inn about the same time that The Tobacco Trail Motel was built.

If they had ever thought that their quaint little motor court in the Pines would end up serving the needs of organized crime (contrary to Sheriff Robin Pridgen's opinion) and satisfying the needs of the Bright Leaf Tobacco Market Mafia, Mr. Gridley would have burned the place down to the ground (like that other innkeeper of a "House of ill repute" tried to do down at the Traveler's Motel).

Cherry Bombs, Silver Tips, Black Cats, and M-80s

As you may recall, every year 'round about Christmastime, the boys in "the hood" needed to blow something up. We would ride our bicycles down to Maurice's Grill on the right side of US-117 and hunt up ol' Red Walston. He was Sue's Dad, and since we all liked Sue A LOT, he liked us. He would stop flippin' those delicious hamburger patties that exceeded the width of the Wonder Bread bun and meet us 'round back. He would scout the parking lot, then go to the trunk of his red '55 Chevrolet and bring out those white cardboard boxes holding 1/3 gross (48) Cherry Bombs, Silver-Tips, or M-80s.

We put that contraband in the baskets of our bicycles, and rode straight to the US-301 bridge over Contentnea Creek. After going through the trash dump behind Lamm's Store, we found glass mayonnaise jars and pickle jars. You remember what we did then? We put some of those "smooth, flat, slick, river rocks" in the bottles. Then one of us would hold the jar lid and jar while the other would drop in a lit Cherry Bomb. Hastily replacing the lid, we dropped it off the bridge, into the water as we perfected "underwater demolition" training.

Another neat thing we did was to light those M-80s, drop them into a two-foot-long galvanized two-inch pipe, follow it with one of Daddy's D-cell flashlight batteries, and "git back." Those batteries must have gone into orbit, because we never saw one re-enter the atmosphere. We even took those pipes, crammed in two M-80s followed by nuts and bolts, and shot them like mortars at ducks in front of Pinky Connor's mansion down at the Mill. We still have most of our eyesight, and much less of our hearing.

Beside Molly's "cracker box house" over in the field behind Helms Truck Lines Depot, we would bury an empty tin can that was about three inches in diameter, much like a hole on the greens down at the Happy Valley Country Club Golf Course. We then dropped in a lit Silver Tip and followed it with a 2½ inch can such as the "orange juice cans" that we used to drink water from. We usually found those imploded wonders out in the field with scorch marks on the sides, and inwardly crumpled edges.

Ol' Donkey Ray Bynum was helping us with our dastardly deeds one afternoon, lit that Cherry Bomb, drew back to throw it, and it went off. He lost the end of his right index finger and thumb, while deafening his right ear. Apparently, his fuse was too short (in many ways). More about ol' Donkey Ray later.

When we ran out of the first three boxes of dynamite, we would go back to see "Red" who probably didn't have any more. I remember one night when we followed an ambulance down US-117 and found that a Lumbee Indian had cut "Red" from side to side. "Red" didn't make it, and we all became a little more galvanized. After that we would go up to Elm City where the single stop light in front of the Post Office was "upside down." That was just a little disconcerting to a poor old colorblind teenager who had trouble enough driving his '55 Pontiac Star Chief "like he ought to."

Lo and behold, there on US-301 was the notorious Essofleet Truck Stop. Not many things were not available at that monstrosity. It was the hub of illegal drag racing, it was the hub of bootleg trucking, it was the hub for "stump hole" white lightning, it was the hub for caseloads of taxpaid liquor, beer, and cigarettes, and it was the hub for almost everything else that was sinful, unhealthy, dangerous, or illegal. For a fee, lurking in the shadows, there was always some old drunk willing to buy beer, guns, cigarettes, or fireworks for us teenagers.

That night after having cashed in our tips, stopped by the gas station, gone by Essofleet and made our "haul," we followed an ambulance to one of the most horrific wreck scenes that I have ever witnessed, and I will spare you the sadness. Froggy Bowen and I found a partial pint bottle of Jim Beam that was lying on the ground right next to one half of the pregnant girl's body and threw it into the woods.

Remember when we would ride our bicycles with clothes pinned playing cards flapping in our spokes up to Raper's Store to buy Mother a fresh loaf of Sunbeam Bread for twenty cents? We had to ride on "the back road" because there was less traffic. After we got past the snarly dogs up at the Williamson's, we would pull in and lean our bicycles up against Ronnie Galloway's barn. Then we would walk over to Raper's, buy the bread, come back and again ride by those snarly dogs with our feet raised up on the handlebars to keep from getting bitten. Mother said that she would change her name if it were "Raper."

That little country store seemed much larger back then than it is now! Mr. and Mrs. Raper sold Winchester shotgun shells for eight and ten cents apiece, and I could buy 2 or 3 per day when I didn't eat much lunch at school. They also sold little cellophane packages of air rifle BBs for five cents. For a quarter, they sold red and yellow tubes of BBs with a crimped end like a shotgun shell. When you bit the cap off the tube, you could squeeze the opening of the tube and dump the BBs straight into the loading port of our Daisy long pump BB guns.

"The Goat Man"

I have saved part of the best for last. Do you remember the "Goat Man?" Ches McCartney was his real name, and he came from Georgia. Twice a year, once northbound and once southbound, an inconsistent, persnickety, scruffy, eccentric, hairy old man with a snarled salt and pepper and chili and beany-weeny beard, greasy Engineer's Cap, mongrel dog, and overalls would bounce along US-301 on his treks between Florida, the Midwest, Canada, and Maine. His wagon resembled a boxcar shaped covered wagon with cloth sides. Sometimes it had one or two car wheels ("slick as a baby's bottom" according to Goat Man), and sometimes it had three-foot steel wagon wheels (Ouch!).

He came by and shared his wealth with us maybe four times before he died in Macon, Georgia. He would call his dog down off the padded bench seat, and allow us to sit up there, but not go inside. He sold postcards, sold what he found along the roadside, and would preach when given the opportunity. Daddy always gave him cash either for his ministries or goat feed. Mother would give whatever food we could spare, and clean green Army blankets.

Before long he would harness six goats and put two on top of the wagon, and six to eight behind the wagon. Sometimes he had as many as fifteen to twenty multi-colored goats: big ones and small ones, hairy ones and slick ones. Our dog, Penny thought not much of The Goat Man, nor his goats, nor the wagon. One year he cried as we buried "Nellie" in the sandspur field on the hillside beside the ditch. Nellie had mothered three of the "kids" that he nourished with a baby bottle, and he was heartbroken at her death. But he was also "a tough old bird." He did not take kindly to teasing, and at some point, he had been accused of shooting (at) some teenagers who had overturned his wagon up near Boston.

What I have tried to recount here in these few pages is but the tip of the iceberg of incidents that befell all of us as we grew up on "Tobacco Trail." Surely there are many stories that each of you remember, and perhaps you remember some of these differently from what I have allowed. Stories about our friends could create volumes. Stories about school days, teachers, cars, customers, jobs, hunting, fishing, Scouting, the swimming pool, family, and living day to day are contained herein. My hope is that by writing my recollections, that each of you will kindle a memory to throw in, throw out, or argue about. Perhaps we can help each other recapture the adventure and excitement that played a part in making us who we are today, and also help our children and grandchildren learn more about "the good life" as we lived it!

Wasn't too bad, was it?!

Michael J. McArthur

The Tobacco Trail Motel

(June of 1947 through September of 1983)

Wilson, North Carolina

Well, I reckon you'da had to've been there!

Growing up in Wilson, North Carolina in the '50s and '60s was a pure, unadulterated blessing in many ways. You were afforded more opportunities for learning than you would have ever thought humanly possible. It was because of the rich tapestry of "inconsistent," hard-charging, borderline personalities who lived there. Why did they live there? Because it was a "Boom Town" of sorts. Wilson was "The Bright Leaf Tobacco Capitol of the World." If you couldn't make a living in Wilson, you just weren't trying. Likewise, if you couldn't get in trouble in Wilson, you just weren't trying. OR you were politically connected, OR your family was born and raised in Wilson, OR your family had lots of money, OR you were the vilest villain in the village. I was fortunate to know them all, maybe too well. Well, maybe not ALL of them, but more than my young boy's share.

Have you ever pulled sand lugs? Have you ever gotten, "The monkey on your back?" Have you ever had snakes fall across your shoulders at 4:00am from tobacco barn rafters? Have you ever gotten "tons" of sand in your eyes from the bottoms of your co-workers' feet on the rafters above as you were "takin' out" a barnful of sticks of Bright Leaf, flue-cured tobacco? Have you ever thought you were gonna die if, "The Boss" didn't hurry up and bring you that "square meal": four peanut butter Nabisco crackers (nabs) in a cubical cellophane package, a large R C Cola, and a melting Moon Pie? Have you ever had ANYTHING IN YOUR LIFE as good as a Pepsi Cola with ice in it, and half filled with salty Planter's peanuts from a cellophane package? Have you ever hit a .22 bullet with a hammer and wondered where everything went? Have you ever used a clothes hanger to wire a .22 long rifle bullet onto the muzzle of your Daisy long pump BB gun, fired it off, and hit anything you were aiming at? Have you ever been shot? Have you ever shot at another human being? Have you ever run from the police? Have you ever chauffeured a bunch of drunks? Have you ever had to swim for your life? Have you ever wondered whether you would see tomorrow?

A Southern Belle and a Merchant Marine

Well, let me tell you a fascinating story about a beautiful Southern Belle, a handsome sailor, a fist full of dollars, two adventurous spirits, and their privileged family.

Wilson, North Carolina, situated halfway between Lower Manhattan, New York, and Miami, Florida provided respite for "them Yankee Snowbirds." Every spring from South to North, and every fall from north to South, they would load up their Cadillacs with appropriate clothing, their canes, and their Poodle dog, and make the journey. My parents operated a "mom and pop," four unit, single-bed rooms, motor court and gas station on nationally acclaimed "Tobacco Trail," US-301, two miles south of Wilson, right in the middle of the Tobacco Belt of America. "The Tobacco Trail" (US-301) was so named by President Franklin Delano Roosevelt in 1938. This was "halfway" for the snowbirds, and Mother and Daddy developed friendships with many of them who would stop and spend the night during their migration: eat at Parker's Barbecue, sling vinegar and BBQ hot sauce to the ceiling out of the tabletop bottles with hole drilled caps, and then head down and bed down at the Tobacco Trail Motel with Mac and Betty. The rooms rented for $4 plus 3% tax, $4.12. Styrofoam cups of refrigerator ice was about the only complimentary service offered other than clean sheets and southern hospitality.

We also had a lot of familiar faces that seemed to appear at our front door or ring our bell at all times of the day and night. A one-inch black air hose (the snake) stretched fifty feet across the driveways, and connected to a ten-inch, bowl shaped "bell" plugged into the 110-volt receptacle under the front window on the world. A car driving at an angle over it would cause a "bing-bing, bing-bing," to roust us out of our comfort into dealing with all kinds of public patrons. Some were tourists. Some were construction contractors. Some were Bright Leaf Tobacco industrial workers. Some were truckers since we had a lot of room to park their "rig." Some were criminals, hiding out. Some were jilted spouses. Some were linoleum salesmen. Some were asphalt roofers. Some were love-birds who stayed only a couple of hours. Some were "carnies." But all were glad to get a clean room for a fair price.

With all its inconsistencies, "the motel" provided a meager existence, not quite a living. Thus, my Daddy would "go to sea" with the United States Merchant Marines for months at a time, leaving Betty, my Mother to "run the motel." And wash the linens. And raise three kids, ages 7, 9, and twelve. Upon his departure, standing in the doorway to our home, Daddy would call me to his side and say, "Now Mike, while I am gone, you are the man of the house. I want you to take good care of your mother, your brother, and your little sister." And with that, he was gone. I have been blessed with the responsibility of "taking good care of" my mothers, brothers, and sisters ever since: male-female, black-white, Yankee-redneck, young-old, rich or poor.

In 1948, my Mother, Mary Elizabeth Robertson (April 24, 1918 to March 4, 1985) had just graduated from New York City's Barnard College for Women, affiliated with Columbia University, Borough of Manhattan, City of New York (that wouldn't accept female students), and moved from Monument Avenue in Richmond, Virginia to Brooklyn, New York. She lived in a small brownstone apartment on West Street which later became the footprint of the World Trade Center. She was a young and beautiful leather goods buyer for Saks Fifth Avenue's flagship store in New York and led a youth group for her Methodist Church near the Port City Docks. Her church Ladies Circle hosted Sunday morning "free military man breakfasts" for weary service members (like my father).

My Father, Captain John William McArthur (February 7, 1912 to January 24, 1990), handsome and uniformed, was an electrician and pump master from Indianapolis, Indiana, serving his country as a Merchant Marine.

His assignment was to keep an ocean-going oil tanker's pumps pumping and the lights either "on" or "off." The lights had to be rigged to "go dark" instantly upon the approach of Japanese bombers or submarines who targeted US fuel tankers.

His ships, known as "suicide rigs," fueled the Navy destroyers and aircraft carriers in ports throughout the world. Throughout their brief courtship, Mac brought "Betty" trinkets and presents from distant ports such as Casablanca, Trinidad, Naples, Paris, London, Turkey, Panama, India, and Venice: porcelain ballerinas, gold wind up clocks, scarves, books, and tapestry. He would bring my brother Pat, sister Kathy, and me presents later on: hats, model ships, lace handkerchiefs. Never could we have imagined the sacrifices and dangers he survived. But he always returned. After all, his fifth cousin was General Douglas MacArthur, as in, "I shall return." (March 20, 1942)

According to Betty's Mother, Maude Lee Rowlett Robertson, it was a "Match Made in Heaven," "in church." Betty married Mac, and at their wedding, received a cookie jar full of cash from spendthrift grandmother, Maude Lee, and a shoe box full of cash from Irish tightwad grandfather, John. They made their home in a small brownstone apartment in the very footprint of what became the World Trade Center. Footnote: in the 1980s, what is left of the McArthur families went and visited the communities surrounding the World Trade Center where the newlyweds dined, worked, and played: Dinner on the Green, Radio City Music Hall, Fifth Avenue, Times Square, Sardi's with their hand drawn caricatures of celebrities (Lucille Ball, Gene Autry, and Bob Hope stick out), and Mamma Leone's Ristorante right down the street at 261 West 44th Street. Daddy always got a charge asking the violinist/serenading budding actor to "Sing Dixie." That was well before the entire neighborhood was blown to smithereens on September 11, 2011, beginning at 9:03am and causing nearly 3000 hardworking, red-blooded Americans to lose their lives.

With this dowry "treasure," in 1947, the newlyweds loaded up their scant belongings and Betty's dog, Penny, into a 1943 Plymouth, and headed south on US-301 to open a Motor Hotel somewhere along the highway in Florida. Well, all that was a great plan until the Plymouth "gave up the ghost" in Wilson, North Carolina. They built their legacy, right there on US-301 (Federally named "The Tobacco Trail"), raised a family, and made a LOT of memories.

Mary Elizabeth's children were special. She attended every theatrical production of all three, all the way through the following seventeen years of their schooling. Daddy stayed home running the motel, and Betty raised her brood. After struggling through Mike (Me), raising Pat and Kathy were, "walks in the park."

Mother and Daddy were honest, hardworking, innkeepers who understood and followed The Golden Rule. Patience was NOT one of their long suits. In 1948, a year before I was born, The Tobacco Trail Motor Court was started as "McArthur's Gas Station" with four, drive up to the door, double bed or two twin beds and a bath, motor court rooms.

My earliest recollection was that the rooms rented for $4.00 a night plus 3% state sales tax: $4.12. Daddy ran the gas station with two pumps and an air hose out front, while mother managed me, my little brother and sister. She managed the motel, much to my grandmother Maude Lee's mortification: "What? A woman? Running a motel?" Mother was the innkeeper, the maid, the desk clerk, the complaint department, the dishwasher, the floor waxer, the toilet scrubber, and everything else that came along, while Daddy ran the station.

Daddy never lost his love of the sea after serving in the Merchant Marines during World War II. Often, when he found it necessary to supplement their income, he would "go to sea," giving me the command, "Now Mike, you take good care of your Mother, little brother, and sister." And I've been doing that ever since, but in a much more broad arena than just my own family.

As a young family we "made up" the rooms, painted the yard furniture, replaced the screens in the outer doors, raked those _____ _____ Red Maple leaves, shoveled ditches to channel the downpours, fought the grassfires started by flicked Lucky Strike, Spud, and Camel butts, tried to plant a garden only once, and shoveled level way too many dump truck loads of glass and rock filled roadside rock hard, clay dirt hauled by the North Carolina Department Of Transportation into "the back lot" beside the incinerator. Daddy always gave the dump truck driver a piece of a pint of Southern Comfort whiskey that some renter/customer had left in their room.

Contract Bridge

Mother and Daddy played Contract Bridge with a bunch of really nice couples at the Wilson Recreation Department: Billy our science teacher and Ella Beaman our Biology teacher, Bill and Mary Hooks, Arnold and Nell Formo, Graham and Peggy Lane, Sam and Pat Morrill with Sammy who lost his life in the 82nd Airborne in Viet Nam, Sam and Maude House, Arthur and Roberta Pritchard, Joe and Sera Brewer, with Mike and Smokey. When they went to play Bridge, Pat, Kathy, or I would man the desk at the motel. Ol' Pat was spinning a yarn one evening as Kathy and I sat on the couch. "Bing-bing. Bing-bing." A blue station-wagon pulled into the driveway. Evidently Pat was too busy to rent a room, so he pushed open the screen door to the house, and yelled to the driver, "We're full." (Not a car on the lot) He shut the door and resumed his story. Kathy was getting ready to go over to The Beefmaster Steakhouse and serve tables. I was preparing to go to Ralph L. Fike to practice for Stunt Night where I was the sound technician. As you can see, we were a busy crowd.

After the legendary peeping tom told Daddy, "Well shoot me, you S.O.B.," they sold Tobacco Trail Motel to Mr. Patel (Indian for "innkeeper"), and moved to Macon, GA in 1988 to be near my sister, Kathy. They left behind the wild neighbors, the Esso Station, Hubert and Hilda Barfield, the Strickland family with their trashy daughter, barking dogs, and crowin' rooster, the Baileys, and the Gypsies. The Gypsies (where The Beefmaster is situated now) would hold alcohol fueled séances, moonlight madness rituals, and all kind of "spiritual hand-woven alcohol fueled events" next door. The entry fee was a case of Pabst Blue Ribbon Beer. Usually it culminated in a bunch of drunks, yellin' and screaming, occasional knifings, shots being fired, and the Wilson County Sheriff's Deputy arriving to quell the escalating uprising. Or when T. H. E. Sheriff himself, Robin Pridgen or his able-bodied ABC Officer cohort, Glenn Stutts arrived, they usually "partook" of the revelry for a little while, usually with "Mr. Green" making a discreet appearance, however briefly.

Money was a transient commodity to those who lived on the fringe. Corruption ran deep at the tobacco warehouses, at the train station, at the downtown hotels, and roadside "hangouts." Those at the top of the food chain subscribed to "The rich get richer," while those on the outskirts, though having their occasional heydays, pretty much lived, "The poor get poorer," lifestyle. I'm told that it was easy to pick up drink bottles along The Back Road, or find them stacked behind the store to whom you were reselling them for two cents apiece. Drink bottles that were not "refundable" usually found their way to a four door, tan '55 Pontiac Star Chief with guys throwing them at road signs. That Pontiac had dents and scratches at an angle across the top from the driver flipping the bottles and them scraping en route to the SPEED LIMIT sixty roadside signs. Dennis's two door '53 black Ford was dented on the right rear quarter panel from the bottle hitting the edge of a Silver Lake sign and bouncing back onto the car at 60mph.

Two of my friends occasionally had to steal a Buick to get to Atlantic Beach on Jr. Sr. weekend, and stowaway at the Oceanana Motel. Pookie had to steal Beatles 45 RPM records from Woolworth's Five & Dime Store on Nash Street, and resell them to our "rich kid" classmates. Another of my stellar friends was known for driving loads of Percy Flowers bootleg to Allentown, Pennsylvania. When he went out NC-42 to the "designated area," a floating Clorox Bleach bottle was tethered by a rope across a fishpond. The position of the bleach bottle in relation to the width of the pond, indicated where the loaded muscle car was parked with a note in it indicating the destination for that load of Mason Jars. You know it! Occasionally one or more of those Timothy Hay packed jars made its way to "other" locations, like NCSU's Owen Dorm room fifty-one. The hauler didn't end up going to prison for that, but he did for stealing and reselling golf clubs down at Wilson Country Club on Contentnea Creek, two miles south of Wilson on US-301.

Somehow, free sets of tires from Kenly, NC ended up rolling under a white '62 Corvair Spyder that spent a lot of time at the Putt-Putt mini-golf course beside the Jump-Jump trampoline center behind The Creamery at Ward Boulevard and Goldsboro Street. Once when Luke decided to host a "pig pickin'," it became J.E.'s responsibility to provide the 75-pound pig. He developed a plan: borrow his dad's Oldsmobile station wagon, put sheets in the back seat, go over near Black Creek behind Barden's Potato House, go into the pig pen with a five-pound ball-peen hammer, knock the pig out, tote him and throw him in the backseat of the Olds, and drive him to Luke's house, and tie him by the leg to the basketball goal. Can anybody see "Murphy's Law" in this plan?

Wouldn't you know it? J.E. ran that Oldsmobile right in the ditch, and the pig lived to oink another day.

More often than not, making ends meet became a little risky, and some of the guys just weren't too real good at keeping that temporary wealth. Gambling was not one of our strengths, but we thought we were "high rollers." Didn't even have a clue on how to throw dice (shoot craps), didn't know whether a "flush" in 5-card-stud poker beat a "straight," didn't know what number you were required to "hit" in blackjack, but did understand what Andy Griffith refers to as, "Odd-Man," in his comedy routine, "What It Was, Was Football."

A favorite pastime in school on rainy days and also out in the smoking area at Ralph L Fike High School, was tossing quarters to the edge of the building. Three or four of us would each "backspin" a true silver quarter toward the 90-degree base of the wall with the winning quarter nearest the building netting its owner all quarters pitched. And we could pull Coke bottles at Raper's Store: seems that the 10-ounce and the 6 ½ -ounce bottles had state capitols in raised letters on the bottoms. Whoever "pulled" the iced-over bottle from the horizontal slot showing the most distant city won the right to have his drink paid for by the least distant bottle puller. A blank bottomed bottle was a loser.

"Shots Fired!"

There were always a lot of shots being fired at different nightspots around Wilson. Some of the store owners had worn out, blued .38 revolvers lying on the countertop or on the ledge of the manual cash registers. Cliven Oakes was quite often either the shooter or the shootee. One time when he was a month's long registered guest at Tobacco Trail Motel in the pumphouse, he got too close to some stolen tires from a warehouse down in Kenly, NC. He had been planning to steal those tires for a while, but just hadn't yet gotten around to it. He ALWAYS had a shady deal or risky plan, and he worked his plans. He told me that he had four tires that would fit my Pontiac Star Chief, but that one of the four was a recap. To a poor boy, new tires were new tires. He told me that these particular four tires were "exchanged" from a friend's car so that a different tread style could be installed. After careful consideration, I determined that statement to mean that my "friend" would be running "stolen" tires, but that mine were "legit." Positive thinking as taught in Psych 101 at North Carolina State University.

I was driving my old Pontiac on Ward Boulevard one night and came to a stop at a stoplight intersection with Tarboro Street. Back then it was just a two-lane city street upon which my school bus made regular stops. I was listening to WKIX, Raleigh, an AM radio station that played a lot of Motown, R&B, and rock and roll. I looked to my left, and lo and behold, there were three of my "acquaintances" having a "discussion." The conversation was already heated to the boiling point. Pushing and shoving led to a fistfight brawl.

Sherman Frazier, Sampson Trueblood, and Cliven Oakes OBVIOUSLY had a problem, right out there on the sidewalk of the Mood Swing Café. The too few neon signs and no other lighting, gave the site a bluish aura of provocative intrigue. Smoke was pouring out from the kitchen exhaust vents, and steam was rising from a manhole cover. As you can well imagine, I was mesmerized by the developing firefight. At that time of night, without much traffic, I sat through another cycle of brown, orange, and white (I'm color blind, remember).

About the time that ensuing traffic caused me to "move on," I saw Sampson grab Sherman off of Cliven. Apparently, right at that moment, Cliven missed a good chance to SHUT UP, and pointed at Sherman. Sherman snatched his U S Army, Colt .45 from his waistband under his field jacket and fired three shots. They sounded and looked like a lightning strike. Four feet of blinding fire flew from the muzzle of that cannon, three times. The roar of the explosions resonated off the surrounding buildings.

Not that I haven't since, but at the time I had never experienced anything like that. Good GRIEF! I pulled onto the shoulder as the brave souls from within the Café poured into the darkness, now lighted by lots of headlights. Squalling tires led many out onto Tarboro Street, headed toward Rock Ridge, home of our former Education Governor, The

Honorable James B. Hunt, Jr. The foolish ones stayed on the scene to see what was gonna happen next. I was smart enough to know that I did not need to get into that mess, but I just couldn't bring myself to shift into gear and leave it.

Pretty soon a single police car arrived. The Wilson Police Officer evidently radioed for the cavalry. He effectively blocked off the victim and got most of the more sober patrons out of his way. I heard the cranked-up siren and saw the blinking bullet red light of the ambulance coming from town on Tarboro Street. There was so much commotion, that the road was now blocked because a young woman (not a lady from the language she was using) had gotten her toes run over while pushed up against a moving Buick Roadmaster. The ambulance couldn't get up to Cliven who was lying motionless, having crawled out onto the edge of the parking lot.

I had a really good flashlight that my Grandaddy John Robertson had bought me when I earned the rank of Eagle Scout in 1965. I went over and got absorbed by the melee. Finally, the ambulance backed up to Cliven, and their floodlights on the back of the vehicle lighted up the bloody scene.

Sampson and Sherman, joined by Sammy Coltraine were huddled up, getting their story straight. And, YES, there lay on the sidewalk what looked like a chrome, ivory gripped .25 automatic pistol. When I first walked up on the scene, that little pistol had not yet arrived, but now it had! Something magical must have happened to the three .45 caliber spent casings, because I looked everywhere for them, and never saw them.

Turns out, inside at the bar, Cliven had "hit on" someone that he shouldn't have. Sherman and Sampson took it upon themselves to right that wrong. Cliven let his liquor do too much talking, and the barkeeper told them to, "Take it outside." Push came to shove, and shove came to blows.

Cliven "allegedly" pulled that .25 from his pocket and pointed it at Sherman. Seems, Sherman was offended. He snatched out that .45 and shot Cliven once in the stomach. That 369 foot-pounds of muzzle energy from that heavy bullet knocked that old boy flat on his back with both his feet up in the air. The next .45 bullet went through the sole of Cliven's left foot which is where all the blood was coming from since Cliven was holding tightly to his bloated belly. The third .45 bullet was unaccounted for until the next day when a fresh gouge was found in the side of the Café. That was one night that I was glad to climb into ol' Bullet and go home.

"Here Comes the Goat Man"

Growing up, we looked forward to a sorta every-other-year phenomenon known as, "The Goat Man Is Coming." As we all were busy about our chores, horns honking out on US-301 drew our attention to "The Super Slab." There on the wide, grass barren shoulder was truly a sight to behold: about fifteen of the ugliest and meanest looking critters I had ever seen, yoked to a "Snake Oil" carnival wagon. Danged if there weren't two more of those goats tied on top. You really would have had to have been there to get the full, foul, photo.

Not to be outdone by the menagerie, the crusty old, bearded wagon-master (Ches McCartney – July 6, 1901 'til November 15, 1998) was usually slumped on the front seat with his black, mid-sized mongrel dog. He walked a lot, while quietly murmuring to his herd. The goat-drawn contraption moved ever so slowly, but carefully. The wagon(s) had three-foot steel wheels with no springs or shock absorbers. The curtained and enclosed carpet covered wagon pitched and yawed over the rain-washed gullies along the shoulder. At the poke-along speed of less than two miles per hour (four miles per day), it gave Goat Man the opportunity to survey the contents of the roadside-ditches. He would find lots of "stuff" that he could re-sell or incorporate into his vast collection of "priceless prizes and possessions." He gave me a rusted M-1 Rifle bayonet in a U S ARMY canvas "dogged" sheath. The sharp point of that blood-guttered knife is firmly stuck in the bull's eye of my ax-throwing target at home, right now.

Goat Man would usually "gee" his herd right into the driveway of Tobacco Trail Motel, where he knew that kind souls (Mac and Betty) would "look atter 'im." We had a fluorescently painted billboard in front of the office that read "WELCOME HOME." Smokey Joe painted the sign in return for his lodging. The first order of business was caring for his animals. While Ches milked his goats, Daddy would help him stake the smelly beasts along the back fence where the grass was always ankle deep (sandspurs, too). Goat Man would untie from the side of his abode, a banged up, Vintage Galvanized #4 Wash Tub, fill it with water for the goats, carefully inspect them for injuries, and then go use the bathroom inside motel room #6. He told us one time, that he had been to every state in the United States, except Hawaii, but had plans to go. He was afraid (no he wasn't), that if he went to Hawaii, his goats might eat the grass skirts off the hula girls.

Goat Man was a colorful vagabon and told us that he was born a farmer from out somewhere in Iowa. His main home was a church near Macon, Georgia. In the early 1970s, he broke his hip in Macon. Relatives of mine operated on him and patched him up. Drs. Waldo Emerson Floyd, Jr., and Waldo E. Floyd, III expertly attended their patient, but Goat Man adamantly refused any form of pain medication: "He eschewed alcohol, and he had a strong desire to experience pain naturally without medication."

He traveled up and down the eastern seaboard of America from Maine to Miami but spent a lot of time in Georgia. He would sit at the kitchen table with Mac and Betty, and spin yarns and reminisce while drinking the last drop of black coffee from the 15-cup Kenmore percolator from Sears and Roebuck. Sometimes Mother had to get up and leave the table when the recitations became too "colorful."

He had "sponsors" who aided and abetted him in his travels, and Mac and Betty qualified. They watched as he washed his clothes in that Wash Tub and hung them on the clothesline that had sparrow nests in the pipe ends, behind #1. They gave him room and board for a few nights. A hot shower (which he needed BADLY), was never found necessary, several good meals (including Parker's Barbecue plates), and good company was able to be withstood for only so long.

He sold postcard pictures of himself for a buffalo nickel, but I never saw one. Supposedly he was a preacher, and he always had a heavily worn Bible in the bib of his overalls, with a bunch of ragged bookmarks sticking out. It looked like it was falling apart. Pretty soon, he became restless, and his now rested goats (smelling not a whit better) became the deciding factor as to when it was time for him to hit the road again. With a cardboard box full of fresh clothing, some food, and ten dollars in his pocket, he bid us farewell.

Michael J. McArthur

Motel Duty

We lived near two families with sets of twin boys within walking distance of the motel: Ronnie and Donnie Taylor and Ronnie and Donnie Williamson. Sometimes they would help us with our chores so that we could go hunting or fishing down at Wiggins Mill. They were a couple of years older which got me in right much trouble, and a lot of experience "before my time." Hunting, fishing, camping, lying, running, chopping (with a sharp True Temper hatchet, I chopped off about one quarter of an inch of my left thumb, picked it up, taped it back on, and popped the clutch)! We were "the neighborhood boys," and were known to partake of just about every form of recreation you can imagine, good and bad. We all worked with our parents, their parents, and neighbors who could pay us a quarter an hour. That's when I got started "makin' real money."

Croppin' Tobacco

Other than my motel duties, "Croppin' Tobacco," also called "Priming Tobacco," was my first payin' job. The farmer I worked for, Elsie Walston had a mule named Sambo that pulled the tobacco "sled" or "truck" along the "truck rows" that ran every ninth row. Two croppers on each side of the truck, "pulled" yellow <u>ONLY</u> leaves, starting at the golden 5-foot plant's base, along two rows apiece on each side of the sled. As the leaves were gathered by the strong hand and placed under the support arm, I found it amazing how much crop could be carried for maybe 30 feet before the cropper walked over and gently placed the leaves inside the burlap "curtains" hooked on each side of the sled.

Then came the most amazingly remarkable part for me: one of the "field hands" would say, "Git up" to Sambo, and guess what! Sambo would bob his head and slowly amble toward the barn. Thirty more feet up the truck row, and the "hand" would holler, "Whoa." There he would stand, waiting until the sled was filled, and the command, "Git up" was given.

At the end of the row next to the dirt path, the field hand would yell, "GEE" for the mule to make a U-turn to the right, or "Haw" for Sambo to make a U-turn to the left, back down the next "truck row." The farmer had a cow, Bessie who could occasionally substitute for Sambo, but she "tromped down too much crop." When it was late in the afternoon, we used to ride on her boney back.

Being color blind served me well those hot summers. The gentleman farmer, Mr. Elsie, might I say, was "quar" about his crop. You didn't tear the leaves, you pulled them. When sorting the massive pile of gold, you didn't kick or sweep the leaves across the pack house floor, you picked them up, gently with your hands so as not to bruise them.

Bernard, the farmer's oldest son, could pick them up by scrunching his toes around the stem which was barely all right. While I was supposed to be "croppin' " the yellow leaves, Mr. Elsie determined that I was pulling too many (1 or 2) GREEN leaves to be tied. That ended my croppin' days. From then on, I learned to tie and hand and hang.

The last year that I worked, part of the season, the mule was out of commission. That meant that the tobacco sled was connected to a Farmall tractor. My color-blind self got the distinct privilege of drivin' that tractor. Thereby giving me a glimpse of those black and silver, State Highway Patrol Fords with chrome, bullet shaped red blinking lights on top, as they cruised between Bill's Drive-In and Parker's Barbecue out on Lover's Lane. I was hooked!

During the early Spring, the tobacco fields needed 5-inch aluminum pipe-fed irrigation which had to be manually moved across the whole field every 36 rows, at appropriate time intervals, usually on a rotating basis with the pipes in an adjacent field. Thank goodness, Wiggins Mill Pond down by Attorney Pinky Connor's plantation never ran dry. You shoulda seen the water moccasins that hung around the pumping station! I know they were Water Moccasins because when they would swim out into the pond, their bodies were visible above the water, and many times their heads were raised about eight inches. I also knew that the fanged inside of their mouth was white like "cotton." Killing them was how I gained that piece of information. The water filled pipes were almost too heavy for an 80-pound boy to wrangle.

When the harvest season rolled around, the first "pull" was what the old- timers called "sand lugs." Sand lugs were the first sprouted leaves at the bottom of the stalk which were the largest on the plant. They were also the roughest to pull: bent way over, summer sun baking your back, sweat running into your eyes, and every sinew in your legs stretched to the max. Being at about four inches off the ground at the stalk, put them lying flat on the sand. The three inches of rain from the afternoon before had splattered white quartz sand onto the tops of the leaves; thus "sand lugs." Talk about nasty, heavy, and aggravating! If the monkey couldn't find you pulling sand lugs, he just wasn't lookin'. One good thing about scouring the ground like that, was occasionally finding centuries old Indian-made arrowheads and spear "points."

I never "got the monkey on my back" which was mild to severe heat exhaustion. One guy even got heat stroke and never worked with us again. Once you suffered "the monkey," your tolerance for back breaking croppin' backer was never the same. A victim of the monkey could still "top" and "sucker" tobacco because that process was done standing up; but you had to look out for Water Moccasins who sought the liquid in the sucker crevices and the five-inch yellow, black, and white Tobacco Worms.

The snakes were never a problem when the mules were in the field. Obviously genetic selection had taught them that a mule would stomp them to death, so they slithered away. "Topping" was the removal of the top, flowering stalk section of the plant which robbed the leaves of production sustenance. "Suckering" was the "breaking off" of tubular suckers which also robbed the leaves of production sustenance. There always seemed to be colorful Tobacco Hornworms on the suckers which eventually morphed into Sphinx Moths, locally called Hummingbird Moths for their hovering capabilities.

Depending upon the size of the field and the availability of empty barns, croppin' tobacco was usually over with by about noon; having begun at 5:00am. All while "we men" were "croppin'," four ladies were "tyin'" 6 to 8 leaf stems with white twine dropping down from balls suspended in wire baskets above the tying racks.

The tied bundles were "looped," side-by-side, tightly onto tobacco sticks, 1" square and 48½ inches long. The sticks were suspended at each end in portable racks that were moved from barn overhang to barn overhang for shade. I am pretty sure there were some stories told and gossip spread during those prime-time sessions.

As the sticks became fully loaded, they were "handed" to a man who would pass the 20-pound stick to another man who would "hang" it on the rafters of the barn, sometimes 15 feet above the ground. If ever there was a time when a six-foot blacksnake could fall from above, onto your head, now was the time. That would usually empty the barn, the "tie" ladies, and whoever else was witnessing.

The Fishing Hole

Down at the fishin' hole one morning on my "day off," I was fishing in a farm pond that had a fallen hollow Oak Tree trunk lying on the bank and extending down into the water beside some Broad-Leaved Cattails.

Always when my cousin Denny and I arrived at the pond, there was a slowly and sneakily slithering snake visible through the hole in the trunk, and an Alligator Snapping Turtle basking in the sun on the top.

This day I was standing barefooted in knee deep muddy water amid blue and yellow flowering Hardy Water Lilies, shooting Blue and Brown Hawker Dragonflies with my Daisy long-pump BB gun. That was the best kind of BB gun, 'cause it held more BBs and was more powerful than the Red Rider, lever action. It had a muzzle end loading magazine that one night launched itself (I didn't do it) into the tile ceiling of our house, thereby leaving a 1" round indention in the acoustic tile.

For 52¢, we used to buy a box of fifty .22 caliber "rifle balls" from Raper's Store across from Parker's Barbecue. Today they can cost as much as $10.00. We would carefully wire a bullet in front of the muzzle of our BB guns and go "bird hunting."

It never worked, but that lead went flyin' "somwhrs." We also would take the cartridges, while not so carefully, lay one on the concrete porch of the pump room, point it in a safe direction, and hit it with Daddy's True Temper claw hammer. Where whatever went on those occasions was anybody's guess. By plan or plain luck, we never killed anybody, we hope. But Kathy did shoot a Helms Motor Lines truck trailer one Sunday afternoon (not that she ever knew it 'til now).

You know it could get awfully hot in those sandy cotton fields in August in Wilson, North Carolina. The Williamson twins and I got a job "hand picking" cotton. We would put on long pants and worn-out shirts and go into the cotton fields after lunch, after the dew had dried, along with about ten or fifteen other laborers.

We had a burlap sack tied to our left hip through the belt loop so it wouldn't come loose and slow us down. Each of us was assigned a single row to "pick," and stuff into our sack. The more experienced adult laborers were assigned two rows: one for each hand, and they had burlap sacks tied on each hip. Theirs was a work of art in that their nimble, strong fingers could pluck ALL the cotton from the bowl with lightning speed.

At the end of the day, everybody took their sacks to a cast iron "cotton weigh-up scale" hung in the middle of three, four-inch saplings arched and tied together like a teepee that Jessie had erected. Some of the adults had picked over 200 pounds. Each of us had picked about forty pounds, and we were pitiful. We whined, we tried to figure out a way to make our cotton weigh more, but never got the chance.

After the first day, were "allowed" to stay home. Our fingers were raw, and we had only earned about seventy-five cents for the day's labor. While out in the field, we had found where Elsie had planted about four rows of those great big, heavy Jubilee variety watermelons. He had sliced four or five up at the cotton weigh in. Those things were deep red with black seeds. They were incredibly delicious.

Thinking about those watermelons, a plan was hatched. We left the Williamson house, skirted the swamp, crossed the canal on our homemade bridge, followed the path, and made our way through the briars and under the barbed wire fence, right into the middle of the watermelon patch. Donnie was the biggest twin, and the strongest. He heaved up one of those forty-pound melons and busted it on the sand. I am authorized to tell you that that was the absolute best tasting watermelon that I had ever before or since eaten, bar none.

But our interlope was cut short. BLAM! BLAM! Elsie was on his back porch with his Field Grade L. C. Smith double barrel 12-gauge shotgun, shooting at us. We saw him break open the breach to reload it. To quote the Bob Hope film actor, Stepin Fetchit, "Feets don't fail me now!"

We ran in three different directions, and not one of us got peppered. At the time we should have known that Elsie was a good six-hundred yards away, and the range on that shotgun was only about seventy-five yards. Nope! We weren't scared, much! Good sense and logic had already left the building when we decided to go over there and steal watermelons, anyway!

Back to the fishin' hole: I had just crawled through the barbed wire fencing, in water up to my knees when, wouldn't you know it? Suddenly, the 2-inch evil head of a Red Bellied Water Snake brushed my leg, and popped up right beside my bare left knee. I immediately put a BB right down through the top of her head as she wrapped her scaly self around both my skinny legs.

After I pulled her out of the water, I saw that she was pregnant. She was almost four feet long and about as big around as a tennis ball. The lumpy midsection made me curious as to her insides. On my way over to Ronnie's and Donnie's, I dropped by the barn to show the snake to the ladies looping and tying tobacco.

They emptied the place.

Then I crossed the path and proudly walked over to Miss Jessie and Mr. Elsie's house and ran all the family off the rickety back porch with the old timey galvanized scrub board and the hand crank wringer Maytag washing machine.

The snake was draped over the barrel of my gun. Noting movement in her midsection, I decided to dissect her. Contained inside were 27 MOVING, individually compartmentalized ten-inch water snakes about as big around as a pencil. Thankfully they were nearly ready to emerge, so I took them in a tobacco twine box back down to the pond and released them. Most of them probably became lunch for some Largemouth Bass and hand sized Speckles (Black Crappies).

"Sea food" and Tobacco Gum

Back to the tobacco field! Now was the time to go get lunch at the cross-roads country store: usually "a box of sardines." Elsie called it, "Sea Food."

Some of us would ride in the bed of the wooden floored pick-up truck, while the "cool" older boys would ride on the tailgate, legs dangling off the back. During cotton season, in order to make "choppin' " less difficult, they would drag their hoes on the pavement to make the edges sharp as razors.

The little rectangular, brightly colored sardine can usually contained ten Scandinavian miniature fish with water, "packed in there like sardines." There was a "key" fastened to the bottom of the can which was pried off with a wooden spoon because your fingernails were long since history. The key was used to engage the scroll top of the can. As you rolled the covering back across the top of the can, you made sure not to spill any of the juice on your worn out, cut off Blue Bell dungarees because, of all things, it smelled bad and drew gnats.

Now you were ready to lift the fish out of the can with the curled tin top and place it onto the Lance Saltine cracker. These both seemed much bigger in size then than now. A Honey Bun, a skinny hunk of Hoop cheese and a Pepsi Cola rounded out lunch.

As soon as possible we exited the store and weaved through the "old men" to get away from the nicotine-stained walls with Buick, Ford, Dodge, Chevrolet, and "Pin-up" calendars (Betty Boop), and Lucky Strike posters (L.S.M.F.T. Lucky Strike Means Fine Tobacco). That store was filled with the stale smell to others, but good smell to me of Sulphur matches and cigarette smoke. Outside there on Route 2 was a packed dirt parking area beneath centuries old White Oaks and a China Berry Tree, known by Southerners as a "Chaney Ball Tree." That gnarled old lightning struck

Chaney Ball Tree had enough dead limbs and branches to fill a "stake truck." Since I was the smallest, I climbed up there with a worn-out True Temper Bow Saw from Stephens Hardware and began cutting out some of the larger limbs, but not the limb with the Robin's nest in it.

Suddenly I whiffed a musky odor. As many snakes as I had handled over the years, I knew that one was close: REAL CLOSE. Sure enough, the rotted cavity behind the limb I was cutting, housed a spooked 4-foot, harmless Black Rat Snake (Remember that Robin's nest?). He launched himself out of that tree, brushed my neck, and coiled right onto the dirt spot where ol' Bernard Walston USED TO BE STANDING, just prior to his larger-than-life, leap of faith.

The shaded dirt was cool to our bare feet as we played "holies" which is a game similar to yesterday's horseshoes and today's Corn Hole. If you can remember, the miracle healing powder known as "snuff," came in small, round, capped, shiny tin cans.

Some of my "extended" family used to run low on snuff which they skillfully placed in the pouch of their lower lip which made them look like they had been slugged in a fistfight. When they ran out of snuff, they would quietly go to "Cap'n Mac's" pipe humidor, grab a pure handful and compress it into a wad, and stuff their mouth with Prince Albert Pipe Tobacco. Back to "holies."

We would dig two holes about the size of a baseball, 'bout twenty feet apart and two inches deep. We had taken the round cap of a snuff can and filled it with lead that we had melted from pneumatic tire wheel weights. And yes, we might have pried one or more from a '63 Rambler that belonged to Carson Outlaw. We would team up and take turns pitching that ½ inch thick chunk of lead toward the opposing team's "hole." We kept score with the first one sinking ten holies declared the winner, which was usually Bernard's brother, Rudolph.

Carson's Rambler came into focus on a number of occasions. Once when his Rambler was parked under the Chaney Ball Tree, it was blocking the view to the north from a Waterbury, Connecticut Yankee, too briefly stopped at a stop sign, who promptly pulled out in front of Andy Parrish's "stake truck."

That same week my neighbor, gentleman farmer Louis Tom jacked up the right rear tire on that Rambler, so as not to be seen, and then carefully lowered it into one half of a CONGO variety watermelon. Of course it allowed the Rambler's skinny tire to spin, throwing watermelon juice in every direction, when fired up and put in reverse.

As recently as twenty years ago, I took my leather bag of "cat's eyes, clog knockers, aggies, steelies, crystals, clouds, tigers, pee-dinks, woodies, and shooters up to the store and "shot marbles" with the neighborhood kids. They had not a clue!

We played box car, ring, triangle, and drop having thrown to the line for deciding who would "shoot" first. Of course at the end of our time together, the boys thanked me, and have done so upon many recent occasions in their adulthood.

Back in the day, when Mrs. Armstrong, my wonderful second-grade teacher at Frederick L. Woodard Elementary School on Kenan Street in Wilson would end our too-short recess with ringing her handbell, we yelled, "GRABS," for what was left in the ring, grabbed 'em and ran like hell. We also had a time with Duncan YoYos and spinning tops, but that story comes later.

Now that we had finished our "seafood dinner," rested up playin' holies, hammered out a little Rock-Paper-Scissors, scrubbed the tobacco gum off our hands and legs, and laid out in the back of the truck, it was time to go back down to the Millpond where two hot, log-built tobacco barns waited to be emptied. Methodically, we gradually emptied the racks of "tied" sticks of flu-cured bright leaf tobacco. The sand that continually fell onto your sweaty neck, eyes, and ears from your co-worker's bare feet on the rafters above was unbelievable. Mr. Elsie had kept the rusted gas burners (used to be wood fired) lit throughout the night before, but had turned them off the following morning. He had gone to the barns during the night to regulate the heat and make sure nothing was on fire. It was still hot and dark in there.

Liberty Tobacco Warehouse

In the early days, before mechanization on "the floor" of the sales warehouses, six leaves of brittle but slightly moist leaves were carefully "bundled" by the older women. They would "grade" the handful of leaves, then take a slightly moist leaf and "wrap" it around the stems, making a "hand." Then these "like graded" bundles were <u>placed</u> onto four-foot square, woven wooden "racks" or "baskets" to be transported to the sales warehouse in Wilson. As teenagers, when we found a "hand" lying in the middle of Tarboro Street, we would stop the car, get out and pick it up: we could sell it for 5¢ at Liberty Tobacco Warehouse. Gasoline was 25¢ per gallon, and ol' Bullet ('55 Pontiac Star Chief) got about 8 - 12 miles to the gallon, depending on how hard I drove it.

Later, after mechanization (forklifts) came to Wilson, and they started accepting tobacco tied in sheets, we piled the tobacco in the "pack house," on the floor onto huge burlap "sheets" to be tied at the top like a hobo's poke (satchel). This allowed the leaves to remain dry while allowing air to circulate and prevent mold and mildew which decreased the value of the crop. These big, 4-foot diameter, round "sheets" loaded with tobacco went to Wainwright's Tobacco Warehouse on Goldsboro Street in the beds of two-ton farm trucks. Mr. Raymond Browning was an auctioneer who lived for the season at Tobacco Trail Motel in the Pump room for $20 per week. He was a smoking, tobacco chewing alcoholic, in cahoots with American Tobacco Company, but could give miraculously guaranteed predictions what a crop would sell for: usually quickly, and for just slightly over "best price." He found a lot of "free" unopened half gallons of Smirnoff Vodka or Gordon's Gin or Everclear 190 Proof Grain Alcohol on his doorstep almost every morning. We carried the empties down to the millpond and shot them floating in the sand pit with our Remington, Nylon 66 loaded with Winchester, yellow box, .22 caliber, long rifle, hollow point bullets. Too often we could hear the 1200 fps bullets ricochet either off the bottle or the water, into the distant unknown.

On more than one occasion, more than one of those 190 Proofs would end up over in the parking lot of Ralph L. Fike Senior High School in the form of a concoction known as Purple Jesus, commonly, and I mean

Michael J. McArthur

commonly called "P J". Most often it coincided with an Atlantic Beach/Emerald Isle weekend event.

Waiting Tables at Parker's Barbecue Restaurant 1963 -1971

When I turned 14, I was allowed to leave the tobacco field and go ½ mile up US-301 near the Wilson County Fairgrounds, where I stood on a drink crate to "draw pints and quarts (quat o' tea)" of dark sweet (only) tea into cardboard containers to be sold, "out the back door" of world-renowned Parker's Barbecue Restaurant. By all standards, I was too young, and "too little" to wait tables because the trays of food were too big and heavy.

I was "Mac" and "Mrs. Mac's" son, so I got away with a lot of stuff. The big guys didn't pick on me too much because not only did I supply the back-door take-out demand for tea, I kept about thirty glasses full of tea for the dining hall waiter's to scoop up without having to independently fill their orders.

All during my duration at Parker's we served every customer with a tall Dixie Cup of water at the time of their arrival. Gifted with large hands (and feet), I could carry eight Dixie Cups of water, carefully placing them in the midst of the awed customers. That is now no longer the case.

Also, all during my time at Parker's Barbecue, we served sweet tea in G L A S S glasses. As you can imagine, occasionally, as a clear glass was scooped into the ice machine, it broke and cut the blood out of the waiter. Immediately, the shivers of glass blended right into the stockpile of ice. What did we do? We scooped all that ice out of the "box," and refilled it with ice from Wilson Ice and Coal Company up by the Seaboard Coastline railroad tracks on Vance Street.

The icehouse was always cold and dark. Big blocks of ice, about the size of twin bed box springs, were rolled out from deep within. The burley, heavy, white-coated worker began chopping the block into smaller pieces that could be fed into a screaming grinder which spit out a big plume of usable ice, right into triple layered, four-foot-tall, open topped bags. We then loaded about eight of these into the Parker's Barbecue catering van and sped back to the restaurant. We dumped the bagged ice into the ice machine and were back in business. <u>Today</u>, when you order your "LCom" (large combination), DM (dark meat), BS (Brunswick stew), FF (French fries), T (sweet tea), your sweet tea is served in a plastic glass.

As a rule, a "Large Combination" consists of White Meat chicken breast, a fluffed-up spoonful of pork barbecue, a ladle of Brunswick stew, a serving spoonful of boiled potatoes, a bowl of slaw, six cornsticks, and beverage.

Back in the day, it cost $2.25.

There was a "candy rack" vendor named E. B. Barefoot who became a Silver Cadillac DeVille driving, self-made millionaire, selling Hershey Bars, Baby Ruths, and Nutty Buddies.

Occasionally part-time waiter Dennis Earl would casually stroll by the rack, scarf a Snickers Bar, throw it from behind his back over his head, and catch it in his apron. He was amazing in many ways.

One Sunday in June, Dennis Earl came to work half drunk, with a bad attitude (imagine that). After filling all the shakers of salt and pepper, the vinegar bottles, the sugar bowls, and the chromed napkin boxes (but not too full), he waited on fourteen tables, took their scribbled Guest Check orders, and did not bother to enter the table number to which that order was supposed to be delivered.

He slipped behind the cash register, he kicked open the swinging door to the kitchen, spiked a handful of clumped up orders onto the nail beside the two big coffee pots, sauntered back into the dining room, wisely avoided eye-contact with Jenny Parker (Ralph's stylish wife), took off his white starched apron, wadded it up, chunked it into the "soda" box beside the trays, threw his hat into the trash can, saluted Head Waiter Donald Williams, shot Tommy Davis "the bird," and said, "I'll see you boys in the funny papers!"

When Mr. and Mrs. E. B. Barefoot came in and ordered his Large Combination <u>dinner</u>, his wife, Mrs. Elizabeth ordered a child's chicken plate (drumstick ONLY). Their bill came to $3.75. Henry Brewer usually sat with them while they ate and would sometimes grab the "Guest Check" bill and wad it up, stuffing it in his pocket.

Then he would tell Mr. Barefoot, "Aw, don't leave a tip. I pay those boys plenty of money." When he did leave a tip, it was a nickel. At that time, Parker's Barbecue paid us $00.40 per hour, and our tips were expected to equal or exceed the basic minimum hourly wage of $1.15.

The restaurant was owned by Henry Brewer (Sue), Graham Parker (Dot), and Ralph Parke (Jenny). These three families created a barbecue dynasty and truly an unparalleled legacy in the fast-growing world of pit-cooked pork barbecue and fried chicken food service. They invented the phenomenon of great food and greater service at a reasonable price. One of the three owners rotated "OFF" every third week. The other two owners worked every other day during their two weeks of duty.

Waiters at Parker's Barbecue were usually teenaged boys, sons of sharecroppers, who needed a job for many reasons. We all subsidized our household income by taking part of our parents' loads upon ourselves. Most of us (waiters) made pretty good money which was never reported to the Internal Revenue Service.

We could make as much as $30 a day working after school. That is a lot of $.50 tips! I was able to buy my brother and sister some clothes that my folks could not afford. Among other things, Kathy got Bass Weejun loafers, and Pat got a belt and some shirts his sophomore year at Ralph L. Fike Senior High School.

Tip Thief

Life was not all fun and games back then, but we managed to get along. Work many times (maybe not often enough) helped keep us focused and out of trouble. Trouble could always find its way in, though. Some of the newer boys would steal tips from the older boys which was frowned upon. We had one named Junior who got caught with a "marked" dollar bill that Donald had planted on table 10L. We knew he had it, because the cashier, Dot (Graham's beautiful wife), saw him pocket it versus put it in the tip jar. We said nothing.

At about 9:10 p.m., half of us, including Junior, went "out back" to the cook pits in the cinder block building directly behind the restaurant. Every night half the waiters cleaned up the dining hall, and half the waiters had to "throw hogs" onto the gas-fired elevated (48 inches) metal "pits" for overnight cooking by Ronnie Galloway. The longitudinally butchered hog halves were hung upon huge steel gambrels (hooks), by slits between their ankle tendon and bone. These hooks were suspended from steel rails about eight feet above the wet slick concrete floor. The hog's carcass had a ten-inch slit between its third and fourth rib at about four feet off the floor. Many times the snout of the upside-down hog-half, touched the floor.

Each of us waiters took turns "throwing" however many hogs Ronnie said "throw" (usually between 10 and 15 apiece. That meant that we would approach the suspended, upside down hog, and if we were right-handed, we would insert our left hand into the ankle slit, grab the ankle bone, insert our right hand between ribs 3 and 4, heave the carcass upward off the hook, and carry the carcass fifteen feet to the pit. Remember that I was small: five feet, four inches – 104 pounds. Some of those hogs weighed almost as much as I did, particularly those with their snouts dragging the floor. I was thankful for those big ol' strong farm boys who took it as a challenge to grab the biggest ones as a show of strength to their cohorts – somewhat of a workout, if you will.

We would then stand sideways to the pit, pivot clockwise thereby swinging the head of the hog away from the pit, and then with all of our might, give a mighty HEAVE and "throw" that hog perpendicularly right up onto the already hot steel grates, skin up. We would then "pack 'em" tightly to one another, and go get our next quest.

Henry's Tenderloin Breakfast

There was the Sunday morning when we all got to work early, and Woody Walston went out to the cooler. He had brought an "Old Hickory" butcher knife and carefully (he thought), carved out about ten pork tenderloins. Aubrey, "Uncle Aub" Shingleton had brought two dozen eggs, and we were gonna cook a feast with corn sticks for breakfast. Unfortunately, on that particular Sunday morning, Henry Brewer, one of the three owners arrived earlier than we had expected. BUSTED! You might never guess what happened next: to our tremendous shock and amazement, Henry got busy, found a large Griswold #9 Cast Iron Skillet, threw some lard in it, rubbed some kind of seasoning on those scraped up tenderloins, and cooked them to perfection. That beat the heck out of getting fired which we all expected and deserved.

Next came time to sit down and feast. Henry thought he was gonna punish us by making us eat each and every last bit and morsel of the filched food. WRONG!! Those ol' country boys wolfed down that food like they were preparing for a game of tackle football out in the back forty. Since that didn't work out like he expected, Henry decided we were gonna hafta pay for the meal.

Our good friend "Mr. June," volunteered to do that, but Henry wouldn't hear of it. At that time, June Brunson was a 20+ year employee, and bulletproof. He just died (84) on September 8, 2020 after 69 years with Parker's Barbecue. He was one of Daddy's Friday night regulars in number 15. During lunch that day we had to go in the woods at Elsie's and scrounge around in the trash pile for flatware that had been carelessly thrown into the trash barrels by most of us! That was not only humiliating, but hard, nasty work (punishment). Well, since that wasn't enough, Henry decided that we would have to stay late that night and oil the floors. When our best friend Sue, Henry's wonderful wife got there, she soon got wind of the brouhaha. She told him, "Henry, I love these boys. You leave 'em be." That ended that!

Tonight, though, throwing hogs was not our only concern. Tonight we had Junior to contend with. Junior had stolen at least one tip off table 10L, and untold others. Tonight we would "break him from suckin' eggs," to quote the incomparable Jerry Clower (just one of our many heroes). Tonight Junior would learn a lesson that he would not soon forget, but survive. Tommy Davis, one of the older (25 yoa) waiters asked Junior how he was enjoying his job. Junior replied that he "loved it." Tommy asked him was he making as much money as he thought he should. Junior replied, "I reckon so." At this point Jimmy Ray (we named him Donkey Ray) Bynum chimed in, "Junior, you are a _____ thief," at which point we grabbed his arms. Tommy grabbed his ankles, turned him upside down like those hogs, and we shook all of his money, keys, cigarette lighter, pocketknife, and two marbles out of his pants pockets. Junior didn't make as much money that night. He later turned out to be one of my best friends, and we worked together and hunted together for years after that.

Donkey Ray's Antics

Donkey Ray could find M-80s, Silver-Tips, and Cherry Bombs by the "1/3rd gross," (48 count) when nobody else could. He lived in Saratoga, NC which he christened "Togeyville." He was related to the owner of Essofleet truck stop in Elm City, and was way too familiar with EVERYTHING that was ALWAYS available at that location. It was not uncommon for many of us (mostly "them") to ride throughout the community and either throw Cherry Bombs at "yardbirds," or scarin' the H out of polecats. Red Walston, down on US-117 at Maurice's Grill near Contentnea Creek usually had his red '55 Chevrolet trunk FULL of those 10" cubed white cardboard boxes full (1/3rd gross) of Silver Tips, Black Cats, and Cherry Bombs. Ol' Donkey Ray was our ring-leader until one afternoon he lit a short fused M-80, drew back to chunk it, and in one fell swoop, deafened his right ear while blowing off the flesh tips from his thumb and pointer. From then on, he was our designated, mangle handed, half-deaf driver. He drove a black '61 Ford, and one night "swerved" home to Togeyville, systematically pushing over every NC Department of Transportation sign, right up to and into his daddy's driveway. The State Trooper, Cecil Simons found him the next morning, passed out in the "rolled and pleated" front seat with an empty fifth of Janis Joplin's favorite whiskey, Southern Comfort.

As a table waiter, Donkey Ray was, according to him, "the best." He was such a clown and humorist, that his customers loved him, and would ask for him upon their entrance to the restaurant. He was a large framed young man, with a sassy stride and cocked head. He "chucked and bobbed" through the Sunday noontime crowds, and balanced <u>on one hand</u>, large trays of "Family Style" barbecue a good two feet above the coifed hairstyles. If he ran up behind a "blocker," he would bounce that tray, the bowls would clatter and rattle, and the offenders would IMMEDIATELY get the H out of his way.

Only once did I see him falter. While holding a large bowl of steaming hot Brunswick Stew in his left hand, he reached across a senior lady's shoulder with his right hand to place a plate of corn sticks atop the chromed (not over-stuffed) napkin dispenser. That Stew bowl tipped and dribbled about three hot tablespoons of bright red stew, right down a lady's open backed blue chiffon "Sunday best." After the commotion died down, it turned out that the lady was "family" to Donkey Ray, and he dodged another bullet.

Rowdies and Two Half Benjamins

Speaking of "dodging:" One Saturday afternoon after having just left the American Legion racetrack across the highway, a crowd of rough and rowdy rednecks came in and made way too much of a racket. Unfortunate for them, and entertaining for us, great big restaurateur, owner, and chief cook Ralph Parker was summoned from the kitchen. Ralph was an intimidating, dark complected, giant of a man who had little (or no) patience. He entered the dining room with his characteristic 20-inch, two-pronged cooking fork. He never spoke a word. As he glowered at the table, at least eight, one-dollar bills and a five began to fly from pockets onto the table. The rowdies made a hasty retreat.

Quess what? They committed an error upon their return the very next Saturday. Well, you know who happened to be their waiter! Donkey Ray Bynum. Never did he mention the previous week's episode with Ralph Parker. Neither did they. They knew better! Upon their exit from the restaurant, a few derogatory comments were overheard about the "service" they had received. Among other things, Donkey Ray had found a single five-cent nickel "tip" with Brunswick Stew smeared on it underneath a business card which read, "You have been visited by The

Royal Knights of the Ku Klux Klan." He grabbed that nickel, ran to the foyer of the restaurant entrance, and spied 'em. They were ganged up at the back of a dust covered, fire-engine red, Ford pick-up truck, laughing and joking. Donkey Ray, in all his radiant glory, bounded over there, threw that nickel into their midst, and yelled, "Here you son of a bitches. You need this worse than I do."

By now several of us were at his side, and we dared them to make a move. Fortunately for them, they for once in their ragtag lives made a good decision: they apologized to Donkey Ray. Arrogantly, Billy-Bob handed him a one-hundred-dollar bill (but with a smirk on his red face). Wouldn't you know it? Donkey Ray tore that Benjamin right in half, and threw it on the gravel parking lot. Apparently, it was not over! Not to Donkey Ray, anyway. About this time, Cecil Simons, our local Highway Patrolman just happened to pull off US-301 into the parking lot. He saw the commotion, and skidded to a dusty stop behind us. Now, you know he was on our side! He "instructed" that crowd of drunks to get into their trucks and get the H out of there, and "Don't never come back!" Worked for us! We scooped up those two half Benjamins, grabbed Donkey Ray by the arms, and we all went back inside.

Dot Parker, bless her heart, was crying and had already called the law. She, like her husband Graham Parker, carried a.38 Smith and Wesson revolver in her pocketbook, and was stormin' out the swinging door to help us when we went stormin' back in. Of course she had to fuss at us a little bit, but her tears gave her away. She was smokin' mad at that crowd of rednecks. Her heralded philosophy was, "Do NOT mess with my boys! Not now. Not no how! Not ever!" See why we loved her?

Friends, the Beach, Ducks, and More

Warren Dixon Barnes

Warren was my best friend. Best in my mind from a personal standpoint, and best in character from everybody's standpoint. Beginning at a young age, Warren Dixon Barnes (April 19, 1949 to November 21, 2020), was just a good person who surrounded himself with good people, or in my case, he found some good. We all liked Warren a lot, and the good thing about him was that he deserved our admiration and respect.

Warren, Bill, and Anne grew up in front of the Seaboard Coastline Railroad tracks under the tutelage of Dick and Romaine Barnes at 1718 Woodside Drive in a small Wilson subdivision known as Forest Hills. Warren's folks were the epitome of Ozzie and Harriett Nelson to many of us teenagers. They were always kind and caring, and Mrs. Romaine would always have a peanut butter sandwich or an apple for us. As they kept a close watch over their own three, they also kept a close watch on those of us with whom their children hung out. Warren and I were the ones upon whom it fell the awesome responsibility of "lookin' out" for our friends who either one. drank too much, or two. drove too fast or both, or three. used poor judgment, or four. paid too much attention to their friends' bad advice; and sometimes committing all four egregious errors at the same time. If Warren was gonna go to the Fike Cyclones vs. Rocky Mount Griffons football game in Rocky Mount, then Mrs. Butler would let Gerald go with him. If Mike was gonna drive his '55 to Memorial Auditorium in Raleigh to see Dionne Warwick, The Four Seasons, or Joe Pope and the Atlanta Tams, then Lew's and David's moms would let them go. Sadly, we lost John Graves, Lew Highsmith, and Harry Liner, and nearly lost several others to automobile accidents. Dick and Romaine were always there to console us.

Warren was a member of the Fike High Homecoming Court, and through the parade, asked me to drive beautiful Co-Chair Carol Ann Hammond and him nestled high atop the exposed back seat, on the rolled and pleated upholstery of a U. S. Navy S.E.A.L.'s 389 cu. in. GTO convertible with two Holley 4-barreled carburetors, and a Hurst 4-speed transmission. After clearing the Parade Route, <u>we had to do</u> a FORBIDDEN fly-by past the grandstand, out onto the field at Fleming Stadium, and back to Fike High School in that extraordinarily L O U D Convertible GTO. Twice, Warren and I, in our sport coats had to jump out, raise the hood and put the single fan belt back onto the pulleys. Turns out that Wilson City Police Officer Ray Hayes was NOT IMPRESSED by the uproariously loud commotion, but Warren and I thought it was great fun.

As our friend Bob Hester maneuvered his Honda ninety motorcycle underneath the stadium's grandstand seating, he asked Officer Hayes, "Where do you want us to park, Officer (pronounced 'Awfcr' by Bob)?" Well, Awfcr Hayes thought Bob had called him "HOSS." Hayes put both his huge, gloved hands on the handlebars of that motorcycle, and explained to Mr. Bob "Class President" Hester that, "Officers of the law deserve RESPECT. You better remember that!" For once in his life, Bob was speechless, but somehow managed to mumble a sincere, "Yes, Sir," with no feeble attempt to explain the mix-up.

Emerald Isle

Emerald Isle (conch shells, crab shacks, and sunburns), Squatter's Campground (tents, no sleep, and underage drinking), Oceanana Motel (pier fishing, pier Grille, and pier game room), Sanitary Fish Market (fried shrimp, sweet tea, and suntanned waitresses), Captain Bill's (hushpuppies, fried Flounder, and suntanned waitresses), and Atlantic Beach (the sandbars, The Ember's Club, The Circle amusement park, and the Pavilion's sandy dance floor) seemed to have magically magnetic properties for nearly all of Wilson's "groovies." Not only after the Sadie Hawkins Day Dance, or during spring break, or during Junior-Senior weekends, but after school got out, everybody who was anybody, "headed down to Morehead City." Down through The Croatan National Forest, traveling too fast on two lane US-70 through Dover and Tuscarora. Some of us would stop for a break at Thomas Haywood's Store in Croatan near

New Bern. There in the edge of the woods, cattle rancher Wilber Herring had fabricated back in the thirties, "The Self-Kicking Machine." Mr. Haywood's laid-back philosophy was that, "If we would kick ourselves more, we would kick others, less." The so called, "One Kicker of a Contraption" consisted of four farmer style, high-top brogans, each tied and mounted at the end of a one-inch steel spoke jutting off a wheel which was connected by a pulley and belt, to a pully and crank that the "kickee" would back his or her butt up to, and turn the mobilizing crank "as fast as you could stand." The world-famous, incredibly effective, amazingly motivating machine now occupies a place of honor inside Raleigh's North Carolina Museum of History, a gift from the Taylor family.

On Surfside Drive, in Atlantic Beach, sometimes it would take a couple of hours to get everybody "settled in." Along about four o'clock, Warren and Elaine would venture out from the confines of Elaine's "compound," and go down to "The Circle" in the center of Atlantic Beach. This notorious circular strip of sandy, salty, asphalt held miraculously invigorating powers of attraction. The cotton candy was so good that it would make you write bad checks. The triple dipped chocolate ice-cream was dished out by the gallon, and was, "as hard as Chinese 'rithmetic." The sights you could see, the aromas you could smell, and the sounds you could hear beside The Emporium, were nothing less than spectacular. "Ray-Bans" were sold on every countertop, but the coolest sunglasses were "Aviator" pilot glasses from Marine Corps Air Station (MCAS) aboard Camp LeJeune, right down across the Bogue Inlet Ferry on US-58. (The B. Cameron Langston Bridge over Bogue Inlet from Emerald Isle to Swansboro was not dedicated until August 24, 1971)

The Marines Have Landed

Speaking of Marines, when they individually or collectively took over the ocean-front Pavilion's dance floor or the eight pool tables, they were a fearsome, formidable bunch – but right many of the girls "liked 'em," – some of the girls liked 'em a LOT. One of the most impressive sights that I ever witnessed exploded one hot Saturday night, right out on the front porch of the Pavilion. Seems that too many of the barrel-chested Marine recruits placed too much of their too sweaty selves, in too close proximity to too many, too young "teeny-boppers." Some called it "bopping." We called it shagging. Some of our mothers had taught us how to shag so that we could "fit in."

Apparently, the eight or ten house-paid, big-boy "bouncers" were no match for the marauding militia. The call went out to the Marine Base Commander.

The passel of partiers jammed all up out front in the street parted like the Red Sea for Moses, when two OD Green Willys Jeep Trucks slid to a stop, right at the Pavilion's front porch. Out bounded eight of the biggest, fatigue uniformed, helmeted, baton brandishing, snarly dog looking warriors ever to lace on a pair of spit-shined combat boots. There was absolutely no mistaking it: <u>they were on a mission</u>. The eight-man squad of Marine Corps, Military Police was there in full force, and prepared to take care of business – <u>THEIR WAY!</u> That mission was to extricate and take corrective action upon any miscreant who dared to bring disrespect to, or tarnish the name or reputation of the United States Marine Corps. Their base commanders worked extremely hard to foster good relations with surrounding communities, and they were not about to let four drunken sailors tarnish that image.

With **MP** emblazoned on their helmets and their white arm bands, one or more had chromed whistles attached by chromed lanyards to their starched and pressed uniforms. Those whistles sent an unmistakable message to "the good ol' boys" who, more than likely, had heard that joyful noise in days gone by. Apparently, these four rowdies either had short memories, or were slow learners. Those **MP** soldiers were not about to let four skinheads succeed in ruining ANYBODY'S night on the beach. These warriors were not bound by some of the "Politically Correct," ridiculously imposed "hamstrings" by which most police officers and sheriffs' deputies are bound. After all, tourists meant tax revenue and income to the summer resort towns of Atlantic Beach, Beaufort, and Emerald Isle. Impressively, the whistles shrilled out a voiceless command to the four offenders. ALL FOUR immediately sprawled eagle, face planted on the saw-dusted and waxed, sandy floor, legs spread wide apart, and fingers interlocked behind their pencil-necked "whitewalls."

I honestly do not know how it happened so quickly and so smoothly. First things I saw emerge from the eight clustered **MPs** were four "stiff as a board," terrified recruits. In unison, they were hoisted up at arm's height, above the helmeted heads of the **MPs**, parallel to the exposed ceiling rafters. Even better than the movies, it was truly a sight to behold: eight uniformed Marines, in tight formation, marching in close-quarter cadence to their war wagons. Not what any of us had expected: the recruits were not characteristically or haphazardly "THROWN" in the style of Chuck Norris and Sylvester Stallone, into the dark confines of the Willys wagons. They were placed there, motionless, quiet as a church mouse. It reminded me of a modern-day comedian who quipped, upon the untimely discovery of his dastardly deeds, "I didn't really know how many of them it was gonna take to whip my ass, but I knew how many they were gonna use!"

The circumspect **MPs** were not disheveled in any shape, fashion, or form. In fact, they were "Cool." They were not "give out." Not NONE. They were polished professionals who had just flawlessly performed their urgently unpleasant mission with the utmost pride and without showing any disrespect, rude, or crude behavior as might could have easily been expected (and which we were all eagerly anticipating). There was not a person on site who could say a negative word about what had just transpired. There was no blood – no broken bones, there was not even any offensive language. However, there was much sincere and deep admiration and utmost respect, and maybe, just maybe, a little bit of wholesome fear instilled into each one of us that fateful night.

The Embers Club at Atlantic Beach

The Embers Club was a cavernous establishment just across the way from the Pavilion. Since "demon rum" was served across the bar along the side walls, patrons had to be eighteen years old to get through the crowded door, much less be allowed to "grab us up a cool one." There were not many of us who did not possess and carefully guard a two-dollar fake ID, or our friend's smudged ID. I coveted Jimmy Williamson's cardboard NCDMV issued Operator's License (pronounced liiizens). I paid him $5 to get me a duplicate. The only hitch was that he had emblazoned prominently there upon the face of his certificate, "Corrective Lenses." Well, you know what that meant. That meant that he was required to wear glasses. No problem! I got me two pair of "Five Points Five and Dime Store" readers and was good to go. Since I was able to see a little bit better, I could also hear a little bit better because of my newfound ability to read lips from further away.

It just so happened that the first night we were inside The Embers Club, that the band performing was "The Wreck of the Old 97," named after a Southern Railway "fast mail train" delivering mail behind schedule, and crashed outside Spencer Mountain (Pop. 37) in Gaston County, North Carolina. Warren and I had cajoled one of the bouncers into giving us a table on the front row. I turned my chair around and was sitting at the feet of the bass guitarist. The band launched into their routine of Mitch Ryder and the Detroit Wheels and Little Richard's rock and roll combo-rendition of "Devil with a Blue Dress / Good Golly Miss Molly." The cigarette smoke was thick as train smoke, and so acrid inside that packed palladium, that I honestly could see no more than twenty feet in any direction. Though the temperature was cool as ice, my eyes were burned shut for most of our time in there. Suddenly, something "smoked me" right in the chest. I opened my eyes and looked down. There, inside my starched white herringbone, long sleeve Van Heusen shirt pocket was a four-inch broken tip off the percussionist's drumstick (still have it): two inches pocked aluminum and two inches hard white plastic. He never missed a beat. Now more carefully, I watched him as he slam-banged the acoustic bell upon which he had hit and broken off the drumstick earlier.

The next night we were more fortunate in that The Embers, featuring lead singer Jackie Gore, percussionist - Bobby Tomlinson, and manager/guitarist - Craig Woolard were performing. I think that night was the first time that I had ever acknowledged "beach music," which became my lifelong favorite: "Sixty-Minute Man" Billy Ward and his Dominoes, ""Little Red Book" The Drifters, "Across the Street" Lenny O'Henry, "Carolina Girls" General Johnson and the Chairmen of the Board, "Last Kiss" J. Frank Wilson and the Cavaliers, "Jamie" Eddie Holland, "Brenda" O. C. Smith, "With This Ring" The Platters, "My Girl" The Drifters, "Hello, Stranger" Barbara Lewis, "Fat Boy" Billy Stewart, "At

Last" Etta James, "Reputation" Little Anthony and the Imperials, and "Reach Out" The Four Tops, being some of my most favorites.

Then Came Purple Jesus

Usually associated with these beach soirees was just a little bit of alcohol. More often than not, some of our brave "girlfriends" would drive up to Rocky Mount and cajole (for $5) some "innocent bystander" hiding behind the Nash County ABC store, to go inside and buy "my Daddy" a pint or fifth of Everclear, 190 Proof, 95% Grain Alcohol. Some of the "amateur pharmacists" would then conjure up a concoction called, "P. J." Paul Cobb was one of those chemists, and was known to imbibe: we nicknamed him "190." The girls were not fond of hard liquor, but sorta liked Purple Jesus.

Many years later, on May 31, 1979, my SHP 58th Basic School Physical Training Instructor and good friend, Master Trooper Pete Peterson (1942 - 1979) along with two Sheriffs' Deputies Roy Huskey (1931 -1979) and Millard Messersmith (1921 - 1979) got shot with a .30-06 rifle and killed over a Purple Jesus domestic violence dispute involving a father and his daughter in Rutherford County, NC. So horribly disturbing, that I still carry the memory!

Purple Jesus was a combination (Not a "mixture." Remember Mrs. Abernathy's painful physics lessons?) of Everclear and Welch's grape juice. I don't ever remember seeing it done, but apparently there were those among us who were good at it, and enjoyed every aspect: illegally buying the forbidden hooch, illegally transporting it, secretly hiding it, illegally mixing it in a bathtub or plastic trash can, and then illegally "gettin' wasted." The outcomes of these endeavors were quite often comical, but nearly always unfortunate. Some of those folks got so sick that Warren and I thought they might die. Some of them wanted to die.

Junior-Senior Weekend 1967

Our fist-fighter buddy Coy Daniel liked P. J. Some of Coy's best friends were George Dickel, Jack Daniels, and Jim Beam. During our Junior Senior weekend at a rental cottage in Atlantic Beach, as a prank, Lew Highsmith, Arthur Stamper, and Doug Champion staggered through the sand dunes with Coy, under the false pretense of some nude sunbathers laid out over by the barnacled shipwreck skeleton. They were "gone." Coy was "tired," so he laid his near naked self right down on the beach. Just before Lew and the rest of us departed, Lew took Coy's right hand and placed it upon Coy's bare chest. "Arkie" was carrying a small leather "Channel Master" transistor radio playin' the popular Boxtops song named "The Letter." Coy and Doug had gotten into an argument over the title: Coy thought it was "The Letter," and Doug thought it was "Gimme a Ticket for an Aeroplane."

About two hours later, when the <u>tide was coming in</u> and we were getting ready to go eat at The Sanitary Fish Market, we went back to get Coy. Thankfully, due to the now foot deep water, Coy, like the sunbathers, was gone. We looked high and we looked low. We looked up toward the John Yancey Fishing Pier and we looked down toward the Triple S fishing pier: he was not to be found. Some of the more sober guys became worried. Some didn't care. And some were in denial that they had had anything to do with this wickedness.

When we went out to get into Warren's white Ford, blue canvassed convertible, there lay Coy: sunburned except where his hand had laid. He was not happy, and from experience, I knew enough to stay out of his reach. Evidently whatever he had consumed was not "Fightin' Likker," or he would have been hard to handle. He was usually hard to handle, anyway. High speed driving had revoked his driver's license for all of his junior and senior years at Ralph L. Fike Senior High School. Therefore I would drive " 'ol Bullet" up to his house and Mac McCall's house (and sometimes Gerald's house) every morning to pick them up and take them to school. They usually played sports or found other rides in the afternoon. I usually had to go to work at Parker's and did not have time to mess with them.

Michael J. McArthur

Pranks and Martha Reeves and the Vandellas

Speaking of pranks, I heard through the grapevine that some of us (not to mention any names, but their initials were Warren Barnes and Doug Champion) might have entered into Ralph L. Fike Senior High School late one Saturday night under the cover of darkness, just before our graduation. I think it was the same night that Martha Reeves and the Vandellas performed their rockin' hot, R & B show on the stage in the school auditorium where we had just held "The Class of '67, Stunt Night." Martha had swilled way too much Crowne Royal, and got in a cuss fight with lead back-up singer, Gloria Williams who was a famous vocalist in her own right – and Martha didn't like it, not nary bit! I was standing right at the side exit door from the auditorium to the parking lot, taking in the show from the best seat in the house. Martha stopped singing "Jimmy Mack" mid-song, and started throwing things: first her microphone, then her shoes. Watching their managers storm onto the stage to quell the riot was a sight I will never forget. This was a full blown "chick fight" long before they became "en vogue." Dresses were torn, makeup smudged, and wigs knocked off. Their language would not fit on their top-selling 45s. Both combatants were what could be called "Toe' up from the flo' up!" There were no injuries, and most of the audience just thought it was a part of the show. I heard what they were yellin'. I was close enough to see the spit slinging. Since I was blocking the exit, I figured I'd better get out of their way. No tellin' what was gonna happen next!

Anyway, "The show must go on." And it did! They finished their gig early. Martha shot Gloria "The Bird," as she stormed out into her white Cadillac Fleetwood, barefooted. In the aftermath of the afterglow, I went over to 'ol Bullet, got in, and drove forward, my front left tire riding up onto and stranding on the top of the 10-inch concrete filled steel parking lot delineator pipe. What a surprise. What a sight. And what a dilemma. Jimmy Blackwell, Charlie Pat Farris, Bobby White, and Bogie Bullock came over, grabbed the heavy chrome bumper, and heaved the front of the car left toward the street, off the pipe (no small feat of strength!). Do you reckon that was embarrassing? The "Heatwave" song that I had just witnessed inside, flooded over me outside. I crawled onto Bullet's plastic seat cover, cranked up, and took off spinning tires.

Our Principal, W. W. (Wee Willy) Woodard had witnessed the whole episode, and asked me about it the following Monday morning when I snuck into the front office to get the American Flag to raise on the pole in front of the school. That pole is the same one that Jenny Lou Lancaster got her tongue frozen to one morning in January that year. Somebody went and got School Secretary Judy Cook's coffee pot, cooled it down at the water fountain, and poured it onto the pole just above Jenny Lou's misery. It worked!

Wee Willy had summoned fearsome Assistant Principal, Dean of Boys, Mr. Thomas Stott who had just recently somehow gotten all four of his Buick tires icepick flattened in the school parking lot during a PTA meeting. Together they asked me if I knew anything about the "four flats," or who the two B&E Felons were that the Wilson Police had chased inside the school the previous Saturday night. Honestly, at that time I didn't know anything about it (and wouldn't have ratted out my buddies, even if I had known their identity). Our English Teacher, Mrs. Fleming's twins, Lou and Wray told me all about it later that day over spaghetti in Mrs. Williford's lunchroom. Isn't it amazing what you can learn in the lunchroom or while riding an activity bus? Apparently, Doug and Warren wanted to "re-arrange" some things inside the school that night, and took that opportunity to do so. Supposedly, at some point there was a full-grown Guernsey cow led up the steps to the second floor where Mrs. Raynor's Spanish Class was held. It was told that getting that lactacious beaudacious bovine UP those steps was much less difficult than getting her DOWN those steps. Apparently, she had become, "nervous!"

All's well that ends well. Doug and Warren split up, and Doug lit out through the smoking area toward the parking lot. Warren flew (track star, remember?) through Mrs. Ella Beaman's hallway, and out beside Mrs. Loretta Parker's (all of my friends were in love with Mrs. Parker - David Woodard and me, especially) new classroom building. The rest of the night he lay in the honeysuckles and briars kinda sorta behind Lou and Wray's house. I'm not quite sure how sunrise treated the boys, but it did shine some light on Warren's torn shirt and the new scratches on his pretty boy face.

Michael J. McArthur

Muscle Cars and Chaperones

One of the good things about being "chaperones" was that Warren and I got to drive our friends' cars: David had a bronze Buick GS-400. Romaine Woodard had a Carolina Blue '65 Stingray Corvette. Lew had a ratty old white Valiant. Tommy Goard had a '67, black vinyl over yellow SS 396-375 horsepower Chevelle with a reverberator on his sound system. Bill Adams had a '64½ black vinyl over yellow Mustang with an 8-track stereo system. Hamp Anderson had a Golden Goat: black vinyl over gold '65 Pontiac GTO with Air Force Jet landing lights in his dual high-beam headlights that got confiscated upon the Esso Station inspection. It also had an air powered spigot on the dashboard that dispensed Black Jack Daniels. One of our country cousins, Ivey Edgerton from Micro had a '67 white Oldsmobile 442 – 455 cu. in. convertible that was probably the fastest car that I had ever driven. John Graves had a '58 rag-top Jeep, in which he was killed while Canada Goose hunting in 1966 in a cornfield rollover at Lake Mattamuskeet with Ken Plummer and Bob Hester. Doug had a '32 yellow Chevy Roadster. Dennis Boykin, our fishing buddy had a black, '53 four door Ford Crestliner that was terribly fast (and it "held" in curves like a race car). Mike McArthur tanked a 1955, four door, two tone brown, Pontiac – Star Chief with a white sun-visor over the windshield and a hydra-matic transmission that, when cramped, could make both back tires "bark" when internally hard-shifting from first gear to second gear (if it didn't bust one or both of the universal joints.) Along with a broken fuel gauge, it also had a red, one gallon can of gas tied in the corner of the roomy trunk for emergencies. Harry Liner (Our teacher, Mrs. Liner's boy) had a black four door Plymouth in which he was killed in 1968.

I was a late bloomer: a small teenager (five feet – four inches tall and 104 pounds at age 17). Warren and I were ALWAYS the designated drivers because we didn't drink at all. Occasionally I would try to drink a beer, but neither was I old enough to buy it, nor accomplished enough to handle it. The next year when Warren and I were freshmen at N. C. State University, I was so little that some of those rednecks thought I was a child prodigy, having been ultra-smart and graduated at age 14. I proved them wrong in the short run! In room 51, Owen Dormitory, Doug had a Mason Jar of Percy Flowers' "hand woven" corn liquor. It stayed in the "medicine cabinet" above the sink, and we took great pleasure pouring a teaspoon full and lighting it. This amazed all our uppity friends. Doug had gotten this hooch from one of our friends who drove a loaded "hot-rod-Lincoln" twice a month from behind a tobacco barn in Lizard Lick to the docks in Baltimore, Maryland.

One night after I got off from Parker's, several carloads of us followed an ambulance north on US-301 toward Sharpsburg. One of the little towns that had only one stop light, right in front of the Post Office. To my dismay, it had the red "Stop" light at bottom of the triumvirate, and the green "Go" light at the top. Warren was truly amazed at how I "hadn't learned my colors in first grade." Being color blind had an adverse consequence while driving. I learned that with a very cheap lesson: from the back seat, Aubrey Shingleton slapped me in the back of the head yellin', "You ran that stoplight, you FOOL." As we followed it, the speeding ambulance crossed a narrow creek bridge in a tight curve. There in a plowed-up yard was a Mach I Shelby GT, midnight blue Mustang, ripped apart by an Oak Tree into a thousand pieces. Natalie Forrester had been hurrying to get home before her 10:00 pm curfew. She hit the bridge railing, and didn't make the curve. There is much more, but I will stop here, and spare her family the grim and gory details.

Snooker and Other Games of Chance

Down the street from Warren, lived Mr. and Mrs. Morris who had two daughters "that were as strong as battery acid," Lynn and Debbie, and their "jock" brother named Boo. Some of the guys who dated these girls would secretly park their cars down near the Barnes' house and sneak over to the Morris house and "watch TV" until way too late in the evening, just like on the Ozzie and Harriett Show. Further down the street lived Gerald and Raymond Butler and their family. Once when Mr. Morris had raked all the White Oak leaves into a huge pile on the edge of the street at the curb, Gerald drove his daddy's station wagon plumb through the leaves at breakneck speed. Two or three days later, after Mr. Morris had re-raked the leaves into an even bigger pile, Gerald again drove his daddy's station wagon through the pile of leaves. Who would have thought that somehow two cinderblocks had mysteriously appeared inside that pile of leaves? It was not a pretty site for days and weeks to come.

What I remember most about Gerald's daddy is that occasionally he would get Warren Barnes, Ken Plummer, Lew Highsmith, Mac McCall, David Woodard, Gerald's brother Raymond, Gerald, and me together and play penny poker. Mr. Butler knew the rules but occasionally, we made up our own rules as we went. Mr. Butler ALWAYS won all the pennies. Over Thanksgiving, without apology, Warren mysteriously dealt Mr. Butler a five card, no wild cards, NATURAL Royal Flush (Spades) one night. Never before and never since have I seen such in a five-card stud game. But who knows? As naive as we all were, for all we knew, Mr. Butler had snookered us. And he was good at making good times, better.

Speaking of Snooker: there were two Snooker tables at The Cue Club. That is where Warren and several of the rest of us learned to shoot pool. Warren taught me how to shoot a "masse" shot: When slightly blocked from being able to shoot the intended ball, and you need to "curve" the cue ball around the blocker, here is how you do it. You chalk up really good, RAISE the back of your cue stick way up, and strike slightly DOWN and forward onto the cue ball thereby causing it to not only advance forward, but to spin to the left or right as your need dictates. In contrast, I taught him how to shoot "jump shots." That is where your cue tip strikes the cue ball, horizontally and well below center, causing the cue ball to "jump" a blocker ball. Like most pool halls, Mr. Morris absolutely prohibited both of these maneuvers due to the risk of the cue tip ripping the felt tabletop covering. "ABSOLUTELY NO JUMP SHOTS. NO MASSE SHOTS!"

I had bought a long, straight grained Ash cue stick for $10.00 with a small leather tip from Emmett Williams out on Airport Road. It was long enough for my arms to adequately maneuver it. I sewed a dark blue corduroy sleeve for it, and kept it on the shelf behind my back seat in the window. If you could successfully shoot "Snooker" BY ALL THE RULES, you could easily shoot 8-Ball, 9-Ball, 6-ball, Cutthroat, or any of the myriad of games conjured up by "the older guys."

Mr. and Mrs. Morris owned and operated "The Cue Club" in an old glass fronted machine shop right beside Billy Clark's daddy's veterinarian office on Ward Boulevard. Lots of good times and better memories were made there. After I got off from work waiting tables at Parker's Barbecue, I would change out of my J. C. Penny, work shoes into my cordovan Bass Weejuns, and drive my four door, '55 Pontiac Star Chief with a hydramatic transmission to The Cue Club. There I would find my cohorts, and kindly remove their daddy's money from those who thought they were pool sharks. By this time, Warren was head-over-heels in love with Elaine Pate. For all intents and purposes, he was out of commission for late night forays into the vast world of skulduggery. "Mischief" might have been my middle name, but "magnanimous" was Warren's. He was such a great guy.

The Nags Head Casino

Occasionally, some of us would be brave enough to venture out to other beach "hang outs:" Carolina Beach, Minnesott Beach, Whichard's Beach, Ocracoke, Topsail Island, Wrightsville Beach, Ocean Isle, and Myrtle Beach. Some of us chose to "try out" what later became The Outer Banks, somewhere east of the Alligator River Bridge, the longest bridge that any of us had ever seen. Some of us had heard of Manteo, The Lost Colony, and Blackbeard the Pirate (Edward Teach). A few of us had heard of Oregon Inlet, The Gulf Stream, and shipwrecks. ALL OF US had heard unimaginable rumors about "The Nags Head Casino."

My college roommate was Jerry Davis (Wee Wink), from Kitty Hawk, North Carolina. His family OWNED The Outer Banks, or so all us poor blokes were led to believe. Wink's Grocery Stores were dotted up and down the Beach Road, and the sons, Jerry and brother Miles were legends on the roads, in the nightspots, on the refuges, and along the silver sands. They were "Bankers;" residents of The Outer Banks. They raced each other. They raced Constable McGuillicudy on the Bonner Bridge. They knew where the freshwater ponds loaded with Pintails were secluded in the Oaks behind the weathered dunes. Seemingly, they knew everything.

One Thursday afternoon (evidently no Friday classes – that week), Jerry and I locked the door, taped the lock (to keep the RA Ralph Birchard – Resident Adviser out), climbed out the window of North Carolina State

University's Owen Dormitory #51, loaded into his white, shiny '68 Plymouth Road Runner, and headed east – Beep, Beep! We went through Wilson, Williamston, Plymouth, Columbia, East Lake, and arrived at the new Lindsey C. Warren Bridge over the Alligator River on the Tyrrell / Dare County Line. The swing section was open, and a string of barges were hauling what looked like white sand (probably land-plaster) down the river. We crossed into Mann's Harbor, dropped down through Manteo, crossed into Nag's Head, and went north through Kill Devil Hills, past Jockey's Ridge and the Wright Brothers Memorial, and pulled in at Wink's Grocery Store on the Sound Side of NC Rte. 158 in Kitty Hawk.

We ate a soft-shell-crab dinner with Jerry's folks, and then Jerry drove us down to Ras Wescott's, The Nags Head Casino. By most standards, it was a little too early for much excitement to be going on upstairs, so we spent our time bowling duck pins and playing pinball with the tourists. The band upstairs was practicing, and we could hear the bass guitar and the saxophones. About 9 p.m., Jerry's brother Miles and Claudia came by, and we all went up that steep, narrow stairway to the dance hall. Ras was known to keep the shimmering hardwood dance floor waxed and polished. We removed our shoes while we could smell the wax granules that were strewn across the hardwood planks. As I said earlier, Jerry and Miles were revered "locals." Ras came and got us, and we went up to the stage and platform from which he operated his "tight ship."

David Ruffin and The Temptations were performing that night, and the place was already packed with teeny-boppers (but eighteen we hoped – maybe), pairs of shy (acting) girls, frattybaggers hawking the girls, and skin headed soldiers – lots of them doin' sorta like they wanted to. Barry Gordy's Motown #1 hit, "My Girl" and "The Way You Do the Things You Do," rocked the house. The volume was deafeningly brutal, but nobody cared. The sights we saw and the sounds we heard will forever live in my mind as one of the highlights of my college career – far exceeding The Embers Club and The Platters in Downtown Raleigh. Far exceeding The Pavilion and Doug Clark and the Hot Nuts in Atlantic Beach.

A friend of mine named Dave Dowdy from Grandy was one of about eight bouncers who worked for Ras. Bouncers ranged in size from lightweight to heavyweight, normal to behemoth, and mild to ferocious in temperament. Dave qualified somewhere in the middle both in size and temper, and he was fiercely loyal to Ras. Ras, I think was partial to Dave for his "people skills." Everybody liked Dave, and "Uncle Dave" would normally make Ras' life less difficult by handling onerous intemperates with finesse rather than bloodshed. But there was a line neither to be crossed nor even approached. That is where the whistle came into play.

Right square in the middle of the party atmosphere, invariably, some "hot head" would become too loud. That was his first mistake. At The Nags Head Casino, you only got two strikes before you were out. Ras was a family friendly concessionaire, and he put up with no junk, or "bad press" as he called it. First thing you know, a loud patron would become rowdy, and then "stumble" into a female or use offensive language, neither of which was acceptable in Ras' establishment. After all, his customers were friends and neighbors, and they were there as Ras' paying "guests."

From his perch atop a platform near the bandstand, Ras could eyeball the entire dancefloor. He not only enjoyed his business aspects, but he also enjoyed the entertainers. When something went awry, Ras was quick to respond: "Get in front of it," he liked to say. One or more of those military "Casanovas" were usually the culprits. And Ras didn't like them "messin' up his show." First, he would send Dave Dowdy over to tell the offenders, "It is time for you to go!" Of course, that went over like a lead balloon. Here stands a five-foot-eight bouncer telling a six-foot-six commando to "Get out." Honestly, you would have really had to have been there to get the full picture.

Ras wore a chrome traffic whistle around his neck on a lanyard, and all of his "locals" knew what it was for. He would turn red in the face, draw in a deep breath, clench that whistle in his teeth, and blow a long, loud, and shrill rush of air, <u>and point his finger toward the offender(s)</u>. Instantly the crowd looked to see what was happening, and who was soon to be in deep trouble. That commando was soon to learn a terrible lesson. Ras had sent his smallest bouncer to tell his largest patron to, "Get out." Bad, but ingenious plan. All eight bouncers descended upon the soon to be bloody site where Ras was pointing. Oh, my God. It went from bad to worse in.7 seconds.

On a good night, the bouncers would merely hoist the commando, deliver him to the blood-streaked stairwell, and introduce him to his immediate departure. On a bad night, when the commando punched a bouncer, the bouncers would kindly deliver the commando to the nearest window, push open the 4'X8' plywood window shutter, and heave the offender right through the unencumbered opening. Look out below. The hood of that '66 yellow GTO was not quite as flexible as a trampoline, but more flexible than the sandy, graveled parking lot.

Those who survived their comeuppance, were scooped up and poured into the back seat of a blue and white 1965 Ford Galaxie, Dare County Sheriff's patrol car, manned, and I do mean MANNED, by Dare County Deputy Sheriff Donnie Twine. I just went to his funeral in 2018.

When a mass brawl broke out (rarely), the bouncers would encircle the rowdy group, and "usher" them down those steep narrow steps. Woe be unto those caught up in the path. At the bottom of the steps, just outside the broken but never shut doorway, was parked that '65 Galaxie with the back passenger door standing wide open. Deputy Donnie Twine, former Golden Gloves U. S. Army boxer, <u>who backed down to no one</u>, served as receptionist/greeter. Donnie would "kindly inquire" as to the age(s) of the miscreants: "19? Get in. 17? Get in, 15? Get out of the way!" I personally witnessed (from curbside) as many as eight to ten bobbling heads being hauled off to God knows where – not to be seen or heard from ever again!

Two years later I went back to Nags Head, but it was a weekday, and only the arcade was open for my enjoyment. The 1960 hit "Stay" by MauriceWilliams and the Zodiacs followed by Willie Nelson's "Crazy," sung by Patsy Cline was playing on the Wurlitzer Juke Box. Next came Levi Stubbs and The Four Tops singing "Reach Out, I'll Be There." When J. Frank Wilson and the Cavaliers cried out "The Last Kiss," I decided it was time to go. Compared to my previous visit, The Nags Head Casino was quiet. Probably a good thing!

Movin' On

Coming along in the mid '60 was a good life. Good music! Crime aplenty, but not a lot for those of us who halfway tried to live by "The Golden Rule." Parents, usually both in the home, raised us to be respectful and law-abiding. There were lots of simple good times. And always somewhere safe to go and something reasonable to do. Nearly all of us duck hunted on Contentnea Creek and the swamps around Wiggins's Mill, and most of us took way too many chances. The millpond was deep, and we were young and foolish. Too many times we put two too many people into boats meant for two. But somehow, we always made our appointed rounds. Warren always hunted from a bushed-up stump near the power lines on Contentnea Creek "at the third bridge" on Downing Street below Bill's Drive-In on Lover's Lane. That is where he and I would go nearly every afternoon in October before the season opened to "count the ducks" that flew up and down Contentnea Creek. Counting ducks and geese has become one of the things that my children and grandchildren just seem to do instinctively. Whenever we spot a **V** of Canada Geese crossing US-70 out near Crabtree Valley Mall, Jenny or John or Jay or Nakayla or Leela or Nolan will say, "Nine, Granddaddy." We could differentiate between Wood Ducks, Mallards, Pintails, and Green-Winged Teal. Bob Hester counted on us to keep him informed with our informal duck surveys.

Wading around in those swamps made men out of boys, as it was extremely difficult to maintain our "upright" composure while sliding off and tripping over underwater snags – IN THE DARK (More on this in a few minutes). There were always obstacles to overcome, but one of Warren's and my favorite expressions was, "The harder you work, the luckier you get!" In fact, my life's mission and also Warren's life's mission has been to remove obstacles and barricades in not only our lives and our families' lives, but from the lives of all with whom we interact.

Michael J. McArthur

"Leave 'em Lay…"

Many times we would meet at the Millpond, go hunting at sunrise, kill a couple of Wood Ducks, be at school by 7:30am, suffer through it, and be back in the swamp behind the A.M.E. Zion Church to hunt until "quittin' time." This church was a hotspot for Sunday afternoon Tent Revivals without the tents. Locals called them "Camp Meetings." Glistening-white Cadillacs, jet-black Lincolns, and an occasional midnight blue Buick Electra 225 would fill the small parking lot, and spill out onto Lover's Lane for at least ten cars deep in both directions and on both sides of the sandy dirt road. Stylishly dressed worshippers with top hats, white evening gowns, stylish women's hats with huge plumes, enormous patent-leather pocketbooks, and diamond studded walking canes would fill the small church house and spill out onto the grassy yard. Several of us neighborhood boys would ride our bicycles down past "Shug's Place," and go into the pine woods across from the church to learn about life. And LEARN we did!

And then the music would commence, and commence it did! The organist had been playing at a fever pitch for a short time, and then, as I recall, chimed in would be the saxophones and the Fender electric guitars. Then the other horns and drums would kick in. This music was so deafening that we boys had difficulty hearing each other whisper about what we were beholding. And then it got LOUD. As the intensity of the music revved up, so did the intensity of the preaching. Someone from inside this raucous debacle yelled out: "Give The Lord his due! He needs your tithes and offerings to get His Mighty work done. These baskets we're passing out don't need your jingle money. They need your whisperin' money." We took that to mean "folding money." At this point, there was so much happening across from our pine thicket that we could hardly take it all in. I am sure that there were people deafened during these Sunday afternoon church camp meetings. We, in our stronghold across the street were nearly deafened. As the preaching throttled UP, so did the excitement of the revelers.

It was a solid, turbulent sea of excitement and exhilaration. Everybody was calling on the spirit to save them from their sins. People were dancing and cavorting. People were violently wailing and sobbing. People were singing at the tops of their lungs. The "unspoken tongue" proliferated. People were coming out of their clothing. And people were "falling out," inside the open doors of the little chapel, and outside in the yard. As worshippers would hit the floor or collapse onto the ground, the black-suited, bald-headed, sweaty preacher would bellow out, "Leave 'em lay where Jesus flang 'em." This went on for two hours or more, and it was getting dark. Time to go, for us and for them. Some revelers had to be carried, barely conscious to their cars.

Apparently, this gathering consisted of one HUGE family. As they departed the scene, they all cried out to their "Brothers" and "Sisters," bidding them farewell and safe passage until "next month." I wondered why there were no ambulances dispatched to the scene. Somehow, the next morning when Pat and Kathy and I rode our yellow Chevrolet, Number 23-C Wilson County School Bus by the church, there were no signs of the melee which had so brutally occurred the day before.

Taxpaid Bootleg and Homemade Hooch

One of our most secret and favorite places to hunt (when we had time to get there) was down below Bill Ellis's Barbecue Restaurant/hang out, on the west side of Downing Street where nobody else much hunted. Ken Plummer and Doug Champion found a "tracked" construction swamp buggy hidden under some tarps at the edge of Contentnea Creek one afternoon, and played "Rat Patrol" with that tank until way past dark. That particular part of the marsh was hard to reach, and guess what: there was a liquor still, deep back in the swamp on an island. A couple of moonshiners had constructed an underwater bridge from the edge of a Guernsey (HMMMM?) cow pasture, out to the liquor still. They had nailed 2X6s with 20-penny nails from one 12-inch Water Tupelo to the next during a summer dry spell so that when the water returned, the 2X6s were submerged. We only found that bridge by accident, years later. That liquor still got raided sometime over the Summer of 1966, and all that was left of the site were 55-gallon barrels with one-inch square holes (many of them) punched through their sides. These demolition holes were randomly whacked by "them G.D. 'Revenooers' " according to Mr. Deans (related to our high-school math teacher). A railroad pickax had smashed the wooden benches, the barrels, the lids, and the boards nailed to the trees for whatever purposes.

This same Mr. Deans sold tax-paid pints of Southern Comfort and Rebel Yell to some of Warren's and my friends (Billy Whitley, Bogie Bullock, Tommy Tucker, Al Rehm, Hoyt Waller) from his back porch up on NC-42 near Buckhorn Dam. When we/they pulled into his Sycamore tree lined, root laden driveway, the secret signal was to open and close the car door three times. He would come out with a double barreled 20-gauge shotgun cradled in the crook of his left elbow, never speak a word, go back in and get what was asked, deliver the bottle, take his ten bucks, go back inside his dimly lit shotgun shack, and slam the door causing his rabbit dogs to wail, and his banty hen chickens to cackle. As Warren and I traveled to and from N C State from 1967 through 1971, we went right by that "enterprise" every Friday and every Sunday.

"Sneak"

In the ninth grade, my daddy and I had built from my plans, a canoe shaped "sneak boat" that we named "Sneak," out of one sheet of ½-inch marine plywood that would fit into the open trunk of my '55 Pontiac. Warren and I used this boat mostly for retrieving dead Wood Ducks floating white belly up, mostly after dark, from murky waters that were over our heads. When the water was only waist deep, we would just wade right on out there, get soaking wet, but retrieve our game. For bigger hunts, Mother and Daddy had bought brother Pat and me an eight-foot aluminum, Dead Grass Green, Sears jon boat (used it yesterday). One afternoon I took Warren and his Labrador Retriever out to his favorite stump, and before I could get back to my pothole blind, Warren shot and killed a drake, Greenhead Mallard. What a prize back in those days. Warren's dog, (Harvester of Happy Valley) "Happy" immediately launched from the blind into the 10-foot-deep creek. He was a very young dog, and he ballistically swam up to the Greenhead, mouthed it, and promptly climbed up onto another stump and ate the duck. All of it. I can still hear Warren lambasting that "sorry dog:" "Happy, get over here. Happy, COME! Happy, I'm gonna kill you. Get over here. Happy, please don't eat that duck!" Warren could see that the duck on his left leg had a bright silver, U. S. Fish & Wildlife, numbered band. Even though this fracas was well within Warren's range, he let the dog live to hunt another day. Happy either ate the band, or it fell into the tea-colored water, never to be seen again.

One of the three owners of Parker's Barbecue trained and field trialed hunting dogs. Like Warren's "Happy," many of Graham Parker's dogs were sired from a long line of expensive breeding stock. They were handsome in stature, and smart. Graham shared with Warren a tried-and-true parable about hunting dogs: "When you are blessed to have a 'puppy' that outperforms all the older, more experienced dogs, cherish the moment. And remember this, at some point in his life, that champion that you are so proud of, will become a puppy. And you cannot do a damn thing about it!"

Texas Gulf Sulfur Company Aurora, North Carolina

Another favorite place for us to hunt was in Aurora, N.C. near Texas Gulf Phosphate and Sulfur Mining Operation. Texas Gulf ran twenty-four hours a day, seven days a week, year-round. Huge excavators with buckets the size of small houses constantly swung on two-inch cables out over the Pamlico River, crashing down and bringing up tons of raw earth from which the phosphate was mined. Occasionally, due to operator error, the cables would snap under tremendous tension, and the "maw" would be flung over 100 yards, "somewhere out yonder in the river."

Part of the refinery process involved fresh water washing the ore from the matrix. Somehow, Tommy Goard and Warren found that there was a "warm-water-canal" emptying from the mill into the lower Pamlico River swampland just off NC-33 near Royal, N.C. Tommy was the kind of friend to Warren and me that, when we needed help, he was always there. Several times he helped me "make up" motel rooms so that we could go rabbit hunting that afternoon down in Elsie Walston's Snipe swamp. In the summer, he would help me cut the grass so we could go bass fishing in Mr. O'Connell's farm ponds that he knew about, and had permission to fish.

In any case, this warm water canal not only had stuff floating in it that the ducks liked, but it was NEVER FROZEN OVER from having been utilized in the heated chemical separation of ore from matrix. This was absolutely a duck hunter's paradise. No matter the temperature; no matter the wind, this place was like a "rare-earth," duck magnet. All kinds of ducks. It granted all species of waterfowl safe haven from the elements, but not from four crazy teen-aged duck hunters. Within the swampy confines of this small wetland, Warren Barnes, Tommy Goard, J. E. Owens, and Mike McArthur began a nearly mythical, four-year odyssey never to be replicated.

Most times I would throw that jon boat in the trunk, and pick Warren and J.E. up at 4:00am. We would wind our way down to Aurora on NC-33 through Greenville and Choco (Chocowinity). Usually we would stop at a dimly lit, all-night gas station on Greenville Boulevard, fill up with gas, put a quart of oil in my old Pontiac, get a big fat greasy sausage-egg-and-cheese, and head on down toward Bayboro. One time I forgot to pay for the oil, and worried all day that there was gonna be a roadblock up near the Lemon Tree Inn in Chocowinity, looking for the oil thieves. Sometimes we would stop by Overton's Store in Bonnerton. The store had the best hoop cheese, and the coldest **Coca Colas** around. It also had holes through the floor where you could see the ground and the hound dogs underneath. Years later I discovered that this store was operated by the mother of one of my Wildlife Basic School instructors, Mike Overton. She always had for sale those "high-brass" Super-X, Mark-V, Magnum 4s that I will tell you about.

We usually took along three or four "grass bags." These were commonly called "toe-sacks" or "gunny sacks" by the locals. We had about six Sears & Roebuck, Mallard decoys in each bag, which could have easily held twelve. At the end of the day, upon our departure from the woods, the excess space was ALWAYS filled with "our legal daily bag limit of migratory waterfowl." If there were more ducks than hunters, one or more of the hunters would exit the woods, load up the boat into the trunk, and drive over to the Bayview/Aurora Ferry dock on NC-306. He would leave a bag of "decoys" by the signpost about halfway back to the swamp. When "the coast was clear," he would return to the swamp and pick up the rest of the hooligans, go snag the hidden bag, and high tail it for Wilson. We always worried about having to explain all those dead ducks that we were cleaning down on the back porch of the pump room at Tobacco Trail Motel. Warren made us promise to eat what we killed, so we decided that we would be extra careful how we "butchered" the meat so as not to let Brandy, Mother's Irish Setter eat any of it while our backs were turned. He was known to do that among other atrocities. But he was Mother's dog, and could do no wrong!

Here we go, back at the beginning. Since the ducks flew into this swamp all day long, we didn't have to get there too very early. Along about 6:00 am, upon our arrival at the edge of the swamp by the creek bridge, we pulled the 8-foot jon boat out of the trunk, put the decoys and paddles into the boat. We jumped in with our guns, and launched into the darkness to find a special slough marked with a broken taillight reflector from Helms Truck Lines. We had nailed them onto a tree way back up on the Spanish Moss laden, jagged shoreline. There we disembarked, grabbed the decoys and slung our guns over our shoulders. We had made makeshift slings from OD Army surplus one-inch webbing. We jammed both paddles underneath the Styrofoam packed seats, and began to pull the boat up onto its edge to wind our way between the water tupelos. We slogged through the knee-deep water, and back out into the deeper openness of the adjacent swamp. Occasionally, in the deeper parts where we could not stand on the muddy bottom and pull the boat between the trees, we had to "bear-hug" the adjacent tree and hook the boat with our feet while pulling it up on its side to slide it through narrow passageways. The next time when we went back, we took along foot-long pieces of treated 2X6s, and twenty-penny nailed them onto the tree-trunk for us to stand on while we maneuvered the boat to where we wanted it.

In the middle of this three-hundred-acre swamp was a four-acre grassy knoll that we christened "The Refuge." It was known to shelter Wilson's Snipe, and Clapper Rails. Yep, we killed and ate them, too. Warren was shooting a Remington 1100, 28-inch full choke, semi-automatic shotgun. J. E. and I were shooting J. C. Higgins, Sears and Roebuck, Ted Williams pump shotguns with modified chokes. J.E.'s barrel was only twenty-five inches long because he had gotten snow frozen into the end of the barrel, and pulled the trigger. Believe it or not, with his barrel split open at the top, he wanted to look for that little brass bead in eighteen inches of snow! We all bought expensive shells because they held a tighter pattern, increased our range, and hit harder: Winchester, Super-X, Mark V, 2 ¾ inch, Magnum #4s.

Do you know what you do when you "ring" a shotgun shell? Well, you take out your Case Sodbuster and carve a "ring" around a shotgun shell somewhere about one inch back from the crimp. This uniformly weakens the circumference of the hull. When fired from your shotgun, the whole end of the shell comes off with the plastic "shot-cup" holding the ounce and a half of lead pellets in a single projectile. This resembles a "slug" component being fired at a deer or across the swamp to cause ducks to lift up and fly toward us. There is really no other way to put it: we were deadly with those firesticks.

Warren's Plunge

Warren always wore what was standard back then: a Ted Williams Deluxe visored – rolled up side-brim, water-proofed, insulated hunting hat, and a brown corduroy collared hunting coat with a sewn-in game bag. J. E. and I wore G. I. Joe's, U. S. Army surplus, Jeep Driver caps and Army field jackets. On this morning, as we plowed through thigh deep water, of course J. E. was in front of the boat. I had my left hand on the starboard gunwale, and Warren was cautiously walking along the edge of the deeply dredged canal, hoping to flush a Clapper Rail or a Snipe. Ker – SPLASH! I looked over my right shoulder and there was nothing to see but that Ted Williams hunting hat, bobbing on the ripples, right exactly where Warren had just been hunting. No problem. At least not for me! Of course, we didn't laugh - much. Ol' Warren swam over to the Bald Cypress root, grabbed it, righted his wet self, grabbed his hat, dumped a half-gallon of muddy water out the barrel of his shotgun, and we got back to the business at hand. For decades, we still laughed about that episode, every time we got together which was way too infrequently. Our good intentions got overwhelmed by life! Warren was much better at time management than anybody I knew.

The Onslaught

As the sun came up, the ducks started flying, by the hundreds! Black Ducks. Banded Pintails. Banded Blue Winged Teal. Gadwalls. Shovelers. Green Winged Teal. Widgeons (Baldpates). Mallards. But no Canvasbacks or Redheads – I never could figure out why. Those prize ducks were "rafted," "kiver to kiver" out on the open water of the Pamlico River during the Bayview/Aurora Ferry crossing. After the initial onslaught waned, during the more cam (calm) time, J. E. found it necessary to shoot at a "Gawk Bird" (Johnny-Long-Legs, Goolagong, Great Blue Heron). We called it a Gawk Bird after the awful, raspy call it uttered. Fortunately he missed (I think). Or it might have been one of the "meals on sticks" that I will speak of later!

A knot of eight Blue Winged Teal pitched just beyond the canal, about thirty yards toward the river. We thought about firing one of those "ringed" shotgun shells in their direction. Guess what! J. E. had brought in his pocket, a slingshot made out of a bicycle innertube, and a handful of Cherry Bombs.

He loaded an un-lit Cherry Bomb with a longer than usual fuse from Red Walston's (Sue's Daddy) "Maurice's Grille" on US-117, into the worn leather shoe tongue "pouch" that we had tied on with white nylon masonry cord. J. E. overextended that tubing back the length of his outstretched arms, and Warren lit it with a book of my matches from Dick's Hotdog Stand on Nash Street in Wilson. J.E. let loose, and the Cherry Bomb fulfilled its purpose well. At lightnin' speed, it traveled beyond the Teal, hit the top of a Water Tupelo, and exploded. This caused the Teal to flush, and fly fast right into our kill zone. Fast is an understatement. Warren picked out and killed two drakes, and I peeled one out. While J. E. and Warren had been rigging that handy dandy, improvised explosive device (IED), I had quietly unloaded and moved J.E.s shotgun from his prop, to over under the edge of the jon boat so he couldn't find it in time to shoot with us. Lesson learned! Cussin' fit, came first. But, lesson learned. Plus a cussin' fit later when two Pintails flared 'cause he "clicked" an empty chamber at them. Great fun!!!

To make an extremely long story short, we killed more ducks than the law allowed. But for every boyhood problem, there is a workable solution. Having been "socked in" to this sticky predicament more than a few times in the past, now we had devised a plan. Not like in the sixth grade when Elmo Walls (Skip's daddy), our local Game Warden had snuck up on and caught Ronnie and Donnie Williamson and me shooting Wood Ducks at 0: dark thirty. As Elmo briskly walked toward us, my plan was to, first, hide my new Lohman Duck Call (still got it) from Wilson Hardware way down deep by the snap harness in my left hip boot. Next, stand perfectly still so that Mr. Walls wouldn't think I was gonna run. Next, hope that my daddy's EXCEL 30-inch, full choke, single shot shotgun would not be taken away from me, and last, answer all questions with "Yes, Sir" and "No, Sir." Somehow that night I did not have to "go to jail, go straight to jail, not pass 'GO,' and not collect $200.00." Mr. Walls was joined by his Supervisor (as they were called) partner, J. B. Duke, and they carefully explained to me, 1. How much trouble I was in, 2. What could happen to me if they arrested me, 3. How much money it could cost me, and four. Be prepared for them to go straight to Tobacco Trail Motel and tell "Betty and Mac." You could have stuck a fork in me, for I was done. My goose was cooked, even before I killed it!

A few years later, I had driven Ol' Bullet down to the millpond behind Shug's Place, unloaded "Sneak," my home-made sneak boat, launched it and paddled across and UP the run of the creek to a hidden pothole that only I knew about. From my kinda shaky duck blind at about six feet above the water, I could see the backside and driver's side of Ol' Bullet shining through the corn stalks and the Spanish Moss. UH-OH!! There squatted somebody, leaning against the driver's door, smoking a cigarette. It was already way too late to be getting "checked" by a game warden. Why I don't know, but I slowly slid down out of the blind, crept low as I could in "Sneak," shoved out into the downstream current of the creek, and found that I had left my paddle stuck in the mud under the blind. I took my trusty, J. C. Higgins, Sears and Roebuck, Ted Williams Pump Shotgun and used it for a rudder and paddled right past 'ol Bullet and the interloper. I pulled over at lawyer Pinky Connor's mansion on the bank near the dam, and called Mother to come get me. Of course I didn't tell her why I couldn't get back to my car. When I did get back, I found where Wildlife Enforcement Supervisor J.B. Duke had left his distinctive size 15 boot print in the sand. Also he had carefully, I'm sure, laid his LIT Lucky Strike cigarette in the crevice between my fender and hood. And yes, it had burned the paint. And yes, years later when I was a Highway Patrolman, I asked Duke's son, a Rocky Mount City Detective what brand of cigarettes his daddy smoked. You got it: Lucky Strike.

"Pass the Pepper, Please"

As it came to pass, out in "The Refuge," we had just "a few too many" Teal, bull Pintails, and Black Ducks in a pile in the middle of a Texas Gulf Sulfur swamp. Just for this purpose, we implemented our plan for treachery. Warren had brought along in a Zip-Lok bag, a "lost shaker of salt" and Romaine's crumpled box of black pepper. With my Boy Scout (Case made) Sheath Knife (my son John has it now, for my grandson, Nolan later), we cut six, two-foot-long, sharp on both ends, green one-inch sticks. On top of a rotted tree trunk, we built a fire from "squaw wood," and lit it with a Herter's flint and steel kit from my vest pocket, inside the Army field jacket. Warren had used up my matches lighting those Cherry Bombs. Squaw wood is the lowest two or three branches sticking out from a live Tupelo. These are called squaw wood because Native American Indian squaws could easily just walk around and gather firewood from the forests, and they had found that the bottom branches of all trees were always dead wood, having been choked by the bark's growth, and easily broken off.

The sun was warming us, but the fire was a welcome relief. Some of Warren's soaked clothing was nearly dry, hanging from a branch near the fire. Those "tidy-whities" didn't even begin to "flare" the kamikaze ducks. We plucked and gutted those three Teal, plus a Wilson's Snipe, a Wood Duck, and an unmentionable. All these ducks have lighter colored breast meat, and not so "rich." The Snipe has a small, dark-meat breast, but juicy. We shoved the six sticks into the mud around the edge of the fire. And just as it always happens, "her-ONK!" Here came two Canada Geese, just above the treetops. This time, my shotgun was over in the boat, Warren was huddled up next to the fire and not ready, and J. E. fired twice, killing BOF'o'em, – his limit (as if he cared? – Not a whit!). To quote one of my farmer friends: for the rest of the day, "You couldn't tell J.E. <u>nuthin'</u>."

The smaller goose, probably the gander was banded by the U.S.F.&W. Service., and we later found out that the honker had been banded on the DelMarVa Peninsula, six years earlier. This meant the Goose was a "Migratory" bird, and not a "Resident Canada." Migratory Canada Geese (Canadas, not Canadiens) are much sought after for their gaminess. Their eyes are so sharp that they are hard to decoy, their plumage so thick, and their muscles so strong that they are even harder to kill.

Back into the Texas Gulf Sulfur warm-water swamp/canal, we took those three Teal drakes, the Wood Duck, the Snipe, and the unmentionable, all "plucked," leaving the oily skin attached, salted and peppered inside and out, and shoved those one-inch sticks into their body cavities. The other ends stuck down in the mud, we leaned them out over the flames, and occasionally rotated them as on a rotisserie. Oil from their skin began to sizzle and drop into the fire. The meat on the drumsticks began to recede with little white bones exposed. It was time to eat! What a feast! Warren, now fully clothed, broke out his salt and pepper. A casual observer would have wondered, "What has come over those fools? Out here in the middle of a swamp, stripping piping hot meat off the bone, and stuffing it into their smiling mouths! They MUST be crazy." You know what? We musta been! GUILTY, Your Honor!

Meanwhile, the incoming ducks seemed opposed to neither the "What on Earth" commotion nor the smoking campfire, evidenced by their continued flight, right down our gun-barrels, into our powder keg. We all had our limits. Warren was always our official/unofficial "guide" for these trips, and 'bout 2:00 he made us (J.E. balked) stop shooting for the day. Like I said earlier, Warren was always, "the good guy."

Dr. Stotesbury's Goose Lodge—Heaven on Earth

In 1964 I peeled the lead goose out of a **V** of seven on Dr. Stotesbury's famous Goose Hunting Farm in New Holland on the south side of US-264 in Hyde County. At age 14 with Boy Scout Troop 222, on a goose hunt at Lake Mattamuskeet, I was on top of the world. We toured the Lake Mattamuskeet Wildlife Refuge's gated "back 40" in Dr. Hester's station wagon, loaded with shotguns and ammunition. Had we been apprehended, we would all still be incarcerated at Camp Butner Federal Prison up in Granville County. My Daddy and brother Pat didn't venture out on that second 12-degree morning, so I got to wear all their extra insulation. They stayed at the lodge and cooked lunch for the rest of us.

Our Scoutmaster was Harvey Vaughan, and our Assistant Scoutmaster was "Mac" Hester (Dr. Joseph McMurray Hester, July 3, 1919 to August 8, 2008). Our Senior Patrol Leader was Bill Vaughan. We were hunting under the guidance of Dr. John Stotesbury who was a colleague of Dr. Hester. Dr. Stotesbury had about ten "box blinds" in his thousand-acre fields. These were constructed with treated 2X4s and ¾ inch plywood, and could comfortably conceal four hunters. The floor was about two feet below the surface of the field, and the railings about two feet above. The perimeter was "bushed" with corn stalks and bull-rushes. Crouching, while peering out between the husks and duckin' down was like a game of James Bond espionage, graveyard hide-and-seek, stealin' Crimson Sweet Watermelons, and playin' hooky from school, all rolled into one. It just could not have been any better to a 14-year-old country boy. Occasionally the incoming cold-front would cause "dust devils" to lift corn husks twenty feet into the air. The 2X12 wooden bench ran the length of the blind, and was just right for kids to stand on and shoot. Labrador Retrievers could easily exit the open ends of the blind and retrieve our birds, but we did not have dogs for that: we were the retrievers.

There was a thick, low fog that morning, which at first, blocked our view across the treetops to the Lake. For whatever reason, the Tundra Swans, ducks, and geese were slow to lift off The Refuge, but about 9:00am we began to hear their calls. Slowly but surely, the birds began to break off into flocks of fifteen to forty. And here they came. Along with my friends Bob and Joe Hester, Kent Anderson, and Bill Vaughan, we had a tremendous hunt, killing maybe 6 Canada Geese and one Mallard (Bill Vaughan). We were careful NOT to shoot an incoming Swan, wings set like an F-4 Phantom Jet, and spectacularly white in the morning sun, ($1000.00 fine).

A wounded or sick Swan was swimming slowly in the "Outfall Canal" just below The Refuge pumping station. Dr. Hester said that it was "a little yellow," probably because it had ingested lead from lead shotgun pellets on the bottom of the Lake (henceforth steel shot requirement). As we pulled into the parking lot off US-264 at O'Neal's Motel, a group of Fifth Avenue camouflaged "hunters" were ganged up around a muddy truck. Dr. Hester let us go over there, and what we saw was frightfully amazing. There lay a Black Bear behemoth sprawled out in the back of a Willys Jeep Truck. He had a through-and-through, .44 Magnum bullet hole blown from side to side of his massive head. None of us had ever seen a bear "up close and personal." It was three times as big as any of us. This made a HUGE impression on me and the other Scouts.

Inside the store they had for sale, about ten or twelve double barreled or pump action, 10-gauge shotguns. Just right for the Yankees. They also had cases of four-inch magnum #2s, 10-gauge shotgun shells. I shelled out two bucks for two shells. All this was also impressive.

As a result of Joe Hester's incessant, perfect calling, and after slipping on the frosted seat and floor of the blind, I was able to raise up and fire once with Daddy's single shot, Excel twelve gauge at the lead goose. I missed, I thought. He set his wings and began a slow descent toward the back of our field. My single #2, magnum shot, downed goose glided into the irrigation canal, and was hearty enough to still be able to swim fast. There were dog-fennels, catbriers, and heavy underbrush along both sides of the ditch, and the escaping goose tried to hide under it or crawl up into it. I jumped into the ditch with my black knee boots quickly filling with cold water. I didn't even feel it! The water was not frozen because it was running so fast the days before had been warm. As weeds slowed the goose, I would gain on him. Finally I determined that if I did not shoot him, that he would get away from me, into the larger canal at the back edge of the field. BOOH- YOW. I carved out a ¾ inch crater across his crown. He was now mine, for good. Lo and behold, there on his left leg was a muddy silver aluminum U.S.F.W.S. band. I cannot remember the banding site or the age or the gender as reported back to me months later. I still have that band threaded onto the leather lanyard of my Canada Goose call. Two of his black webbed toes were missing, perhaps having been caught in a trap, or bitten off by an Alligator Snapping Turtle as a gosling. As small as I was, and as big as he was, I do not even remember having any trouble throwing him over my shoulder and running a hundred yards back to the blind. Along the way I had to jump back into the ditch because a flock of geese was crossing Bob Hester's and Kent Anderson's blind, thereby resulting in two Canadas falling like rocks from the sky. That black dirt dust clouded the sky upon their impact.

Have you ever tried to "pick" a wild goose? Well, "It's no daisy," to quote the famous Doc Holliday. There were some local hearty farmers who "picked geese" for $3.00 apiece. They offered to "swinge" the goose and gut it and wrap it for another $1.00, and Daddy sprung for all of it. Mother baked it with stuffing, apples and onions, and our family ate that goose for Christmas Dinner that year. It had to have been delicious, or at least everybody said it was!

As I recall, J.E. shot at a Double Crested Cormorant on that hunt, and from that point forward, all of us on that expedition have referred to Cormorants as "Owens Geese." That night we held a kangaroo court hearing within our Troop, and found J.E. guilty as charged. We sentenced him to hard labor, and to clean up Dr. Stotesbury's Goose Lodge where we were staying. You know full well that in order to avoid his excessive whining, we should have just done it ourselves!

Michael J. McArthur

The Peeping Tom

The story I am about to relate to you is scathingly hellish, sensitive, senseless, and tragic for all concerned. Parts of it will be totally unbelievable. My only recommendation is for you to please understand that these horrendous events occurred in the 1960s in a climate of respectful peace and pleasant harmony. In those days there was little tolerance for inconsistent and inappropriate behaviors. This was "back in the day," when there were true and certain consequences for messin' up. When not only did "offenders" (as they are called in today's tolerant society), not only did they know right from wrong, they understood <u>not</u> <u>what MIGHT happen to them</u>, but what was most assuredly <u>gonna</u> happen to them, <u>when</u> they got caught (NOT **IF** THEY GOT CAUGHT).

Law enforcement agencies still had seasoned officers training new officers, and instilling in them basic principles of fairness based upon good judgment and common sense. Go try to find an abundance of that in today's mixed-up society. Officers "back then" understood the value of living a good life, representing yourself and your agency in an acceptable manner, and projecting a good image for others to see. This attracted the cream of the crop to become interested in becoming a law enforcement officer. Not only was law enforcement respected because most of them deserved it, but the officers worked to maintain that image. They understood that they, their wives, and their friends would stand in line at the grocery store right beside potential jurors who might have to determine the veracity of their testimony at a trial.

As it is with all professions, each officer has his own preferred "specialty." Some can investigate and interview witnesses with the best of 'em. Some can teach and train new officers basic safety protocols and investigative procedures. Some can "give chase" during high-speed pursuits, and live to tell it. Some can do administrative duties for the right reason, the right way, the first time. And then there is Hogan. The "gumshoe" trash magnet who just happens to attract every form of malady imaginable, through absolutely no fault of his or her own. Why is this? To quote Patrick Swayze (Dalton) in the 1989 roustabout movie "Road House," "Just lucky, I guess." I knew many of these characters during my career, and worked closely with two who are indelibly etched into my catalog of memories (good and bad!).

In Wilson, North Carolina, we were fortunate to have a plethora of "opportunities" to make a living and/or make the living worthwhile. Among many other things, there were tobacco farms, tobacco warehouses, tobacco workers, tobacco trucks, and too many times, tobacco thieves. In the dark of night, it was not uncommon to hear of a sharecropper's platform of sheeted Bright Leaf Flue-Cured Tobacco going "missing." After the owner exhausted his "abilities" to strongarm those who he thought responsible, the landline call went out to the High Sheriff of Wilson County, Robin Pridgen. One way or another, by hook or by crook, the light of truth eventually emerged. Then it became time to decide whether to forgive the indiscretion because the thief was your mother's son by a previous marriage, or resort to any of a dozen other options. Most often tears washed away the blood. Occasionally there was a late-night fire of mysterious origin. Road rage occasionally played a role both before and after the fistfight. And then there were the bullet holes through and through the brand new red and white '64 Chevrolet SS Impala, 327 cu. in., 300 hp. four speed. I looked through 'em. I didn't see them going in, but I saw the holes not too long after they busted out.

Out on "The Tobacco Trail" designated US-301, there were about ten Motor Courts. The kind of overnight accommodations where the renter ran across the bell hose upon driving onto the property, alerted those of us working the desk, paid for a night's stay with cash, "registered," and drove right up to the door of "his room." Mac and Betty McArthur, my folks built it, owned it (along with Wilson Banking and Trust), and operated The Tobacco Trail Motor Court, later to become Tobacco Trail Motel. In other parts of these musings are some specifics concerning most of the more mundane aspects as they presented themselves. In this writing I will discuss several of the more sensational, extraordinarily unusual, astonishingly dramatic, and genuinely chaotic events that occurred on that hotbed of life's challenges.

It started in 1965. We heard rustlings in the dog fennels beside the fence in the vacant lot beside our "mom and pop" Tobacco Trail Motel. As the years began to unfold, rumors began to circulate concerning neighborhood hooligans roaming nightly, the "No Tell Hotel Row." This was a conglomeration of about ten, drive-up-to-your-door, low budget motels along US-301, south of Wilson. As it always happened, one night, as my family and I sat at the dinner table eating fried chicken and barbecue on white paper plates from Parker's Barbecue right up the road, a frantic knocking occurred on our heavy wooden front door. This door by its nature was heavy and heavily scratched on both sides. It was the only way in and out on the front of the Sears & Roebuck reconstituted house that Mac had bought from the United States Army on Fort Bragg in Fayetteville, North Carolina. He had it transported by Green OD tractor trailer trucks up 301 to Wilson in 1948. From within this asbestos sided structure we operated the motel and eked out our meager existence.

Of course, Brandy, Mother's wild as hell Irish Setter "went off" when he heard the yelling and pounding on our front door. Did I mention scratches on the inside and outside of that door? Early one Sunday morning when a drunken customer and Brandy were "toe-to-toe" on the front porch, Daddy opened the screen door and said, "Get in here, Stupid." The customer jumped into the house, and Brandy jumped off the porch. The customer was soaking wet. In his stupor, as he crossed the motel lot, he saw steam rising from the 16' by 32' swimming pool (The Cement Pond) as he called it). In he jumped along with two bullfrogs that cleaned up the bugs, then got on the top ladder step and jumped out.

On this night, with someone banging on the door, all three of us kids were hushed as a crying woman, mad as fire, told Daddy of how she had gotten the H scared out of her over in #10. She was from Raleigh and in town for a teacher's conference. Her school's principal had instructed her to stay at The Tobacco Trail Motel because the owner "looked out for" his customers. Mac (my Daddy) was a gruff, muscular, intimidating sailor who put up with NO "JUNK." Well, he also was a kind- hearted father figure to all the downtrodden waifs and strays, down on their luck, who managed to find their way to our front door. Apparently, this tiny twenty something year old, young woman had been standing at the bathroom sink brushing her teeth, when she saw reflected in the mirror, the imprint of a man's distorted face pressed tightly against the opaque, pebbled windowpane. Perhaps he could get the pupil of his eye close enough to the glass to see between the ripples. I do not know of anything that happened as a result of that report. Daddy could find nobody over behind the <u>northside</u> building, but there was an unplanted field with six-foot-tall "dog fennels" growing thick behind the Tiger Lilies across the ditch back there. We were familiar with that field and the Esso Station hillside, because that was where plum bushes grew and yielded the sweetest plums we had ever eaten. These plums were so sweet that the honeybees, wasps, and ants stayed drunk from too much nectar. That is also where I nearly sliced my right ring finger off as I slung a nineteen-inch jagged piece of broken tailpipe toward the junkpile.

Throughout southside Wilson, rumors were emerging about an alleged "peeping tom" making the rounds of creeping and peeping behind the motels spread along the "super slab." Remember Brandy? He was a hunting breed, and he was attuned to almost everything that happened at that motel. Also attuned were the pair of Northern Mockingbirds in the hedgerow of ten-foot Ligustrum shrubs along the four-foot-high fence running down behind our house and numbers 1 through 8 on the <u>southside</u> of the motel. When we heard the Mockingbirds tune up at 3:00am, we knew something was afoot. Turns out that it was **Rhoadie Mack Rountree**, the suspected peeping tom. He could secrete himself inside those ten-foot bushes where Mother's Cedar Waxwings feasted, across the fence line on the Strickland property, and peer across the 8-foot expanse between him and the bedroom windows of guest rooms numbered 1 through 8. We found evidence of where he would sit on a broken cinderblock and patiently smoke Pall Mall filtered cigarettes, waiting for a light to appear inside one of the rooms. He would then make his move.

From his perch, in the dark of night, he could see the backside windows of all eight rooms. Upon a light appearing in, say #4, he would quietly creep along the hedgerow, enter into the hedges, and gain a vantage point from which he could peep into the window. Even though there were venetian blinds inside all the windows, he could see around the edges, or when possible, through the open slats. We found that the underbrush directly across from each window was compressed flat against the underfoot dirt from his standing in one place for periods of time. Also, there were cigarette butts littering the ground.

The Kenwood Motor Court was the last of about ten motels on the right side of US-301 before Contentnea Creek spilled out of Wiggins's Millpond. The Kenwood changed hands about six times as the years wore on back in the '50s and 60s. Some German immigrants bought the twenty units, and honestly made a good attempt to modernize it. While working the late shift, Rueben, the owner of the motel (short for 'motor hotel') was lounging in his Lazy Boy red leather recliner, reading the Wilson Daily Times, and drinking a Budweiser Beer. His chair was in the living room, just behind the small cubicle office attached to the front of the building, and accessed through a narrow doorway. During a rainstorm, his wife, Sonia was "working the front desk," just around, and out of sight through the doorway to "the office." During a busting thunderstorm, a masked, armed robber burst into the office from the driveway, and pointed a silver pistol at Sonia, demanding all her money. Upon overhearing the commotion, Rueben eased out of his chair, unpocketed his own silver .25 caliber, semi-auto handgun, and <u>without looking</u>, <u>much less aiming</u>, stuck the pistol through the doorway and around the side molding. He fired three shots in rapid succession, and the pistol jammed. Upon entry into his office, he found he had shot Sonia once in the buttocks, and absolutely no sign of the robber! You just cannot make this stuff up!

In late1968, Rhoadie Mack Rountree was sighted on a Saturday while secretly peeping into Ginny Shaddee's bedroom window down at the Kenwood Motor Court where Harvey and Hart Wiggins used to live and let me ride their pony, Sport. When called to the scene of the peeping allegation, as was often the case, our Wilson County Sheriff's Office deputies were unable to overtake and arrest Rhoadie Mack because he was "fleet of foot." At our Tobacco Trail Motel home, we had a Channel Master Police Scanner which monitored and broadcast forty channels. Channel #1 monitored the Sheriff's dispatcher, #5 monitored the Sheriff's "car to car," #8 monitored the Highway Patrol, #10 monitored the Wilson City Police, and so on. On this particular night, we heard the dispatcher send four deputy sheriffs to the Kenwood for a reported "disturbance." Sure enough, Rhoadie Mack had been sighted "in the area." Deputy #1 responded, "I got the Coke machine." Deputy #2 responded, "I got the pool house." Deputy #3 responded, "I got the back side." And Deputy #4 responded, "I'll run him out." Rhoadie Mack was known, when sighted, to run into a thick patch of bushes up beside the office building, and crawl through a drainpipe toward the Millpond.

As you can well imagine, to the officers, this was not "their first rodeo," when it came to the game of trying to catch Rhoadie Mack. Deputy #4 slid to a halt in front of the Kenwood office, and ran into the thick bushes just as Rhoadie Mack approached from the opposite side. Rhoadie Mack was a huge, lanky, muscular man, but a scared deputy sheriff with shaky hands, and a drawn .38 six-shooter was enough to turn him around. He headed for Stuckey's Pecan Store on "The Back Road," across the front lawn beside the swimming pool. Out jumped Deputy #2 who fired four shots, hittin' him not nary time. Oh yeah! Did I mention that Rhoadie Mack carried an 11" sheath knife with a six-inch blade on his belt which was now clutched tightly in his huge right hand? Again, Rhoadie Mack was turned back around. By now Rhoadie Mack was in second gear and leaving pock marks in the lawn every time the "taps" on his boots hit the ground. Out jumped Deputy #1 who fired twice before Rhoadie Mack ducked around the side of the building, around back where Deputy #3 emptied his "hog leg." Six bullets flew, and Rhoadie Mack hit the dirt. He was not shot, mind you, I just think he either slipped, or his feet ran out from under him. The rookie deputy was able to pounce on him as the others "piled on."

Not six months later, Rhoadie Mack was "detected" by those persistent Mockingbirds, back again behind #4 at our motel. Daddy called the Sheriff, and Robin Pridgen and Wilson County ABC Officer Glen Stutts quietly rolled into the driveway of the Strickland House next door. As T H E Sheriff positioned himself where he could observe the fight, Glenn Stutts entered the area of bushes where Rhoadie Mack was known to hide while sitting on that cinderblock. Glenn was not a big man, but he had a huge reputation, and he proved it that night. He was wearing all black clothing and creeping along, when his sixth sense spied Rhoadie Mack just across the fence line on the Strickland property. Like a panther, Glen "went on" Rhoadie Mack, snatched him across the wire fence, and dragged him out to the Sheriff, like a good Labrador Retriever/Pit Bull mix.

After pulling just a small jail term (his fourth) for getting arrested, he got out of jail and returned to his hunting grounds. The very next Wednesday night we heard the Mockingbirds fire up, and we turned Brandy loose. He ran down behind #4 and barked a few times, but came on back to the house. Two days later Brandy lay dead from having ingested some form of poison. That was the last straw. Killing my Mother's Brandy! This heinous act was designated as, "First Blood."

It was the fall of 1969, and I was a sophomore at N. C. State University, living in #51 Owen Dormitory, studying Forestry and Ecology. As was known to happen, I came home every weekend, driving my 1955 two-tone brown and white, Pontiac Star Chief with a visor over the windshield (not cool at all). I could wait tables during Sunday lunch at Parker's Barbecue and clear $50.00 to $80.00 in tips. I didn't even sign in or work "on the clock." Every Sunday I just showed up and took care of business, handling my "regulars" who looked out for "their N C State waiter." That left my Friday and Saturday nights, "open." Occasionally Ralph, Henry, Graham, or Bobby Woodard would call my folks and tell them that the restaurant needed my help, and I would go in.

I could make more money at the pool table at Emmett's on Airport Road than I could waiting tables. The Cue Club was a high school hangout, and had its own "teeny-bopper hustlers" from whom I always took their Daddy's money. Mr. Morris had two daughters, Lynn and Debbie who the guys classified as, "strong as battery acid." Earlier on Friday and Saturday nights, before their curfew it was fun to hang out, and beat the wannabe "hustlers" out of their money. Then at about 11:00 p.m., my friend Dennis Boykin and I would go to Emmett's where the <u>real</u> money was on the table.

One Saturday night, before I went to the pool room, I stopped at Service Distributors gas station for a tankful ($5.00 worth) of $00.28 per gallon gasoline. That was up from $00.25 per gallon. Outrageous, I thought. Just before I left the gas station, **Rhoadie Mack Rountree** sauntered in, and took a seat on the windowsill, overlooking the highway, smoking his characteristic Pall Mall filtered cigarettes. I slipped out and went on down to The Creamery at the intersection of Ward Boulevard and Goldsboro Street where my "older, rich" friends hung out. Tommy Goard, Jimmy Blackwell, Charlie Pat Farris, David Woodard, Bill Adams, Doug Champion, Steve Williams and several other "cool ones." I had Daddy's "four notched" 1911 U S Army, Colt .45 semi-automatic pistol safely stowed under my front seat. None of us were bad guys, we just liked showing off. Doug had a yellow '32 Chevrolet, Tommy had a '67 black vinyl over yellow Chevelle SS-396, Bill had a '64½ black vinyl over yellow

Mustang GT, Hamp had a convertible '66 Pontiac 389 cu. in. GTO, David had a '68 400 GS Buick, Steve had a '68 Oldsmobile 442 convertible, Romaine had a Carolina blue '66 Corvette Stingray, and there were several others. Ray something had a white '62 Chevrolet Corvair Monza Spyder, but still "qualified."

After leaving The Creamery and speaking with the owner and my good friend "Pink Pearl," Earl Wilson, I went up to the Wilson Recreation Department where the SARDAMS (MADRAS spelled backward) were playing for a teen dance in the skating rink at the Teen Club. Of course, Bert Gillette and Patti Ruffin were the chaperones. There was an ill-fated stop sign right out there in front, where my best friend Lew Highsmith had gotten hit head on in his white Plymouth Valiant, only to be re-constituted with a Mack Truck radiator proudly protruding through the hole cut out in the replacement hood. Lew's Daddy hated Highway Patrolmen, and when one moved in across the street, Lew and his family had to move across town.

Apparently, no, <u>obviously</u> I didn't come to a complete stop at the stop sign in front of Wortley Herring's house. Notorious Wilson Police Officer Ray Hayes was working security at the venue, and was sitting in his patrol car (not his usual Harley Davidson) headed into the parking lot, opposite from the direction I was traveling. I saw him when he put his foot on the brake to start the engine. I nailed my old clunker. Up past the Wilson Presbyterian Church, around the side where I met as a Cub Scout in Den four with my Mother, out onto Kenan Street, and across to Nash Street headed west. Occasionally I would glimpse the revolving blue light on Ray's white cruiser running parallel with me. I sped on past famous "Dick's Hot Dog Stand," and on out US-58 toward Silver Lake. By then I was not sure where Ray had "lost his way." I turned left onto Airport Road, and slid in behind Emmett's Pool Hall, closing the gate beside the trash barrels behind me.

About that time, a terrible thunderstorm lit the skies, and torrential rain began to fall. Inside the POOL HALL, as I sat on a chromed barstool at the "Shady Lady" PINBALL machine, both my inner thighs cradled the chromed steel front legs. My hands were activating the flippers. Suddenly, a flash of lightning and a thunderous clap, knocked me from my perch, flat on my back in the middle of the concrete floor in front of the juke box. I was dead. In the pitch black, with both hands, I grabbed my head. Having a Beatles style haircut, every strand of rich brown hair was standing straight up off my scalp. Momentarily when the lights came back on, I was able to sit up. David Lucas lifted me up, but I was unable to stand. Cramps in both thighs buckled my legs. They laid me on a pool table and rehabbed my legs until they felt stable. To this day, the spiderweb of blood vessels are still raised up to the surface, and visible. Scarred by a lightning strike when I should have been home! That became the most important lesson I learned that evening, but "the night was still young."

Supposedly, about ten minutes later, Ray Hayes and his blue lights came by Emmett's at over 100 miles-per-hour, not to be heard from again that night.

Having used up my good luck for that night, I went home early. My folks wondered, "Is everything OK?" Without telling too big a lie, I joined my brother Pat, sister Kathy, and her friend Pam Brooks as we launched into a rousing game of Parcheesi. Yep! Sure did. Kathy and Pam were planning a slumber party that night down in #8, and after losing, got mad and went on down there with a strict admonition to, "Lock both locks on the doors." Pat and I shared a bedroom beside the living room where we used to sneak to the door and watch Red Skelton, Bob Hope, Dinah Shore, and Ed Sullivan television weekly shows across the top of our parents' heads on the 12" by 14" black and white screen.

About 3:00 am, the Mockingbirds piped up, thereby rousing both Mother and Daddy. Without turning on any lights in the house, Daddy went into Kathy's bedroom on the back corner of the house, and could see right down behind rooms numbered 1 through 8. There was a bright half-moon that night, and there, right behind #4 was the shadowy form of a man crouched down below the window from which light was pouring. I heard Daddy as he whispered to Mother, "This is it. I have had all this I can take." He came into my room and got me up. He loaded Pat's new Winchester pump shotgun with three #4 Magnum, high brass shotgun shells. I loaded three #4 Magnum shotgun shells into my J. C. Higgins, Ted Williams Special, Sears and Roebuck, High-Standard pump shotgun. "Cap'm Mac" formulated a quick plan of action that would prove effective. Once again, before the night was over the old cliché of, "All plans are good until you hear the first shot, and then everybody panics," (General George

S. Patton), came into play. The panic was not registered in the hearts and souls of either Cap,m Mac or yours truly. Just as we planned it, we executed our plan. The only panic was more than evident in the bloodied criminal.

"Won't Nothing Come of It!"

During this entire 5+ year episode, Daddy had been in constant communication with ABC Officer Glenn Stutts and the elected Sheriff, Robin l. Pridgen. As time drug on, **Rhoadie Mack's** escapades were not only gaining momentum but notoriety. His escapades were becoming mythological and somewhat of a folklore. Not only was it horrifying to the victims of his peeping, but it was becoming embarrassing to local law enforcement. On two occasions, Sheriff Pridgen told Daddy, "Mac, we can't catch that bastard. If you get a chance, shoot him in the legs to slow him down a might. **Won't nothing come of it!**" As you can well imagine, this was not too dynamically challenging from my soldier father's point of view, but it was raucously alarming to my "Southern Belle" mother, Mary Elizabeth Robertson McArthur, from Monument Avenue in Richmond, Virginia. She was incensed that the High Sheriff of Wilson County would impose upon her husband, and ultimately her 19-year-old son, the GARGANTUAN burden of shooting a derelict "to slow him down a might." Was there no other less violent solution? Why didn't THEY (deputies) shoot him? What if Daddy killed **Rhoadie Mack**? What if Mike killed **Rhoadie Mack**? What has my world come to?

All the while, the constant nighttime terror was challenging the dozen or so innkeepers who felt the chill of being entrusted with the safety and wellbeing of their renters. All the while, **Rhoadie Mack** was laughing and joking about his escapades with his sleezy cohorts up at Service Distributors gas station. All the while, a tempest was brewing, but **Rhoadie Mack** just didn't see it coming. His shady buddies even told him, "**Rhoadie Mack**, one of these nights somebody's gonna blow your damned head off, and won't nobody give a damn."

As the frequency of intrusions escalated, it became apparent that the perpetrator was fearless. The other side of that coin is that the necessary remedies were being formulated, not only by law enforcement but by innkeepers. Some innkeepers bought attack dogs, but you can imagine how "dicey" that can be in the hands of those who mean well but just can't seem to make it happen. Some bought expensive lighting and motion detector alarm systems. Some hired unarmed (wink – wink) security forces. Some cut down and removed all hiding places such as bushes and trees. Some erected elaborate fences which were no contest for spry, six-foot, four-inch **Rhoadie Mack Rountree**. And more than a few innkeepers were carrying pistols "to defend themselves." As you can see, the beam of this light was intensifying and becoming more focused, and it was not gonna be a pretty picture.

Well, by now both Daddy and I were fully armed and loaded. We exited the house through the front door into the thick, humid night air. The moon "gave a luster of midday to objects below." We walked together over to the front of number 1, and I stopped to allow him to proceed west down the driveway to the front of number 8 where Kathy and Pam were sound asleep. Upon arrival at his destination, Daddy threw up his left hand to motion for me to begin my approach behind #1 toward #4 where **Rhoadie Mack** had been spotted. It was showtime!

As I rounded the corner and lined up behind #1, I could see **Rhoadie Mack** still pressed up against the windowpane of #4 where two carpenters were sleeping. **Rhoadie Mack** had his hands cupped against the now darkened windowpane, and was so intent on peeping that he did not see me until I was behind #2 and slowly walking in his direction. With an unrecognizably hoarse voice, I yelled, "STOP, or I will shoot." With both hands he pushed away from the right-side window frame and ran west behind #5, #6, #7, and #8. I can still hear his feet pounding the dirt as he ran. I fired twice with no apparent results other than accelerated beat of feet. I was less than twenty yards from him. I hit him both times as evidenced by the patched-up wounds treated by the medical professionals the next day over at Wilson Memorial Hospital.

Now at breakneck speed, he rounded #8, right into Daddy's line of fire. I watched Daddy shoot three times, only hitting him twice, at most. **Rhoadie Mack** ran on through the gate, past the pump house, and out onto

"The Back Road" behind the motel. I was now chasing an unknown quantity, purported to be armed and dangerous (11" sheath knife). And I had just shot him!

There he was!

In the brightness of the moon and with my adrenaline heightened sensory perception, I could see the whites of his eyes, crouched on the centerline of the asphalt pavement. He was squatted down and twisted to his left, inspecting his bloody lower legs and their wounds. His pantlegs were shredded. I can see his face right now as he looked up in my direction. That is when I saw the knife in his left hand with which he had attempted to cut the material from his clothing. His pantlegs would not go over his combat boots. The moment seemed frozen in time. He took an ill-fated step toward me, and mumbled something. I raised my shotgun as he looked me straight in the eye. The knife was pointed straight at me. At twenty yards, I shot him in his left elbow, just above the knife. Even in the coal black dark, the #4 magnums, found their mark. The knife went flying from his fist, found it later in the ditch. He spun to his left and fell to the ground. I'll never forget that muffled sound.

I was now out of ammunition. I ran back to the house to get more shells, and Daddy arrived at about the same time. He had heard **Rhoadie Mack** scream on my last shot. I had heard nothing. My adrenaline surge, and spiked tunnel vision had kept my focus on that knife coming toward me. Upon arrival at the house, Mother had already called the Wilson County Sheriff and they were on their way. It seemed like an hour, but was probably less than ten minutes before three deputy cars rolled into the motel parking lot. The deputies immediately got their five D-cell, Ray-O-Vac flashlights and their Ithaca Model 37 pump shotguns out, and we cautiously proceeded back down the lot toward The Back Road. Mother was hustling Kathy and Pam out of number 8, and back into the house. They were all scared and crying.

As the deputies and I (now unarmed) approached the spot where I had last seen **Rhoadie Mack**, there was nothing to be found but a pool of smeared blood and a few pieces of tattered clothing. But the blood trail was evident as it led into the half-harvested tobacco field. The deputies decided to contact the North Carolina Department of Correction Prison Unit up on Ward Boulevard across from Watson Electric. Their kennel waged a notorious pack of bloodhounds having just tracked down two bank robbers through Toisnot Swamp up by the Tuberculosis Sanatorium on US-301 North.

Bloodhounds and Flashlights

Upon arrival of the tracking dogs and two burley prison guard handlers, again we went down to The Back Road where **Rhoadie** was last seen. The two dogs approached the blood stains, and near 'bout jerked their handlers off their feet toward the tobacco field. They crossed the ditch, and entered a "truck row" where the mule hauled the curtained tobacco sleds during harvest. The leaves had been cropped about halfway up the two-inch stalk, leaving almost three feet of clearance below. The white sandy dirt reflected the moonlight almost like a silver corridor down through the field as it led toward the woods beside Bill Ellis's (April 25, 1933 to February 27, 2017) Barbecue Restaurant. Also evident on the white sand were blood splotches about the size of fifty-cent pieces. These splotches were about six or eight feet apart as they led the dogs toward the woods.

Suddenly, about 300 yards into the field, both dogs locked up, and simultaneously threw their noses into the air. The leather leads became slack as their handlers caught up with them. One of the handlers said, "These dogs need to rest a minute!" WRONG!!! Without any warning, both dogs took off <u>across</u> the plowed rows in a southwesterly direction. Those poor old handlers had all they could do to keep them under some semblance of control. The out of shape Deputies with their shotguns were having trouble running diagonally across the rows, combating five-foot tobacco plants that were heavy with sap and wet with dew. The dogs had "winded" their quarry. That means, the scent on the ground was not nearly as strong as the scent coming "on the wind" from across the half mile wide field.

Having "winded" **Rhoadie Mack**, the dogs let out a guttural howl, and one broke his lead to his handler. The other dog now was right on the heels of his companion, and the handlers were in a total and complete state of exhaustion.

But there in the Honeysuckle and Poison Ivy, lay **Rhoadie Mack Rountree.** Soaked in blood and wet from the top of his head to the bottom of the single combat boot on his left foot. He was nearly comatose. His speech was slurred and mumbled, something about, "Those son of a bitches what shot me." His eyes were closed, and he could not see who was present (I was glad). The glaring flashlights were trained on him, and his night vision was not only impaired by the blinding lights but by the almost empty fifth of Rebel Yell bourbon lying beside him in the honeysuckle vines. The surprising thing was that the whiskey in the clear jug was not the characteristic brown, but clear in color with beads rolling around along the edges. Not only was this man injured, physically, he was totally "rernt" spiritually by the bootleg he had acquired at 4am from "Bit" at "Shug's Place" over on unpaved Lovers Lane. "Bit" was our housekeeping assistant for the motel, and when she ran out of snuff, she would come in the house, go over to the player piano, open Daddy's Grabow pipe humidor, and grab a handful of tobacco. She would crush it into a "wad," and pack it into her left cheek.

It came time for the now brave and manly Deputy Sheriffs to scoop up **Rhoadie Mack**, and "perp walk" him over to the ambulance parked in the driveway at Bit's sharecropper's house. Away he went to Wilson Memorial Hospital over on Tarboro Street. His escapades were over for that night, or so we thought. That night will forever live in the chronicles of my memory, and remind me of the grotesque pain and suffering dealt to many in this world through the bad decisions they choose to make, and can't seem to resist.

Back at the house, Sheriff Pridgen spent a long time talking to Daddy about what had led up to the incident, how it unfolded, and what lay ahead: court and other ramifications. I was sent to my room where Pat and I huddled, trying to listen to the intense conversation in the living room. Apparently, the Sheriff was satisfied that the knife had played a major role in our decisions, and that the end result justified the means. He also implied that he thought this might be the end of the **Rhoadie Mack Rountree** Saga in Wilson NC. He was wrong.

Over at the hospital, **Rhoadie Mack** was still stinking drunk on bootleg moonshine. There is an unmistakable, characteristic odor associated with a human drunk on white lightnin'. He was a fairly good patient in that he was in fact so drunk that he could barely move. One of my high school duck hunting buddies Ricky Tee was the Emergency Room male nurse that night. He was just back from Viet Nam where he had served as a U S Army field medic during the Tet Offensive of 1968. There was not much that he had not seen when it came to traumatic wounds and absolute carnage. So, it became his lot to remove the clothing from "the shooting victim." I kinda thought that was an unfair depiction of what lay before him on the gurney under the bright lights that night. As he used those surgeons' scissors to cut the pantlegs and waistband off the trousers, lo and behold, what did he find? Other than no form of identification, in the right hip pocket he found a "shot all to hell," fourteen-inch telescope. Imagine that!

Upon further examination, he told me later, "There was not a square inch of hide on the lower portion of that man's backside that did not have a puncture wound and a shotgun pellet in it. His left elbow was forever ruined, and nearly in need of amputation." The Medic's "Hippocratic Oath" prevented his re-telling that story, and I was glad of it. **Rhoadie Mack** was ultimately assigned a private room (because of his proclivities) "up on the floor." That next night, while pulling his IV stand in his right hand, he casually limped down the hallway, peeping into other patients' rooms, and making them feel uncomfortable with his leering mannerisms. The hospital administrator, Dr. Simons (the OB-GYN who had delivered me, Pat, and Kathy) called Sheriff Pridgen, and told him, "**Rhoadie Mack Rountree** has got to go!"

So now **Rhoadie Mack** was inmate number 4527676 in the Wilson County Jail. Wouldn't you know it? **Rhoadie Mack** was able to peer through the bars, into the cells of his fellow inmates. That might not seem too odd to many folks, but there are times and circumstances that do not merit one man watching another man as he uses "the facilities." One of his "jail neighbors" had grown up near **Rhoadie Mack** near Middlesex, North Carolina, where **Rhoadie Mack** was known to string women's underwear between the utility poles and in the branches of the trees in his yard. "Jail Neighbor" said something to **Rhoadie Mack** which caused **Rhoadie Mack** to move too close to the cell bars separating the two inmates. That turned out to be a mistake. The "jail neighbor" grabbed **Rhoadie Mack** and slammed his face against the bars, opening a huge gash across **Rhoadie Mack's** now broken nose. Soon, but not soon enough, **Rhoadie Mack** bonded out of jail and went home or somewhere.

Thanks to my Contract Bridge playing parents, their friend Arnold Formo hired me as a part time employee at a pallet manufacturing plant in Wilson on Saturdays. We made Oak wood pallets for use by the tobacco warehouses. We also made collapsible containers out of planed Oak wood slats. Planing those slats nearly deafened me, and I am "so afflicted" to this day. Guess who was one of my cohorts as we manhandled those heavy products: Woodrow Rountree, **Rhoadie Mack's** second cousin. He asked me about shooting his cousin the weekend before. I disavowed any knowledge of it, but acknowledged that I had heard about it. I never went back to that jobsite again.

Wilson County Fair Exposure

The Wilson County Fair was scheduled to come to the fairgrounds the following weekend, the second weekend in October. There are so many rich and exciting stories surrounding this phenomenon that I cannot begin to tell you any of them right now. But one is relevant to this whole, sordid, ever developing **Rhoadie Mack** saga. The American Legion fairgrounds hosted many events during the year as fundraisers to support their efforts with veterans and military families. The half-mile oval dirt racetrack was legendary in the racing circuits and eventually NASCAR enthusiasts recognized some of the drivers as having started their careers in Wilson, NC. The car dealerships used the fairgrounds to preview their newly arriving automobiles. The biggest draw and the most anticipated event was the county fair.

Among the multitude of attractions were the grandstand "Can-Can Follies," the "Wild West Show," the blood-sweating hippopotamus, and the Hoochie Coochie shows. Where do you think **Rhoadie Mack** found employment? Yep! You got it! "The Ladies of the Nile" was near the back of the fair midway, and not really too close to any of the children's attractions. The so-called music coming from the oversized speakers was unmistakably bawdy. The customers ranged from high-school boys to bib-overalled farmers. The requirements for entry were sober countenance and eighteen years of age. Guess who the ticket agent was, and the one who determined eligibility: **Rhoadie Mack Rountree**. After the sultry women came out on stage for a brief display of "their goods," they sashayed back into the tent. At a designated time, the show was sold out, a chain was stretched across the entrance, a slate board was erected that read, "Next show – 9:30," and tickets were no longer sold. Where do you think **Rhoadie Mack** went? You honestly will not believe it.

The honky-tonk music cranked up, and the yelling from within the gaudy tent escalated. **Rhoadie Mack** was not to be seen. Three "too young for admittance," high-school boys were ostracized and humiliated beyond belief, only to have their encounters enhanced and bandied throughout the Ralph L. Fike Sr. High School cafeteria for the next three weeks. Some of those stories followed the boys to their graves. Wilson Mayor Ralph el-Ramey's daughters, Gwen and Terri just happened to watch them being physically ejected in a cloud of dust from under the tent. Of course they didn't tell anybody!

Where was **Rhoadie Mack**? He was not inside the tent for the show. He was around BEHIND the tent, standing on a stack of wooden Yoo-Hoo drink crates, PEEPING "Kilroy was here" style over the edge of the tent, between the walls and the big-top canopy. Now, go figure. Had he been "rehabilitated?" Had any of his perverted ways been addressed adequately to supplant his lecherous leanings? Was he a 10-50 looking for a 10-20? (Accident looking for a place to happen)

All this rendition of tasteless tales and tawdry implications finally came to a head after the following "Parting shot," in more ways than one. About a year later, one late evening in July, a customer at Tobacco Trail Motel came up and told Daddy that he had seen a tramp and heard "rustling" behind his room, number 6. The customer was obviously a military man, and Daddy told him to go down to number 8, round the building and chase the intrusive SOB toward the house where Daddy was armed and would be lying-in-wait. Well, just as Daddy got his .45 and got back to the driveway, here came **Rhoadie Mack**, running as best he could with over 200 pellets of #4 lead shot still embedded deeply inside his body, ligaments, and joints. **Rhoadie Mack** ducked the **Coca-Cola** machine, crossed by the bug light, broached the driveway, headed for the Esso Station beside the swimming pool, and fell (I think) flat on his face. Daddy was on top of him like a duck on a June Bug, holding **Rhoadie Mack** with one hand, the other with the hammer laid back on that .45. "If you get up, I will shoot you!" **Rhoadie Mack** pushed Daddy off him, jumped to his feet, extended his arms, and screamed, "Well shoot me you son of a bitch." With that he resumed his flight up the ditch bank, under the guy wire supporting the neon sign, across the Esso lot, and out of sight up toward The Huntington Motel and Service Distributors.

A year later, the Tobacco Trail Motel was sold to Mr. Patel, and became part of a chain, The Relax Inn. Mother and Daddy moved to Macon, Georgia, and lived happily ever after.

Michael J. McArthur

Hard Work and Other Blessings

The North Carolina State Highway Patrol—North Carolina's Finest—

Get Ready Michael John McArthur

State Fair Stories

Patrol car: There was once a time in 1983 when I was NOT allowed to go to Raleigh, N C to work traffic at the N. C. State Fair, and spend Thursday through the NEXT Sunday to work a demanding traffic direction detail under the notorious 1st Sergeant Thomas T. Jeffries. By not allowing me to go, my NCSHP, Troop A, District III 1st Sergeant THOUGHT he was punishing me, and he got some imbecilic infantile pleasure from it. He had the unmitigated nerve and the audacity to plot against me. During the 1982 District Christmas Party he told me that he "had taken steps" to ensure that I would NOT be working any more N. C. State Agricultural Fair assignments while I was a member of his District. When the Troop C Captain Bobby Clark learned of it, he threw a Tasmanian Devil hissy fit. I had worked that assignment for over seven years. I knew "the players." I knew the infrastructure and the exoskeleton of the "powers that be." I knew where Crabtree Valley Mall was, and how to dodge the majority of traffic jams to get there, and where to find parking when there was none. I knew Governor James B. Hunt, Jr. and his staff and friends who regularly came to the fair, needed special parking spot(s), and free admission. I knew most of the Legislators, and knew what to ask to validate their credentials and what license plates to "look out for." I knew where State Troopers and their families were allowed to go, how to get there, how to get through the admission gates for free, and just generally, how to "keep the right wheels greased." Back in the District, my fellow Troopers who "covered for me" in my absence (Late wreck calls, two counties to patrol, more distance to travel, etc.) had cry babied to their Sergeant that, "McArthur is gone all the time and we have to do our work plus his." Imagine that! Well, as it turned out, one of my District lll Trooper buddies who was originally assigned to the arduous detail, was not happy about it, and had called his "sponsor." Guess what! Troop C Captain (110) called the Colonel (100), 100 called Troop A Captain (108), 108 called my First Sergeant (A-311), A-311 called my Line Sergeant (A-322) (A-311 really didn't want to have to tell me that he had been trumped), and finally A-322 called me and "Voluntold" me to pack my bags, I was going to Raleigh, North Carolina to work a traffic direction detail at the N C State Fair. Not only was I going to work the assignment, but I was gonna work Gate 11, the celebrity eyeball of all assignments at the most popular and highly respected "grand entrance" of the outrageously magnificent State Fair. A-311 couldn't quite wrap his fat head around all that transpired, but he filed his trepidation, angst, and vexation in a special place to be retrieved at a later, more opportune moment when he and his pigheaded fathead friends could retaliate against the insubordinate (defiant) subordinate. This was but one more "tool" to be deployed at a later date, November, 1988, by those who were no more than "Bean Counters."

Well, upon notice that I was to travel to Raleigh and stand for inspection at 1400 hours on Wednesday, <u>three</u> days away, I had <u>four</u> days of preparation to do. I had to get a regulation haircut. I had to paint my Smokey Bear "flat hat" shiny black. I used gloss black and silver paint on all the equipment in my Black and Silver Patrol Car (shovel, ax, pry bar, storage box, spare tire, rifle rack, file box). The craze at the time was white letter tires with red lines along the sidewalls. That meant painting white the raised and bordered letters (Pennsylvania Patrol Pursuit Special), and painting red the small, bordered track that ran all the way around the tires – all four of them. It just so happened that my good Troop Captain had authorized me to install, at my own expense, chromed spoke wheel covers. The small Ford "hubcaps" were flat gray in color and looked like soup bowls. Perfect. My "spokes" could fit right over the top of them, leaving my "issued" hubcaps in place. This became important a week later. One of the shortcomings of those factory Ford chrome wheel covers was that, under the stress and physical strain on the wheels during high-speed pursuit, or just power spinning to pursue a violator, those spokes would "turn loose." That would mean, I would have to remember all the places I had done extreme maneuvers, and the next day go back and look in the side ditches and fields for my errant wheel cover(s); usually missing from the front right tire. Under really extreme driving conditions, sometimes I would lose two. Raleigh Auto Parts, Inc. Junkyard on US-70 East in Garner got used to me calling (I still remember the number 1 (919) 832-4646) and asking "Pop" to hold any and all that he happened to haul in on wrecks. In a successful attempt to prevent their loss, on each of the four tires, through the spokes in three locations I would insert, and zip tight reinforced nylon tie wires normally associated with the "ties" that I used for auxiliary handcuffs. I kept one wrapped inside the headband of my Smokey Bear hat, and four additionals run down through the headliner upholstery for quick access.

Well the next step in getting ready to go to the N C State Fair assignment was shining my "brass." "Brass" included a lot of stuff. My four chrome .357 shell casing valve stem caps, my four chrome .357 Magnum shell casing door lock knobs, my twelve extra bullets in a leather bandolier attached to the handle on the inside of my back driver's side door, and all the chrome appliance features that Ford Motor Company had sent me, plus a few that I made that way, like the chrome Ford hood ornament adorning the nose of my "Control Car" as my outlaw buddies called it. That included using Simichrome silver polish on my badge (with a 5/8^{ths} inch piece of black plastic insulation on its peg to make it ride at the proper elevation above the left pocket flap), my whistle-chain, my two Cross pens, my nametag, my "Serving Since 1974" plate, my tie tac, my collar stars, my belt buckle, my handcuffs, my snap covers, my hat badge, my hat strap buckle, my belt mounted six metal piercing brass plated 158 gr. extra bullets (Lone Ranger), my wedding band, my watch, and my car keys. Of course, my Smith and Wesson nickel plated Model 19, .357 Magnum duty weapon got extra attention by ensuring the face of the cylinder was completely free of gunpowder residue. A fresh coat of oven baked, polyurethane on my pistol grips was always a crowd pleaser. You would honestly be amazed, as I was, at how many members of the adoring public, young and old, but especially school aged children would "fixate" on our holstered "hog-legs".

Patent leather accessories had to be cleaned with Ronson lighter fluid, and shined with Johnson's paste wax. The untreated edges of the leather goods had to be blackened with Sanford black Magic Marker. I had to make sure that my "hidden" extra handcuff key, taped to the inside back of my 32" Sam Browne belt was securely in place in case of an emergency.

My forbidden "CONVOY," that miracle worker, spring loaded "persuader" occasionally got scuffed up on things like headlights, driver windows, teeth, and noggins. It had to be "maintained," painted with "Leather Luster," baked in the oven at 120 degrees, and buffed to a high luster. After the Crime Control liberal lawyers "took them" from us, many of us were so thankful when Colonel John T. Jenkins returned our convoys to us to carry in our hip pocket that was especially designed for the device. Mine, with all its scuffs, torn leather, and sprung spring is currently in my desk drawer here at the office. Did I forget to mention the highly polished solid brass knuckles that we only carried during most night shifts so that the Sergeant couldn't see their outline except for the "wear marks" on the Confederate Gray pocket exteriors?

Funny thing about those armor piercing bullets. Our highly esteemed and ferocious Highway Patrol Armorer, First Sergeant John T. Rowe was a stickler about "his guns." They better be clean. They better be lubricated correctly. They better be accessible, and not encumbered by too much stuff on our Sam Brown duty belts. And above all else, they better contain and use the correct ammunition. Wouldn't you know who unexpectedly walked up behind me in the cafeteria line. Here I was, the all-powerful Basic School Team Leader, with all my lowly cadets having been seated with their rationed breakfasts, facing each other without speaking or expression. Up comes a gruff First Sergeant and snatches those Lone Ranger bullets right off my belt. He didn't even speak, and I definitely knew better than to speak. Besides, I had six more just like them in my patrol car. I think maybe that was when First Sergeant John T. Rowe coined my from then on moniker, "Supervision Challenged."

Now that my uniforms were heavily starched and freshly pressed, my 1983 Ford Crown Victoria (known as our "Crown Vic") needed some / a lot of attention. Starting at the top, the blue light lens had to be cleaned, waxed and buffed – inside and out. These lenses are what the college kids used to brazenly steal off the tops of our cars while parked at The Toot 'n Tell-it restaurant in Garner. During coffee breaks, we would get word of those blue plastic globe lenses turning up at the sorority and fraternity houses at ECU, NCSU, UNC-CH, Duke, and Wake Forest, full of burned popcorn. The revolving blue light's chrome base and coupling ring, and the take-down light had to be shined with Simichrome. Even the six foot "whip" antenna and coiled spring had to be shined and polished. The model airplane rubber wheel on the motor shaft that turned the light spindle had to be replaced because it made the light spin so fast that it wore out the factory components periodically. The three coats of Meguire's wax needed one more layer on the full car body, including the door jams. Before I could take the car to Raleigh, I had to take a toothbrush and brush the dried white paste wax from around the chrome lettering and the red pin stripe that my buddies John Atwater and Felix Chambers had applied. The chrome bumpers, door handles, and even the trunk lid keyhole cover needed some Simichrome. All the window glass and light lenses needed two treatments of Rain-X for extra shine and bug repellant. All four wheel-wells needed scrubbing and a fresh coat of Gloss Black spray paint. The chrome wheel well trim needed some Simichrome. The hood surface, the decklid and the top of the car needed one more coat of Meguire's because it would suffer from the razor-sharp clay grit that settled on it from the racetrack, and was just like sandpaper if you rubbed it on the black and silver surfaces.

The motor had to be power washed, painted, waxed, and shined. Every year I always was assigned and drove a new car. In sixteen years on the Highway Patrol, I was assigned fifteen new cars which I kept for maybe 10 to 14 months apiece. Of those 15, 9 got wrecked somehow, either by me, a violator, or another Trooper. Since it was in such good shape, my car would always be recalled and re-assigned to a cadet upon his or her graduation from Basic School. My unmarked cars would be re-assigned to newly promoted First Sergeants. Always when I needed to drive an unmarked car for any number of "special assignments," like President Reagan's visit to NCSU, Princess Anne's visit to Roanoke Island (during which I was pictured with her in LIFE Magazine), or escorts for surviving families of "killed in the line of duty" law enforcement officers, my First Sergeant was quick to relinquish his nicotine and coffee-stained unit. He knew it would come back to him either wrecked or immaculate, and he never really knew which it would be.

Polished Chrome Wire Wheels and the Commotion They Wrought

Little did I know it, but those chrome wire wheels would inflict pain and agony upon WAY TOO MANY "higher ups" on the Highway Patrol during the next two weeks "at the fair." Believe it or not, in Raleigh the rules tend to vary, not from day to day, but sometimes from hour to hour. Sometimes it depends on where you are stationed. Sometimes it depends on who your First Sergeant is. Sometimes it depends on whether you have a "sponsor," and how much horsepower he or she has. The Brass is not really afraid of anybody, but horsepower behind a Trooper can sometimes benefit his sergeant (thereby benefiting both). Anyway, on about day three of the eleven-day N. C. State Agriculture Fair, the "you know what" hit the fan. The total number of Troopers assigned to the State Fair detail usually ran about 75 to 100 strong. This week I, along with thirty-nine others, worked days (9am 'til 3 p.m.) the first five days, and then we worked nights (3 p.m. 'til 11 p.m.) the last six days.

Like I said, on about day three, my First Sergeant, the man in charge of the whole fair detail, First Sergeant Tommy Jeffries slid up to my post at Gate 11 on Blue Ridge Road. Right there, prominently displayed beside the turnstile, for all to admire, was a brand new 1983 Ford Crown Victoria with only 850 miles on it. Not only was it new, it sparkled from the Mike McArthur treatment, throughout. Sergeant Jeffries called me off the centerline with an obvious look of sinister glee. He had some good news, and some not so good news. The Troop Commander of Troop C, Captain Bobby Clark had received a complaint about a State Highway Patrol Car parked at Gate 11 that was not in compliance with Highway Patrol regulations, policies, and procedures. Regulations require that patrol vehicles not be altered without permission. They must comply with guidelines set forth by SHP Communication and Logistics (C&L) Major Fred Patton (40-year veteran SHP). That prohibited high speed carburetor jets from being installed. That meant not inverting breather covers for "sound effects." That meant not painting tires. That meant not installing chrome hood ornaments. That meant not installing Ford Race Team steering wheels. That meant not taping red "pinstriping" on the silver sides. That meant not having your name "decaled" below the driver's door handle. That meant not "gearing up" your blue light spindle to about four times the manufactured spin. That meant not installing blue lights inside your grille in front of the radiator. That meant not upgrading standard headlights with $40.00 halogen bulbs (4 of them for which I traded an entire years' worth of "authorized state paid wash jobs" at Edenton Shell Station with owner Allen Swanner). But most importantly to Captain Clark, <u>on that day</u>, that meant NOT DISPLAYING CHROME WIRE WHEEL COVERS.

Apparently, just the week before, one of Captain Clark's "fair haired" sissy Line Sergeants had requested and been denied permission to run chrome wheels on his patrol car. You may recall that my Captain had authorized mine. But that didn't matter when I crossed into Troop C from Troop A. "Golden Boy" had just left my post and gone straight to "his" Captain and cry-babied that there was a patrol car over at Gate 11, and people were crowded around it and making comments about the fact that it was the "Purdiest Patrol Car that they had ever seen." The bad news that Tommy brought was that I was to meet Captain Clark over at the Troop C Garage, IMMEDIATELY. When I rolled up, it seemed that all the mechanics in all the bays immediately took their morning break so that they could witness the upcoming fusillade of "directives." First, Captain Clark complimented the appearance of those, "God damned hubcaps." Then he really went off. Some of his friends later characterized him as "spinning to and fro, and jumping from one foot to another like a Tasmanian Devil." He then wanted to know who had given me permission to violate Highway Patrol Policy and Procedure? I did not throw my Captain under the bus (a learned technique), I merely allowed Captain Clark to continue. His next directive was that "You are setting a bad example (bad example??) for the Highway Patrol. Carry your ass back to Troop A."

Like "The Gambler," Kenny Rogers sang, "You got to know when to hold 'em. Know when to fold 'em. Know when to walk away. Know when to run." I, totally out of character, meekly got back into the most beautiful patrol car in the whole State of North Carolina, and drove it back to my post at Gate 11. Since I had been pulled away, Tommy had manned my spot and was still on the centerline. From my unauthorized back seat toolbox, I retrieved a pair of unauthorized wire cutters. I went to each of four tires and clipped three unauthorized nylon zip ties. 'AYE, Caramba! Presto! Ta- daaaa! There sat four "issued" silver "soup bowl" "hubcaps." Long story short, this whole episode had transpired over maybe 30 minutes. Sergeant Jeffries made his Captain aware of the freshly rectified colossal boondoggle. Mike McArthur was freed to fight another day! After all, this was at most, a minor transgression in the big scheme of things. Thanks to Tommy Jeffries. He was truly a man among men, and a good friend forever. He again saved the day! What a great friend and supervisor.

Patrol Car Wrecks and other Calamities

"The Good, the Bad, and the Ugly"

In April of 1979, I was assigned a new 1980 Chevrolet. When I went to Raleigh to get it, I had to transport two First Sergeants, B. G. Price from Elizabeth City, and Jim Minton from Ahoskie. The reason I was getting a new car, is that about a month earlier **On March 10, 1978** I had wrecked while in pursuit of a dark blue Lincoln Continental. I really think it was blue, but not quite sure. I am color blind, having fooled all my employment entrance examiners for both the Highway Patrol and the N C Wildlife Commission's Law Enforcement Division.

On this fateful/glorious night, First Sergeant B. G. Price, and my buddy, Chief Juvenile Probation Officer Robert Hendrix and I had just left the Sound View Restaurant in Roper where we had eaten a late dinner prepared by renegade Chef Bob Furci, which included fried Raccoon, baked Opossum, and mushrooms that his and Edna's two daughters, Tina and Melanie had picked from the surrounding lagoons. Sergeant Price was complaining about the cold wind, and Robert was suffering with a stiff neck. (SIDEBAR: Sadly my absolute best friend, Robert Hendrix beat COVID-19, dodged the flu, but passed away on May 28, 2021. May he and Marvis rest in peace)

On the way back to Chowan County, while traveling north on the extremely narrow, "old" Albemarle Sound Bridge, we met a speeding, dark blue Lincoln Continental in our lane of travel. After narrowly avoiding a head - on collision by striking the concrete bridge railing, I backed a quarter mile off the Albemarle Sound Bridge, executed a power spin, near 'bout slid down the thirty-foot embankment, and took off south on NC-32, woefully inside Washington County, "in hot pursuit." The Lincoln now had a good half mile jump on us. As I built my speed over the next half mile, I buried the needle at over 140 mph. Remember those Mopar carburetor needle jets? At this point I did not have my blue light or siren activated because, well I did not want the driver of the fleeing vehicle to know, just in case he didn't know, that I was back there, "atter 'im."

As I approached Oak Grove Baptist Church parking lot on my right, a white Pontiac, which was the front of two vehicles in the approaching lane turned left across in front of "us" into the church driveway. It looked long enough to be a Trailways Bus with a U-Haul trailer, and it was in slow motion. I mumbled, "Jesus Christ, Sergeant!" I jammed the brake, stood the car on its nose, let off the brake to steer behind the turning vehicle, and split the difference between the rear of the Pontiac, and the front left headlight of that second northbound car. It was a T-total, 100% disaster. Simultaneously, I busted the rear of the turning Pontiac, and the front left headlight of the second car, shearing the skin off its driver's door. Also in slow motion, it looked like two buckets full of debris arced across my windshield, snagging on and breaking off the wiper blades and chrome trim. The Pontiac spun full circle in the church parking lot. The second car skidded off the road into the east side ditch. At this late point in the game, I reached down and activated my blue light as I skidded (controlled braking) over 400 feet to a stop, headed south, still on the roadway.

All three of us forced our doors open and jumped out of the smokin' car. B. G. put on my coat, and Robert's neck was instantly cured! B.G. picked up the microphone and yelled, "Williamston, send me an ambulance!" He jumped back out of the car. I heard Telecommunicator Supervisor Harold Riddick manning the console at the Highway Patrol Communication Center respond, "10-4, A-311. 10-20?" B.G. yelled at me, "Where the hell are we, McArthur?" I yelled back, "NC-32 near Pea Ridge in Washington County." I was as busy as a one-armed paper hanger checking on the conditions of the two partially clad drunken Pontiac occupants. The partying occupants of the second car were now milling about, surveying the war zone. The passenger of the second car, Forest Tex Williams asked his driver, Jesse McCrae Barnes, "Didn't you see that blue light?" How could he, because it wasn't on! Forest Tex screamed, "Well I saw it!" He turned around and saw it <u>after</u> I turned it on while screeching to a "controlled braking" halt. You have to realize that at 140+ miles per hour, you are "outrunning" your siren. Your blinking revolving blue light cannot be seen over the glare of the bright halogen headlights. None of the four, partying folks were hurt. None of us were hurt. Three cars were totaled in the pitch-black March night. Only one headlight, the front right on the second car worked anymore.

Well, as the saga dragged on, first came the Washington County Fire Department and about forty volunteers who illuminated the scene with their heavy duty, jacked up, 4-wheel drive "spotlighted" pick 'em up thunder merchants. We were only about 500 yards from their station. Next came the Washington County Trooper, A-445 Ricky Stallings and his Sergeant, A-411 Floyd Owens. Next came the retired former Trooper now Sheriff, Jim Whitehurst. Next came Perquimans County Trooper A-345, Y Z Newberry. And lo and behold, among all the rest of the inhabitants of Blood Alley, next came the Troop A Commander, 108, Captain Carl Gilchrist. It turned out that just a few months earlier, Sergeant B. G. had used unorthodox political means to get promoted and then transferred back to Elizabeth City from Bertie County after he shot and killed one of two well deserving ne'er-do-wells who had brought a knife to a gunfight. One of many surprises that night: <u>Captain Gilchrist didn't like any of this</u>. Captain Gilchrist also didn't particularly care for me because I was gone teaching cadets in Raleigh way more than I was "catching him some drunks in Chowan County." (Apparently all the drunks were in Washington County.) Captain Gilchrist had come to the scene of this fiasco in a misguided attempt to ascertain 1. WHY a District III car was out of his jurisdiction inside District IV. And 2. WHY had the wreck happened in the first place. And three. just maybe he could find a good enough reason to give both B. G. Price and Mike McArthur "a little geography lesson." (Commonly called an administrative transfer to a new duty station.) I was thankful that ol' Tex Williams had told the good Captain, "Hell yeah, I saw the blue light. I don't know why Jesse didn't."

Now, as the dust was beginning to settle, I went over and surveyed my beautifully ruined black and silver 440, 1978 Plymouth Fury. I reached through the knocked out rear driver's side window to get my coat. Just like the window: Gone! This totaled car was already "red lined" as the single most expensive "per mile" patrol car in the State of North Carolina, according to 40-year veteran, Major Fred Patton in Raleigh Highway Patrol Headquarters. Something about two tiny NASCAR approved MOPAR carburetor needle jet valves that somehow "came from the factory" over at the Rocky Hock Speed Shop. High Speed equated to high gas consumption. Later, one of my misguided Line Sergeants would accuse/question me about siphoning Highway Patrol gasoline into my lawn mower but "That brings on more talk," as ol' D.C. Forehand used to say up at Hettie Mae's Country Store. Every sheet metal panel on that car was scratched, crushed, or dented EXCEPT the top with that blinking blue light and the trunk lid.

Fortunately for me and perhaps grudgingly for him, Captain Gilchrist had already contacted the Troop A Garage Foreman Pete Cox in Greenville to bring me a "spare car," which was standard procedure for circumstances such as this. Unknowing whether I would ever see my '78 again, I got what I could out of it, and sent it on its way to the junk yard. The crowd was dissipating, and it was time for me to get ready to return to Chowan County and drop off Sergeant B. G. at his tan Plymouth at the Edenton Police Department. Y Z asked B.G. if he wanted to ride with him, or McArthur. "Well, Y Z you know I am a little bit superstitious. I rode over here with him, and I guess I better ride back with him." I was glad because I needed my coat back. B.G. and Robert got into the spare and we headed back north across the Albemarle Sound Bridge. B.G. was seated in the "shotgun" seat. He leaned forward and took from his hip pocket a lucky number 13 inch, leaded, leather covered, scarred up, flat "Texas Slap Jack." He laid it on the seat between us. Looked straight at me and said, "Never again, under any circumstances short of treason, are you to turn this patrol car around with me in it!" Silence all the way to the "us-opened" Dining room of the Coach House Inn for the first of about four cups of coffee for B.G. and Robert. We had to get our story straight. Until he died, B.G. would tell others, "This is the Trooper who near 'bout got me killed!" Of course, I was quick to assert, "Now Sergeant Price, you know that I am the one who **saved** your life that night! That bunch of drunks were the ones who near 'bout got you killed."

The Continental got away. Never to be seen again, because I looked. Hard! The State of North Carolina ended up paying all sorts of bogus medical claims. The Pontiac drunk only blew a .07% two hours after the wreck. He got paid for his car, and a voluntary dismissal on his DUI. Forest Tex got paid for his car and a "Get Out of Jail Free" card for his "assistance" during the accident investigation. Once again, ol' B.G. slipped under the beam on Captain Gilchrist's radar. And I got the cold shoulder from Captain Gilchrist for the duration of his career.

Back to the story about my driving Sergeant B.G. Price and Sgt. Jim Minton to Raleigh to pick up our new cars: We were driving B.G.'s old, unmarked Plymouth to be repainted. He was seated in the back seat with two seat belts on. Sergeant Minton was trying to fit his big self into the front right passenger seat. As he opened the door, I asked him, "Sergeant Minton, aren't you scared to ride with me?" His response was a gruff, "Hell. You can't scare me." B.G. piped up from the back seat, "The Hell he can't." End of story.

Bean Counters

"**Bean Counters**" is what Troopers called their supervisors who, from our Weekly Performance Reports (HP-201) tallied arrest citations, numbers of HP-308s (warning tickets), numbers of DMV 349s (wreck reports), numbers of cars stopped, numbers of hours spent on patrol, number of hours spent in court, number of hours spent in training, number of hours spent delivering Traffic Safety Information Programs (TSIs), number of TSI programs given, and number of Driving While Impaired (DWI) arrests made (these used to be DUI - Driving Under the Influence arrests). My First Sergeant once told me, "McArthur, you can 'pen' a 201 with the best of 'em."

Most Bean Counters rely on simplicity because they subscribe to the KISS principle: "Keep It Simple, Stupid." They believe it is easier to measure a Trooper's level of performance by counting how many tickets he writes, rather than take into account the number of enforcement contacts he performs, the accuracy of his paperwork, the quality of his presentations, his reputation for fairness and, his general countenance and overall performance.

One of the highly offensive and dumb questions that Sergeants used to ask us on Sunday nights was, "How many drunks did you catch me this week?" They would lift up the bottom right corner of our Weekly Performance Report (HP-201) to see how many drunks we had charged. There was always competition among the eight districts within Troop A as to whether the First Shirt had adequately motivated his Troopers to work on arresting drunk drivers. Whenever a new unmarked car was to be assigned, it always went to the "high arrest" Trooper. Whenever an experimental Radar came to the District, it always went FIRST to the high arrest man. If two people wanted the same week of vacation, or the same weekend off, the high arrest man always got his preference. Whenever a really good Special Assignment was posted, the high arrest man always got it. Whenever the high arrest man made an error, it was always covered up or forgiven, hence my "geography lesson" and new duty station in Raleigh, C-III at the Training Center.

Wreck Reports and Those Who Can Read Them

My wreck reports were legible, accurately drawn, and well worded for the benefit(s) of the many stakeholders who used them for analytical research and fact-finding. Not meant for poorly educated supervisors who could barely read and write to start with. Prime example: "Vehicle #1 collided with rear of vehicle #2 which sideswiped vehicle #3, before coming to rest against the rear of vehicle# 4, immediately prior to vehicle #1 then skidding to rest in the northbound lane of NC-32 against the passenger side of Vehicle #3." Clear as mud, right? Sometimes you had to make it "interesting." Ultimately one of my highly sophisticated DMV-349s ended up on the agenda of one of our worthless District Meetings. The First Shirt read my narrative and began berating the "anonymous" investigating officer, and how confusing it was to him, but that he had sent it on up to Raleigh, anyway. I immediately stood up and claimed it, bit my tongue as far as what I REALLY thought, and sat back down. Benjamin Franklin Chappell had taught me, "You can't fix stupid." Later, and justifiably so, the wreck report was utilized as a training tool in the SHP Basic School during their two week, half day Accident Investigation block of instruction. I put it there, of course, because I was the instructor. Wreck Reports (DMV-349s) were the product of Accident Investigations performed by Road Warrior Troopers. Actually, many times "reports" were all they were, not investigations, because the Trooper had as many as two, three, or four wrecks "waiting on him" to get there and take over.

One of my duties on the road was to mentor newly assigned Troopers for a six week "training period" as their "Field Training Officer." Joel Siles, a college graduate from Saint Augustine's University came to me "fresh outa' basic school." I will tell you more about him in later episodes, but one of the most amazing things that did not happen during his training, was that he and I did not get dispatched to, or called out to a single traffic accident during his six weeks. Most of that time we covered two counties: Chowan and Perquimans. We even volunteered to cover Perquimans County for Y Z Newberry when our shifts overlapped: no wrecks. Wouldn't you know it. The very first night Joel worked alone, he was sent to a single car fatality on Snug Harbor Road in Perquimans County. A: he didn't know where Snug Harbor Road was. B: he didn't know how to manage the scene. C: he didn't know how to get the wrecker on the scene. D: he was a little bit (no a lot) superstitious, and the poor driver was dead as a doornail, out in the woods somewhere E: the rescue squad looked to him for direction concerning the still in one-piece body – clueless. F: Joel was smart enough to get help from the local Deputy Sheriff on the scene G: his accident report was a work of art: one car, one curve, one lifeless body.

Michael J. McArthur

Joel Never Had a Wreck From Which He Didn't Learn Something

Over the next few years North Carolina State Trooper Joel Anthony Siles learned a lot about wrecks, being intimately and actively involved in several himself.

While at home watching the late news, Ditmar Weid, a Williamston Dispatcher called Joel to a shooting and chase on Cannon's Ferry Road about fifteen miles north of his and Loretta's home on Bowens Road. In his haste, he didn't change into his uniform. Our Sheriff Troy Toppin and Deputy Joseph Byrum were chasing a stolen U-Haul van/truck toward The Punch Bowl, and the occupants were throwing stuff out the back and shooting at the Sheriff in pursuit. Deputy Byrum was hanging out the passenger window and had emptied his 5 shot S&W.38 Special revolver, and was now empty. He got Sherriff Toppin's revolver and shot it dry. Now they were just "witnessing" the event. Joel was now in a hurry. He could overhear the frantic radio calls for help on his 39.10 frequency walkie talkie given to him by Little Man Broughton, the Sheriff in Perquimans County. He was scheduled late shift that night, and had taken our BRAND-NEW MR-9 "moving radar" home with him, still mounted outside the rear driver's side window. Never to clock a speeder again.

Upon passing H. L. Bond's house on the north end of Macedonia Road, Joel entered a 45mph curve to the right at about 70mph. I cannot remember whether one or two Whitetail Deer were also navigating that portion of roadway, but it spelled disaster for Joel Anthony Siles and his shiny Black and Silver. He rolled it at least three times, through the ditch, across three strands of barbed wire fencing, and into the wheat field. He left an impressive set of skid marks which paled in comparison to some he left a few months later in Columbia, NC.

The U-Haul eventually wrecked up against a Purdue Chicken House. Everybody was out of bullets. The van driver and his shooter girlfriend were injured, but captured. Before Joel could join the party, he had to hitch a ride home and get into uniform, then he had to come get MY patrol car, then he had to make a sad report of his totaled patrol car, and then he had to anticipate the for sure to come tribunal. And the sun had not yet risen. Later that morning when the First Shirt and Lieutenant went to the accident scene, can you believe it? Two Whitetail Deer crossed back across Macedonia Road in the opposite direction from the night before. I told Joel that it was obvious that he was living right. I also told him that I was extremely disappointed that he had torn Chowan County's ONLY radar unit all to H.

BEAR SWAMP, GRACE, AND TEN FOOT CORN

Joel had a propensity to drive fast, mostly too fast. My patrol car was faster than his, though. What with all the swamps, canals, and hog pens, the narrow-paved cart paths in Chowan and Perquimans Counties were not exactly designed for "fast." Somehow, he managed to get from point A to point B, but sometimes it was not pretty. Take the time he was over in Perquimans County traveling east through Bear Swamp on a dirt road with ten-foot-high corn standing in the fields on both sides. You guessed it: curve in the Bear Swamp roadway plus soft sand plus Joel Siles. He put MY PATROL CAR so far out in a corn field that it was not visible from the right of way. Those stalks of corn, after being run over, miraculously partially stood right back up. Now he had to figure out what to do. He walked back out to the unfamiliar road in the absolute middle of nowhere. No houses in sight. He knew there was no civilization in the direction from which he had just traveled. He started east again toward some trees. Sure enough, there sat a little whitewashed single-story shotgun shack with an antique black Studebaker parked under the old Oak Tree.

Have I mentioned that Joel was a black Trooper? Yes, he was! And he was the very epitome of a handsome, dark skinned, muscular, physically fit North Carolina State Trooper, proudly wearing the dark gray uniform for which he had worked so hard. There were not many men like Joel in the rural South in North Carolina. Well he walked his dusty self right up onto the front porch of that house. Therein sat a prim, very tiny, white lady of about eighty years. Her lace collar was white as snow, just like the wisps of white hair neatly coifed around her silver spectacles under a black doily cap. In the lap of her long black dress she clutched her well-read Bible. She was not really prepared for anybody to come a-calling, unannounced. When she heard footsteps on her porch, even though alarmed, she got herself ready for whomever might have encroached upon her countrified slice of paradise. Joel knocked on her door. She stared at him through the curtained rippled, bubbled panes. Joel knocked. She stared. Joel took a step back. She stepped back.

Joel, bless his heart, was by now COMPLETELY gotten away with. He had wrecked his training officer's shiny patrol car for no good reason. He was pretty much lost. He was at a standoff with an unknown quantity. He needed help. He wanted to get that car out of that field to see if it was damaged. He didn't want to tell anybody unless it was absolutely necessary. And this little lady would not speak to him, much less offer any aid. It didn't even appear that she had phone lines running next to the single electric cable attached to her gable's end roofline. Right about then, he heard a tractor coming down the road. He turned to walk toward it when the tiny lady asked, "What are you doing out here? You don't belong here." Joel stopped, turned around, and it was apparent that he was upset. She detected that. Joel told her he had run off the road into the cornfield, and needed to get some help to get it back on the road. She told him to come back up on the porch and she would call her grandson with his tractor. Guess what! That was her grandson coming down the road on his tractor. He had been disking a field across the bottom, and had seen the cloud of dust that Joel had raised.

After the car was pulled back onto the road, Joel was back "10-8," ready for service. He always remembered that scared, maybe, little lady who ultimately came to his aid. He took her a box of candy. He also washed and waxed MY unharmed patrol car.

ROCKY HOCK AND A DEAD BLACK CAT

Joel was good for "making amends." One sunny Sunday afternoon in downtown Rocky Hock, as we passed Greenleaf Farms and approached Bennett's Millpond, a jet-black tomcat chasing a gray female sprung from the right-side road ditch. Blip-blip. Have I mentioned that "Spunky" was just a little bit, no – A WHOLE LOT superstitious? Well he was. And here we were right in front of David Ober's house, with David Ober, the cat's owner, in his bib overalls, rocking in his rocking chair on the slanted porch (Slanted so rain would run off it). Of course we stopped and backed up, placing the scene of death right behind us. We got out and surveyed the damage: "To the cat, you fool, NOT your Patrol Car!"

Dead as a hammer. And jet black, too. Oh, my! What a fiasco! There was only one thing to do. We approached Mr. Ober who never cracked a smile, never missed a beat in his rocker, chewing tobacco with evidence all over his white T-shirt and the edge of the porch. I started with, "Mr. Ober, we are so sorry." And he stopped me. MACARTHUR, you didn't do this. HE DID." Mr. Ober was a well-known "character" in his communities which included Valhalla Station, Rocky Hock, and Bennett's. Parts of these communities were known for late night Ku Klux Klan rallies, cross burnings, dynamite, and bootleg liquor stills. Of course, Mr. Ober was not akin to any of this, but we were not too sure at this point. We were on pins and needles.

Mr. Ober directed his attention to Joel. "You ain't t' to blame, neither. It's that damned cat's fault. If'n he hadn'ta been chasing that "other cat," he wouldn't a got hisself kilt." Well, we were kinda relieved, but not completely. We went out into the road, scraped up the cat and all his innards, and gently placed the carrion on the shoulder right BEHIND Joel's car. From his trunk, Joel retrieved his freshly painted, shiny black and silver True Temper, Highway Patrol issued shovel. Right there on the shoulder of RPR-1222, we took turns digging a nice grave for this stiffening lothario. Into the bottom of the pit we gently placed the dead cat. We covered him up, replaced the layer of grassy sod, and tamped it down with the shovel, careful not to step on the gravesite. Joel was struggling with this whole episode: On a Sunday afternoon, in the middle of Rocky Hock, North Carolina, having run over a jet-black cat right in the presence of its bib-overalled owner, and now getting scruffy digging a grave on state property, and burying his victim. We re-entered our ride, and proceeded toward NC-32. Joel had made it clear that he was not gonna drive over that grave, and he never looked back.

CHRISTMAS AND THE ART OF COMMUNICATION

Joel had a tremendously kind and cordial personality. He could and would help anybody and everybody. Because of this, he was respected in both the white and the black communities. He enjoyed his "calling." Sometimes the calling was a little too loud, especially when members of his own race thought he should cut them some slack. He was as fair and impartial as the day was long. To Joel, he had a job to do, and he was good at it. One Sunday afternoon he was up in the yard of a house where a raucous

Christmas Party was raging. It seems he had followed a suspected hit-and-run wrecked car, registered in Waterbury, Connecticut, right into the driveway, and the driver had jumped and run into the crowd. Those in the yard were "friends" of mine, having known each of them for five or six years, and yes, having arrested five or six of them, five or six times. But Joel was not M A C A T H E R. Joel was the "new"Trooper. That Sunday, I was just reporting for duty at 3 p.m., gonna work late shift. Leaving Virginia Fork, I happened to roll right up onto Joel standing toe to toe, and nose to nose with Bull Stanley. I got out of my car, went over there and told Bull to go inside. We got the young female out from behind the beer kegs, and I put her in Joel's car. I backed out, and headed toward town. As Joel backed out with his suspect in custody, in my rear-view mirror I watched him as he put his car into gear, he rolled his window down, stuck his head out the window, and stuck out his tongue at the crowd. Well, he might as well have thrown a 4-foot rattlesnake into their midst. They started jumping up and down and yelling. Joel's "presentation" was excellent, and I heard him exclaim as we drove out of sight, "Merry Christmas to all, "Clark Dark" won his fight!"

Princess Anne Visits Manteo

And then came the most colossal of them all. In 1984, Princess Anne, "The Princess Royal," the only daughter of Queen Elizabeth II and Prince Phillip, flew into Manteo, North Carolina in Dare County during their 300th celebration of the First English Colony. The Princess. after having narrowly survived an attempted kidnapping in 1973, you can imagine the level of security by which she was surrounded. Add to that the indomitable force exhibited by The Royal "Queen's Dragoon Guards." When I was fortunate to attend a security briefing, you will not believe what their "Chief" told us in the thickest English brogue you can possibly imagine: "My good Ladies and Gents, let me explain our mission as guests upon your shores. First and foremost, we aim to ensure the safety and wellbeing of our Princess Anne AT ALL COSTS. In America, you can determine your next ruler with a simple election. WE CANNOT! On behalf of Her Majesty, Queen Elizabeth II, I thank you for the elaborate collaborative efforts between our homeland, Great Britain and The United States of America. We have communicated extensively with and through the British Embassy and your Governor's Office, your Federal, State, and local jurisdictions, and the United States Armed Forces. Back to our mission: <u>We aim to ensure the safety and wellbeing of our Princess Anne AT ALL COSTS.</u>" Well! Those of us fortunate enough to be in that room THOUGHT we had heard his message; gotten the point! Then he added, "Upon any breach of security that might possibly endanger our Princess Anne, our Guards are charged to immediately seize control and handle it decisively." And then he added: "In the event that decisive action becomes necessary <u>FROM OUR POINT OF VIEW</u>, our recommendation is for each of you to fall flat on the floor! We will kill everything from waist high, UP!" Now THAT my dear friends got EVERYBODY'S attention. While dreadfully plain, it was equally powerful!

North Carolina Democratic Senator, President pro tempore Marc Basnight (05/13/1947 - 12/28/2020) was the organizer and the sparkplug whose foresight was responsible for logistic and professional courtesies, BY THE THOUSANDS. And he was good at it. Truly a Godsend, North Carolina lost him to Lou Gehrig's Disease in December of 2020. His office planned the celebration, and ultimately was responsible for its great success. Of course, the North Carolina State Highway Patrol had well over 100 Troopers assigned to the various security and traffic management details. Some were outlying traffic posts. Some were "external" security, and some were "internal" security. We were all "vetted."

About a month in advance, I had the great idea that I would contact the British Consulate's Office in Virginia and ask about royal protocol. The call was made, explicit instructions given, and ultimately the printed version made its way to the Troop A Commander's Office in Greenville. Apparently, I had "exceeded my authority." I think this qualified me for the first-place award in the "No good deed goes unpunished," category.

When we arrived in Manteo, we found that all the manhole covers had been welded shut. All Dumpsters were removed. All buildings had been searched and secured by a notice upon the exterior. Strange looking men and women with long coats covering bulges were walking around without a smile. There seemed to be an atmosphere of anxiety, but nobody spoke it

Michael J. McArthur

That Breathtaking Moment Oven the Croatan Sound

The morning of the event arrived and about thirty of us were at the Dare County Regional Airport, anxiously awaiting the arrival of the swarm of dignitaries. The Governor, the Congressional delegation, the Cabinet members, the bigshots, the pipsqueaks, and everybody else who had been stricken by Royalty Fever. Most importantly, senior members of the Queen's Dragoon Guard huddled quietly inside the air traffic controller's office. The Princess would soon arrive. Under spitting rainfall and lead gray skies, moderate gale force winds (33 knots = 44mph) arced out of the southeast. Her Majesty's personal jet circled and approached runway #1 from the west. The Leer Jet's approach and ultimate landing was a gut-wrenching sight to behold. The jet appeared to be dropping like a rock, out over Croatan Sound. It seemed to pause. Then it turned and twisted as the winds pushed it north from the southeast side as it banked into perfect alignment with the runway, and scrubbed tires on the wet concrete. Amid the dead silence, an audible gasp of relief arose amid cheering from the spectators. It brings emotion to the forefront even now as it is recounted.

Agona Rules!

When assignments were revealed, I was lucky! As I somehow knew I would be, I was assigned to escort Miss Cora, Marc's Mother, "anywhere she wanted to go, anytime she was ready." When she wanted to go to the Queen Elizabeth II Gift Shoppe over the bridge on Ice Plant Island, we went to the Queen Elizabeth II Gift Shoppe over the bridge on Ice Plant Island. When she wanted to share a secret and hug with Princess Anne, we shared secrets and hugs with Princess Anne. When she wanted to sit alongside Princess Anne in the Royal Limousine, she sat alongside Princess Anne in the Royal Limousine. While she was in the limo, I was asked to keep the crowds back for a moment. At that precise "moment," New York journalists from Life Magazine arrived and captured that Trooper with his arms spread wide, holding back the masses, smiling from ear to ear, ogling the ongoing pageantry as depicted in their October issue. Andy Griffith was standing just to my left, but keeping a very low profile. The photograph ended up in that month's Life Magazine issue with Geraldine Ferraro, Vice Presidential candidate on the cover. Miss Cora, as she was affectionately known was a Dare County idol. She was a rock star to Paul Green, "The Lost Colony" playwright. She was a mentor to all the youthful actors and actresses including Andy Griffith. And above all else, Miss Cora was <u>rock solid</u> to the "locals." She mastered and launched in 1937, the persona of "Agona," the love-struck Native American woman on <u>The Lost Colony</u> cast, who knew more antics and pulled more tricks on the naivetes than a star crazed monkey on a ten-foot flagpole.

Michael J. McArthur

Westbound and Hammer Down

Joel Siles was assigned a celebrity traffic post, and served us well, just as we had trained. Along about 4:00 p.m., he and I were relieved from our assignments, and ordered to return to Edenton, just as I was cruising past his US-64 post. We motored westbound with the hammer down. I don't know if you have ever traveled through Buffalo City and East Lake, North Carolina. US-64 is straight as an arrow, thirty-six feet wide with 10-foot canals on each side, and relatively few driveways. An eccentric senior lady lived up one of the dirt driveways, and for years had "adopted" hordes of Black Bears who lived and fed along her property. Sadly, sometime in the dead of the following winter, she ultimately "fed" one time too many.

Other than an occasional <u>photographed</u> long tailed black panther soaring across the asphalt from canal to canal, a few fat alligators feasting off commercial fish offal in the slough beside the Alligator River, some monstrous Dare County Black Bears with cubs, an occasional magnificent Bald Eagle, and a few "relocated and collared" Red Wolves, there isn't much to interfere with traffic on this "super slab." Joel was right behind me at a careful 115mph. Lo and behold, there on the right shoulder was the proverbial, unmistakable, stranded motorist. A pale blue Ford Pinto with what appeared to be smoke coming from under the hood, with a man and woman scratching their shaggy heads. I slowed to a smoking brake pad stop, and Joel blew past me. I activated my blue lights and emergency flashers, backed up about a quarter of a mile, backed in behind the Pinto, and offered emergency roadside assistance. The man was handicapped, and the woman had just poured water from a gallon jug into their radiator, and the steam was rising. They told me that they would be "awright" because they had to stop and do this ritual about every 50 miles. They were thankful for the snake infested canal full of tea colored, leaf-stained brackish water. I remounted, left the pits, and re-entered the race west on US-64. As I passed through Alligator Crossroads approaching the N C Wildlife Resource Commission's Futch Game Land Waterfowl Impoundment just over the Alligator River Bridge, I heard an ominous sound on my SHP 42.10 radio frequency.

Joel was in trouble. He should have been 10 miles ahead of me in Pea Ridge, but he wasn't. Apparently, as he entered Columbia, he still had his speed "up" just a little. A petite senior citizen, a commercial fisherman's widow, traveling east on sixty-four had turned left across in front of his screaming Black and Silver traveling west. As I rolled up to the scene, I could see smoke coming from both the Buick Electra 225 and Joel's patrol car. Four wheel locked up skid marks with a jagged ending led up to the crumpled, totaled patrol car. Debris covered all four lanes of travel, and traffic was stopped. Papers were blowing in the wind. People were running. Lights were flashing. Arms were waving. And it got worse from there.

The little widowed lady had gone to the Piggly Wiggly in Plymouth around noon that day and eaten lunch at The Golden Skillet which she did every other Saturday on her twice monthly vittles run, after her Social Security Check finally arrived. Joel's face was bleeding, his tie was dangling, and he had blood running down his uniform shirt. The peg on the back of his hat badge had dug a two-inch gash in his bedecked forehead. That Smokey Bear hat did not survive the encounter when his hard head hit something harder inside the car. The driver of the Cadillac appeared motionless but alive. She was softly crying, and family members were assisting her while holding her diminutive hands. I will never forget how soft and kind she appeared in the midst of her near-death experience.

I am not quite sure how all those cans of Campbell's Soup, Jolly Green Giant string beans, Maxwell House Coffee gallon cans, Irish potatoes, rutabagas, artichokes, seasoning meat, toilet paper, Mary Jane hamburger buns, busted RC Cola bottles, gallons of Maola milk, Crisco lard, melting ice cream, individual pork chops, busted bags of Pillsbury flour, and magazines could have possibly been inside that car, but they weren't any longer! Everywhere I looked were strewn items from the Piggly Wiggly,... and car parts. Lots of 'em. Right in the middle of the highway, next to one of Joel's chrome wheel covers, was a black patent leather purse, unscathed. I picked it up, and delicately turned it over to a local Sheriff's Deputy who appeared to be a family member of the woman. Columbia is too small to have a police department of its own, and the Tyrrell County Sheriff's Office covers the town's jurisdiction.

As you can well imagine, traffic was backing up in both directions and the sun was setting. The road was choked with jacked up pickup trucks, massive tractor trailers (one of them filled with Tyson Food's hogs going to market), tourist packed motor homes, rickety campers, John Deere green tractors, and PEOPLE. After I had finished checking on the lady, shaking my head at Joel, and kicking groceries and grille plastic out of the two eastbound lanes, I got traffic moving, however slowly. "Rubber-necking" gained new meaning that fateful day.

Here came the Highway Patrol "Brass'" as they patrolled back to Raleigh. They were very professional, and let us do our jobs. The day ended with everybody going home. The Royal Princess flew out to London. The little lady recovered to shop another day. And Joel survived another calamity. When I went to check on Joel in Chowan Hospital, all the "what if's" came to the forefront. What if the brakes had been better on the patrol car? What if the lady wanted to sue Joel? What if the lady died? How bad is my Patrol Car? Was Joel gonna lose his job? And finally, "Mike, what if you had still been the lead car when we entered Columbia? You woulda hit that Buick." My unfiltered unabashed response was, "Joel, if I had been in the lead, that poor lady would have still been in the checkout line at Piggly Wiggly when we blew through Columbia." I also told him that I had recovered his chrome breather cover and his four chrome wheel covers for later installation.

My Friend, Trooper Lin Godfrey

Lin Godfrey was a Trooper from Currituck County who came from a privileged background: his family farmed "BIG." He finished well in his Basic School and was immediately assigned Executive Protection for Governor James B. Hunt, Jr. at the Governor's Mansion on Blount Street in Raleigh. Upon satisfactorily completing that assignment for about a year, he chose for his duty station to be Edenton, NC, A-III. He and I worked closely for a number of years. He was a single Trooper and had made many friends during the course of his assignment here in Chowan. He always wanted to be transferred to Currituck so he could help with his family's business.

Lin developed a close friendship with an Edenton Police Officer named Shadrack (Shack) Small. Shack aspired to become a Trooper, and spent a lot of day and nighttime in the front right of Lin's Black and Silver as a "ride-along" law enforcement officer. During the SHP application process, Shack spent a lot of time "training" with Lin. One cold May night, Lin chased a blue pickup truck south on NC-32 near Valhalla in excess of 100mph. NC-32 is straight as an arrow. The speed was not necessarily problematic. Something happened. The car steered to the right, steered to the left. Steered back to the right and hit the ditch bank. It went airborne for over 100 feet, and came to rest in the middle of a cottonfield.

North Carolina is in, "The Cotton Belt," and Fahey, Butch, Joey, and Carroll Byrum had already planted their world-famous cotton crop. The little plants were about three inches above the ground. That patrol car hit the ditch bank so hard that it sent a slicing sheet of quartz sand horizontally across that field, right underneath the flying patrol car. When the sun came up, it was time to extricate the smashed-up car from the middle of the field. In a meticulously careful manner, so as not to damage any further the crop, Kojak (Milton Jordan) managed to snake the cable from his winch along the perfectly level portion of the plantless field, up to the rear of the car. Did I say plantless? YEP! That sheet of sand had cut every cotton plant off even with the ground. Think "weed-eater."

Both Lin and Shack were injured. It appeared that they had been seatbelted in, but Shack's face had hit something. Could he have been driving? You be the judge! From then on, many of us referred to Shack as, "Weed Eater."

CHRISTMAS FRAUD, AND SHAKEDOWN GONE AWRY

Lin was accustomed to driving his yellow Corvette, and it handled just a little differently from that Dodge patrol car. One Sunday afternoon, in an attempt to do a quick "turn around" on North Oakum Street in pursuit of a speeding violator, he backed into an unoccupied blue 1974 Chevrolet Nova partially parked in the street. Well as a result, we let the speeder go and got out of the Patrol Car to inspect the damage to the Nova and our patrol car. Bumper-to-bumper. Zero damage to either car, but here came the owner of the Nova. He was well known to the law enforcement community. He was an accomplished thief and prevaricator. He said he wanted to take his car to Edenton Motors for an inspection to determine the extent of the damage. Wouldn't you know it! The car needed $800.00 worth of suspension work and a $400.00 paint job from the scratch on the front left fender that didn't come close to alignment with the patrol car bumper. Lin told the SOB that he would pay him $300 for alleged damages, and the crook agreed. About six months later, on Christmas Eve, the crook called me at my home and wanted to know the name of the Insurance Company that insured State Highway Patrol cars. I told him that he should contact Trooper Godfrey, and gave him Lin's number. I called Lin and gave him the "heads up!" I didn't hear anything for about a week until the SHP Troop A District III First Sergeant called me at home about 2:00 and asked me to meet him at the Elizabeth City Office after I checked 10-41 at 3:00 p.m. I did not have any idea what the Sergeant knew I had done, but I knew full well the facts of what I had done. So here I go to Elizabeth City. On the way, my sidekick, Y Z Newberry had a car stopped up by The Bear's Den and Hillcrest Gardens on US-17. As an assistance gesture, I pulled in behind him. He laughed as he approached my car, just like he always did. "Well, it looks like I am gonna have to start investigating ALL the wrecks in Chowan County from now on." Again, he laughed. But I didn't. It seems like Y Z had been in the District III office that morning (which he often was) when the owner, in his blue corduroy Zoot Suit had met with the First Shirt about his "wrecked" Nova at the hands of Trooper Mike McArthur and Trooper Lin Godfrey! THE GOOSE WAS LOOSE!!!

    With my mind racing, I drove on over to Elizabeth City. The First Sergeant was not in a good mood. He began by reading to me the State Highway Patrol Policy and Procedure Manual concerning truthfulness. Then he read to me the "Canons of Police Ethics." By now I was not in a good mood either. I didn't let him know that Y Z had already let the cat out of the bag about a week earlier. My opening shot was, "Sergeant, don't ask me something that is gonna put you in a bad position for having mishandled this case from the beginning." You see! I already knew that Lin had told the First Shirt about the incident, and the First Shirt told him to just leave it alone, pay the crook his $300.00, and maybe it would go away. Well, guess what! It didn't. Evidently the crook needed some Christmas money, and thought he could fraudulently shake-down the SHP into a monetary settlement.

The First Sergeant changed his tack, and asked me where was Godfrey on his day off? This now being January, it was during the height of Currituck County's bountiful migratory waterfowl hunting season. Lin, in addition to being a State Trooper, was a licensed duck hunting guide with the County of Currituck, and the N C Wildlife Resources Commission. He and his partners managed four blinds on Currituck Sound. Lin had a hunting party of six from Memphis, Tennessee, at $350.00 a head, inside his Monkey Island duck blind, in the shadow of the 1875 Currituck Beach 162-foot Lighthouse in Corolla. But did I tell the First Shirt that? Nope. Lin was in violation of the SHP Policy and Procedure "Secondary Employment Guidelines." And it gets worse.

Two days later, our SHP Zone Major calls the First Shirt. The crook had called The Ivory Tower in Raleigh, and attempted to speak with the Colonel who relegated the call to the Zone I Operations Major. The First Sergeant's drawers were in a wad, Lin's drawers were in a wad, and my drawers were in a wad. I had not immediately notified my first line supervisor of an alleged violation of SHP Policy and Procedure AND violations of Chapter 20 of the North Carolina General Statutes. N.C.G.S 20-154, Failure to see before backing, PLUS N.C.G.S. 20-166, Hit and Run and Failure to Report an Accident. Well, now I was beginning to think that my back and neck had been injured in the "wreck." But did I mention that? Nope.

In the wind up, the crook went away, Lin got a verbal warning/reprimand, our First Sergeant came away clean, and Mike McArthur got a "Get Out of Jail Free" card for not having thrown The First Sergeant under the bus by his knowing that the Sergeant had given Lin unethically bad advice.

Kudzu Closeup

Bill Martin and I sat side by side during the 58th Basic Highway Patrol School in the Spring of 1974 at the University of North Carolina, Institute of Government in Chapel Hill, NC. The line-up was Harold Lee (Pole Cat), then Bill Martin, then Mike McArthur, then Billy Ray McCloud. We had a grand time among ourselves as we were all about the same age and had each come from meager backgrounds. Chapel Hill, North Carolina might as well have been a foreign country, and from some of the sights we encountered over the years, maybe it was. Getting up at 5am to be on the field by 5:15am, and rooming in adjacent rooms, we all were buddies. We covered for each other, inspected each other's displays, stood for test runs, and basically got to know each other better than some of the flashes in the pan with whom we were thrown.

Bill and I were working the State Fair one year, and were lodged at the high-rise Howard Johnson Hotel on Glenwood Avenue across from Crabtree Valley Mall. When we were relieved from our traffic direction posts at around 11:00 p.m., it was ALWAYS a race to get back to the HoJo. Blue Ridge Road, to put it mildly, became a little crooked with ravines alongside the million-dollar mansions of Kid Brewer and Seby Jones. Going into a curve, Bill got "tapped" from behind by a nameless colleague, and spun into the Kudzu laden ravine. Well, as you can imagine, there were at least twenty-five more Black and Silvers either just ahead or coming along that same road at the same time. We emptied four trunks of their 15-foot chains to begin the extrication maneuver. My chain is either still lost in that ravine, or in the trunk of someone else's car.

Upon a quick inspection, the only real damage was to the front passenger door. NO PROBLEMO! Over at C&L Headquarters, about two miles away was a whole FLEET of highway patrol cars, some new some old. Bill needed an old door, and the shade-tree mechanic at the body shop in Garner said that he could switch them out before Bill's shift began the following afternoon. SOMEBODY went "shopping," made a "midnight requisition," and "found" a "perfect match." Who needs sleep? "Clean door" went to Rock Quarry Road. As "per instruction," "Clean door" was installed onto needy vehicle. All's well that ends well! Not quite!! The gray paint on the needy vehicle was just a little darker than the gray paint on the "clean door." At this point, I can honestly, (wink – wink) say that I do know what happened next. I heard some rumors, but that is all I know and all I ever heard about it, and all I will ever divulge. If you can believe that over 40 Troopers never spoke of the incident again, all I can say is, "Bless you!"

The Shootout

Firefight on Governor Ehringhaus Road

In October of 1986, the Striped Bass fishing season was in full swing. Trolling Yozuri "Wonder Breads" beside the Albemarle Sound Bridge and the Chowan River Bridge was productive, but finding "birds" (Sea Gulls) "working" schools of Rock Fish could produce monsters when jigging "down deep." Folks from all over America come down here to fish the Chowan, Roanoke, Cashie, Middle, Perquimans, and Alligator Rivers, all of which feed into the Albemarle Sound. In Plymouth, right up from Domtar what used to be Weyerhaeuser Paper Mill, in Martin County is a small mom and pop motel named, Sportsman's Inn. Good friends, good food, good fishing, good bear hunting, and the list goes on. Two Rocky Mount fishermen had gone out to The Golden Skillet for dinner in Plymouth, and upon their return, drove their 1985 Gray Chevrolet Caprice Classic up to the door of room #14, right between #12 and #15. (You know what their room number should have been.)

As they unlocked and entered the room, three robbers, one with a red bandanna over his face, armed with 13-inch, Old Hickory butcher knife (I've still got it) followed and pushed them in. During the robbery, a 6-inch barrel, blued Model 19 Smith and Wesson, .357 Magnum revolver was found in the nightstand. It should have been in one of the good ol' boy's pockets, right? Anyway, the Chevrolet owner had the barrel of his own gun rammed down his throat. His money and his keys were taken, along with his pistol and half a box of jacketed hollow point (JHP) bullets. The robbers hastily fled in the Chevrolet, eastbound on US-64 toward Plymouth.

At about 8:00 p.m., the call went out that three armed and dangerous black males had robbed the motel in Plymouth and were headed east on

Michael J. McArthur

US-64 in a gray 1985 4 door Chevrolet Caprice Classic. I had one just like it at my house: my family car.

At this time, about ten members of the Chowan Edenton Optimist Club were inside the American Legion, Post #40 "Show Barn." We were constructing "Mr. Peanut" on a chicken wire frame, stuffed with brown napkins. The caricature of which was to be mounted in the back of Harold Lloyd Bunch's pickup truck that I had just HAD WASHED and waxed the week before. That atonement to Harold Lloyd came about because the week before, I was on NC-32 near Pembroke Creek at Brayhall investigating a wrecker wreck and had parked my patrol car in front of Harold Lloyd, on the slick shoulder. That was where Gaither Williams's red wrecker hauling a red Oldsmobile had run off the road, overturned, and rocketed the muddy Olds' right back out into the roadway, upside down. About that same time "Rabbit" Leary came driving along in his Momma's Thunderbird, right through the muddy scene. Rabbit's license was permanently revoked. I knew it. He knew it. And he knew I knew it. When my eyes met his, he floorboarded it. Fishtailing in the muddy roadway. Throwing mud all over everything within 100 feet. YOU KNOW NOT! MUD ON MY UNIFORM? MUD ON MY PATROL CAR? OH, _____!

I jumped my muddy self right back into my patrol car, sharply cut my wheels to the left, and floorboarded that 440 Magnum. That car spun around on a dime, and the chase was on ("Rabbit", remember?). He hurtled up to Valhalla, slooded left onto Rocky Hock Road, crossed Rocky Hock Creek Bridge, and cut to the right into David Ober's pumpkin patch. You should have seen those two-foot Jack-O-Lantern pumpkins bouncing that Thunderbird around. Some were launched into the air, others were splattered. It was more than Rabbit could bear. He was not as afraid of me as he was Mary Frances, his 300-pound mother who just happened to come along. In order to save Rabbit's life, I arrested him, handcuffed him, and put him in my car. Mary Frances got there just in time to threaten (or promise) him, "Son, I'm gonna kill you!"

As we were, back to the wrecker wreck. When I got back to the muddy creekside, my slot was still available among the pickups and the ambulance, and the fire truck, and the volunteer firemen. Uh-Oh! The entire front end of Harold Lloyd's NEW fire engine red Ford Pickup displayed a solid muddy facade. No visible headlights. No visible glass windshield! And you know how that happened: as a result of my "power spin." Thus, the Highway Patrol (Mike McArthur) paid for his wash and wax job.

The fact that Harold Lloyd's truck was so shiny and bright was the reason his truck was gonna transport "Mr. Peanut" in the John A. Holmes Marching Aces Peanut Festival Parade three days later on the 4th of October. Harold Lloyd was a member in good standing of the Optimist Club, and when the call about the armed robbery over in Plymouth came out, I said, "Come on, Harold Lloyd, let's ride down to the Albemarle Sound Bridge to see if they come our way." He declined, saying that I would probably be out all night, and that he had to trailer one of Scott Harrell's (January 3, 1928 to January 23, 2018) 42-foot Albemarle Sport Fishing Boats up to Baltimore, Maryland the next morning, early.

I got into my patrol car, and heard chatter on the radio that there had been no sighting of the robbers in the Chevrolet. I shot on down NC-32 to the north end of the 3.5-mile Albemarle Sound Bridge. I called A-445, Ricky Stallings who was working Washington County, and asked for an update. He was stationary at Pea Ridge on US-64 about three miles south of the bridge. We decided to meet on the south end of the Bridge and set up surveillance in anticipation of the Chevrolet. I drove onto the bridge and went about a half a mile and met an '85 Chevrolet that looked blue, or silver, or gray, or green, or pink, or chartreuse. Come on! It's nighttime. And I'm color blind. Gimme a break!

What the heck. I figured that it was probably NOT T H E car. I activated my blue light, and backed off the narrow bridge. As I power spun into a northbound heading, there T H E car was. OOOPS! Stopped on the right shoulder in front of Sandy Point Beach Club.

I was much too close for comfort. I pulled in behind the Gray Chevrolet just as a red bandanaed black male with sunglasses and doo-rag stepped out with a pistol in his hand. There, in human form, stood death itself. With no time to radio anybody, I exited in a low crouch, and ran to the rear of my patrol car, .357 in hand. When the robber exited his Chevrolet, the interior overhead light came on, and the bell started ringing. There in the front seat was another black male with sunglasses, barely visible, peeping over the back of the front bench seat. He yelled to the stationary driver still standing in the doorway, "KILL THAT MOTHERFUCKER!"

And where was robber #3? Little did I know, but he was in a car that pulled in right behind my patrol car as I came to a stop. He had followed me off the bridge. By this time, with no help in sight, I had to do an immediate assessment of my chances of survival. I could rely on no one else, because it was that nobody but Ricky knew where I was, and he was waiting on the other end of the world for me to get there. Little did he know that I was in a fight for my life against at least three armed and dangerous robbers, in the dark of night, waist deep in a ditch, with a six-shot revolver, a flashlight, six extra bullets, and no shotgun. MY BAD!!!

By now the driver was crouched down and <u>pointing his cocked pistol, COCKED PISTOL toward my steering wheel</u>. He had to overcome the glare from my self installed halogen high beams and the take down light mounted on the front of my blue light dome. The mystery car parked behind me slowly pulled back onto the roadway and proceeded north. I stayed beside my front right fender and took in all that was facing me. I figured that I could kill the driver with one or two shots, and the passenger with one or two shots, but where was that third robber? Was he hiding in the back seat? I had to save as many bullets as I could, just to be as safe as I could, BUT LETHAL.

During this interchange, I tried to open my passenger door to radio for help. It was locked. By now I was in a cool rage. Three robbers, six bullets. No radio access. No help on the way. Nobody knew where I was. And did I mention that it was dark? Very dark? As prepared, I took my patrol car extra key out of my front right shirt pocket on my whistle chain, and unlocked the passenger door. I had disabled the interior light activation switch, so I was not immediately blinded AND ILLUMINATED. The radio handset was on "car to car," channel 4. I called Ricky to, "Come over to Chowan County, RIGHT NOW! I've got 'em."

I turned back to the robbers, and in a hoarse voice, I yelled, "GET BACK IN THE CAR. DO IT NOW!" <u>My training had kicked in.</u> Surprisingly, the driver re-entered his car, slammed the door, and the interior light went dark. That was scary, too. Evidently, when an "additional" voice reached the driver from the right side of the patrol car, he figured that there were more than one of me back there, and he was outgunned. I should have killed him. I should have killed him. <u>I should have killed him!</u>

The Chevrolet took off spinning tires and throwing rocks onto me and the front of my car. I didn't care. I ran around the back of my car and re-entered the driver's seat. And "took off spinning tires and throwing rocks" northbound in pursuit of the fleeing felons. I stuck my .357 in the crack of the passenger seat rather than reholstering. Again, MY BAD. During the accelerated ride, it vibrated right between the seats, right onto the floor of the back seat. They had about a half mile jump on me, but I was closing the gap when I heard a faint, "Tap. Tap. Tap." It sounded like the slamming shut of my gasoline fill cap when I pulled away from the pump and had left my flap open. Times three!!! When my patrol car reached the spot on the roadway where the Chevrolet had occupied at the sounds of the taps, my air conditioner sucked in the odor of gunsmoke. Damn. They are shooting at me! "Williamston, I am traveling north on NC-32 in excess of 100mph behind that robbery vehicle, and I am being shot at! I need some help out here RIGHT NOW!" I've got the tape of my radio transmissions from the event at home.

I continued to gain on them, and again I heard. "Tap. Tap. Tap." Then the interior light in the Chevrolet came on. Then I smelled gunsmoke again. "Williamston, they have shot at me six times, and I am still behind them traveling north into Perquimans County on NC-37 in excess of 100. I need some help out here, RIGHT NOW." I slid down in my patrol car seat, peeped through the steering wheel, and retrieved my pistol that had slid into the back-seat floorboard. I DROPPED BACK! WAY BACK! They and I were the only two cars out there in either direction. We flew past Calhoun Jordan's racecar shop. As we approached Les Jones' shot house and gambling hideout where he had been shot and killed two years earlier, I saw six flashes come from the passenger side of the Chevrolet, in rapid succession. And I smelled strong gunsmoke. The interior light came on again. They were reloading that .357 Magnum.

As we were now in Perquimans County and approaching the T intersection with US-17 at The-Five-Mile-Y, I knew they were traveling much too fast to make the turn. The Chevrolet locked up all four wheels in a cloud of blue smoke. At that precise moment in time, a WINN DIXIE tractor trailer was traveling north on US-17, and approaching the same intersection. He too saw that that Chevrolet wasn't gonna make the turn. He, too slammed on brakes creating a cloud of blue smoke, STOPPING in a direct line of my sight to follow the Chevrolet which was now in the edge of a soy-bean field, having made the T intersection into a crossroads intersection. I skidded to a stop, just south of the intersection as the tractor trailer saw the error of his ways, and got the H out of there. I got my Ithaca pump 12-gauge riot shotgun out of my trunk and a box of 25, #4 buckshot cartridges. Now it was my turn.

When I came around the corner of my car, I could see two men running across the field in four-foot-high soybeans. They both stopped, and one of them turned and blasted two .357 Magnum rounds in my direction, and immediately dropped down out of sight for the next hour and a half. I started emptying that shotgun in the direction that I had last observed the felons. Ricky Stallings screeched to a stop and started putting on his bullet proof vest. "Ricky, get your shotgun and start shooting. They are right out there in the edge of that field." He started shooting, and I emptied my shotgun again, that being all twenty-five rounds. By now the air was deathly still, painfully quiet, with a heavy haze of gunsmoke shrouded like curtains.

The Highway Patrol Telecommunicator Chuck Rogerson was a relatively new dispatcher, and he followed Highway Patrol protocol to the letter. He was a blessing to me and others that night. By now he had at least 100 Highway Patrolmen on their way. He had SBI Special Agent Dwight Ransome coming from Bertie. He had Ronnie Stallings with his ten-man Emergency Tactical Response Team and dogs coming from Hertford County. He had bloodhounds coming from the Department of Corrections in Creswell. But none of them were there yet! Suddenly, out of nowhere, my hunting buddy, Calhoun Jordan pulled up beside me and asked me what he could do to help me. He had heard the shots and the siren go by his house. He had a million-candlepower spotlight and a Remington, 742 BDL .30- '06, ten shot, scoped semi-automatic rifle on the front seat of his truck. He immediately became the most important man on the planet. He took that rifle and emptied it into the soybeans, TWICE. Fire was shooting out the end of that rifle barrel at least SIX feet, and it was music to my ears. He ran out of bullets, but went home to get more.

That fateful night, years before he became Dare County's Sheriff, Hertford County Task Force member Doug Doughtie ("believes in accessibility") was "Boots On The Ground." He had Dare County Deputy Sheriff C. C. Duvall in the air in the Dare County helicopter. As he courageously hovered forty feet over the bean field, the "wash" from C. C.'s helicopter beat down those four-foot beans near 'bout flat. There lay one of the culprits.

Here came ANOTHER gray, 1985 Chevrolet Caprice. This one drove right into the thick of the melee, and before it came to a complete stop, out jumped a GREAT BIG BLACK MAN. Special State Bureau of Investigation Agent Dwight Ransome was on the scene and with his "command presence," he IMMEDIATELY took control. He rallied the troops and empowered the officers to capture the thugs who were still in the beanfield: "GO GET THEM AND BRING THEM TO ME!"

I looked north toward Elizabeth City and heard <u>and saw</u> a Hertford City Police Officer, Corporal Tim Spence headed south on his way, about two miles up the road. Then I heard, on my scanner, his Hertford Dispatcher tell him to "Stand down! Return to your assigned jurisdiction." His headlights dipped, and he turned around and went back north. By now, Harvey Williams and the whole Town of Edenton Police Department night shift was arriving on the scene. Before he got stuck to the axle, my Sergeant Potts ordered all officers to surround the field. The Fire Department from Hertford arrived on the scene, and a very good friend of mine, Chief Aubrey Onley came up to me and asked, "Cap'n Mac, what do you need me to do?"

I was still standing in the doorway of my patrol car with my shotgun at the ready. Lo and behold, as I surveyed the damage, I realized that I had fed all twenty-five rounds through that pump action shotgun, but had only popped the cap on about eighteen of them with the other eleven live rounds lying on the ground. I quickly picked up "the evidence," reloaded my gun, and waited to see what was gonna happen next.

About now Sergeant Potts took my .357 away from me. My shotgun was seized. And I was ordered to sit inside my patrol car and begin writing a narrative. I was defenseless, or so my supervisors thought. I reached into my left hip pocket and retrieved my .22 Magnum, two shot, High Standard Derringer. My wife, Becky had given it to me upon my

Michael J. McArthur

Valedictorian graduation from the 58th Basic Highway Patrol School. We also had given its consecutively numbered twin to Trooper R.L. "Pete" Peterson who had been shot in the head on May 31, 1979 in Rutherford County. Sadly, he never got the chance to pull his out of his left hip pocket, but he had it!

For the most part, I was O K. The ensuing clangor and rakehell chaos that proliferated that night had not yet affected me. Not yet. I was still taking care of business. The confusion, the anger, the fear, the dust in the air, the loud noises, the gunpowder, the yelling, and then sudden quiet of my patrol car interior was cataclysmically challenging. I almost felt like I was in the third person, on the outside looking in.

Look out! Here came Chief Onley and Sid Eley manhandling a struggling black male with a red bandanna around his neck. His shirt was ripped open, and his head hung down. This was an earth-shattering sight to me. What made it even more momentous was that .357 Magnum revolver stuffed behind his belt buckle against his naked belly. Somehow in the confusion Chief Onley had slipped into the edge of the field without being noticed <u>and without getting shot</u>. When the beans got blown down, he had crawled on his hands and knees right up to the thug, and pounced on him as he was trying to bury the pistol. Aubrey drug him out of the field. Sid Eley grabbed one side and together they, "brung 'im to me," right through the astonished onlookers.

As I sat at the wheel of my patrol car, I was eye-to-eye with that pistol. Aubrey and Sid hadn't seen the pistol. They wanted to put the thug in my back seat. I jumped out of my car, rounded the back bumper, and slammed, SLAMMED the thug's face into the trunk lid. I yanked that pistol out of his pants, and put it in my pocket. I don't remember putting the handcuffs on him, but somehow he ended up crying that, "These handcuffs are too tight." Yeah. Right. Agent Ransome came to the thug's rescue. He put him in the caged backseat of his State Bureau of Investigation patrol car.

When I went over to the wrecked fisherman's Chevrolet, I looked in the front right floorboard. There were twelve spent .357 Magnum Remington shell casings. The half box of bullets was now nearly emptied but still had five live rounds stuck in the Styrofoam. The "Old Hickory" 13-inch butcher knife was on the floor in the back seat. I picked up the knife and the twelve empty cases and put the "evidence" in my trunk. Earlier I had emptied the sand caked .357 cylinder, and found two spent casings, and four live rounds. The gun was so jammed up with sand and soybeans that it could no longer fire. I still pause and reflect when I look at those fourteen spent shell cases in my evidence locker.

Hearts were pounding. Exhaustion was setting in. Things were beginning to look up. The second of three thugs was captured walking down US-17 about an hour later by Sheriff Little Man Broughton and a Perquimans County Deputy Sheriff. The third one was captured about a week later in Richmond, Virginia. I borrowed a quarter from Perquimans County Sheriff, Little Man Broughton, and walked over to a lighted phone booth that was in the parking lot of Doug Cale's Five Mile Y Country Store, to call home. By now it was almost midnight. Becky was home with Jenny (10) and John (5). When she answered the phone, it was obvious that she was already awake. She had had a premonition that things were stirring. I gave her a brief rundown, and assured her that, first, I was all right and not injured; second, that we had captured two of the three, and third, nobody else had been injured. I was not sure when I would be able to come home, and it turned out that it would be around 3:00am. Not bad. A few minutes after I hung up, a "friend" of hers (Katie Lewis) in Weeksville called Becky. Katie had been listening to the police scanner and overheard the entire episode. She "just wanted to make sure Mike was all right." How about if that call had gone to Rt. 3, Box 201H just ten minutes sooner!!

As Agent Ransome was pulling away from the scene, he stopped and asked me if there was anything else he could do for me. **What a man!** The cavalry was beginning to dissipate, and I still had paperwork to begin. Sergeant Potts was standing over by my patrol car, looking in the grille. Had I been hit? Evidently NOT. There were no bullet holes in my car. I wonder where those fourteen hollow points went. Thank goodness that, according to Agent Ransome, the two that he had in custody were "high as a Georgia Pine on Crack Cocaine." Jailer Onley motioned for me to come over to the passenger side of my car. There, for all to see, was a MAGNIFICANT imprint of a head, right in the middle of my trunk lid. There were scratches on the fender from the sights and cylinder of the fisherman's .357. There was an impressive pile of spent 12-gauge shotgun shells that had been kicked out of the sandspurs onto the shoulder of NC-37.

About a week later, I was again, back at the Optimist Club meeting on Monday night. Our "Mr. Peanut" parade float had won second place at the Peanut Festival. Harold Lloyd said that his pickup truck had weathered the torture fine. I asked him, "Harold Lloyd, don't you wish that you had been with me last Wednesday night?" He chuckled, "No, I don't think so. When the shooting started, there would not have been room in the floorboard under the dash of that Patrol Car for you and me both." He was right!!!

About a year later, I got a $500.00 check in the mail from North Carolina Farm Bureau Mutual Insurance Company, made out to Trooper Michael J. McArthur. It seems that there is an ongoing policy of Farm Bureau to award $500.00 to anyone who is responsible for the "recovery" of one of their insured stolen vehicles. A single income household of almost any State Employee can always use $500.00.

Senior Resident Superior Court Judge Thomas S. Watts, and Judgment Day

Along about that time, court cases were becoming imminent. The robbers, all three of them, had been charged with many, many charges in Washington County, Chowan County, and Perquimans County. In the back room, State Appointed Defense Attorneys for the three agreed to a squirrelly plea bargain: the defendants would plead guilty to the robbery charge in return for voluntary dismissals without leave on all others. Senior Resident Superior Court Judge, The Honorable Thomas S. Watts of Elizabeth City was the presiding Superior Court Judge on the bench when the cases were called. He himself had just the week before, been the victim of an attempted assassination (A Muslim with a sawed-off shotgun inside the bar inside Courtroom #3 in Pasquotank County). For many reasons, security was tight in that courtroom that Monday morning in Plymouth, NC. SBI Agent Ransome and the fishermen painted a vivid picture of the circumstances surrounding the robbery the night in 1986 when all this mess happened. To a hushed courtroom, I held up the fourteen spent .357 cases, and recounted the facts surrounding the 7.8-mile chase and the ensuing gunfight.

After all the evidence presentation and a 30-minute recess, Judge Watts took the bench and made several very profound statements: 1. "You three men deserve no mercy." 2. "The State of North Carolina has given you unduly warranted consideration." 3. "You will all be very old men with white hair before you get the chance to take another shot at one of MY HIGHWAY PATROLMEN." With that, he gave each of the two that had been in the Chevrolet over fifty years apiece in the custody of the North Carolina State Department of Corrections. The third defendant was declared to have been a "Youthful Offender" at the time of the robbery. PLUS, he had "volunteered" valuable information to law enforcement which had greatly enhanced the strength of the evidence. He had, in fact, been inside The Sportsman's Inn. Then twenty minutes later he had in fact been inside the mystery car that had pulled up right behind my patrol car on the side of NC-32, the night of the gunfight. He only got three years active with twenty-four months supervised probation. Sadly, after he got out of Polk Youth Center in Raleigh, he returned to his home in Washington, N. C. On a rainy Easter morning, he climbed through the bathroom window of an apartment in Greenville, raped and killed a three-year-old child. For that he was sentenced to death, and executed in about 2013.

Post-Traumatic Stress Disorder and a Brighter Future

During maybe 8 to 10 years after this chapter in my life, I struggled with very low-level symptoms of post-traumatic stress disorder (PTSD). The shots that night had missed me and my car, but somehow hit home about a year later. Believe it or not, strands of hair began to regularly appear on the floor of the shower every morning. Gunshots in the night woke me up in a cold sweat. Gunshots and the smell of gunsmoke on the firearms range caused blurred vision. Dove hunting and the associated gunshots were bothersome. Fireworks on the Fourth of July caused my hands to tremble. Shortness of breath, diminished eyesight, and hearing loss can also be symptomatic, but I attributed them to aging. What did change as a result, was my level of tolerance for unprofessionalism and poor performance. My patience became "off the bottom of the charts." Some of my best friends were also struggling with their poor supervisors and worse working conditions. I felt comfort in knowing that I was not alone.

All of these circumstances caused me to begin thinking about changing careers. I was very fortunate to have available to me my first choice, right there on the Highway Patrol. During the previous several years, I had gotten a bad dose (and had had my fill) of Sergeants, Captains, and the like who seemed to prevail in the face of all PERILS. I decided that teaching Highway Patrol Cadets in the Basic School in Raleigh was how I could finish out my career (two years), and maintain some level of sanity and dignity. **Little did I know that I would soon get a rash of significant help with some life-altering decision making.**

Smokey Bear Hats

"Don't Touch 'em"

One of the most popular forms of headgear for any law enforcement officer is the flat brimmed, belted and strapped, RCMP "Mountie" style, "flat hat" with the agency's badge centered on the front. On the North Carolina State Highway Patrol, we call them, "Smokey Bear Hats." During his or her spare time, from the moment a Cadet is issued his or her new, "Smokey Bear hat," it is rarely off his or her head. During "Supervised Study," it is on their heads. During dorm maintenance, it is on their heads. During "breaks," it is on their heads. During bathroom visits, it is on their heads. Nothing is as representative of their hard work as is that Smokey Bear Hat. They protect it and guard it with their life. THAT IS WHO THEY BECOME upon graduation from Basic School. THAT IS WHO THEY ARE as they patrol the State's highways. Upon retirement, THAT IS WHO THEY ARE FOR THE REST OF THEIR LIVES.

But along the way to retirement, **THINGS HAPPEN.**

Take the time that a friend of mine was directing traffic at the intersection of NC-54 (Hillsborough Street) and Youth Center Road, right out across from Tanker's Grill near Burke Brothers' Hardware. Jimmy was standing on the centerline of NC-54, doing what an experienced State Trooper does: maintaining his command presence and letting the traffic work itself, as long as it will. Along came a yellow Granville County School Bus, loaded with teenagers. It slowly turned left onto Youth Camp Road. This particular afternoon traffic was being assisted prior to a Thursday evening horse show at The Governor James B. Hunt, Jr. Horse Complex on Trinity Road, right behind the North Carolina State Fairgrounds. You would honestly not believe the great numbers of events hosted at these two locations, YEAR-ROUND.

As the bus slowed to allow an "OFFICIAL" golf cart to enter onto Youth Center, and the bus inched forward, out from the third window on the bus, came a long skinny arm and tousled head of hair. Guess what he was reaching for. You got it: the Smokey Bear hat. Jimmy's back was to the bus, and he did not see what was happening until he felt the snatch on his hat. Think about it: this could have had a disastrous outcome. And it did. But not for Jimmy. Jimmy wheeled around, caught that kid's arm, and let go when he heard and felt the "SNAP." The hat fell to the pavement.

As you can imagine, after LOTS of in-depth investigation. After LOTS of paperwork. After LOTS of bureaucratic red tape. It must have ended well. I never heard anything else about it.

"Just Too Drunk"

One Sunday afternoon, after getting a report of a drunk on a moped dodging in and out of cars in the parking lot of Whiteman's Country Store near the United Piece and Dye Works on the Chowan River, I patrolled from Arrowhead Beach about a mile over to the local hangout. Whiteman's was the neatest kind of store. It had everything: guns, ammunition, fishing gear, nails, tools, heating and air conditioning supplies, plumbing supplies, and oh, yeah. It had the best, fresh cut meats and local vegetables around. It also sold Daddy Ruth's seven layer "Pig Pickin" Cakes for $15.00. Paul and Nina owned and operated the store from 5am until 11 p.m. Try to see if you can find that kind of store now 'a days.

As I pulled onto the lot, there zipped Polecat, right out from under the grease rack at Robert Wiley's Auto Repair Shop which was attached to the store. When he saw my Black and Silver patrol car, unexpectedly, he slammed on the moped brakes, and flipped it onto its side. He crawled out from under it, and held up both fists as in the caricature of Sonny Liston and Joe Lewis. There was a jovial crowd already assembled in the lot who had been watching Polecat's antics (and hoping he would not run over their child or hit their vehicles). Polecat had a big nose, and it was already bleeding. As he tried to dance around like Mohammad Ali in the boxing ring, his feet got tangled up, and he fell onto the gravel surface. Again, he crawled himself up into a fighting stance.

This was more than I had bargained for, but as the old saying goes, "Some things you <u>have</u> to do, and some things you <u>get</u> to do." (Mary Scott Perry Haigler) This was one of those things I was "privileged" to get to do. Or so I thought.

In the dusty lot, I unadvizedly (stupidly) walked over to Polecat. "Polecat, what in the world is going on?" We were friends. I figured that when he saw me and heard my voice, he would calm down. Nope. He raised both arms like it was a stick-up and lunged at me. I caught him around his fighting chest, AND HE KNOCKED MY SMOKEY BEAR HAT OFF MY HEAD, ONTO THE DIRT. Now you know what had to happen next. But it didn't. Polecat was **"just too drunk"** for me to whip his butt, particularly right in front of the families out to get some ice-cream at Whiteman's on a hot Sunday afternoon.

I wrestled Polecat, kicking and screaming like a little girl, to the rocky ground. Blood and snot and tears and arms and legs flying. I put the handcuffs on him, and put him in my patrol car. Robert came out, got the moped and rolled it into his shop. My black tie had been ripped off. Blood (Polecat's) was on my shirt and on my face. Like I said: we were friends, and always were right up until the day he died of cirrhosis of the liver.

All the way to jail, Polecat cried and asked me to forgive him. All the way to jail, he asked me to take him home instead. All the way to jail I was thankful that I had not had to knock his head off. He was **"just too drunk."**

SNAKE WORSHIP AND DRAG QUEENS

I live in the Cowpen Neck section of Macedonia, right beside Beaver Dam Creek, and what used to be known as "The Rattlesnake Crossing." One afternoon I got a call to "go get Bo Didly" who was driving a white Oldsmobile Toronado, and terrorizing our community. Sure enough, when I went out to my patrol car, there he went: up to Advance Community Building, right by Macedonia Baptist Church (mine), turned left at Po Jack Leary's, slid into his yard and past his porch. As I pulled up, he made a mad dash for his front door, but he didn't make it. I snagged him, and threw him back out into his yard like those iron man wrestling matches you used to see on television.

This rattled him just a little bit. He was still interested in getting into his house, but his wife was holding the door shut and screaming at him. Not to mention the fact that I was standing there in my blue jeans and t-shirt. Something clicked in that dazed head of his. He threw his arms up like I was holding a gun on him, which I was not because I did not have one (except that .22 Magnum derringer in my hip pocket). He yelled at Locke Carraway, "Go get my shotgun." He was gonna kill his wife who happened to be Locke's baby sister (not kill me, thank goodness).

He walked over to me and attempted to hug me. I quickly sidestepped him, and he fell to the ground. He just lay there. After a few minutes, he got up and we began a conversation. The reason that he was driving to start with, was that he had been at a party on Wildcat Road, and "IT" (the party) got out of hand, not him. Guns came out when a rattlesnake was spotted. Bo Didly's religion worshipped snakes, and Bo thought he would go capture that 3-foot serpent. Just as he got down in the ditch, and near the serpent, Locke Carraway had shot and killed the snake with a .410 shotgun. Do you want to know just how close to the rattlesnake that Bo Didly was standing? The entire .410 load of buckshot had passed through one side of his pantleg and out the other side without touching the skin and bone therein. Now that is close, dear reader.

I mentioned Locke Carraway in this short story because Locke and I "go way back." I had known Locke since 1974 when he at Carroll Smith's Northside Auto had fixed the radiator on my 1973, 455 cu.in., white over blue Buick Riviera. He lived in a curve on Wildcat Road, and I drove by his house at least six times a day. Locke stayed drunk on weekends, but he usually stayed drunk at home. One afternoon, as I approached his house, here he came around the curve with that Cadillac in a broadside slide. He rolled it twice right in front of me, and ended up thrown out in his brother, John Carraway's yard.

Locke experienced a compound fracture of his right upper leg. The bloody white femur was poked through his gray mechanic uniform pants. Locke was trying to get up and walk, again, **JUST TOO drunk** to acknowledge the severity of his injuries. Locke had lost his glasses, and could not see me, but knew my voice. When Rescue Unit #1 with Ed Taylor arrived, Locke would not let them administer aid. This episode went on for about ten minutes that seemed like an hour. Locke finally let them work on him. He was transported to Chowan Hospital where a blood alcohol test was administered: 0.17%. Not as high as I thought it would have been, but then again, Locke's liver was in such a compromised state that the oxidation of ethyl alcohol was less effective, thereby giving him less tolerance, but the same level of drunkenness. This is a science that is taught to Chemical Breath Test Operators during their Two-Week Breathalyzer Certification process. It is called, "Pharmacology of Alcohol" and those of us who know, could tell some "interesting" stories concerning the "drinking subjects" and "The Controlled Drinking" exercises.

At 2:00am, about a year later, lo and behold, after receiving a second call about Locke driving drunk, I pulled into his yard right behind him off the roadway. I confronted Locke just as he exited his Cadillac (He liked them). Locke was obviously "**just too drunk**." He wanted to know who had called me. I knew, but didn't tell him it was his own _____. Locke was about as strong as he was wide. He was ALL MAN. As I pointed to my Patrol Car, I told him to, "Have a..." BLAM! With doubled up fists, he knocked me flat on my back. It was so dark in that yard that I did not see it coming. My Smokey Bear hat got knocked off my head AGAIN. From his previous broken leg, he was unable to run, but he got inside his house before I could gather my wits and overtake him. For the first time in my career, I called, "Signal 25," on my Highway Patrol radio. That meant all cars working and within the sound of their radio were to travel to Edenton, to help a Trooper in trouble.

The door was locked, but the lights were on inside the house. Locke was inside a bedroom situated at the front of the house, and I stood outside his window and watched him packing a suitcase. He had locked the bedroom door, and somebody was banging on the door to which he yelled, "Get the _____away from that door or I will shoot you." At this time he had a large black revolver in his hand, which he then placed into the suitcase.

The cavalry swooped in on Poplar Leaf Road, Edenton, NC: Edenton Police Officers, Deputy Sheriffs, Trooper Ray Potts, three armed citizens, a nosy neighbor, and my father-in-law, Ray Beckler. One of the Edenton Officers kicked the front door off its hinges. Inside that front living room, sat 8 adults and one little girl wrapped in a blanket in her mother's arms. Those nine people were facing three pointed shotguns and five drawn pistols. Those who were seated misguidedly stood up. As weapons were brandished from side to side, people screamed and dropped to the floor, side to side like dominoes. The yelling and screaming was so loud that none of us could hear it. Trooper Potts kicked the hallway door open and the bedroom door open and pounced on Locke. Out he came in a heap. A scuffed-up heap. And he had lost his glasses, again.

The rest is pretty routine. The Cavalry loaded up more than their weapons, and went back to their normal duties. Trooper Potts and I "escorted" Locke out of his house as the family members feebly tried to stop us. Locke was breath tested and went to jail. Trooper Potts headed back to Elizabeth City but got re-directed to a personal injury wreck on US-17 near the Five-Mile Y. I went to the Emergency Room at Chowan Hospital for a back injury. I called Becky to let her know the facts just before the Emergency Room exploded with wreck victims.

Seems like when it rains it pours. As I lay embarrassed in the OB-GYN cubicle in the Emergency Room, hooked up to IV solutions, my friend Dr. Leibert E. Devine came in and told me that he was going to have to move me into the hallway. He had to make the room available for some female wreck victims who needed the electronics and diagnostics on the wall in my room. I was walked out into the lobby of the hospital, laid out onto a sheeted Naugahyde couch, and my IV bag was adhesive taped to the wall above my head, right below the television.

After getting their sorry selves kicked out of the beer joint, three women had pulled out of the Hillcrest Gardens night club into the path of a Naval Aviator (Jet Pilot) on his way to Oceana Air Station in Norfolk, Virginia. Hillcrest Gardens had a sign in front of it with their motto: "THERE IS NO REST AT THE 'CREST'." That is except in the back rooms where ladies of the night plied their trade.

The confusion of the three mouthy wreck victims was about to get on everybody's last nerve. Suddenly I heard Dr. frVine, really a great guy, say too loudly, "Look, Bud. You quiet down or be arrested." Here was my good Doctor friend making threats. The three "women," none of whom were injured were not "women" at all. They were gay male cross dressers; women wannabees. Here I had been "bumped" into the hallway for three "drama DRAG QUEENS." OH, well. I reckon you do what you gotta do. I finally made it home that night and took my two days off for that week.

SLOPE NOSED KENWORTHS, AND GALE FORCE WINDS

"MAN, I ALWAYS WANTED TO DO THAT!"

Normally, on a hot summer's day, a lot of Piedmont dwellers go to Nag's Head for fun in the sun. Most take the southern route on US-64 through Plymouth, Columbia, and East Lake. Some take the northern route on US-17 and US-158 through Edenton, Hertford, Elizabeth City, and Southern Shores. On this particular afternoon, there was not much traffic on the Edenton Bypass. It was still only two lanes, before the additional lanes and miles of cable guide rails were installed from the Bertie County Line all the way to the Perquimans County Line.

I had stopped for speeding, a '67 red Chevelle, SS-396 four-speed convertible. Contained therein were two young Wilson County School teachers who recognized my name, and knew my brother Pat and sister Kathy from having been their teachers at Ralph L. Fike Senior High School. As I stood on the shoulder at their door, I was vulnerable to vehicular traffic then traveling north on US-17. Due to being only two lanes, I could not adequately park my patrol car in a manner to give me that ribbon of safety between its front left fender and the violator's door. CB radios were the craze back then, and usually when Troopers stopped cars or were visibly "working" traffic in an area, the CB would "light up." I know, because I had one. My "handle" was, "The Phantom," then "Silver Bullet," and then "The Gray Ghost." I had already heard CB chatter to the effect that I was out there working RADAR on US-17.

Here came two "18-wheelers," slope-nosed Kenworth tractor trailers. As I leaned against the Chevelle, they passed so fast and so close to me, that their "draft" blew my Smokey Bear hat into the front seat of the convertible. For a moment, I was thunderstruck. What was I gonna do about that? Well, I decided to continue my enforcement contact and allow the S.O.Bs. to continue northbound. I listened to my CB as they "communicated" about what they had just done. They rounded the curve up at the Five-Mile- Y and were now out of sight. Now my plan of action was initiated. I bade, "Happy Motoring," to the teachers, mounted my patrol car, and headed north into Perquimans County. On the CB, I continued to hear about the two tractor trailers having blown the Trooper's Smokey Bear hat off his head. One of the Kenworth road jockeys said, "MAN, I always wanted to do that."

I caught up with them, and pulled them BOTH over by the sawmill in front of Hillcrest Gardens (Remember, "THERE IS NO REST AT THE 'CREST' "). I got them out of their trucks, and they both had round "graphs" clutched in their hands. The conversations began in earnest. Neither one of them really had much to say. From my patrol car open window, they could hear my CB chatter. They knew their goose was cooked.

This was a time in history when truckers were not required to have Commercial Driver's Licenses (CDLs). Later, CDLs were nationally required and had recorded against them all the infractions and violations that the licensed possessor had accumulated. These two 'ol Arkansas rednecks each possessed in their ragged wallets, at least 8 or 10 different states' operator's licenses with their true name and false addresses. Also contained therein were at least 20 or 30 hundred-dollar bills. I so hoped that one or both of them would not try to "slip me one" like had happened to Trooper Charlie Mims who right at that time, happened to be pulling up alongside this roadside three-ringed-circus.

We talked about their speed. They didn't want to. "Trooper, you know we won't speedin'." And I agreed with them. By now I had asked each of them to provide to me and Trooper Mims a valid Class A Driver's License that had been issued to them by a state in which their privilege to drive had not been previously revoked. I later found out that these two boys lived beside each other in Wynne, Arkansas. One of their uncles owned and operated "Pluck-A-Duck Hunting Lodge," where Tommy Jeffries and my son, John, Jeff Mullen and his son Dusty, and I had hunted just a few months earlier. The weather had been rough: so cold (4 degrees) with gale force winds, like the kind that blew my Smokey Bear hat off my head, that the six-dozen Snow Goose decoys tipped over and froze sideways in 2-inch ice on the rice patties.

Lucious and Junior fumbled and fumbled, and finally each produced a valid Class A Operator's License issued by different states. I told them that I was charging each of them with Reckless Driving, Exceeding A Safe Speed, and the second driver with Following Too Close. In their grubby little hands, they each produced nice round graph paper covered with zig-zagged lines. Sure enough! They had not been speeding. The graphs showed that they had each been traveling 55mph which was the speed limit. HOWEVER, the graphs also showed that at 2:30am that morning they had been running 91 and 93mph respectively. At 4:10am they had been running 84mph. And at 5am they had been running 88mph. I asked them if their tires were rated for that kind of speed. Lead driver, ol' Lucious told me, "Man! Don't you see 'KENWORTH" wrote on the side of that tractor?" Junior still wasn't talking much.

Lucious was older, but Junior was just an "Arkansas young'un." Lucious's voice was raspy and low like a bayou bullfrog's. Junior's voice was recognizably less colloquial and more high pitched. He was the one who had earlier said over the airwaves, "MAN, I always wanted to do that." Shame on him! SHAME ON HIM! I asked ol' Charlie Mims, "Did you hear what Junior said on that CB about, 'MAN, I always wanted to do that.'?" "I'm 'fraid so!" Like I said, SHAME ON HIM. Before we all parted ways, I told Charlie and those two, now jovial rednecks, "MAN, I always wanted to do that!"

Charlie said, "Let's go get on the CB, name these two yahoos and identify what they are driving, and tell the listeners what happened during this enforcement contact gone bad for two truckers. Charlie used to tell me that one of his favorite sounds was when he stopped a speeding 18-

wheeler, and the driver locked his air brakes: "Ch-chshshshsh!" He had spent WAY too much time standing in the hot sun directing traffic for hours at the time at an accident scene where a tractor trailer driver had done something stupid.

THE FOLLOWING TWO PARAGRAPHS ARE EXCERPTS FROM THE BOOK COMPILED BY RETIRED NORTH CAROLINA STATE HIGHWAY PATROL MAJOR WILLIAM S. ETHERIDGE, AND TITLED, "A North Carolina State Highway Patrol History." The excerpts are contained on page 30.

The 246-page spiral bound book is not copyrighted, and was dedicated on May 1st, 2019. With Major Etheridge's permission I have been allowed to share the following two paragraphs.

THE 1929 UNIFORM BADGE, AND ITS EXTREME SIGNIFICANCE

"The badge of the North Carolina State Highway Patrol, worn over the left breast on the uniform shirt, is an emblem of achievement, responsibility, and authority. It identifies the wearer as a member of a nationally recognized traffic law enforcement agency for excellence. It identifies a member's rank and represents achievement in that the wearer had demonstrated those special qualities required of "North Carolina's Finest."

"Thus, the badge of the North Carolina State Highway Patrol is worn with pride. It is a symbol of Courage, Commitment, and Intelligence: Courage to live dangerously, to do a lonely job, deal with life and death crisis at any hour anywhere in North Carolina, in any kind of weather; Commitment to the cause of highway safety, law enforcement, and service; and Intelligence to make safe, sure, and dependable decisions."

I certainly could not have said it any more eloquently.

Michael J. McArthur

Speed Timing Devices

The Other "STD"

RADAR is an acronym for Radio Detection And Ranging. Law enforcement and military forces use RADAR for speed detection and ranging vehicles, aircraft, and boats. More commonly, the North Carolina State Highway Patrol uses UHF DOPLER **RADAR** to detect the speed of vehicles traveling upon the highways. This is a tool they use to make the roads more safe for travel. When a "**RADAR** Certified" Trooper uses RADAR and detects a speeding vehicle, after it meets all the pre-enforcement criteria, a citation or arrest can be made upon the driver of the vehicle "clocked" at whatever the violation required.

Troopers ALWAYS wanted to have their own **RADAR** units mounted or installed in their own assigned vehicles. Way back in the early '60s and 70s **"Speed Watch"** incorporated two air hoses stretched across the highway at a predetermined distance from each other, and when a speeding vehicle crossed the "whammy" lines, a stopwatch (I've still got mine) mounted on a board indicated the speed of the vehicle crossing the hoses. It was a messy, tedious, and time-consuming method of speed detection and enforcement.

Then along came **VASCAR** which is an acronym for Visual Average Speed Computer And Recorder. We called these units, "The Silent Killers." There were no hoses to be seen. There were no radio frequencies to be detected. A **VASCAR** operator had merely to visualize a speeder, compare it to the time it took to travel a measured distance, and flip switches to the best of his well-trained abilities.

When we no longer used Speed Watch, and few of us used **VASCAR**, it became almost too easy to play "Catch Up." We could mount **RADAR** onto our cars, go out to a "cabbage patch," and pick however many "easy ones" we needed to keep the sergeant off our butts. Seasoned violators utilized **RADAR** DETECTORS. These small units were the scourge of State Troopers. We didn't like them. We didn't like people who used them. But then again, it was a game we played. We could sit in our marked or unmarked patrol cars and the **RADAR** unit would clock violators traveling

Living Out Loud with Grace, Grit, and Gratitude

toward us or away from us. Either high speed or low speed could sometimes indicate that the driver was drunk.

My "Partner in Crime," and good friend John Atwater would operate stationary **RADAR** in the Uwharrie Mountain range on the side of NC-49 in Stanley County. He could visually monitor and estimate the speed of vehicles below as they passed his "hideout." When he visually detected a vehicle traveling at a high rate of speed, he would wait until the vehicle was going away from his location, and instantaneously activate the **RADAR** signal. He called this "Shooting fish in a barrel." When the speeding vehicle was only traveling maybe 12 or 13 miles over the limit, and when the **RADAR** signal produced a reading, <u>I F</u> the brake lights came on, that meant that the speeder was utilizing a **RADAR** DETECTOR. That driver was SURE to get a speeding ticket to make up for the ones he had avoided while using the RADAR DETECTOR. If, when the **RADAR** signal was activated with a displayed result, and the brake lights did <u>not</u> come on, John would let that one go. On Wednesday nights, John would work that stretch of NC-49 because he knew that Professional Wrestlers, members of the World Wrestling Federation would be traveling between their homes in Charlotte, NC and Channel 5, WRAL Rasslin' bouts in Raleigh, NC. John was a huge fan of professional wrestling, and would occasionally get asked to come ringside and speak with Ric "Nature Boy" Flair, Hulk Hogan, and The Great Bolo. I always wondered what the Great Bolo would pull from his tights. John told me: nerf brass knuckles. John stopped, I didn't say "caught" so many wrestlers that many of them knew him by first name, and he knew theirs. Apparently, John was a DUKE fan. He wrote UNC-CH Head Basketball Coach, Roy Williams three speeding tickets on that stretch, and Michael Jordan, two. He also stopped a speeding Carolina Blue pickup truck with twelve Carolina Blue shovels carefully "mounted" in the bed. They were late en-route to Chapel Hill for the ground-breaking ceremony for the Dean Smith Center. They arrived "later."

One of the fun things we used to do was let the high school track team members run for speed detection in our **RADAR** beam. One of the fastest sprinters that Trooper Robert Allen (November 6, 1940 to July 12, 1976) and I ever clocked was his Reverend Ashby Browder (September 17, 1942 to September 22, 2020) of Immanuel Church: 20mph. Reverend Browder preached Robert's funeral too few months later, and has since died in December of 2020.

Smokey Blackouts

During the fall, some of our State Parks and Military Bases conducted what they called "controlled burns" in their Loblolly Pine forests. These fires burned so hot that they created their very own weather systems within the many thousand square acre perimeters of the blazes. Lots of tornadoes, quakes, and violent thunder and lightning storms were produced, and the N C Forestry Service and others had to contend with those life-threatening situations as well. The fires would occasionally leak out of bounds, and helicopters and C-130 airplanes would be called to drop fire retardant and water upon the errant inferno. Firefighters mounting the ground assault had to be prepared for the air attacks from tons of water that occasionally killed the professionals.

Smoke from these fires was oppressive. It would burn your eyes. It would reduce visibility to zero. It would distort sight and sound effects., and would form monstrous "columns" up into the atmosphere. When the smoke met more dense weather patterns, occasionally the smoke would be forced to ground level like a croquet wicket. Several times during my career, we had to contend with extremely dense and hazardous (for a number of reasons) smoke plus fog: SMOG. I have had to enter these hundred-acre, highway covering SMOG areas to extract wreck victims. We located them by their "hollering" through the nighttime particulates. I would get someone, usually a fireman to walk on the shoulder, in front of my car with his hand on the hood. Upon locating victims, he would slap my hood. All the while we could hear other motor vehicle accidents occurring on other paved portions of the roadway. Sometimes drivers would wreck, get out of their cars to inspect the damage, and another vehicle would come along and knock cars out of sight of their owners, "somewhere out there in the fog." As I sat in my "invisible" Patrol car, my **RADAR** unit was clocking cars traveling either toward me or away from me at unnerving speeds.

Death Notifications

One of the most delicate and humbling functions ever performed by State Troopers is the arduous task of notifying family members and loved ones of the untimely deaths of someone close to them. Usually a Trooper will ask for assistance from a local pastor or even better, the pastor of the deceased. Of course, WAY BACK THEN there were no cellular phones, and just a very few roadside payphones. "Word" did not travel as fast, and many times, in order to contact someone for help, we had to send someone from the scene or go ourselves to get whatever it was that we needed to perform our duties.

Midway Fiasco

School Teacher: Billie Gray Womack and her Father, Bill Womack, Jr.

The opening day of school in Chowan County was always fraught with traffic delays, too many big yellow school buses, upset Mamas, and confusion. Buses were late. Traffic patterns were unfamiliar. Motorists were crying as they dropped their child off for his or her first day. Teachers did not know their students yet. And on this day, it was raining cats and dogs. I was at Chowan Middle School investigating a fender bender. My Trooper buddy in Bertie County was at a tractor-trailer wreck in Merry Hill at the intersection of US-17 and NC-45. A speeding northbound Mustang on US-17 had skidded through the stop light and underneath, between the tires of a semi-trailer loaded with logs on its way to Weyerhaeuser Plant in Plymouth, NC. The Mustang continued north without its top, and without all the body parts that should have been attached to the driver. The wreck scene was chaotic. The Trooper was fresh out of Basic Training. The rain was oppressive to victims, workers, onlookers, and "evidence."

I was sent over to assist, partly because the car was registered to an Edenton resident. Immediately, upon arrival, I knew the car and I knew who owned it. It belonged to a very nice and refined schoolteacher friend of mine who I had just seen at Chowan Middle School. The log truck had jackknifed onto L. E. Brown's Texaco Station and knocked down the utility poles which put electric wires and cables across both US-17 and NC-45, AND THE GAS PUMPS. Did I mention that it was raining?

After getting a thorough picture of what the Bertie Trooper was going through, I approached the Mustang. It had traveled into, underneath, and up against some pine trees in a small clump. There, inside, was a bloody conglomeration of books, clothing, papers, drink bottles, food wrappers, an open Bible to the book of Psalms, and a very dead single occupant, mostly in the back seat. His clothing was ripped open. His pants pockets were empty: NO IDENTIFICATION. No one in the surrounding rain-soaked crowd knew the man. After speaking with the Bertie Trooper, I volunteered to go to Chowan Middle School and notify the vehicle's registered owner.

Upon arrival at the school, I went to the Principal's office for assistance. Principal James Herndon and I had played softball, volleyball, and basketball together in the Recreation League. He and the schoolteacher were related by blood. I explained to him the uncertainties surrounding our mission, and let him make the call as to how to proceed. I honestly did not know who had been driving, but that he in fact had been killed, instantly. It was gonna be a long morning. We attempted to bring in the teacher's pastor, but could not make contact. Her father was outside in his workshop without communication. As we walked down the hall toward the teacher's classroom, we thought that asking her to report to the school library might be less ominous.

Apparently, there was an air of subdued grief in the room upon the entrance of the schoolteacher. She immediately cried out, "Oh my God. What has happened?" We comforted her as best as we could, but the urgency of her plea overtook us all. We explained that her car had been involved in a serious traffic accident over in Merry Hill, and we were unable to determine who had been driving. She immediately blurted out, "My husband was driving my car to work this morning at R J Reynolds, AVOCA." We began to relate to her the seriousness of the accident when she stood up, and screamed, "Oh, NO! Oh, NO! Oh, NO. Oh, my GOD. Oh, my GOD! MY BROTHER WAS DRIVING IT TO A DOCTOR'S APPOINTMENT IN GREENVILLE!"

She slumped down onto the couch in a fit of desperation and disbelief. To this day I am at a loss to come up with a better way to have handled the notification, but I am sure there had to be one.

Joby Johnson's Five Lives

Pedestrian: Joe Boy (Joby) Johnson

Lots of bad things happen in the dark of night. Some by mistake, some by intent. And some by a combination of factors. Take a pedestrian trying to get home, but **JUST TOO drunk** to know where that is, since it tends to change from week to week.

APPENDAGE: On September 10, 1982, Joe Boy (Joby) Johnson, Ruby Kaye Johnson and several friends and family had been "drankin' " at Slow Boat and O'Vivian Oakley's house on Brayhall Road. Keep in mind that "shots" were "available" at that house. Also keep in mind that the "shots" were not tax-paid liquor, but "stump-hole" homemade "bootleg" corn whiskey. But according to many, this was "good stump-hole," meaning that it had not been "run" through a condenser (radiator) with lead fittings. Well, as usually happened, Joby got mad at Slow Boat over Ruby Kaye.

For a short background, a few years earlier in the '70s, Joby had gotten into a "knock down – drag out fight" with one of the Stanleys. As he was known to do, Joby pulled out a fish gutter knife. Apparently, he had brought a knife to a gunfight. Then Stanley pulled out a short (14 inch) 12 gauge "Topper" shotgun. I've still got this shotgun. It had a 3-inch barrel, and a 3-inch stock. It also was held together by a bolt, not a pin. Being a single action weapon meant that the hammer had to be cocked or "laid back" as the lingo goes. The hammer would not stay cocked because the gun was totally worn out. Stanley had taken one of his mother's half-inch wide plastic belts, and threaded it through the trigger guard BEHIND the trigger. He then buckled it, and pulled it forward with constant pressure on the back of the trigger as he held the forearm with his left hand. With this technique firmly in place, he could successfully "lay the hammer back," and keep forward pressure on the trigger with the belt in his left hand around the barrel.

Joby was a slow learner when it came to using good judgment. He swung his knife at Stanley. Stanley didn't shoot him. Joby swung again and fell down. Stanley didn't shoot him. Joby got up, raised his knife over his head, and took one too many steps toward Stanley, and grabbed the shotgun. Stanley released the pressure on the belt, the trigger "quivered," and the hammer fell onto the firing pin. Joby was "gut shot." He fell forward. At Unit B, a wing of the old Edenton MCAS Hospital, Joby "laid up" for about a month. He was a medical marvel. He had survived being nearly cut in half with his hand on the barrel of a 12-gauge shotgun when it discharged a load of #5 shot through his navel. As a result of this massive wound right in his belly, Joby would sport an "appendage," a hernia if you will, for the rest of his life. This hernia became one of his many "trademarks." When happy, he would pull it out. When sad, he would pull it out. When sober, he would pull it out (that was not very often). When drunk, he would pull it out (that was quite often).

Standing in the middle of Dillard's Mill Road one night, while I was training Pat Mitchell, Joby staggered right up and folded himself onto the stationary front bumper and hood of Pat's patrol car. When he rolled off, guess what he had in his hand. Guess what the first thing Pat saw when he ran up to him. Pat thought that this appendage was an injury just having been sustained. Funny, but not funny. About 1988, I was testifying inside the 1980 Chowan County Courthouse. At lunchtime I went out to my shiny Black and Silver, got in, and here came Joby. Ruby Kaye had abandoned him at the pool hall inside Choke's Grille on Oakum Street. He needed a ride up to Cannon's Ferry. I just happened to have in my "unauthorized" toolbox, the sawed-off shotgun which Joby had had his hand on when it went off. I raised it up for him to see. He stumbled backward so hard that he did a backward summersault. I didn't see Joby for months.

LINNY PERRY: Quite often, Joby's alligator mouth would get his hummingbird butt into a lot of trouble. His wife, Ruby Kaye gutted Blueback Herrings for Linny Perry at the Perry-Wynne Fishery and Cannery on the Chowan River in the small hamlet known as Cannon's Ferry. Joby was forbidden to go upon the premises. Imagine that! Well

Ruby Kaye controlled Joby's disability "check." She never gave him what he wanted. He always was mad at her. So, he went to the Cannery. Linny Perry asked/told him to leave. Joby pulled out an "Old Hickory" 11-inch butcher knife with a 7-inch blade. That big knife was a big mistake. Linny Perry was a big man. Linny pushed Joby backward right into the fish cleaning vat, and "baptized him until the bubbles came up." But Joby survived.

SIDE VIEW MIRROR; Joby did not have a driver's license. I don't know that he ever had one. I do know that occasionally he would drive when his brother Joe and/or Ruby Kaye were much drunker than he was. When he couldn't find something to drive, he would walk, stumble, stagger, wobble, or shuffle either on or beside the road. As he approached Teeny Boy Perry's Store one afternoon, evidently he got too close to the roadway or was in it. The side mounted, side view mirror of a Mack Truck caught Joby right in the back of the head, sending him eyeballs over elbows into Teeny Boy's Store parking lot. Again, he went to Unit B for a brief stay. Again, he survived the encounter.

FATAL: But this time was different. Slow Boat was mean as a snake, and slow as molasses; thus, his moniker. He was also hardheaded according to Phil Long for whom Slobo farmed. This night Slobo had physically thrown Joby out of his shotgun shack on Brayhall, followed him out into the yard, and thrown him out onto the roadway. Joby started walking toward Hancock Station. Out on 32, right along where the road floods during hurricanes, for some reason, Joby either fell or lay down right in the middle of the southbound lane.

I heard the call go out to Chowan County Sheriff's Deputy Melvin Evans, "10-56 (pedestrian) in the middle of NC-32." I headed that way. Before I could get there, Deputy Evans was calling for the Rescue Squad to be dispatched. Upon my arrival, there lay Joe Boy Johnson, badly injured, and a white van partially on the roadway with its emergency flashers activated. There were no skid marks leading up to Joby. Upon further investigation, I determined that upon the arrival of Deputy Evans to the scene, he had activated his blue lights and emergency flashers. He had (and still had) his bright lights on in an attempt to locate the pedestrian. Pete Townsend of Townsend Furniture Company had been traveling south on NC-32 after making a furniture delivery in Rocky Hock. Pete's view was obscured, blinded by the bright lights of Deputy Evans's patrol car. Blip – blip.

Joby was wearing black pants, a dark plaid flannel shirt, white socks, and had lost his shoes. A Chowan Hospital Registered Nurse, Mrs. Josephine Nixon was huddled over Joby monitoring his vital signs. I determined that it would have been almost impossible for Mr. Townsend to have seen Joby prior to impact. The roadway was beginning to become cluttered with rescue units, fire trucks, and volunteer firemen.

Most motorists had been re-routed through Brayhall Road. As we waited, I walked toward Edenton and spoke with the motorists who were backed up in the northbound lane. Deputy Evans was standing beside Joby. I instructed each of the northbound motorists to proceed with caution as they continued up NC-32. There, in a dark blue Chevrolet Corvette sat a friend of mine, Jehovah John Johnson. Joby was his brother, and Jehovah John was unaware who was lying in the roadway. I had to tell him. Jehovah John looked down, as if in prayer, and pulled onto the shoulder of the road. Together we walked up and knelt down beside Joe Boy. Jehovah John grasped Joe Boy's hand and felt a response. I think that Jehovah was satisfied that he had reached his brother in time to let him know that he was loved.

Medical Examiner Dr. Leibert E. DeVine pronounced Joe Boy dead. He ordered a medical heart blood alcohol screen which came back at .11%. I clipped a patch from Joe Boy's pantleg and shirtsleeve. This would come into play some years later in a civil action pertaining to Joe Boy's death. He was only forty-three years old, and he had not survived.

Deputy James Walter Peal, Jr.

Back in the early '70s, there were not but so many law enforcement officers stationed in any of the "so called finger counties" of northeastern North Carolina. Budgets were tight. The exhibited need was, at times not massive. Training was almost non-existent. And those of us who had answered this calling could barely pay our bills with our low salaries. Many of us worked part-time jobs, sometimes two.

Some Wildlife Officer friends of mine were eligible for and received food stamps to feed their families. The expenses associated with law enforcement many times meant buying some of your own equipment and supplies. In many parts of the state, the cost of living far exceeded what was reasonable pay for a newly sworn officer. The usual solution for this was for counties to hire and employ locals who had already acclimated themselves to their jurisdiction, and already had living accommodations.

Such was the case for Washington County Deputy Sheriff Walter Peal, Jr. (April 1, 1926 to October 16, 1986). Walter was a full-time Deputy and a part-time hardware salesman. He knew every nook and cranny in Washington and Tyrrell Counties, and he knew most of the people. Anytime you needed anything from " 'cross the Sound," Walter was the "go to" man. Walter and his family were living proof that the simple life was healthy and good. That is until evil encroached and took Walter's life and that of his daughter, Regina seven years later.

It was a Thursday night, and I was working RADAR on US-17. I clocked a brown Oldsmobile at eighty-eight miles per hour. The female driver had received a call from her boyfriend's girlfriend, and was returning home to "get to the bottom of this." She was a shift supervisor at the Perdue Chicken Plant in Lewiston in Bertie County.

She had borrowed a co-worker's car to go home because her car had been impounded for drunk driving. Her license was revoked, and she had the odor of an alcoholic beverage on or about her person. All her stars had become misaligned, and she was now handcuffed, sitting crying in my patrol car.

As I pulled up to the Magistrate's Office, I was dispatched to a motor vehicle accident on the Albemarle Sound Bridge, 10-33 (Emergency). The road was blocked. Multiple injuries and possible fatalities. It was now dusk, and the light was fading fast as it can in the fall. (A-354, 10-33 (emergency). 10-50 (Motor vehicle accident) multiple PI (personal injuries), possible F-Frank (fatalities). 10-53 (the road is blocked). 10-51 (wrecker) and 10-52 (ambulance) 10-17 (en-route). A311 (First Sergeant) and A-322 (Line Sergeant) 10-42 (off duty). 10-26 (your estimated time of arrival)?

Suddenly, things took a turn for the better for my speeder. I unhandcuffed her, gave her back her keys, and told her to, "Get out." I did not have to say it twice. I took off for the Albemarle Sound Bridge.

On October 16, 1986, life was good for Walter. He was sixty years old and was taking two of his daughters, along with his baby granddaughter to dinner in Edenton, NC. A drunk driver traveling south on the NC-32, Albemarle Sound Bridge crossed the centerline and hit Lori Peal's northbound car head on. Lori was driving, Walter was the front passenger, and Regina and the baby were in the back seat. The impact pushed Walter into the headliner post, Lori into the steering wheel and windshield, Regina into Walter's back, and catapulted the baby, Crystal through the windshield and sixty feet down the bridge. The roadway was completely blocked, railing to railing.

The first car to arrive at the scene found the blanket, heard and discovered the baby therein. Having been blanketed in a car seat, the injuries were not too terrible, thank goodness. Walter was obviously dead. Lori was semi-conscious, and Regina was motionless. On a Friday night at 6:40 p.m., there is right much traffic on the Sound Bridge. Motorists going to and returning from work at Weyerhaeuser Paper Mill in Plymouth. People traveling to and from other employment. People traveling to and from the Outer Banks. People traveling to and from local restaurants and entertainment venues. All this to say, there was chaos on that bridge on that night. The wreck happened at dusk as I determined the next day when a photographer, Alan Asbell worked the scene with me.

When rescue squads got there, the scene was so much more graphic than they were accustomed to, that I had to direct them to what was most important. Not Walter. Lori and Regina were transported with the baby first. I cannot say for sure, but I think they went to Washington County Hospital in Plymouth. That is where I interviewed Lori a few days later. The mouthy drunk went to Chowan Hospital at my direction. I would "see" him later.

There was so much traffic stopped on the bridge, and everybody's doors were open, that ambulances, police officers, sheriff's deputies, and wreckers could not get to the site. While health care volunteer providers saw to the wellbeing of the accident victims, I made it my job to clear at least one lane of travel in preparation for the arrival and departure of emergency responders. By moving the drunk driver's car to the west side of the bridge, it would make the northbound lane of travel most attractive. There, right in front of me was a large red 6-wheel Coca-Cola delivery truck. With his permission, I hooked my patrol car chain to the chassis of the drunk's car, and to the front bumper of the Coke truck. There was an off-duty Virginia Beach Police Sergeant on the scene who took charge of clearing the northbound lane.

Slowly, the Sergeant directed the Coke truck forward toward the wreck. That allowed for the truck tires to turn at an angle as it prepared to back south toward Washington County. Of course, the chain held, and the Coke Truck backed gently south. As it skidded along, several of us pushed on the side of the wrecked car to get it to go in the prescribed direction. <u>Blam-a-lam</u>. The Coke truck backed right into the grille of a brand new 1986 silver Cadillac, Coupe deVille. The absolute least of my problems! But the northbound lane was clear.

As this fiasco was unraveling, I walked south along the motorists waiting in line to get through the scene. There, in a pickup truck were two young men, patiently waiting clearance to proceed. <u>They were Jimmy and David Peal.</u> Walter's two sons. Regina's and Lori's brothers, and the baby's uncles. I happened to recognize them. Jimmy was soon to become a Washington County Deputy, and David (March 9, 1957 to December 22, 2014) was an aspiring North Carolina State Trooper (now deceased). I stumbled, but caught myself on the driver's door sill. "Jimmy, David, that wreck up there has killed your Daddy." They immediately jumped from the truck and got to their family members before transport. It was a scene straight out of a horror movie. There was absolutely nothing that any of us could do. Everybody was crying. Everybody!

There were car parts, clothing, plastic, spare tires, ripped off tires, 12-volt batteries, and people covering every square foot of that bridge. I told those folks to start picking up debris and throw it in a pile behind Lori Peal's car. Somebody took it upon themselves to throw every single piece of debris right over the railing of that bridge, but it made the way clear for Carroll Smith's wrecker to hook up to the rear of the wrecked car. Carroll had just driven south through the accident scene and gone to Washington County to turn around so that he would be headed back north to tow the vehicle to his shop in Edenton.

Guess what! His wrecker was inexplicably stopped half-a-mile south from us on the steel section at "the draw" of the bridge. HE WAS OUT OF GAS! WHAT NEXT? Carl Lane, the NCDOT Bridge Attendant had a three-gallon gas can full of gas, and dumped it into Carroll's wrecker. Teamwork! Right? When Carroll got back up to the wreck scene, he was focused on getting Lori's car turned around so that he could tow it from the front with the rear wheels rolling, and it worked.

When my Sergeant Jim Farmer and I cleared the scene, all the wrecked cars were gone. All the debris was gone, all the on-lookers were gone, and the roadway was back in serviceable condition. We went straight to Chowan Hospital. When I looked in the chart of Ivey Lee Jones, I found that his blood alcohol level was still at a.13%, two hours after the wreck. He had gotten off work at Cianbro-Williams Bridge Construction Company at 5:00 p.m. He had passed the hat among his friends and gone to White's Country Store on Base Road in front of the airport and bought four cases of Miller High Life beer in 12-ounce cans. Six concrete finishers had drunk it all, but Ivey Lee Jones still had one empty container in his 1980 Chevrolet, and one "for the road."

Sergeant Farmer and I prepared our interview strategy, and it worked. After having had his Miranda Rights explained to him, Ivey Lee answered all my questions in a manner that he accepted full responsibility for the wreck. First, "Which way were you driving on the Albemarle Sound Bridge? How fast were you driving? Where do you work? What time did you get off work? Who bought the beer? Who drank the beer? HOW MUCH BEER DID YOU DRINK?" Did you have anything to drink after the accident?" The rest is history.

Chowan County Magistrate Carlton Perry prepared misdemeanor warrants for Death by Motor Vehicle against Ivey Lee and placed him under a $400.00 secured bond. Ivey Lee posted the $400.00 bond and was released to go home and recover from the serious injuries he had received in the wreck. The Chowan County Grand Jury indicted Ivey Lee on Felony Death by Motor Vehicle. On June 1st, at age 42, Ivey Lee Jones pleaded guilty to Misdemeanor Death by Motor Vehicle. He received a two-year sentence with recommended work release. He had to pay Walter's widow,

Molly Riddick Peal $5000.00 restitution, "for the immediate family of the victim."

During a Civil Trial many months later, under the professional guidance of Attorney M. H. "Hood" Ellis, the Cianbro-Williams Bridge Construction Company was found culpable, and a Jury ordered it to pay to Walter's family 1.8 million dollars for his wrongful death. This came two months after Regina, who had never recovered from her devastating head injury, died as a result of injuries sustained in the October 16, 1986 wreck. A second wrongful death claim was never pursued against Cianbro and Ivey Lee Jones.

Lori never recovered emotionally. Her injuries were so devastatingly horrid and painful that she led a miserable life, and has since died. Molly, Walter's widow died of a broken heart. David, divorced, fell and hit his head on his hearth and died. Jimmy and grandbaby Crystal still live in Plymouth.

Ivey Lee Jones has not held a regular job since getting out of prison. He blames me personally for his misfortunes. On holidays, in his drunken stupors, he would call me at home for ten or more years and cuss me out. About two years ago, as I sat here in my office as the elected Clerk of Superior Court, he came in and asked for copies of his criminal file. He appeared disheveled and moved with a limp. His clothes were dirty and ragged. He did not recognize me as I spoke to him, and I would not have otherwise recognized him had he not told me his name.

Suffering Alongside Death

Chatham County Oil Tanker Drowning

In 1971 I was a Wildlife Enforcement Officer (Game Warden), stationed in Pittsboro in Chatham County, NC. Chatham was a large conglomeration of small, hardworking communities. Some worked in the trucking industry. Some worked at textile mills. Some worked at chicken processing plants. Some worked in agriculture and logwoods. And some were simply commuters to jobs elsewhere in the triangle of Raleigh, Durham, and Chapel Hill. All these jobs necessitated travel, and the roads, other than US-15-501 and US- 64, were narrow through rocky soil, and crooked around gulleys and ravines full of Kudzu. One of my best friends tried to keep his best friend from dying early one evening on the Pittsboro-Moncure Road. Trooper Leonard Meeks ran off the road and hit some huge, unforgiving trees. Many times, my friend, Trooper Tommy Jeffries has told me and relived his valiant efforts to save Leonard's life, but to no avail. He told me of passers-by who would not stop to help. Communication efforts were lacking. I had heard the call on my scanner, but did not respond because there was no urgency indicating a wreck had occurred. The forlorn ghostly empathetic feeling and disgust of death without comprehension; never to be rectified.

When a human must stand and witness another human breathe his or her last breath, a part of the observer dies, too. Second guessing and "what if" scenarios are replayed forever in the survivor's mind's eye. Such was the case, again in Chatham County where a fuel tanker tractor trailer "Suicide Jockey" drowned in his own cargo. It was a snowy night with two feet of accumulated wet snow blown into drifts across US-15, 501. I will never know what happened. Neither will anyone else

I was driving my issued International Scout, 4-wheel drive jeep north on 15-501 to a reported capsize on the Haw river in Bynum, NC about five miles north of Pittsboro. As I topped a hill, I could see strange appearing lights at the bottom. A fully loaded stainless steel diesel fuel tanker had jackknifed, skidded sideways across the two lanes, collided with and come to rest against the red clay embankment. Upon my "by chance" arrival, the scream of the Cummins Diesel engine was horrendously deafening. I was twenty-one years old and knew nothing of diesel engines. The ignition key did not stop the engine, and thankfully the transmission was either blown or in neutral keeping the head high wheels turning like a buzz saw. My Wildlife Commission Radio was not "manned" by telecommunicators. Our only responsive units were our co-workers. My Supervisor, "Cuckleberry" Jones heard my call for assistance, and ultimately sent every available rescue squad, Sheriff's deputy, and Highway Patrolman to the horrifying scene.

On impact, the entire cab had folded forward, off the chassis with the driver's seat and the control panel nearly covered by the falling snow. The diesel fuel was spilling out of the tanker's fill cap and the air was filled with the smell. Somebody finally cut the fuel off to the engine and the tandem wheels stopped rotating. The windshield was punched forward from the inside out, still attached to the rubber gasket. There lay the driver, pinned under the front chrome bumper of the cab with nothing but his trucker boots extending above the snow, FEEBLY KICKING. I pulled as hard as I could. One leg then the other, then both, to no avail. His boots came off, and apparently, he was not wearing socks. His feet were wet and oily. I pulled on his jeans. I went to my Scout, got my shovel and tried to dig him out. He was pinned between the frame of his truck and the rock-hard shoulder, head down in the ditch. His front wheels chocked the ditch, and the fuel filled the ditch. He drowned in Diesel fuel, right there before my eyes. The Coroner's report listed "Drowning" as his cause of death.

Mrs. Constance Goodwin

While Y Z Newberry and I were doin' what he called, "Patrolling our beat in a military manner," he got called to assist a stranded motorist on the Four Mile Desert Road in northern Perquimans County.

Naturally, since his county was characteristically, "out of control," I got called to a wreck in front of Gabby's Restaurant on US-17 in Perquimans County.

An extremely nice man and his lady friend had just left the "Hootenanny" and pulled from the driveway of the restaurant out onto US-17, right in front of a northbound Chevrolet. After maybe 100 feet of skid marks, the Chevrolet T-boned the couple right in the driver's door.

Surprisingly, there was not a whole lot of damage, but both man and woman were fragile, in their late 70s. Mrs. Patty Madrey, a Certified EMT, heard the collision from inside the restaurant. She immediately came to the rescue of the injured couple. The Chevrolet driver was uninjured.

Patty was wearing a sequined, glittery jacket. She was known for her bravery and by her jewelry: big diamond rings and diamond bracelets. Without hesitation she applied pressure to the bleeding driver's face. His blood ran between her fingers, all over the rings and bracelets, and down her forearm, dripping from her elbow. To say she was dedicated is an understatement. She was given a towel which she wrapped around the still seated driver's head, turban style. She next turned to the female who appeared to be halfway OK. I was relieved that she was talking, and alert enough to her surroundings. She gave me her house keys for safekeeping.

The ambulance arrived, both were stretchered into the unit and headed to Chowan Hospital. Upon my arrival, the man was sitting up, eyes closed, but softly speaking. The frail woman had taken a turn for the worse, was unconscious, and even though intubated, she died right there on the gurney. She had never been removed onto the hospital bed. Her sons never got to the hospital before she passed, but I shared with them the calm that she had displayed, and that she appeared to suffer no pain. Also, I shared with them that she had had the best of care, and that the emergency responders had focused on her and comforted her during her last moments. I gave them her house keys.

Miss Patty met in maker in 2021.

I Feel "Eel"

For many years, the five mile stretch of US-17 from southwest to northeast through Chowan County was only two lanes. Working RADAR on this mini "Super Slab" became an attractive job pursuit for Troopers in Chowan and Perquimans Counties. We worked together on late calls and wreck calls, so we might as well work together to enforce the speed laws where it was relatively safe: straight highway, extra wide shoulders, and boxed off in Bertie and Perquimans Counties with narrow crooked roads that SUDDENLY opened up for passing and making up lost time behind a tractor and twelve row disks. Need I say more?

The News and Observer, published in Raleigh, NC, ran a story that statistically showed that the stretch of US-17 that ran through Chowan County had the highest number of speeding tickets written per mile in the whole state. When Butch Whitley worked early shift, he wrote speeding tickets on US-17 in Chowan County. When Joel Siles worked late shift, he wrote speeding tickets on US-17 in Chowan County. After dinner, the Perquimans County Troopers would come over and write speeding tickets on US-17 in Chowan County. Keep in mind that most of these speeders were running 75mph or more. If we took time to write one at 65/55, we were missing one at 87/55. You be the judge.

I took great pride in showcasing the North Carolina State Highway Patrol as a dedicated and hard-working organization. My sergeant told me early in my career that, while on duty, activating that blue light neither decreased my gas mileage nor increased my overall safety. He was right. Too many of my friends have gotten hit by oblivious "passing motorists," mesmerized by those ten or more flashing blue lights. There were times that upon re-entry to my patrol car after just having issued a citation, my RADAR would indicate ANOTHER SPEEDER. Usually I just made my speed estimation, executed a U-turn, and pulled the new acquaintance over before the first speeder had even gotten underway.

A Dark Cloud?

About 1985, North Carolina introduced and passed US mandated legislation that would require drivers to wear seat belts. Later everyone had to wear them, but the first statute only required the driver's compliance. For a whole year, law enforcement officers could only write HP-308s (warning tickets) for violators. I wrote some of my friends three or more warning tickets. Guess what! On June 1 of the next year, North Carolina's mandatory seat belt usage law went into effect. Violators had to pay $25.00 when convicted. Cap'n Murray Tynch told me upon my writing him his first seat belt ticket: "MacArthur, I've got more $25.00 than you've got ticket books!" And he was right.

Again, guess what! I wrote some of my friends three or more $25.00 tickets. The first week, just to impress upon Chowan County the importance of wearing your seat belt and motor vehicle law compliance, I wrote <u>FIFTY</u> seat belt tickets. This was not only unheard of, but earth shattering when those tickets hit the Troop Commander's desk on the following Tuesday morning. What I thought was "a good job," apparently "hung a dark cloud over the whole state." If Mike McArthur was writing fifty in one week in the smallest county in the State, some of those other "hot-shots" should be writing more than a paltry three or four. I thought it was amusing, but not really many others wearing the gray uniform thought so!

One year, the State Highway Patrol launched a "See and Be Seen" campaign to alert drivers of speed law enforcement. It was just before Christmas Holidays, and there was always some law enforcement initiative aimed at motor vehicle law compliance, especially getting drunk drivers off the road. Chowan County did not really have that many drunk drivers, partly because we knew most of them personally, having captured them and taken their license "last year." So in an effort to support the initiative we had to "improvise." That is, "perform a lot of enforcement contacts." This year I decided that warning tickets were a Great enforcement tool. On the Sunday night before the initiative took effect, I took ten warning ticket books of twenty-five each, and "primed" them. I wrote US-17 on them, stamped them with my name, and filled in my registry number: 2188. This number used to be indicative of how many Troopers had preceded you upon being sworn in.

Monday morning, I hit the highway "wide open." My plan was to write 100 warning tickets, but it would depend on my "other" assignments during the week. Sure, I would have accidents to investigate. Sure, I would have blood relays to transport. Sure, I would have arrests to complete. Usually the week before Christmas can be up and down. School is out, and people take vacations. There was plenty to do, though. The first day I wrote 30+_ warning tickets and maybe two regular 200s (Traffic Citations). During the rest of the week I wrote two drunk drivers, six or eight speeders, one or two stop sign violations, one or two licenses revoked, four or five no operator's licenses, four or five expired tags and insurance and inspection tickets, and investigated two motor vehicle accidents. I called it a "TICKET SALAD." It had a little bit of everything in it. The real kicker came when I tallied my warning tickets for the week: it came to 202, two hundred and two warning tickets. Almost all of them were for speeding at least ten over the limit. Some were for loud mufflers, slick tires, and rolling stop signs. The response from The Highway Patrol Sergeant? "You have put a cloud over the whole State of North Carolina." Sound familiar?

Back to the **eel truck wreck**. After having worked a 3 p.m. to midnight shift on a Thursday, I went home. I had not gotten to bed when the phone rang. Margie Allen who lived about 200 yards off the US-17 Bypass called and said that she just heard a terrible wreck and people screaming out her back door on the us-17 Bypass. I put my uniform back on, and as I was getting in the car, I heard the phone ringing inside the house. I picked up my radio handset and told T-Comm Supervisor Burris Taylor at Williamston SHP Telecommunications Center that I was on the way. Upon arrival, in my headlights, I found a laid over tanker truck tractor and trailer, and a Pontiac torn all to pieces. There were maybe 10 other people running around the scene for an unknown reason. As I walked into the melee, I discovered the nature of the commotion. There were thousands of two-foot-long eels slithering all over the asphalt in the eighth inch of water that had not yet run into the side ditch. People in the Pontiac were screaming for help. The tractor trailer driver was gathering his belongings from the sleeper of his cab.

This accident scene was just about one-hundred-yards north from the concrete bridge over Pembroke Creek. The side ditches were full of slippery eels that were sliming down to the creek. Some were being helped with bystanders pushing them and their slimy selves right over to freedom. The three of the four occupants of the car were still screaming. The driver was obviously dead at the wheel. It seemed to be especially dark that mournful night, and the excruciating bedlam at that wreck scene was overwhelming.

Somehow, with the help of Chowan County Sheriff's Deputies, we got the southbound lane of travel open. All of the occupants of the Pontiac had been transported to the Emergency Room at Chowan Hospital on NC-32. Robert Sawyer's big truck wrecker was coming from Elizabeth City, and Felix Chambers was hauling the Pontiac to Nick George Chevrolet. Those eels that didn't make it to Pembroke Creek stunk up that section of US-17 for weeks and weeks.

Michael J. McArthur

In the Emergency Room (now referred to as "The Emergency Department"), you cannot imagine how things were "jacked up." Doctors, numerous doctors were hunkered down over patients. No doctors ever relished the thoughts of getting called out at 4:00 am, but called out they were. Some of the white uniformed attendants were neonatal nurses. Some were Laboratory and Radiology technicians. Some were front desk registrars. Some were plain clothed, having been called in for their emergency management skills. There was not a calm area in the unit. In fact, there was enough bustling, hustling, and tension in the rooms to cause concern. Surprisingly, communication was relatively low key: those who were supposed to be talking were professionally issuing orders. Those who were to fulfill those orders were professionally making things happen. Very impressive.

The only real noises rising above the din, were the wailing and crying out pleas from the wreck victims. With the doctors and nurses and everybody else doing all they could, as always there was one patient who, seemingly the least injured, was DEMANDING that somebody come over to his stall and get him some water. Without much to do, I walked over, pulled open the curtains, and there sat what appeared to be a patient not having been involved in the wreck. I handed him a small cup of water, and told him, "Shut up! There are people dying in here." He shut up! For EVER!

About five minutes later, a blood curdling scream came from behind those very curtains from which I had just exited. The charge nurse, Lucy Daniels, having had just about all she wanted from that troublesome patient, went over opened the curtains, and there lay wreck fatality number two. Now, there were only two patients still alive of the original four. Medi-vac helicopters came from Louise Obeci Hospital in Suffolk and flew the younger of the two patients to Obeci, while East-Care came and lifted the elderly man to East Carolina University Medical Hospital in Greenville.

As you can imagine, my next two weeks were full of interviews, report writing, newspaper recounting, and intense scrutiny revolving around the physical aspects of the horrendous motor vehicle accident. Environmental folks from Environmental Protection Agency came down from Washington, D. C.. They were concerned about pollution and the reintroduction of thousands of eels into the Inland Waters of North Carolina. Jump suited hardhats plus Ivy League Suited National Traffic Safety Board investigators came and required that we block off US-17 so that they could complete their thorough investigation. The whole scenario was ripe for various interpretations, with only one story coming from the single communicative survivor: the tractor trailer driver. I believed his account: the Pontiac had at the very last minute, driven completely into the path of his Peterbilt Tractor.

As time went on, the fates of the two survivors from the Pontiac occasionally came into conversation. I can relate to you that their fate and their conditions were never far from my thoughts, having witnessed firsthand, the severity of their injuries, and wondered at the time how could they have survived. For almost three years, the two victims lay comatose in assisted care facilities: one in Richmond, Virginia, and the other in Roanoke, Virginia. Much to my surprise though, on a Monday morning when I was appearing in Chowan County Criminal Superior Court, I received a call from our SHP Telecommunicator, Harold Riddick, asking me to telephone a law firm in Cincinnati, Ohio concerning the two survivors. They were no longer survivors. They had each died earlier that morning within an hour of each other, about 3:00am.

Doesn't that sound bizarre? I thought so. I notified our Governor's Highway Safety Program, Traffic Safety Unit in Raleigh, and asked them to determine what my next step should be about having to submit an "Amended DMV-349 (Traffic Accident Report)." Their requirement was for me to submit another "349" and list the final two occupants as having died as a result of the accident. Easily done. Case cleared.

During my next several years as a Trooper, I had many opportunities to share final moments with folks. It could be said that these were unfortunate experiences involving the untimely deaths of friends, neighbors, and strangers, but I considered it a God given gift to "be there" for them. We prayed.

I think that you have gotten the picture from these rather lurid depictions. Perhaps I will get motivated and share more later… if I live that long.

Michael J. McArthur

The North Carolina State Agricultural Fair

Calling the Cavalry

Amid all the Coronavirus Pandemic doom and gloom, here are some cheerful anecdotes to lift your spirits.

For fourteen of my 16 years on the State Highway Patrol, I had the good fortune to be assigned to work for the notorious 1st Sergeant Thomas T. Jeffries as a Trooper / traffic control officer at the N C Department of Agriculture's world-famous North Carolina State Fair. Somebody asked me once how I had drawn that "Special Assignment" so many times, year after year. My response? I quoted Patrick Swayze's response in the 1989 movie, "Road House," to "Doc," when, upon seeing all his scars and degrees, she asked him, "How's a guy like you end up being a bouncer?" "Just lucky, I guess."

The First Shirt near 'bout had raised me in law enforcement, he knew I knew local geography (where things were), and he always stationed me at Gate 11 on Blue Ridge Road, the celebrity eyeball of the two-week event. Across the street from my post was a small V.I.P. parking lot where we put dignitaries, law enforcement families, and our own families. A young Sheriff's Deputy from Orange County came over and told me that there was a blue Chevy Nova parked beside the "BOOZE-IT AND LOSE-IT" Operation Eagle command center. Believe it or not, contained there-in were "four long-haired hippies smokin' dope." When I approached the car with white smoke pouring out of the four open windows, they suddenly sat up straight as if in a movie, on command. Immediately, I had them each interlock their hands and fingers behind their heads, and place both their feet either on the back of the front seat, or up onto the dashboard. The young Deputy was instructed to go back out to my marked Black and Silver Patrol car, open the door, pick up the radio handset, depress the button and ask for "assistance at Gate 11 from A-354." When an unknown voice echoed throughout the N C State Fairgrounds, it brought the cavalry, "Pronto!" This was my last night on late shift, and I had just transferred custody of the four malodorous potheads into the custody of the floating C-111 Black Moriah car for transport to the Wake County Magistrate's

Office. That Trooper was soon to be elected Wake County Sheriff Donnie Harrison. At that point I thought the "main attraction" for the evening was over.

BUT, NO!

About 8:00 that night I took my meal break, and went straight to "Tony's." He sold hot sausages, pizza, and chili cheese steaks. He was situated right beside the Baptist Church vendor who sold jumbo fried turkey drumsticks. I had gotten to know Tony in years gone by, and he already knew how many slices and what kind of pizza I liked: "Two slices, extra cheese, pepperoni, and light sauce." He also was a magician with his Dexter Butcher Knife as he prepared the meats and vegetables for his dishes. I would always give to him my **Case** "Sodbuster" pocketknife for him to put a razor edge on it. Upon his returning it to me, he would grin and say, "Swing it through the air! Hear those screams? Molecules being sliced in two."

Upon my return to Gate 11 on Blue Ridge Road, I put new batteries into my flashlight, and replaced Adam on the centerline. It was a cool night in October of 1984, and the traffic was, "thicker'n thieves at a dogfight."

A Sheepdog, Fireworks, and a Torn Tunic

A 30s something father of three driving a two tone, Chrysler station wagon on Blue Ridge Road in front of Gate 11 at the N C State Fair in Raleigh in October, 1984, failed to see your's truly standing in the roadway givin' it my best Trooper Pete Peterson form to signal him to, "Get movin!". It was about 9:30 pm and the night air was beginning to chill. This poor man, his true love, a sheepdog, and three head of curtain climbin' crumb snatchers were too absorbed "oohing and aahing" about the $15,000.00 fireworks display lifting up out of the dirt/clay packed racetrack underneath the Corvettes in "Joey Chitwood's Hell Drivers." The dew had settled a heavy layer of red clay dust onto the station wagon's windshield which had been parked back in the Tanker's Grille parking lot over by the Southern Coastline Railroad Tracks on Hillsborough Street. To give him just a small amount of credence, just maybe he couldn't (or didn't) see me. Every night I too, was covered with that red mud from the top of my Smokey Bear hat, to my shoulders, to my patent leather chukka boots, scorched and charred by the explosively burning molten phosphorous from the 50+ road flare lane delineators. During night shifts, not only our uniform patent leather chukka boots, but our pantlegs had holes burned through them. During the eleven-day assignment, a Trooper worked six nights (3-10) and five days (9-3), or vice versa.

Can you believe it? Somehow, as I was turning toward the other pedestrians, the Chrysler hit me from behind. I scrambled/rolled up onto the hood, up over the windshield, and onto the top where my Smith & Wesson stainless steel handcuffs got hung up in his luggage rack. He slammed on his brakes, and I then rolled back across the windshield and wipers, and down onto the hood. His young'uns were screaming, and there was enough chaos right then and there for three world's fairs and a billy goat ropin' contest! My traffic direction partner "Street" McCoy by this time was at the driver's door. He snatched it open, snatched the driver out, and the car kept goin'. Mom had to apply the brakes. Screamin' young'uns were witnessing "Street" beatin' the you know what out of their daddy, right there in the middle of Blue Ridge Road. I sprang from the hood, pounced on Street's back, and yanked him away.

Talk about apologetic: that deer in the headlights driver was cryin' alligator tears with a bloody nose and a torn tunic. After quick assessment, I determined that no dope smokin', slicked down yuppie drivin' a clunker station wagon full of his beautiful family through the bumper-to-bumper snarl at the N C State Fair could possibly hurt a North Carolina State Highway Patrolman. Street and I scooped him up, brushed him off, threw his butt back into the station wagon, saluted him, and gave him the famous "Happy Motoring" send off.

The next day, during "muster," Captain Bobby Clark motioned me over to the side. Turns out that the station wagon driver was a friend of the Captain. Dope toker had told Captain Clark how lucky "dad" had been during the previous night's episode, and that Trooper McArthur was to be commended for not bringing "serious charges" against the poor old driver who was "doin' the best he could" with that crowd and a barking sheepdog in his car!

Wolfpack Placard, and "You Can't Get There From Here"

Later in the day, I was sent to the intersection of Blue Ridge Road and Trinity Road to assist with two busloads of impaired gifted children. Their buses were parked at the Highway Patrol Communication and Logistics lot, and the sight impaired, hearing impaired, and physically handicapped groups of V.I.P. children were to be loaded onto the tractor powered shuttles for "The Grand Tour" of the fairgrounds. Turns out that one of the children was a niece of Trooper Adam Coleson who was assigned traffic direction responsibilities in that intersection. We decided that I would direct traffic while "Mr. Big Shot Trooper" shepherded the entourage. He stood six feet five inches, and represented the State Highway Patrol with class and dignity while seeing to the needs of the tiny little children.

Out on the blacktop, in the middle of the intersection, from up toward the railroad tracks, here came a North Carolina State RED Lincoln Continental with a single occupant. His front bumper prominently displayed a "North Carolina State Wolfpack Club" license plate. His left turn signal (onto Trinity) was blinking. That could not happen because, at that moment, we had five lanes of traffic (shoulder to shoulder) coming out from an N. C. Governor James B. Hunt, Jr.'s Horse Complex event. The elderly Lincoln driver was determined to turn left as a "RESIDENT" placard would normally allow him to do. I told him, "Sir, You can't get there from here; not right now."

Traffic continued to pour out of Trinity onto Blue Ridge Road. Some of it really wanted to go north, but was forced to go south. And the "RESIDENT" should have been able to see that. But he didn't. Now, who was I to interrupt the established traffic pattern?

I tried to ignore him, hoping he would go on north toward Crabtree Valley Shopping Center, and loop around to get to his residence. But, NO! There he sat, waving that "RESIDENT" placard, and blowing his horn. Blocking a whole lane of northbound traffic. My partner was directing traffic around the Lincoln when it began to inch forward, as if to turn onto the muddy shoulder, in the face of oncoming traffic. What in the...? I stepped off the centerline toward the front left fender of the Lincoln, now only inches from my uniform pantleg. I heard his tires grind the rocks on the asphalt as he turned his wheels sharply in my direction. Slowly and intentionally, he drove into me, pushing me and forcing me to step backward.

At this point there immediately exploded a multitude of options available to me, and damned few available to him. He had just intentionally collided with a pedestrian, and much worse, he had, "... unlawfully, willfully, and feloniously assaulted a law enforcement officer." N.C.G.S. 14-33, (c) (4).

What to do!?!?!? What to do!?!?!?

By now, through— no fault of his own, the light bulb in this man's head had apparently screwed itself all the way in. He stopped. I pounced three paces to his rolled-up window, and he lowered the glass. I surprised him, and even moreover, I surprised myself. We glared at each other, and then I laughed! Apparently, he was having a bad day, probably soon to worsen. He was speechless when I asked, "Can I help you?" "Jesus Christ, man. PLEASE! I just want to go home!" **Don't we all!**

I stopped all traffic then upon Blue Ridge Road. Trooper Coleson stopped the influx of traffic from Trinity Road. The poor old gentleman took three back-ups to turn that land yacht 180 degrees around. Trooper Coleson directed him to, "Go to Hillsborough Street, turn right, and head toward Cary, NC. Then wind around onto Edwards Mill Road and get home safely. And, by the way: Happy Motoring!"

Mrs. Louisburg and the Magic of the S H P Helicopters

A few years before this incident at the T- intersection of Trinity Road and Blue Ridge Road, there was another incredible circumstance that fell upon the State Highway Patrol. Five other Troopers and I were directing five lanes of one-way traffic out of Gate A and Gate B of Carter-Finley

Stadium after an NC State Wolfpack versus UNC - Carolina Football Game. Traffic was bumper-to-bumper, and flowing smoothly. A perfect time for a "street savvy" Highway Patrolman to get the H out of the way. Our only real responsibility at that time, was to ensure the safety of the hordes of fair going or fair returning pedestrians. And there were thousands of them parked inside the football stadium parking lots. On a coordinated signal, six Troopers would enter the two parking lot intersections, inside the pedestrian crosswalks, and methodically stop all vehicular flow.

During our morning briefing, we had been alerted to the strong possibility that a ritualistic initiation for prospective Hell's Angel Motorcycle Club membership would be conducted sometime during that day. It would involve the armed robbery of the State Fair admission coffers. We were extremely vigilant. Already we had seen some "bikers" go across the road onto the fairgrounds proper. Just looking at them, they did not appear to have bulky concealed weapons, but their "weapons of choice" could have easily been smuggled through the gates in "biker babe's" pocketbooks.

It had rained earlier in the week, and had decreased the size of the usual crowds. But, today! Today was picture perfect, no wind, and not a cloud in the sky. Both of the Highway Patrol helicopters from our Aviation Unit were in the sky overhead. Channels 5 (WRAL) and 11 (WTVD) had their Eye in the Sky news helicopters hovering over the massive crowds, traffic snarls, and tailgate picnickers. RDU (Raleigh Durham Airport) was experiencing mass confusion and lock-down because an unidentified small black plane had entered some restricted airspace over the fairgrounds due to the presence of certain unidentified international dignitaries. Duke University was playing against Clemson just up NC-54 in Durham. Wake Forest University was playing Virginia Tech up in Winston Salem. East Carolina University was playing somebody just down US-64 in Greenville. That was FOUR major Atlantic Coast Conference (ACC) football games within two hours of the State Fair. And this was the last Saturday of the fair. There was a food fair of some description happening in downtown Raleigh. All this is to say that, well I don't know what to say about it. You tell me! I do know that there was not much preventive patrol being performed that day. All the Troopers were directing traffic at one of many special assignments.

About the time when hundreds of pedestrians were jovially plodding wearily either toward or away from Chitwood's racetrack, and we thought we had it ALL under control, above the roar of those Dodge 440 Hemis, frantic SCREAMING reached our ears. There appeared to be an unauthorized "huddle" right in the middle of MY asphalt! A very pregnant young lady had passed out in the turn lane – in the center of the five lanes of bumper-to-bumper traffic feeding Carter-Finley Stadium. Apparently, she was related to everybody in Louisburg, because they were all crowded around "Their little Amy." This menagerie was blocking at least four of the five lanes, and we could not tell if the expectant mother was dead or alive. Just when we thought nothing else could happen, a medical doctor with a stethoscope around his neck, stepped off the shoulder toward the mayhem and twisted his ankle. Down he went!

Now we had two patients to deal with. The "backed-up traffic" was patiently waiting, and the roadway stretching from the asphalt obstetric delivery site toward Communications and Logistics up on Blue Ridge Road was completely barren. Somebody at Patrol Headquarters ordered one of our helicopters to "Right now, you go sit down in the roadway on Trinity, load up the patients, and get that GD traffic moving." Well, I do not know whether that was the right thing to do, but I do know that that is what happened. SHP Aviation Sergeant Chuck Boyd (former US Army Huey Helicopter Viet Nam War combat pilot) performed exactly as ordered. The young mother was regaining her composure, and her family was happy to allow her to get scooped up, and get medical transport, if you could call it that. Away they went. Rex Hospital was only about two minutes away. I am unsure of what ever happened to the good Doctor. Back to the NORMAL chaos: business as usual!

"Country Come To Town"

I suppose you have figured out that there was never a dull moment when assigned a traffic direction detail at the nationally recognized, world famous North Carolina State Agricultural Fair. Particularly if you were fortunate enough to draw a post at a pedestrian crosswalk. My friends in high places always looked out for me, and put me "close in." I always appreciated the fact that I could talk to the folks, welcome them, and give them encouragement as to what they could expect inside those chain link gates, and ultimately how to find their way to North Hills Mall, Thad Eure's Angus Barn Steakhouse, or Crabtree Valley Shopping Center.

Out on the asphalt (in the road, as we called it), directing traffic was a totally different and invigorating experience. We had to keep our eyes open – WIDE OPEN. Some of those motorists were "country come to town," and were not accustomed to either the volume of cars, the associated pandemonium, or that six-foot mountain of a man in that gray uniform. We were only trying our best to help make the day less stressful for over a ninety thousand fairgoers PER DAY. Add to that the AMTRACK Silver Meteor which ran through the fairgrounds on its way from New York City to Miami, Florida. Those speeding bullets paid not one bit of attention to Highway Patrolmen or their blue lights.

Some of those drivers, if you could call them that, didn't keep their eyes or their minds on the road. A uniformed officer in the roadway was not something they were accustomed to seeing or much less, responding to. When you add into the equation that it was misting rain, it was nighttime, flashing lights of every color were everywhere, there were at least five lanes of traffic going every which way, there were at least seventy five phosphorous burning bright white, road flares emitting bright distraction and clouds of pungent smoke, the kids were screaming in the back seat, Mom was giving chin music with inaccurate directions, and, lo and behold, there stood a North Carolina State Highway Patrolman. He was holding his red-wanded two D-cell flashlight straight up beside the palm of his other hand indicating that the driver was to STOP.

I can tell you, just like thousands of other police traffic directors, that this was a bad spot in which to find yourself. Some of us called it, "No man's land." That is because the pavement belongs to vehicles. Traffic cops are merely an intrusion into space reserved for rubber tires, not chukka boots. WAY too often, we had to jump out of the way of a cruising Chrysler loaded with good people who never saw us. What was the remedy for that flagrant insurrection? Very little! We could "run" them down, but then we would leave our traffic post vulnerable to more incursions, and our partners in peril.

Michael J. McArthur

D-Cells and "HAPPY MOTORING"

One of the things that I found amusing, not that I ever participated in such, but can verify its authenticity, often involved D-cell batteries. Immediately after you jumped out of the way to keep from getting hit by that Chrysler, and realized that you had not been scuffed up or killed, what was your next step? If your Model 19, Smith & Wesson, nickel plated, six shot, .357 Magnum revolver was snapped in and holstered on your right hip, you reached into your left front pocket and retrieved one or more dead silver Ray-O Vac, D-cell flashlight batteries. With the utmost of care and respect for "others" in the roadway, it was known to happen that one or more D-cells were hurled in the general direction of the now departing Chrysler. The driver was totally oblivious that he had committed such a grievous transgression, but that Highway Patrolman knew full well how close he had come to missing dinner that night!

If, in the unlikely event that the battery collided with its target, and in the even more unlikely event that the driver stopped, then it came time to "put up or shut up." In true American Baseball League fashion, the battery had met its mark, the driver had stopped, and now a "conversation" ensued. Many of the "pitchers" employed the worn-out strategy, "The best defense is a good offense." Immediately the driver was made fully aware of the serious nature of his offense. And yes, the penalty could/would be severe. And maybe, would the driver be willing to make amends with a sincere apology. It could go a long way toward atonement and rectifying this Mell of a Hess. Of course sugar could have melted in the motorist's mouth. If, by chance, there was physical damage to the Chrysler, "Oh, it's nothing," according to the relieved driver. Just another opportunity for a good Trooper to brush off the driver, send him on his merry way, and deliver the tried and true euphemistic admonition: "Happy Motoring."

One "SLIM JIM" Is Just Not Enough

Living Out Loud with Grace, Grit, and Gratitude

It just seemed like the State Fair always afforded boundless opportunities for the uniformed members of the North Carolina State Highway Patrol to provide valuable assistance to "stranded motorists." Invariably some poor mother of four had locked her keys inside her car, and was late to pick up her husband's mother at work. As would usually happen, she would approach us right when there was not time to stop what we were doing, and go and help her. The partner Trooper was on lunch break, and traffic was backed up out of sight. As you know, we would find a way, or "improvise" as our good Sergeant Thomas T. Jeffries would encourage us.

Just when we got her passenger door unlocked, she stood the heavy four-year-old on the seat, and shut the door. She got the twins by their hands and then heard the, "CLICK," heard 'round the world. The four-year-old had re-locked the four doors.

This family had just moved to Cary from South Carolina with Carolina Power and Light Company (CP&L), and obviously struggling to "get it together." Just before they left Charleston, the wife had experienced a flat tire out on I-26 Expressway. When she got out to look at the damage, that same four-year- old had locked her out, he alone in the car, she on the side of the road, with the motor running. Under no circumstances would that child unlock that door this time because he had gotten spanked for unlocking the door at an inappropriate time earlier in the week. What do you think we did? Sergeant Jeffries and I unlocked the door again, removed the keys, handed them to the mother, and bid her, "Happy Motoring." We returned to our post quickly before another calamity could befall that poor woman!

Most of us had at least one unauthorized "Slim Jim" hidden in our well-organized trunks. These were one-inch-wide by twenty-four-inch-long strips of stainless steel about one-sixteenth of an inch thick. They had a handle on one end and a series of hooks and notches on the other. If, in the strong unlikelihood, that we knew what we were doing, we could "magically" slide that Slim Jim down through the window molding adjacent to the glass, and unlock a locked car door in less than fifteen seconds. H O W E V E R The other likelihood was that we didn't know what we were doing, and while that Slim Jim was down inside the intricate locking mechanism inside that Mercedes door, it would either mess up something expensive, or get "hung up" in the intricate wiring. During my various attempts over sixteen years, I watched two of my Slim Jims return to the residences of the cars' owners, one in Rocky Hock, and the other in The Seafood Capitol of the World, Calabash, NC.

Again, all's well that ends well. There's more, but the statute of limitations has not expired. ☺

Gilchrist Bank Robbery Exercise SHP Hostages

You'd a Really Had ta' Been There

"Do Fewer Things Better"

Some of you may remember North Carolina State Highway Patrol Captain Carl Gilchrist, 108: Troop A Commander in Greenville. He had the audacity in 1984 to "summons" me to Greenville loud and clear, through Williamston Radio Telecommunicator Alex Jones: "Williamston, to A-354 (me). 10-25 (meet in person with) 108 at Troop A Headquarters at 1400 hours." Well, as always when these calls came in, we already knew what we had done, we just didn't know what the good Captain knew we had done. Perquimans Trooper, Y Z Newberry called me on the Sheriff Julian "Little Man" Broughton's walkie talkie radio on the blocked frequency, "Well MacAther (as he called me), what on earth have you done this time?" I assured him that I was lily-white, and we both had a good laugh. After I dumped out my patrol car of "things" that weren't supposed to be in there (like extra guns, tools, Slim-Jims, binoculars, the child safety seat, etc.), I drove "carefully" to Troop A Headquarters in Greenville.

Upon my arrival in "the pit," I found Captain Gilchrist out in the garage talking to Pete Cox. This was not a good sign. This meant that what the good Captain had to say to me was not for general knowledge, and not meant to be heard through his closed office door. We shook hands and walked over to the gas pumps, well out of earshot. He began with how he, "didn't expect all 'his' Troopers to be perfect." Right then and there I knew this was not gonna be pretty. He went on to say how he thought, "I had a bright future with the Highway Patrol, and that occasionally, our White Horse stumbled. It was up to us to determine how we would learn from experiences such as what he wanted to talk to me about." You know what? About two years earlier, my short term First Sergeant Pinky Lane, A-311 had said those identical lines to me. I can only guess that they had attended (but not learned much) the same "First Line Supervisors School," conducted in Chicago's Northwestern Traffic Institute. Before I could think, my incorrigible self blurted out to "Pinky", "Well if I have to be the kind of SOB that it takes to be a Sergeant, I don't think I want to be one." He yelled back at me, "I don't think you have anything to worry about. Get out of my office." Upon my hasty retreat, I found Mrs. Delores Kemp, our wonderful Troop A-III Steno IV, wiping tears from her eyes. I wasn't sure whether she was laughing or crying, but I knew better than to stay around to find out!

On this day in Greenville, I found that apparently, one of my "good buddy" fellow Troopers had complained to Captain Gilchrist about having to work harder to cover my shifts in Chowan County during my four-month long term special assignments at the SHP Basic Schools in Chapel Hill and Raleigh. The Captain went on to say that he knew how important it was for me to continue my heavy involvement in Community Policing in Chowan County. That it was important to have a healthy family life and to be active in Macedonia Baptist Church (how he knew that I do not know). Also my involvement as an Eagle Scout and a Scoutmaster was important for the image of the Highway Patrol. He understood that I was responsible for raising the money for the Fourth of July event put on by the Chowan Edenton Optimist Club. That as a charter member of the Advance Ruritan Club, I was doing some great projects, and "Making my community a better place in which to live," after the hurricane that had just blown through.

He finished up with, "You know, all these things are important. All these things are obviously better suited to a young man like yourself. My only suggestion would be for you to maybe consider, D O I N G F E W E R T H I N G S   B E T E R!!!" Well, he might as well have just "cut to the chase," and said, "Trooper McArthur, you are not writing enough tickets." From that day on, when I was fortunate enough to be working the roads in Chowan, Perquimans, and Gates Counties (always by myself), at the end of every week, I turned in double or triple the normal number of citations and warning tickets as my fellow Troopers. I well understood and could comprehend the "Reasonable Level of Production," spelled Q U O T A! During Christmas week of about 1982, I conducted over three-hundred motor vehicle stops, wrote twenty-eight HP-200s (citations) and issued two-hundred-and-two HP-308s (Warning Tickets). These numbers were twenty times the numbers generated by any other Trooper in the district. My Sergeant told me that this "Put a cloud over District III." I generated these accelerated levels of production in a successful effort to make my end-of-year totals equal to or greater than my co-workers. I could "play the numbers game" with the best of them, if for no other reason than to keep my Sergeant and Captain off my ... case.

The Future Colonel

Captain Carl Gilchrist had a beautiful family. His "little girl" as I remember her, had a younger brother, Michael, who ultimately was a cracker jack, top of the heap kinda guy that I coached through the 78th State Highway Patrol Basic School, where he finished first in his class. He never forgot it. He became T. H. E. Colonel as a Republican, and bit the dust when Democrat Governor Roy Cooper went in. He successfully developed and advanced previously sluggish projects during his tenure, not the least of which was development of a better employee performance measurement / management tool.

40 Miles of "Git Back"

During his 78th Basic School, one of many highlights of the training was our Bank Robbery / Hostage Negotiation exercise. I made Cadet Gilchrist one of the gunmen for the six cadets designated as robbers. True to movie mogul form, while escaping from "the bank," he hung out the window of the getaway van, firing .38 Special, Smith and Wesson blanks. Unfortunately, two lab-coated female SBI (State Bureau of Investigation) forensic technicians walked out of their facility at, apparently, a bad time. OOPS! <u>Unknowingly,</u> they had stumbled right into the middle of a much-publicized "extreme training exercise." Guns were blazing, as the women ran for cover, and the handguns evidently got unloaded in their direction. As you can imagine, the "you know what" hit the fan, full throttle. GREAT LEARNING EXPERIENCE. (and great fun).

During the daring daylight robbery of Building #5 Bank, two pencil-necked cadets had been taken hostage. The whole gang (6 robbers + 2 hostages) holed up in an old sharecropper's shotgun shack behind the driving track. All the SHP Headquarters Brass from The Archdale Building (the Ivory Tower) showed up to witness these spectacles, and got ringside seats. Soon to arrive at "the hostage incident, the "cavalry" of pursuing cadets (6 Black and Silver patrol cars full), loaded with adrenaline pumping cadets, surrounded the entire seedy, weedy site. One member of the posse entourage, Cadet Lewis, a good ol' boy from Franklin in Macon County colloquially told our Major Robert Barefoot, "Major, if you will just let me go git my squirrel rifle, I'll come back here and kill ever' one of them son of a bitches."

Well, as an "Evaluator" for the exercise, Trooper Mike McArthur, had unlimited access to the shack, and smuggled secret intel inside to "my" cadets. You knew I would, didn't you? Anyway, red-headed Brenda, one of the two cadet hostages was a petite female, that everybody really liked (DO NOT mess with Brenda!!!). When I went inside the hideout, there was a sheet wadded up over in the corner. I checked it real close for "contaminants," and spread it out on the dusty wooden floor. I sketched the enlarged outline of a brassiere onto its white surface, took out my razor sharp "tactical" knife, and carved it out. Then, I found a 1" x 1" x 4' Bright Leaf Tobacco barn stick, tied the "flag" to it, and gave it to Gilchrist. He brazenly waved it out the hole in the broken panes, and yelled, "HEY, you S.O.B.s. We've got your little girl Trooper in here. Go ahead and shoot all you want." All the 78th Basic SHP cadets later autographed the "flag," and presented it to Major Bob Barefoot, the Director of all SHP Training.

Guess what happened when all those fun-loving, "sophisticated," "Gold Badges" – Captains, Majors, and Lieutenant Colonels spied that "flag." IMMEDIATELY they had to "intervene." If you think that that wasn't more fun than a barrel full of buzzed monkeys, you'd better think again. In the "wrap-up," old Macon County mountain boy yelled, "GIT BACK," "fired" one shot and "killed" the ringleader Michael Gilchrist, who got to sit on the bench for the remainder of the exercise. In preparation for his future brilliant career, he learned a lot about "sensitivity" and "intensity" during tactical operations. He also learned just how incredibly unpredictable, seemingly intelligent men can act when women are involved.

H U G E life lesson for everybody.

Michael J. McArthur

Michael J. McArthur

People's Bank Robbery and Billy Spruill Shooting

The Bank Robbery

Isn't it strange how nothing ever really "goes south," until you are in a position to least manage a viable response? Such was the case one hot Tuesday afternoon in "uptown" Edenton, North Carolina on June 1, 1976. The sun was shining, school children were at the marked crosswalks beside John A. Holmes High School, and People's Bank was being robbed.

That's right! The North Broad Street Branch of People's Bank and Trust Company was being robbed by two men with guns. They had "Big guns," to quote the tellers, "stuffed under his shirt." During "business as usual," for the fifth time that day, two men with masks over their faces, one with a handgun, entered the front door of the small brick building at 4:45 p.m.: quitting time. The taller and older man (32) walked directly to one of two surveillance cameras in the corners, holding a "Withdrawal" slip in his hand, and taped it over the camera lens. He then pulled a second gun, a Smith and Wesson, blued .38 Special revolver from his waistband underneath his open shirt tail, and handed it to the second robber.

The two tellers, Mearplene Peebles and Delois Fajer, had ducked down, and were hiding behind the countertop shelves. Little did they know that the older robber had already robbed several banks and shot bank tellers across the south, from Texas to Florida. He was a Georgia prison escapee for an armed robbery conviction, and had other robbery charges pending. The younger man, Asa Pike (22) jumped up onto the teller station like a real outlaw, and pointed his .38 revolver at the two women. He placed duct tape across both tellers' eyes and told them to, "Shut up!" By then, Delois had activated the hidden surveillance cameras with her foot, and the whole scenario was recorded, entry to exit. Mrs. Fajer bless her kind heart, after having safely retired as a bank teller in Brooklyn, New York, come back "home," got robbed and retired from People's Bank in Edenton. She then went to work part time at RBC-Centura. Wouldn't you know it: she got robbed for the second time on a Tuesday at the RBC bank behind McDonald's Restaurant, mid-day, during the lunchtime rush. Two crazed soldiers carrying M-16, fully automatic

Living Out Loud with Grace, Grit, and Gratitude

rifles entered the bank, hit Delois with the rifle, hit Carlton Perry with the butt of the rifle, cleaned out the vault, and got away clean!!

On that day in the People's Bank in 1976, the two robbers had been inside the bank <u>and filmed</u> on four previous occasions - THAT DAY! Then they went and sat on the curb across the street and waited for the perfect time to go into, and rob the bank. Also at that time, a very young man named Frank Halsey, Jr. entered the bank to make a deposit. He was hit in the neck and taken hostage. The younger robber filled a bag with money from the cash drawers, and the vault was never breached. There was more money in the register trays than the bag could hold. While stuffing the bag, tens and twenties fell onto the bank's floor. This made the man mad. He yelled for the other robber to come help him, but the decision was made to run.

The Chowan School's crossing guard had seen the two men enter the bank with their masks on. She had yelled for someone to, "Go get the Police." Guess what! They did!

About that time, the two men, wielding their handguns, released their hostages and exited the bank's front door, right in front of the Crossing Guard who screamed and ran into the high school parking lot. The two robbers went south on Broad Street, and then turned right onto West Peterson Street, dropping tens and twenties onto the sidewalk as they divvied up their loot. The young guy had given his .38 pistol back to his partner who had stuffed it into his waistband. There was a trail of money lying on the sidewalk and blown up under the bushes hours later.

Edenton Police Officer Billy Spruill (died from aneurysm on January 11, 2021) and off duty Police Officer Charlie "Chuck" Alexander (deceased) were "patrolling their beat in a military manner," when Police Dispatcher William A. "Bozie" Adams yelled into the console microphone: "Billy, People's Bank on North Broad Street has been robbed. Two "robbers." He didn't say, "112. 10-65 People's Bank, N. Broad Street. Two black males armed with handguns. One wearing a white T-shirt, and the other wearing a blue and white plaid button up shirt." Billy heard it, and got the message.

Billy and Chuck were only about a block away, and when they turned off Broad Street onto W. Peterson Street, they saw the money blowing in the wind, and saw two black males walking away from them toward the

Vine Oak Cemetery on Granville Street. At this point, there was no time to radio for help. It was Billy (six shot,.38 Special Revolver) and Chuck (unarmed) against two armed and dangerous brazen bank robbers.

What to do!? Billy rolled his marked patrol car to a stop beside the two men, and stepped out of his driver's door. The older robber, Otis Hobgood (32) shoved his bag and the money toward his partner, pulled both handguns from his waistband and began firing both guns at Billy. Chuck immediately departed the scene on foot, back toward the high school. Already hit by gunfire, Billy crouched down behind the protection of his patrol car, and low crawled/dragged himself toward the back of his patrol car. The shooter approached the front bumper of the car just as Billy raised up and shot three times through the back glass and windshield of the car at the robber. The robber ducked down and continued counterclockwise around the car. By now the two adversaries had completely circled the car, and the robber continued firing through the door panels at Billy. He shot Billy in the hip, and also shot Billy's Mace canister off his Sam Brown leather belt.

Billy bravely raised up and fired his weapon until it was empty. My good friend J. Robert Hendrix arrived on the scene with his S&W.38 Special, but was unsure of who was who UNTIL he saw Billy, bloody, lying on the asphalt, and the robber continuing to fire his Browning Hi-Power 9-millimeter through and through the vehicle. The robber ran toward the railroad tracks beside Albemarle Ford Company warehouse. Police Captain Harvey Williams (September 13, 1935 to August 7, 2014) screeched to a halt, and stepped out of his marked Patrol car parked nose to nose with Billy's. Immediately, a bullet grazed one of the trees beside Captain Williams, and he dove onto the pavement. As Hobgood fled, he shot back at Captain Williams, and Captain Williams fired one round at the fleeing robber. He missed, he thought. The robber vanished into a weeded field with four-foot-high broom straw and dog fennels throughout. Officer Jeff Knox with a shotgun out the window, and Sergeant Gussie Wayne Mizelle (June 20, 1940 to August 7, 2019) pulled up, jumped out and took cover, Jeff underneath the car. Three shots rang out! More pandemonium!

Back at Billy's Chevrolet, Robert Hendrix was tending to Billy who was bleeding profusely from his gunshot wounds. The contents of his canister of Mace aerosol had emptied into and onto the wounds and all over Billy's left side. The extreme burning sensation was affecting Billy, Robert, the firefighters, and the angel nurse in white, Mrs. Josephine Nixon (February 13, 1920 to December 25, 2006) who had stopped to help Billy. Edenton Fire Captains Hawk Crummey (November 24, 1932 to March 20, 2018) and Melvin Lane (October 5, 1937 to April 21, 2016) were squatted down holding pressure on Billy's wounds to stem the flow of bright red blood. Thank goodness that an ambulance arrived quickly, and the two Emergency Medical Technicians were able to somewhat neutralize the extreme chemical burns with medical saline solution from their "Go Bags." Billy was transported to Chowan Hospital where he was treated for gunshot wounds to both legs, despite the still lingering nauseous effects of the Mace spray. After months of surgeries and a prolonged recovery and rehabilitation, Billy was able to return to work. He didn't last long before the post-traumatic stress symptoms and pressure from his wonderful wife Peggy and daughters Amy and Melanie caused him to leave law enforcement for a more mundane, and better paying job with a fuel company. He later returned as the Chief Deputy, and retired from the Gates County Sheriff's Office in 2015.

The Cavalry Arrives

By now, there was a raucous commotion as "the cavalry" began to converge on the scene. Evidence, important evidence, was spread over three blocks: money, empty shell casings, witnesses, and more empty shell casings. Parts of Billy's leather goods were lying in the street. Two spent CS Tear Gas canisters were in the edge of the weed field. Blood was splattered on the side and inside the Patrol Car. Blood was smeared on the pavement. Spent Emergency Medical Technician (EMT) first-aid supplies were strewn throughout the crime scene. Diamond sized pieces of shattered General Motors Safety Glass were strewn up into the yards of houses, and all over the paved portion of West Peterson Street. Edenton Fire Chief Luther C. Parks (July 8, 1923 to February 2, 1997) and his men had taken the lead in preserving the crime scenes. They had Emergency Vehicles and uniformed Firefighters guarding the spectacular scenes with their lives. Police Sergeant Joe Norman took a squad (just like he did in the United States Marine Corps) and secured the perimeter. Everybody wanted to know about Billy. And Chuck, where was Chuck? And was he shot, too? Chuck had, in fact fled to several house porches in the neighborhood trying to get a weapon, but was unsuccessful. Everybody wanted to kill whoever had hurt Billy. Billy was a "Best Friend" to all of us. He never failed to stop and help anybody and everybody. And now he's gone! So sad.

I was "that new young Highway Patrolman, Mike McArthur with his beautiful wife, Becky." Becky and I had been married just about ten months on September 11, 1974, when Colonel E. W. Jones sent us to A-III, Edenton, N.C. My first thoughts: "Is that still in North Carolina?" Little did any of us know that our lives would be changed so dramatically just two years later. Billy Spruill was one of the first to come by our apartment at 309 North Broad Street to welcome us. Robert Allen and Ben Chappell were the other Highway Patrolmen stationed here in the Cradle of the Colony. Our daughter Jenny was born in January of 1976, and was asleep in her crib when the bank robbery shooting started. Becky and she were in for a sight as the robbery events unfolded just one block over.

I had overhead on the 39.24 frequency of my Channel Master Police Scanner that the bank had been robbed, and I got there while the gun smoke was still fresh and being compounded. Captain Williams was still crouched down behind the passenger side of his patrol car with his issued revolver trained on where he had just seen the shooter go down in the chest high weeds. The other, younger robber had vanished, but had kept the bag full of money, or what was left of it. The bag and some of the money were later recovered in one of Tom Shepard's ((March 16, 1925 to May 3, 2019) Warehouses over at Chowan Feed and Seed. Police Officer Louis Brothers was on the scene, and had a loaded, un-plugged old Remington on a Browning Patent Frame, 12-gauge semi-automatic shotgun trained on where his Captain had told him to "keep watch."

"CLICK"

As I drove my Black and Silver around the debris in the roadway, the robber raised up and fired twice at me and the rest of the officers in the street. Officer Brothers pulled the trigger on his shotgun, but had failed to load a 00-Buckshot into the chamber: **CLICK**! (one of the loudest noises that was heard that day!!) The robber ducked back down, now having performed a "recon" of sorts as to what was about to get turned loose on him. From heavy concealment, he fired twice more, and then once more, effectively keeping everybody pinned down behind their cars and other cover.

State Highway Patrol Trooper Raymond M. Potts arrived amid the cloud of chaos. He and I huddled behind one of my friend's houses, across the street from the weeds, and put a plan together to bring this thing to an end. We both had our SHP issued Ithaca Model 37, 12-gauge, pump shotguns loaded with five, #4 Buckshot. Our S&W Model 19, nickel plated, .357 Magnum revolvers would be our secondary weapons of attack. At that time in our careers, we had not been issued bullet proof, body armor. We could have used it to implement our plan more safely.

As time wore on, more officers from surrounding townships and State agencies arrived on the scene. Alcohol Law Enforcement (A.L.E.) officer Virgil Williams, amid gunfire, skidded his patrol car into Wiley Waters' Black and Silver patrol car. There was a HUGE amount of risk and danger in the air. "Incoming rounds always have the right of way!" according to SBI Special Agent Tony Cummings. Nobody was safe from gunfire had it erupted, because nobody knew where the shooter was. In a process to eliminate where the shooter was NOT, Trooper Potts and I spread out about thirty feet apart and entered the weed field. With our shotguns shouldered, safeties off, index fingers beside the trigger at the "ready to fire" position, we cautiously "slow-walked" into the thick cover.

There he was!

Lying on the ground just ahead of me lay a shirtless black male. Tens and twenties were lying on the ground at his feet. I am sorry to admit this, but I put a cussin' on him that would embarrass six Navy S.E.A.L.S. and the galley cook. He lay motionless. Again I yelled a string of obscenities at him. He lay motionless. Trooper Potts came over and we pounced on the shooter's bloody torso. He lay motionless.

Apparently, when confronted by "the cavalry" out on the street and all around his hideout, the shooter knew that his time was up. He had killed a police officer. He could not escape. He could not win a gun battle (after all, how many bullets did he still have left?) Now it came time to make some decisions:

1, Raise his hands, give himself up, and face the death penalty, or 2. Shoot it out, and run like H, or 3, Bring an end to his life.

He had chosen #3.

After having been abandoned by his fellow bank robber, lost the money, shot it out with two police officers, gotten shot in the leg, and finally reached a hiding place surrounded by 30+ people who were yelling that they were gonna kill him, the shooter took the coward's way out. He rolled onto his back, took that Browning Hi-Power (13+1), put the 9mm muzzle on the center of his chest, and pulled the trigger, TWICE. AND LIVED! Both bullets were embedded, side by side, about five inches into the soft ground below a massive hemorrhage of bright red blood. He was not shirtless, but the front was ripped open, and made it appear that he had removed his blue and white plaid shirt. That hole in the back of that shirt was impressive. An autopsy was later performed at the University of North Carolina Memorial Hospital in Chapel Hill, and the Medical Examiner ruled the death a suicide: two bullet holes through his chest and exiting his back, plus a self-inflicted bullet wound from his right temple and exiting the left side of his head. He had sparkling bits of diamond shaped General Motors Safety glass matted in his hair. He had on a pair of AT LEAST size 15 black and white, Converse All-Star Tennis shoes that were smeared with blood, resting on some of the bank's currency.

After having twice failed again in his miserable life, the hardened criminal now took the blood splattered Browning Hi-Power and placed the muzzle into his right ear. This time, when he pulled the trigger, his lights went out. The exit wound on the left side of his head was even more impressive than the exit wound on his back through that shirt. He had effectively changed his mind, from inside his skull to outside his skull. Trooper Potts and I made a quick assessment, and backed slowly away from the steam rising from the corpse. Now came the painstaking task of collecting the huge evidence inventory and recording what had transpired. That task belonged to the North Carolina SBI, Special Agent William (Bill) Godley. Why? It honestly appeared that a "police involved shooting" had occurred. And it had! Captain Harvey Williams had not missed. When firing at the fleeing suspect, he had, in fact, shot the robber through and through his right upper thigh. The robber had not flinched, thereby causing Captain Williams to think he had missed. On the range, Harvey Williams NEVER missed. This man, Otis Hobgood was an experienced, career criminal. His prison time in Georgia had turned him against the option of returning to "hard time."

When I returned to my Black and Silver, it was still running, and the air conditioning was a welcome relief. My Line Sergeant J. R. Deans approached me in my car, while another Sergeant approached Trooper Potts. We were quickly debriefed, and told to begin writing a painstakingly detailed narrative of what had transpired. A local well-meaning "individual" had related to our late-arriving Sergeants that, "Those two Highway Patrolmen went in that field and executed that poor man." Imagine that! Even back in 1976!!

Michael J. McArthur

GSR—Gun Shot Residue

Sergeant Deans had, in fact arrived at the scene of the corpse discovery in time to see the blue cloud of extreme profanity rise above the dog fennels. He asked whether the deceased had heard any of it, and I told him, "I sincerely doubt it." Sergeant Deans said, "Well the rest of Chowan County heard it." Stuff happens, Right? About a week later, our SHP Captain in Greenville, Carl Gilchrist gave Trooper Potts an opportunity to tell what happened on that fateful day. The Captain wondered why our hands had not been swabbed by the SBI for gunshot residue (GSR). Apparently, he too had heard that Ray and I had gone into the field earlier, and killed the robber. After intense de-briefing from the Captain, our independently produced narratives analyzed and corroborated, our weapons were returned to us. After having successfully dodged another bullet in more ways than one, we were freed to go and fight another day!

As the afternoon wore on, a small portion of the bank money was collected. The shell casings were cataloged, the blood was scraped and photographed, and the witnesses were interviewed. Billy's bullet riddled patrol car was hauled to the Police Department by Albemarle Ford Company's wrecker, driven by J. C. Stillman. Those of us who were still at the scene now became focused on where the other robber had gotten off to. Witnesses gave us the name of the younger robber, Asa Pike. He was the grandson of a local Baptist Church Minister. In New York, Pike had recently become involved with his cousin (now very recently deceased – like forty-five minutes ago) over selling marijuana. Apparently the two of them had hatched the scheme to rob Peoples Bank in broad daylight to finance their amateur pharmaceutical operation. The preacher's son had never handled a firearm, therefore the reluctance of his older cousin to trust him with that .38.

Bloodhounds were summoned from the North Carolina Department of Correction, Creswell Unit. Upon their arrival with two burley handlers, we figured that it was just a matter of time before we would get a chance to capture bank robber number two. Over behind one of the neighbor's houses, we heard what must have been a 12-gauge shotgun blast. Yep! Sure was! Where was that masked man? And he needs to know that we have guns, too! Anyway, those dogs were leashed onto 30-foot leather leads, and turned loose. They ran. They sniffed. They howled. They growled. They hunted. They doubled back. They "winded" a scent while winding their handlers. The handlers told us that, "The Department of Corrections (DOC) 'Rules' prescribed a 20-minute rest." "Let's let the dogs rest a spell." Yeah, right! To paraphrase the thug in the 1969 Classic movie, *Butch Cassidy and the Sundance Kid*: "Rules? There ain't no rules in a 'gun' fight." After a five minute "sit-down" we went back into the neighborhood where we received very little legitimate help or credible information. After all, Asa Pike was a preacher's grandson, and a local boy.

The "Porcupined" Patrol Car and Three Self-Inflicted Fatal Wounds

Back down at the waterfront, behind the Edenton Police Department, Billy's car had been thoroughly "gone over." There were probably fifteen 10-foot wooden dowel rods that had been threaded through each and every bullet hole by SBI Agent Godley, thereby tracking which holes had come from which direction, belonged to which bullet, and perhaps whose gun. Pictures of that "porcupined" car left an indelible scar on my memory.

The next day, Wednesday June 2, the preacher surrendered his grandson to the Edenton Police Department. Of course the young man was very polite, and very co-operative. His having been involved in a violent felony resulting in the death of a perpetrator, made him eligible for a capitol murder charge. As you are well aware, as a youthful offender with a clean record, he was allowed to plead to a lesser felony. He pulled some time up in Polk Youth Center on Blue Ridge Road in Raleigh, and he is now back in the community.

Edenton Police Sergeant Billy Spruill was released from Chowan Hospital the following Saturday, June 5, 1976. He underwent numerous surgeries over the next period of time, along with the associated rehabilitations. North Carolina's Attorney General, The Honorable Rufus

Edmisten came to Edenton and visited the local hero while in the Recovery room after one of his surgeries. Of course, Billy was humbled while thanking the community for having come to his rescue, and continuing their prayer ministry over him and his family.

My young wife, Becky, holding our 5-month-old daughter Jenny, had watched much of the activity through the kitchen window of our new second story apartment at 103 W. Carteret Street. Never a dull moment in the life of a North Carolina State Highway Patrolman, or his family either. We would go on to chase a recklessly driving doctor's son at 120+ mph, encounter a triple fatality - head-on crash on NC-32 at Christmastime, dodge deliberate vehicular assaults, field credible threats, and apprehend drunks and motorcycle marauders from the driver's seat of our 1973, 455cu. in., white over blue Buick Riviera. Like I said, never a dull moment.

More later!

Building a Better World at $6.00 Per Hour

NCSU and the Angel Farm

In 1970 I lived in Garner, NC, supposedly finishing up my last year at N C State University in the School of Forestry, Environmental Ecology. I worked for Davidson-Jones Construction Company and William C. Vick Construction Company. The owners were friends, and whichever company had jobs, we would work for that company. I worked as a Laborer ($6/hour), a Carpenter's Helper ($8 per hour), a Safety Engineer and Timekeeper ($10 per hour) for Tommy and Jimmy Vick, William C.'s brothers.

Beginning in about the month of March 1970, a fleet of Gregory Poole's Caterpillar Excavators, Earth Movers, Bull Dozers, and Euclid Dump Trucks carved a huge crater in the red clay, right in the middle of the North Carolina State University Campus between Reynolds Coliseum, Carmichael Gymnasium, Alexander Dormitory, and the Student Supply Store. We were the prime contractor, along with hundreds of subcontractors. We built the Banks C. Talley Student Union Center which has become the showpiece of the University. There were radius walls. There were half walls. There were concrete caves, solid glass enclosures. There were eight-foot ceilings. There were forty-foot ceilings. There were theaters. There were multiple elevator shafts. There were daunting geometric and architectural challenges (NCSU remember?) throughout the building.

Designated as a "Laborer," I did all the climbing, hauling, retrieving, pushing, pulling, toting, and whatever else that the too fat, hung-over, alcoholic, diabetic carpenters wouldn't/couldn't do. For weeks at the time, I rolled LARGE wheelbarrow loads of concrete from the thirteen-yard capacity trucks to the dump site at the end of a wooden twelve foot elevated, four-foot-wide, double railed, solidly built wooden bridge. All us "wheelbarrow jockeys" (8 – 10) had to make sure we didn't get too close to each other, or too close to the edge of the 100-foot bridge, because the 200-

Michael J. McArthur

pound wheelbarrow could easily tip and launch my 125-pound torso right over the edge. We were like ants: three loaded wheelbarrows going south, three empty wheelbarrows going north, one wheelbarrow loading, and one wheelbarrow dumping. This was dangerous as H. After we dumped the heavy concrete out of the wheelbarrow into the 12-inch wall cavity, Zeke would drop the 10-foot vibrator cable down the hole to evenly distribute the "mud" and not leave "honeycombing" when the oiled forms were removed. Inside these fifteen to thirty-foot-deep, forty-foot-long, twelve-inch-wide cavities which would transform into interior walls, were hundreds of miles of ½" steel "re-bar." These encrusted rods varied from 3/8ths inch to three inches in diameter, and were custom fabricated at the steel mill to strict specifications submitted by the architect, Clancey and Theys to ensure appropriate wall durability and strengths. Modifications and "innovations" were often crafted by ironworkers with steel, eight-inch wire spool "holsters" from which they could strip however many feet of wire they would need to "tie" the bars to one another. Most, but not all workers wore leather gloves to protect their scarred, muscular hands from the sharp points of the "tie-wire" which they skillfully, with lightning speed, "tied" all the steel together inside the forms. If right-handed, the holster was worn on their left hip, and a pair of Klein or Channel-Lock side cutter electrician's pliers cut and "wropped" in their right hand.

After about two weeks, I was "promoted" to a carpenter's helper. That also meant that I did all the climbing, hauling, retrieving, pushing, pulling, toting, and whatever else the too fat, hung-over, alcoholic, diabetic carpenters wouldn't/couldn't do. But I didn't have to roll concrete anymore. BUT when the daily concrete "pour" was in progress, each loaded truck had to have a "slump test" performed on its load. To perform the test, an open bottomed, upside down funnel like stainless steel conical tube (looked like a space capsule) was placed on a sheet of three-quarter inch plywood on the packed red clay beside the dual wheels near the truck's hydraulic chute. The driver/operator would carefully "chute" the apparatus level-full of concrete. I used a twenty-inch stainless-steel 10-millimeter rod to tamp <u>25 times</u> the concrete into the super full, topped off tube. Immediately I would lift the tube from the wet concrete, and the concrete would "slump" into a mound. I had to measure and record the EXACT height of the "slumped" concrete (four-inch slump was ideal) to ensure that the concrete about to be delivered was the correct "strength:"

not too "wet" and not too "stiff." Next, I got to fill and screed four, six-inch cardboard cylinders, tamp 25 times, and record the time, date, location, and shipment number on the side of the cylinder. They were placed under the tool shelter, and after 28 days, the "plugs" were shipped to Froehling & Robertson's testing laboratory to be compressed/busted apart. This was a strength test that required a rating of "sufficient," or the entire fabricated floor and/or wall had to be "torn out." It was VERY important that I did the slump test accurately, or a "bad" load of concrete could cost William C. Vick hundreds of thousands of dollars.

When not testing concrete, like on rainy days (there were a lot of them), I would help carpenter Rupert May "hang doors." Large "3-6" (36 inch) and "4-0" (40 inch) wide, oak-veneer doors probably weighed 50+ pounds. They came "backed" and "mortised" for hinges, but occasionally required slight modifications. "MAC," my father had bought for me an almost complete set of carpenter tools: Disston cross-cut handsaw, six Stanley wood chisels, True-Temper claw hammer (not big enough for framing rafters), Stanley hack-saw, box-cutter, screw drivers – tri-square – framing square, Crescent wrenches, Vice Grip pliers, Channel-Lock pliers, Klein Electrician's side-cutter pliers, four-foot Belkamp level, Craftsman standard socket set, Black Diamond cross-cut flat bastard milling file, Miller Falls 12-inch wood rasp, Keen-Kutter hatchet, Yankee Push Drill, Lufkin "Red-End" folding 6-foot rule, and a Wilson Hardware Nail Apron. That weekend while home at The Tobacco Trail Motel in Wilson, in preparation for this new job, I went over to Westwood housing subdivision off Raleigh Road, and went in the scrap lumber pile of a house under construction. There I found four 1" x 8" planks, long enough to build a top-hinged toolbox with a slit in the top to accommodate the short end of the Framing Square sticking straight up.

I used those wood chisels (still do), to custom fit those EXPENSIVE doors, and was accountable enough to be trusted to do them right. Do you know what a "sling psychrometer" is? It is a hand-held instrument that measures relative humidity and dew point in a given location, like the offices and classrooms under construction in the Student Union Center. It was critically important that the humidity level from rain or snow did not cause those doors to "warp," thereby causing them to be replaced. I would walk into an appointed area, take out the sling psychrometer, moisten one of two thermometers, sling the thing around for thirty revolutions, and then read the relative humidity. Not once in about a year did I find an unsuitable reading of relative humidity.

Those very doors were sent "unfinished," to be installed and then to be "clear coated." Thompson and Thompson, the painting contractor that won the bidding process, submitted a bid of about two-thirds that of his competitors. Turns out that he had counted the doors, determined the square footage, and figured how much finish he would have to purchase and apply. He forgot to multiply his square footage by two: <u>both sides of hundreds of doors</u>. William C. Vick kindly accommodated his error, and still got an excellent job for a fair price.

Out of the "Field" and into the "Office"

As a junior at N C State, evidently that imposed upon me the apparent ability to do accurate paperwork, and I even got a raise. After a while, leaving the red mud and concrete, I became the timekeeper and worked out of the office trailer up beside Alexander Dormitory and behind the Student Supply Store where drop-dead beautiful Hazel Stancil worked as a cashier. All the guys loved Hazel. She was a dark haired, tan, farm wife from Smithfield, and her daddy was a member of The Royal Knights of the Ku Klux Klan. She always had a great big smile, and country ham-sweet potato biscuits under a red-checked hand towel in a woven rush basket on a shelf under her register.

Those with Whom We Work

On the jobsite, first thing every morning I called the roll, and determined who was (or wasn't) present, and gave to each his (only males) numbered, round badge. I clocked them in and clocked them out at the end of the day or whenever they left. If they needed a new hardhat, I had 'em. If they needed a loan, I had a small "petty cash box" from which I could loan them $10 that had to be repaid the next day at 7:00am or they would be sent home. Delmo Ballance gave me a $20 bill and unsuccessfully asked me to show that he had worked on a day when he hadn't. He was the Job Foreman, and was responsible for duty stations and assignments. Great guy that everybody liked, but had a serious "dranking" problem. He came in one morning and went over to the equipment shelter and got Edsel to pour about two inches of gasoline into a cardboard Dixie cup. Edsel only had one eye, and was deathly afraid of snakes: big ones, little ones, live ones, dead ones, and even the rubber ones that we would slide under his door, thereby not letting him easily exit, BUT HE DID! Great fun. Delmo went around back by the LULL (front end loader), and poured this gasoline upon his genitals. Apparently, he was more scared of his condition than the resultant extreme burning sensation. Can you imagine? He told Tommy Vick that, "Well, it worked last time." Do tell!!!

Our jobsite was an absolute beehive of activity: sheet rockers, Watson Electric electricians One of them my friend Tommy Goard), plumbers, brick masons, concrete trucks, glass installation crews, painters, inspectors, engineers, N C State faculty, iron workers (bad animals), front end loaders, back hoes, insulation deliveries, and the list goes on. I learned a lot: how to "tie" steel re-bar, how to "oil" concrete forms, how to build scaffolding, how to mix mortar, how to pull wire, how to bend conduit, how to solder copper, how to back-plane doors, how to document progress from the vantage point above all that was happening after walking twelve-inch I-beams at eighty-nine feet elevation to get there, how to get out of the way, how to stay out of the way, when to be quiet, when to give assistance, and most importantly how to get along with "inconsistent" people on their level, in an unfamiliar and many times "edgy" (understatement) work environment.

Learning Things the Hard Way

One hot afternoon, when a flat-bed semi-trailer of Sanford Bricks rolled onto the site, I went out and showed the grizzled, bearded driver where that particular load was to be dropped. I volunteered to go get the LULL front end loader to "off-load" the pallets of bricks. I am not real sure what he said, but it was something like, "You stupid, SOB. Get the H out of my way!" I did so, quickly. His mechanically equipped, remote controlled robot put that entire load of bricks on the ground in about ten minutes, and his "Big Red" Mack Truck left me in a cloud of red dust, licking my wounds. But I had learned something new.

Many times, deliveries of forty-inch wide, 80-foot-long steel I-beams would be delivered with Raleigh Police escort after 5:00 p.m., sometimes at midnight, to avoid rush-hour traffic. That meant that I got to stay overtime, unlock the gates, and watch the physics unfold. Our "contracted," highly skilled, T-shaped "Tower Construction Crane" operators "lived" up there in those cabins at the top of the T. Those guys could manipulate those cabled hooks, and untie your bootlaces with their hydraulics and mechanical engineering prowess. They teamed with their ground "engineer" who both radioed and gave hand signals for the deployment of their loads. For some reason, occasionally those 40-inch-wide beams sported barefooted young women wearing pink hard hats and "Daisy Dukes," "walking" atop those air-lifted beams. This was for show, I think, because I never really understood why else she would have been up there. She came along with the "pop-eyed" truck driver, and he along with the rest of us watched her like a hawk (with good reason). His strategy was for her to assist with beam placement by walking her 90-pound self out to the "high-end" of the beam to "level it off" for placement on the ten-inch Oak ground timbers. 90 pounds? Somehow, it actually did make a difference. For whatever reasons, we all appreciated her "efforts."

After those beams were strategically placed upon their Oak beam spacers, they had to be numbered according to date, and specific installation site. All the auditorium beams went alongside Alexander Dormitory. All the bowling alley beams went parallel to the Student Supply Store fence, and so on. Mechanical Engineers flew in from Omaha, Nebraska and performed "X-RAYS" on the eye-apparent cracks along the surfaces. Sure enough, there were fatal flaws. Back to Peden Steel in Garner they went. The next shipment also had what appeared to be streaks of small cracks. These superficial cracks were only cosmetic in nature, but they needed repair (grinding out, and welded over). We contacted Mike Brakefield and James McLaughlin over at Contractors' Supply in Cary, North Carolina, and they shipped to us six brand new "man sized," handheld electric grinders. Grinding out cracks and overtime were in my immediate future. Peden Steel was paying the bill on this, and they were paying $20 per hour (the company only paid us $18 per hour). William C. got his "finder's fee," I reckon.

This work started at daybreak and ran all day. Saturday morning came, and all we "grinders" met at the now defunct Finch's Family Restaurant at 401 W. Peace Street, almost underneath Raleigh's Capitol Boulevard Bridge. Future Attorney General Rufus Edmisten and several high-powered Democrats were all in there preparing for their chores in the North Carolina General Assembly a few blocks south. That afternoon, as I was listening to WKIX, 85 a.m., Raleigh's Top Disc Jockey Pat Patterson was spinning his colloquial yarns as usual. This day he launched into the esteemed Representatives and Senators over at the Legislative Building on Jones Street. He allowed that, while washing his hands in the men's bathroom, two legislators came in. Uncharacteristically tactfully, he said that as he observed them in action: he had finally found a Legislator who knew what he was doing!! Big, canned laughter. Pat died a few years ago (January 02, 1936 – January 15, 2017) as did News and Observer Columnist Dennis Rogers (1942 - August 08, 2020: both will be highly missed.

Grinding Steel and the Co-eds

Our bunch of rag-tag, redneck, vagabonds told a few lies, we drank our coffee, ate our country ham, scrambled eggs, grits, and cheese biscuits, gathered our strength, and went over to the NCSU Student Union jobsite. We tried to work until zero dark thirty, but Virginia Wilkinson, Candy Peachy, and the crybabies over in Alexander dorm couldn't hear their Lynard Skynard and Rolling Stones over the roar of the huge generators and those screaming machines. The grinders' rooster tails and spiraling sparks lit up the night, and were an impressive display of awesome harnessed power, "turnt loose." After that one long day, I determined that that job was best left to those fearless, full grown, beer gutted country boys. I was whooped.

During the day when I wasn't doing time sheets or "slumping" concrete, I was the designated "Safety Engineer." That meant that I would venture out onto the massive jobsite in search of laborers not wearing their hardhats, unanchored scaffolding, dangling lines, protruding nails, or inadequate walkway railings. Ropes or cables stretched across sidewalks and corridors were always a problem. Loose lumber, trash, and tools were always underfoot. We didn't worry so much about OSHA inspectors as we did about somebody getting hurt, and then mad, and then assaulted, and then prosecuted, and then fired. Water in the alcoves was unhealthy and slick. Unauthorized "visitors," particularly female visitors would bring termination, but a lot of those good 'ol boys really didn't seem to care.

Every day, outside the jobsite along the 8-foot perimeter fence, the sometimes scantily clad female students suffered a barrage of "compliments." It became a spectator sport to watch and laugh at the exchanges between the rednecks and the street-savvy co-eds. Whatever went out from inside the fence, usually was launched back even hotter and more precise, "in language a child could understand." I really think that some of those girls could hold their own, whether in a heated exchange or a knock down drag out!

The Angel Farm and the .22 Caliber Rifle Gunfights

Speaking of co-eds, William C. Vick's 20-year-old daughter was a sophomore, and Class President over at Meredith College on Hillsborough Street. Our company got the job of remodeling the stage area of Jones Auditorium with new lighting, seating, sound acoustics, and curtains. We had to unbolt from the floor at least 300 cushioned chairs, and either break or grind off the quarter-inch threaded mounting posts. As I used one hammer's claw on the post, I hit that face with the face of another hammer. These two highly tempered steel surfaces striking each other at high speed caused a $1/8^{th}$ inch chip of steel to fly deep into my left forearm. Off to the medical tent, and a surgical removal by a rough old, retired World War II Marine Corps nurse – solid as a rock. It took her all of three minutes to scalpel that steel out, and she was back to watching, "The Young and the Restless." I did something similar about two years later over at The Cineplex Movie Theater at North Hills Mall, and the piece of steel is still inside my left thumb. From my perch atop the N C State Student Union, I could read show times and what movies were playing as shown on the Cineplex movie marquee through the lens of my Northern Tool "optical transit level" on a tripod used for leveling the steel beams.

Next, we had to suspend acoustic tile and "baffles" from the auditorium ceiling on 3/8th inch threaded rods. In order to correctly angle all those 4' by 8' panels, I had to buy two 7/16th inch Snap-On chrome ratchet wrenches to advance all those 7/16th nuts, seventeen and a half inches above the end of the inverted protruding black painted rods.

Construction sites are full of opportunities for somebody to get hurt or killed. Luther Heard was a consummate "concrete finisher." He had his customized five-gallon bucket in which he carried an assortment of finishing tools: cold chisels to gouge out imperfections, brick trowels to mix and smooth repairs, brushes with which to sling water onto his surfaces, and abrasive stones to use with elbow grease when grinding off raised irregularities. Occasionally his hand-held, brick-sized grinding stone would become grooved or pitted. Much to the chagrin of our bosses, he was found to take his super-hard stone over to the brick masons. They would use the $600.00, twelve-inch diamond carbide blade on the circular brick saw and "resurface" the face of his stone. Doing this would take off about half of the blade's diamond matrix at the same time. Bad for business.

Luther was always one to help anybody. One late afternoon, he held a 2"x 4" against a steel beam and used the "RAMSET" to "nail it" 60" above the floor. The RAMSET is a pistol that uses red (light weight), yellow (medium weight), or purple (heavy-weight) .22 caliber blank cartridges to propel the inserted 3", case hardened pin through the stock (2"x 4") into the base (steel I-beam). Training taught us that the RAMSET had to be held exactly perpendicular to the stock so as to prevent "ricochets" and errant pins flying through the air like crooked bullets. Luther loaded the gun with a purple load and a collared 3" pin, placed the 2"x4" against the steel, activated the RAMSET by pushing it tightly against the wood, and pulled the trigger. That 3" pin went into the 2"x4", struck a knot in the board, angled off, scratched against the steel, and came right back out and into Luther's stomach, lodging in his kidney.

Luther was out of work for about two months, but came back, strong as ever. It is hard to keep a good man down, but easy to put a worthless man down. And we had some worthless men on the site. They would come in to work drunk, riding with their cousin, intentionally fall down and twist their knee, and have to visit the site nurse. She was hard as nails, but understood the civil liability of returning a supposedly "injured," low-life, brain-dead, slacker to full duty.

Holidays always spilled over into the following Monday morning, "no shows." Word would reach us that one or more men had gotten into a fistfight or gotten cut over their "babes" or bootleg liquor, or both. It was not uncommon for Wake or Johnston County Deputy Sheriffs to arrive at our office trailer, wanting to "speak with" one of our workers. Word traveled quickly throughout the jobsite that "Five-O" was "up front." More than one of our workers were known to climb the fence or hide in trucks to escape capture. Many times, the worker was led away in handcuffs. He was fully aware of what he had done, but we could only guess.

Usually one or more workers had wrecked his car over the weekend, the brakes had "locked up," the wheel had run off, or their bride had run off with their "ride." Since most workers lived in family-based communities (Flowers Hill – as in Percy Flowers, Crocker's Nub, Stancil's Chapel), usually family came to their rescue. It was "ups and downs," "ins and outs," and "arounds and abouts." Always a "you won't believe this," preceded the explanation of whatever calamity had befallen them: there was never a dull moment, and it was never their fault.

Calhoun Garrett and his cousin Jimmy played Cowboys and Indians on the Bright Leaf Tobacco farm with .22 caliber rifles: not trying to hit one another, but to see how close they could come with bullet placement. The barber who cut my hair the morning I married Becky was one of the cousins, and usually participated as an Indian in these "range wars." The hay lofts and tobacco barns all had bullet holes. The wagons and tobacco "sleds" all had bullet holes. And my barber's daddy's '55 black Chevrolet Bel Air had a bullet hole in the trunk lid, right beside the keyhole. These Garrett boys were cousins of the Daughtry boys, one of whom made the ill-fated pass at Bill Ellis's (Bill's Barbecue) sister Jenny, and ended up getting shot by Bill and his M-1, .30 caliber carbine.

Meanwhile, back at the Angel Farm, the next assignment we got was to remove two dozen banks of colored lighting for replacement by another subcontractor. Surprise, surprise! All those 4-inch round blue light lenses fit right into the grille of every one of my patrol cars for the next sixteen years.

Before we left Meredith College, the guys called it, "The Angel Farm," we got the contract to build eight dormitory rooms down the center of the attic of one of the all-girl residence halls, Heilman Hall.

As you can well imagine, there were some "good ol' boys" who were not allowed to even set foot upon that hallowed ground. They were uncontrollable, and we needed to keep the job: not lose it because of rowdy rednecks.

One hot afternoon about two o'clock, Foreman Calhoun Garrett stormed up there and called us all to go to the parking lot. Calhoun came from Crocker's Nub in Johnston County. He had grown up on Flower's Hill near Stancil's Chappell, and reportedly was one of Percy Flowers' liquor still operators. His cousin, who allegedly drove hotrod Lincoln's laden with "stump hole," moonshine, bootleg liquor up to Baltimore, cut my hair at Man-Mur Barbershop on Hillsborough Street the morning I married Becky, November 10, 1973.

We reminisced about the good ol' days of dove hunts, Daisy long-pump BB guns, pickin' cotton by hand, stealin' watermelons, and "priming" tobacco with sand lugs and mules. He and several of his cousins played cowboys and Indians with .22 rifles – not to hit but come close to hitting one another with "rifle balls."

Bill Ellis's Barbecue, "Miss Wilson," and Gunfire

Late one night at world famous Bill's Barbecue over on Lovers' Lane when it was still a deeply furrowed dirt road, one of the Daughtry cousins put the make on Bill Ellis' sister, Jenny. Upon the rebuff, the Lochinvar called "Miss Wilson" a witch with a capital B. Then he made the nearly fatal mistake: he told Bill, "I'll come back tonight and burn this GD place to the ground."

Well Bill did not take kindly to that little remark. Bill had a white cinder-block smoke shack out back of the restaurant in which he cooked his barbecue and Brunswick Stew. Later that night Bill loaded his .30 caliber, Singer made M-1 Carbine, finished off a pint of Southern Comfort rotgut, and went to "cookin'" in the smoke shack.

It wasn't ten minutes before here came four of the Daughtry brothers, driving a white '62 Plymouth Valiant. They "cruised" around the restaurant just like we all did earlier in the evening. On the next loop, as they slowly came to a stop in front of the smoke shack, someone inside the vehicle, mistakenly I am sure, flicked a Zippo cigarette lighter for some unknown reason. I know it was a Zippo because I found it (still got it) just after the melee.

Bill vaulted through the door into the driveway, dropped down on one knee, and emptied the 15-round magazine into the now vacating motor vehicle.

He shot two of the four inside. Didn't kill nary a one.

They went about three miles over to the Wilson Memorial Hospital on Tarboro Street. A friend of mine was an Army Medic retired and working as a male nurse in the Emergency Room. He later told me a lot of things about that night: one of the shooting victims had already dug one of the .30 slugs out of his arm; the other shot brother was already planning retaliation; one of the uninjured was still hiding out in the Valiant; and the fourth brother was crying like a little girl.

During the commotion and the bloodletting, the medical staff called the Wilson County Sheriff's Office. Soon to be incarcerated for gross incompetence and corruption, Sheriff Robin Pridgen came out and investigated. He later praised Bill for not allowing himself to get, "kilt by that Johnston County trash."

Allegedly, Calhoun later broke into my house up on Old Wake Forest Road and stole a 20-gauge double barrel, Spanish made shotgun and a

Remington 742 BDL .30-'06 scoped rifle. The shotgun has never been recovered. The rifle was recovered twenty-two years later at "Po Jack's" Bear hunting camp / liquor still operation in Pantego during a BATF, U S Marshall, DEA, Drug Interdiction Raid. It was loaded, hanging on a cotton picker spindle just inside the kicked in back door. When I went down to Beaufort County Sheriff's Office to recover my rifle, I found it different from when I had had it. Now it had a brand new Tasco 3x to 9x variable scope on it, and the bolt mechanism was completely worn out to the extent that it now rattles when I shake it.

Anyway, back to the Angel Farm. The way he stormed into the attic, we figured Calhoun was gonna fire every last one of us. We all knew everything that we had done, but we didn't know what Calhoun knew we had done. Turns out Rupert May had gotten a complaint on himself turned in to the Chancellor. He had used "ugly words" while digging a trench across the gravel roadway beside the Wainwright Music Building. Rupert's version of what he said: "The handle broke out of my shovel." Calhoun tried to tell the Chancellor that his men were known for "calling a spade a spade." The Chancellor snapped that that was NOT what Senator Tony Rand's daughter had heard: "This GD, MF shovel ain't worth a _____." Rupert immediately earned the distinct privilege to go over to Mr. Vicks house in North Hills to sandblast all the oily soot out from under the whole interior of his basement where the oil furnace had caught fire, scorched all the subflooring and joists, and blown out four windows.

Roof Jobs, Bad Brakes, and a Slipping Clutch

Occasionally we had to resort to unconventional methods to get the job done. The Garner Baptist Church roof pitch is about a 12/12 which equates to a 45-degree slope. In addition to being unwalkable, the rain gutters are least thirty feet above the ground. There were at least twelve flaps of slate gray Certainteed Architectural style shingles that had been blown off the roof leaving a patchwork of black splotches. Jimmy Corbett was the chairman of the board of deacons, and told Mr. Vick, "We can't have that. Please send someone over to fix it before Sunday morning services." This was Wednesday afternoon. I was one of the few employees who had a valid driver's license, so here I go in the company tool truck with Rupert May, over to Garner Baptist Church to see what had to be done.

That Company Truck was a Two Ton International dump truck and always was half loaded with wheelbarrows, scaffolding, trash, and 2"x 6" concrete form boards. Those 2"x 6" form boards usually stuck off the back by about five feet. That meant they needed red warning flags tied to them. Did we have flags? Nope. We stopped at Krispy Kreme, got a dozen doughnuts, and I tied a gallon milk jug to the end of the longest scaffold board. Here we went on Peace Street, under Capitol Boulevard, and up the hill toward Glenwood Avenue. Are you familiar with the steep grade on westbound Peace Street at the stoplight on Glenwood Avenue? Good GRIEF. Here I was, trying to drive a straight shift, worn out dump truck with a slipping clutch. When I stopped on that 30-degree slope with my left foot on the clutch and my right foot on the brake, my next thought was, "How am I gonna get my foot OFF the brake and onto the gas pedal while popping the clutch and not roll backward onto the hood of that MG Midget right on my back bumper?" It was not a pretty sight! I activated the emergency flashers, levered the parking brake, and shifted into neutral. I raced the motor which caused black smoke to envelope the MG. She got the message. She backed up and drove to the left around me, head on into traffic, across the centerline. I think she did that so that she could adequately flip me the bird while squalling tires past me. Rupert got out with his coat in his hand, waved traffic to a halt, and I popped the clutch, lurched through the intersection, and veered left onto Glenwood. Wouldn't you know it! One of the cross-braces for the scaffold bucks slid right off that steel bed, missed a motorcycle, and skidded onto the pavement (thank goodness). Rupert grabbed it, raced after me, threw the brace into the truck, jumped in, and off to Garner Baptist Church we went.

Turns out the church had four unopened packs of Certainteed, Architectural slate gray shingles left over from the original roofing job just three years earlier. Preacher Bob Thomas, and the Chairman of the Maintenance and Grounds Committee Jimmy Crakorn met us in the parking lot, showed us the damage, and pointed to their equipment shelter where a 40-foot aluminum extension ladder was mounted on the back wall. Do you know how heavy that ladder was? It was a Commercial grade roped ladder, so it was plenty heavy.

Rupert put on his leather tool belt, grabbed a caulking gun with a cylinder of black roofing tar, and slung five shingles over his shoulder with a 30-foot length of half inch nylon rope. When asked, he told me he had his granddaddy's hawkbill knife in the torn bib of his overalls. Think about that! Have you put it together yet?

After manhandling that ladder, and slamming it against the shingled roofline near the gable end, up it we went. Rupert tied the rope around his waist through his belt loops, and so did I. He topped the ladder, low/slow crawled up the east side of the roof, over the peak, and down the west side to the first patch job. You know what I did, right? I anchored him with a taut rope from the east side. Well, you know his knife had to get loose, and it slid down the roof, right into the gutter. You also know that he needed a knife to cut the plastic end off the caulking tube and to cut the shingles. I threw my Browning pocketknife that my brother Pat had given me for Christmas onto the west side of the roof, and it slid down right into Rupert's hands. He had to cut almost all of the plastic snout off the caulking tube because he did not have a nail long enough to puncture the freshness seal at the bottom. Now all scratched up, my new knife was next used to slice tabs off the new shingles to be nailed and stuck onto the darkened splotches.

Job well done! NOPE! Not quite. Now I had to advance up the east side toward the peak of the roof, so that Rupert could scoot down the west side and retrieve his granddaddy's knife. Guess what. The rope wasn't long enough. Was I gonna crest that peak and lower Rupert to the gutter? Not a chance. Besides, the wind was picking up. I maintained rigid surveillance on my side of the roof. Rupert threw his caulking gun and hammer and spare shingles to the ground, and low crawled up the west side and down the east side of the roof. We wisely untied from each other, and down the ladder we went. Now we had to manhandle that two-ton ladder to the west side, and carefully lean it against the gutter. The angle of the ladder against that gutter had to be minimized so as not to crush the rim against the facia. Did I mention the wind? I chocked the ladder. Rupert went up and got his knife. Down he came. We put that ladder back under the shelter, got back into the truck, and swore that we would quit before we ever did that little trick again. But wouldn't you know it? We had almost the same assignment about five months later but on a much smaller scale, and less slanted roof. A corner grocery store on Oberlin Road behind Cameron Village Shopping Center had sustained tree damage, and needed shingles replaced. We did that one on a Saturday morning so we could get time and a half pay.

Crabtree Valley Mall and "Juaquin"

Over on my other job with Davidson and Jones Construction Company, I found myself in the company of more commercial quality building projects. With these projects came a more experienced and accountable work force. The superintendents were usually N C State engineers, with assistants who managed the work force. They instilled in their employees a certain level of pride in their product which was a breath of fresh air for me.

On the jobsite we were required to conform with OSHA guidelines or be fired on the spot. We all had color-coded hardhats so that everyone knew what we were supposed to be doing and/or where we were supposed to be working. My hat was blue (driver's license, tools), and I still have it. Labor Unions were becoming an issue, and there was really no middle ground: you were either "in" or "out." You were either "for" or "against." The "group" within which I worked was "against," unionization, which meant that we were the "favorite sons," of the company. We were afforded more flexibility and favor when it came to decisions concerning days off, vacations, work assignments, etc.

Many of the pro Union guys carried .25 caliber, "Star" chrome-plated, ivory-gripped, semiautomatic pistols in the bibs of their Blue Bell overalls, and in the glove box of their Buicks (of course management didn't know that). Everybody did not have pick-up trucks, but there was usually an arsenal behind the seats, or sometimes hanging on plasticized black hooks bolted above and below (but visible) through the back window. Usually a scoped Remington 742, 30-06 rifle and a Browning A-5, 12-gauge shotgun hung visible, while a Stevens sawed off 12-gauge double barrel shotgun and a length of "tow" rope hung on the back of the front seat. Usually a knife of some sort was somewhere "close at hand." You think I am joking, don't you!

My job title was "Carpenter's Helper." I had my own tools, and some education, and a driver's license. My experience was greater than most from my history with "MAC" at the Tobacco Trail Motel, Henry at Parker's Barbecue, and Tommy at William C. Vick Construction Company. My salary started out at $12 per hour, and was higher than most others. My main partner was a 30-year-old carpenter named Joaquin (WHA-kin). He was a German immigrant who had been a stowaway on a freighter from England just a couple of years earlier. He was fighting to get his "Green Card," and was all about doing things right so as not to raise any red flags. He spoke broken English, but his skills were immaculate when it came to precision craftsmanship. We were assigned to construct the "radius" china display walls that continue to this day within Hudson Belk at Crabtree Valley Mall on Glenwood Avenue in Raleigh, NC. The Mall was built beside, over, and around Crabtree Creek, which rose to 10-foot flood levels during torrential rains from hurricanes, or Saturday afternoon summer thunderstorms. For that reason, we left little on the ground floor that could be stolen or damaged by the hooligans or the contaminated floodwaters.

Joaquin became known to most of us as "James" so that he would blend in, and be less noticeable as "different" from the rest of the crew. We had some structural steel framing to do which exceeded my skill set, but not ol' Joaquin's. He sent me to see Braxton the quartermaster, to fetch three twelve-foot pieces of 2-inch angle iron. When I returned, he told me to take the oxy-acetylene cutting torch, and cut them into 19-inch segments. Well, I did not know how to do that, and it was lunch time. During lunch, he taught me how to light the torch, fine tune the flame, and maximize the heat by tilting the angle of the tip into the stock to more quickly "cut it." The welding goggles dimmed the available light, but allowed me to maintain a visual on the prescribed cut. That was a lot to learn, but also a lot of fun. Unlike Joaquin, I did not have a pencil shaped soapstone marker to indicate where to cut. He sent me over to the freight elevator where several broken pieces of ¾ inch sheetrock were piled up. I broke off quarter sized pieces and put them in my nail apron. When sharpened on a cinderblock, the white sheetrock mark was not only visible during the cut, but would not burn off.

Joaquin had asthma, and would occasionally get sidetracked by his breathing apparatus. At this point he was welding those 19-inch angles at 24-inch intervals to the main beams. He told me to finish welding them, but I didn't know how to do that either. Again, during lunch, he showed me how to insert the #4 rod into the Hobart electrodes attached to the 50-foot Lincoln electric welding leads. Despite extensive security measures, one or more of those copper "leads" got stolen about every month or so. Supposedly, folks burned off the insulation and sold the copper. A friend of mine had heavy duty battery jumper cables fabricated from welding leads. Even on the coldest day and the most completely dead battery, they could effectively jumpstart a vehicle when others would not.

I had never been around a welder nor welded anything. Joaquin showed me how to "ground" the I-beam, place the tip of the welding rod near the spot to be welded, nod-drop the welding shield over my face, and slowly "burn" the weld. After work that day I practiced welding (running a bead) along the "short ends" that were to be re-cycled. Naturally I burned pocks in all my clothing from the hot molten steel "popping off" the weld because I let air get trapped between the pieces. After much practice, Joaquin let me weld the 19-inch cross bars along the top of the suspended frame. At five-foot-five inches, Joaquin was a little "height challenged." These last welds were just a touch too high for him to reach. By standing on my toes, I could reach the weld. I was wearing worn out tan Sears and Roebuck construction brogans with the soles "duct-taped" on. While on my toes, my pantleg rose above the tongue of the open topped brogan, and naturally you know what happened. A piece of red-hot slag fell from the weld, right down into the open top of my brogan. Naturally I stepped down thereby pressing and retaining the heat from that scalding steel as it burned a half-inch crater into the front of my ankle. It self-cauterized, and never bled. DID IT HURT? A LOT! Big scar to this day!

The Methodist Orphanage and "The Car with No Top"

Great Kids and Great Fun

Over the period of several months, Joaquin would be absent, and I would be pulled over to other jobsites. Over on Glenwood Avenue was the Methodist Orphanage, established in 1899 to serve parentless children in the Piedmont. Many of these children were handicapped, hearing impaired, blind, or challenged in one form or another. They were housed, fed, and schooled, all right there on the beautifully landscaped parklike campus. Each residence hall had its own house mother or father. These poor but bright, humble children had a lot going for them that they had never had before. They had friends, food, clothing, encouragement, guidance, and most importantly Christian love. They were SO thankful for anything that was done for them, and they didn't mind asking. They all had jobs: washing clothes, cooking meals, cleaning house, painting walls, tutoring smaller children, mentoring, and lawn maintenance.

My assignment was to go to each residence hall and classroom building to determine what needed to be repaired, replaced, or removed. Wiring was the most common disorder, while broken glass, leaking plumbing, and "scrubbing" doors were contenders. It was extremely cold that time of year, and the warmth of those coal fired furnaces was welcome. My G I Joe's Army Surplus olive drab field jacket didn't quite cut the cold when outside for extended periods of time. Mid-afternoon I found the laundry building was equally warm from the furnaces and ironing facilities. Some of the bedrooms had 6 to 10 quilts on each bed. During the winter, drafts from broken windows presented many problems. Blowing snow and ice accumulated inside the attics and bedrooms, and filtered down through cracks in the wallboard.

After delivering my lengthy list of needed electrical, plumbing, heating, cooling, and structural repairs, I took the liberty to document each house or building's glass repair needs. I had replaced many, many broken windows in my life – some mine, some others'. The window molding, the push pins, the glazing, all of this was not only needed, but workable.

I got Rupert May over there, and it became our mission to measure, remove, and replace all broken panes in all structures. Rupert was one of too few cohorts who could dependably find nineteen inches and 11/16ths on my 35-foot Lufkin tape measure. Just inside most of the broken windows were golf-ball sized granite rocks, not from the paved roadway, but from the parking spots alongside almost every building. Over in the laundry building, where it was nice and warm, were wooden crates of 2-foot by 3-foot panels of new 1/8th inch thick window-pane glass. Also, there were dry-rotted cardboard cases of nearly dried up window glaze under the century old, four-foot-high, slope topped glass cutting table. The framing square and the tools were vintage in nature but priceless in value. The broken-off Red Devil, wheeled, glass cutting tools were 100% worn out. That weekend I went to Burke Brothers Hardware by the Seaboard Coastline Railroad tracks on Hillsborough Street near the North Carolina State Fairgrounds and bought four brand new glass cutters. We had a lot of work to do!

Over the next two weeks we were able to completely re-glass every building that needed repairs. I would drive my '68 white Buick LeSabre convertible straight to the Orphanage, and Rupert would meet me with the company truck with our tools. Most mornings, some of the children would wait for me at the laundry building. They wanted to ride in "that car with no top." Yes, it was cold, but ride they did; yelling, laughing, and waving to their friends. At lunch, there was a corner, mom and pop lunch counter/store out on Glenwood Avenue. There was where I learned what a "walking taco" was. A walking taco is a small cup of micro-waved chili dumped into a plastic bag of nachos, mashed up, and eaten with a soup spoon. They also sold unfiltered Camel cigarettes for $.25 per pack. Rupert would buy a dollar's worth which came to $1.03. He never had the three pennies, and the Greek immigrant, Mrs. Sakas would fuss, but let it go.

Next Stop: The North Carolina Highway Patrol

In April of 1973, just before I reported to the 58th Basic Highway Patrol School at the University of North Carolina Institute of Government in Chapel Hill, I notified my boss that this would be my last week. He thanked me for my work, and said that he had some bad news. Joaquin had been welding sheet metal roofing onto the Glenwood Avenue side of Crabtree Valley Mall when, somehow, he had become electrified. As he attempted to break the circuit, he had run across the metal surface, and the nails of his boots had burned tiny heel print holes into and through the decking. He fell over the edge to his death.

As my career developed toward professional law enforcement, the risks that I had faced while working in construction became more significant in that they had provided procedural learning experiences. Coping skills are learned traits that must be developed to enable survival while living our lives, answering our "calling," and enabling others. Today's world is not a safe place, but through God's grace and hard work, I have survived. How can I help you?

Throughout this collection of essays, please know that all that you see and read, and the thoughts that are proffered, will represent my best attempt to share my life's story with friends and family.

Michael J. McArthur

Benjamin Franklin Chappell Rides Again as Only He Could

From Harley Davidson Choppers to Black and Silvers to Piper Aircraft to The Pearly Gates

Ben was a unique kind of guy who made life interesting/challenging/amusing/humorous/exciting/entertaining/ and most of all FUN. He defied the odds in many ways. When absolutely NOTHING was happening in Northeastern North Carolina, Ben Chappell could get something going in ways that only he could imagine, and he had a vivid imagination. I quote him almost weekly: "When there's no excitement, just generate a little."

When the, "much smarter than us," Highway Patrol brass decided that our traditional 1929 badges needed to reflect modernized gender correctness, they, without our consultation removed the "PATROLMAN" inscription, and replaced it with "TROOPER." Ben didn't like that. He refused to wear it. In fact he was a little more vocal about his dislike than any of us thought he should have been. Ben liked to refer to himself as a "Patroleum," some vernacular that he picked up on the other side of the tracks. He liked to portray himself as one who kept the wheels greased and made things happen. Little did I know that I was subliminally but joyfully picking up way too many of his character quirks. And it has made my life and that of others, "interesting."

The State Fair Rebel

He and I, along with seventy-eight other Highway Patrolmen, worked traffic for First Sergeant Thomas T. Jeffries at the N. C. State Fair for fourteen years. It was nothing to hear/see Ben come rumblin' / cruisin' past my post at Main Gate 11 on Blue Ridge Road, wearing a Motorcycle Club leather "Colors" jacket that did not cover up his black striped, grey uniform pantlegs. Grinning, he was sitting astride a thunderous chopped and raked monster that belonged to some guy or gal with whom he had "connected" (and given special parking privileges), and "borrowed their HOG." He would cruise the entire fairgrounds, Joey Chitwood's Hell Driver compound, and all over North Carolina State University's Carter-Finley Stadium, defying supervisory authority. When the sleek Seaboard Coastline Railroad trains would roll by his post out on Hillsborough Street next to Tanker's Grille up by Burke Brothers' Hardware, he would key his SHP 42.10 frequency radio handset microphone and broadcast, for all to hear – including Crissman (KIB-895) at Raleigh Radio, the train whistle as it poured out across Blue Ridge Road and Polk Youth Center, and Gregory Poole Caterpillar Dealership.

Ben arrived in Chowan County in the Summer of 1974, and departed in the Summer of 1975. He and Robert Allen were the only two Highway Patrolmen stationed in Chowan, the smallest county in the State, and Robert and Margie were struggling with Robert's terminal cancer. Ben was chosen to become my SHP Field Training Officer for six weeks on the road. I arrived on September 11, 1974 and my first assignment was to direct traffic with Robert and Ben around the American Legion, Post 40, Chowan County Fair. This was on US-17 south of Edenton near Frank Jones Fruit Stand. After I sent about ten yankees into the fairgrounds parking lot, they eventually came out on the other end, and Ben called me on the radio: "Don't MAKE 'em go to the fair if they don't want to!" After about two weeks, First Shirt "Pinky" Lane turned me loose. For the next fifteen years, any time I got crossed up, run up on a stump, or became "supervision challenged," all I had to say was, "Ben Chappell was my training officer, and this is how he told me to do it." Without exception, I got a blanket, unadulterated PARDON. Immediately, no further questions Your Honor.

Michael J. McArthur

Ben's Bi-monthly Inspections, Dejections, Injections, And Rejections.

One cold Monday afternoon, during our bimonthly inspection, about eight of us were in the District Office parking lot, to get "inspected, dejected, injected, and rejected," according to Ben. Ben was late getting there. Imagine that! About a week earlier, we had all just signed a "MEMO" from Colonel E. W. Jones that we were to wear our seat belts AT ALL TIMES, NO MATTER WHAT! Well, as Ben descended on the parking lot, sliding tires as he turned sharply to miss Ray Potts patrol car, we all noticed something: Ben's driver side lap belt was unfastened and dangling out the door, the buckle sparking as it struck the asphalt. First Sergeant "Pinky" Lane, already infuriated with Ben for any number of reasons, ran his fluffy self over to Ben's still closed car door. Ben promptly reached over with his right fist, and slam locked the door! This was almost too good for words. We all still laugh out loud when we think about that spectacle. One: Ben late and locking up all four wheels. Two: the sight of the seat belt buckle sparkin'. Three: "Pinky" Lane running while fire engine red. And Four: Ben slamming that lock down and peepin' out at "Pinky."

There was another occasion when those bimonthly inspections came into focus. Apparently one of the Troopers was missing seven of his issued .357 Magnum bullets from his spare box of fifty. When asked, he said that he had shot a snake in his yard, an injured deer out on US-17, and oh, yeah: he had given two of 'em to the waitress at the Pizza Hut. That boy suffered a long afternoon, but not as long as the afternoon suffered by a parking lot shooter. Seems like, the Line Sergeant was conducting a preliminary inspection before the Captain arrived from Greenville to really get down to the brass tacks. As our Line Sergeant stood at the open patrol car trunk, and inspected the Ithaca Model 37, 12-gauge pump shotgun of one of his men, a "good-ol'-boy" crept up behind the Line Sergeant. Just as the Line Sergeant raised the muzzle of the weapon and looked down the barrel, "good-ol'-boy" fired off a 12-gauge round from his own shotgun. Line Sergeant yelled, dropped the gun, and figured he had just blown his own head off. He turned around, and "good-ol'-boy" was already halfway across the parking lot. You REALLY would have had to have been there to get the full effect of that hilarious calamity.

Language a Child Can Understand, Part One

Ben represented the truest meaning of, "Supervision Challenged." He really never met a "First Line Supervisor" that he didn't dislike. Once when he was in Gastonia, NC Harold Riddick at Elizabeth City SHP Telecommunication Center dispatched him to a three-car wreck in Rocky Hock. Not many of us remember the three primary telecommunicators that ran the E-City show. Harold Riddick, Donnie Lane, and William Earl Scott treated "Their Highway Patrolmen" like their very own sons. Since the Troop A District III First Shirt's office was inside the same building, those "Dispatchers" as they liked to be called, looked out for us. They always knew when a "storm" was brewing, and somehow, ol' Ben was usually at the epicenter, Ground Zero! They would call us and tell us "the scoop." Once in 1973 when Ben was serving his characteristic "eleven months in any one location," he took the liberty (Imagine that), of going over to Gum Neck near Columbia to visit a friend. Well the visit turned into an all-day affair, and the E-City Communication Center called A-345 from about 10am that morning until about three that afternoon. He was on duty and finally answered his radio. William Earl told him to travel to the E-City Office IMMEDIATELY. En route, he met up with his partner in crime, Y Z Newberry at the DMV Weight Station where believe it or not, a LOT of Highway Patrol business was concocted/contrived/conducted. Of course, Ben was oblivious to WHY First Sergeant John Thomas wanted to see him. Y Z, amid his characteristic laugh, told him. Ben went on over, took another tongue lashing, and upon his return, shared with Y Z at the Weight Station that "That SAGINT explained to me in language a child could understand where my patrol area was." Later, First Sergeant John Thomas, A-311 was overheard saying, and I quote: "That G D Ben Chappell is like an unguided missile. If I can ever get him back in A-III, I'm gonna' give him some guidance!" as he pounded his oversized right fist upon his underused cluttered desk. Turns out that it got so heated in the office that William Earl got up to go witness whatever was about to happen. Seems like Ben told "Jooohn" as he liked to call him, "First SAGINT you MIGHT can have for insubordination, but you can't have me for breakfast." Things went downhill from there. It wasn't long 'til ol' Ben got that little SHP geography lesson.

What Cassette Recorder

Ben had a liking for country music that he must have picked up from the Blue Ridge Mountains which he loved. He took it with him into the U S Navy and then out onto the highways and byways of The Great State of North Carolina. One of his favorite songs was the 1974 version of Billy Swann's "I Can Help." We would play this over and over on the rickety old juke box at Jiggs White's Barbecue Stand in Hertford, North Carolina where we would go to meet one of Ben's many partners in crime, The Honorable Jimmy E. Stallings, The Mayor of Edenton, for a free double barbecue sandwich (hopefully before ol' Jiggs got too "happy"). Ben would bellow out, "If your child needs a Daddy, I can help," and all us good ol' boys would holler.

Another of his favorites was the 1966 classic from the Bobby Fuller Four, "I Fought the Law, and the Law Won." He had this song recorded on a little black and silver cassette player that he had hidden from the Line Sergeant underneath the front seat of his black and silver patrol car. When he would catch some notorious poor soul like alleged moonshiners Billy Ned Harper or Eugene Dean Keene, up near the famous entertainer Wolfman Jack's Palace on the Yeopim River in Puzzletown near Belvidere; or just down the "crik" beside acclaimed, legendary New York Yankees Pitcher, Jimmy "Catfish" Hunter's baseball diamond (Wolfman Jack was married to Jimmy's neighbor), Ben, as only he could, would create a slow burn in his "prizner." He would activate his recording and the handcuffed hooligan would have to endure, "I fought the law, and the law won. I fought the law, and the law won," all the way to Aubrey Onley's Tri-County Jail in Elizabeth City by "Chauncey's Pawn Shop."

Wouldn't you know it, that cassette recorder came in handy on other occasions, also. Ben and I were investigating a deer wreck on the Rocky Hock Road where three young high school girls had, in reality gone into a rain slick curve too fast and hit the ditch. When the wrecker got there, and before any of their parents got there, Ben put all three girls on the cluttered back seat of his Congo Cruiser, secretly activated the tape recorder, shut 'em up in there, and he and I started measuring skid marks. Well you just wouldn't believe what those girls moaned, right there in the very shadow of THEIR Rocky Hock Baptist Church: "You KNOW you didn't tell him you were trying to miss a deer!!! I told you were going too damned fast. You are gonna get us all locked up!" When Ben re-entered his car, rewound his recorder, and played the contents. ALL THREE burst into tears. All three young girls are now mothers of young girls, right here in Chowan County. We all laugh out loud when we meet at the Chowan County Fair, Waterman's Restaurant, or the Winn Dixie.

During Ben's time in Chowan, he made some lifelong friends who still inquire, "How's ol' Ben Chappell? Do you ever hear from him? I remember when...." He also made some lasting memories among the bad guys. One of those was Herbert Chappell (<u>defiantly</u> not related to Ben, except for the sake of dispute). Herbert operated "Herbert's Boogie Joint" in downtown Center Hill (Ben called it 'Sinner Hill'). For sale within Herbert's bodega were marijuana wrapping papers and incense sticks, so you know what Ben thought of that! Well, one hot afternoon, Ben was almost totally empty on gas, just like Special Agent Bill Godley of the North Carolina SBI on more than one occasion. We didn't have enough to get us to the Department of Transportation pump in Hertford, so Ben hatched a great idea: We decided to "Boogie on down to Uncle Herbert's" as his psychedelic poster beckoned, and fill up. The Amoco gas pump quickly delivered over 20 gallons of regular gasoline into that black and silver patrol car. Ben slid into the store, used his State of North Carolina yellow credit card, and manually ran the card and receipt paperwork through the "grinder" as he called it... before "Uncle Herbert" could intercept him. As we were remounting our vehicle, Herbert ran out on the front stoop of his store, hopped up and down like the Tasmanian Devil, and ripped up the gas receipt, telling us, "Don't y'all 'so and sos' NEVER come back in my store agin!" What do you think happened next? We drove straight to Cisco, siphoned that twenty gallons out into Ben's El Camino, and the rest into that Harley Davidson. Ben's only lament was that he had not filled up at Herbert's with "hi-test." Next, we drove over to Earl Smith's Rocky Hock Grocery Store, bought two pounds of center cut country ham from Mrs. Bernette Smith, two scoops of chocolate ice cream on a cone, and again filled up the patrol car. Ben said he wasn't about to "let Herbert give the State that full tank of gas."

Language a Child Can Understand, Part Two

On one Thursday night, Ben secretly confided in me that he had a "meeting" that he had to attend somewhere west of I-95. Wouldn't you know it, a bad wreck on the Albemarle Sound Bridge required that the on-duty Chowan County Highway Patrolman be dispatched. I was at home on my day off, and I got a call from Ben at a pay phone somewhere in Gastonia with the (704) area code. Could I please go handle the wreck? Wouldn't you know it? Turns out that "Pinky" had a tough act to follow, having succeeded First Sergeant John Thomas and his legendary "personnel management style." When Ben got through with his Sergeant "Pinky" shellacking, Ben stood up straight, cocked his head even more to one side, and sneered, "First SAGINT, you can have me for insubordination, but you can't have me for breakfast!" We can only imagine! After licking his many wounds, Ben AGAIN told Y Z Newberry and Charlie Mims, "You know what? First Shirt 'Pinky' explained that to me in language a CHILD could understand."

One Sunday night, when we took our "too light" reports over to the District Office, Ben slyly switched Cross pens at the MEMO sign off board, with our Line Sergeant J. R. Deans because on account of that Ben's own pen wouldn't work. Within minutes of our expedient flight, the good Sergeant called us back to Elizabeth City to swap out Ben's pen that "looked like Chappell used it to scrape the mud out from between the spokes of his Harley Davidson motorcycle." As Sergeant Deans (A-322) was calling us (A-345 and A-346) on the radio, at 100 miles per hour, Ben rolled down his window and stuck his microphone out at arm's length, keyed the mic, and yelled, "10-9, A-322, we're 10-1." (Repeat, Sgt. Deans. We're unable to copy.) We never went ANYWHERE at the posted speed limit. Ben's driving talents consisted of slidin', sloodin', fishtailin', power spins, bootlegs, and generally just wreaking havoc, one way or another, anywhere and everywhere. The first night I trained with Ben, he took me across the 3.5-mile, narrow two-lane Albemarle Sound Bridge at speeds over 140mph. It looked to me like the other end of the bridge was constricted to a point, and we would not make it through the tiny opening. Next, we toured through the dirt Bear Swamp Road, at times cleaning out the ditches on both sides of that "hog path." He could do more tricks driving a car than a monkey could on a ten-foot flagpole.

The Checking Station

This was the same week when on Monday, Ben, Charlie Mims, Buck Kelly, Y Z and I were holding a checking station on US-17 in front of Gil Underwood's apple orchard, where one night Charlie found it necessary to shoot a "flying black snake" that I had mistakenly thrown at him. Back to the checking station, in the middle of the road, as the northbound traffic began to back up toward Edenton, Ben jumped into the southbound lane and gave highly demonstrative hand signals (like he learned at the State Fair) for the entire line of traffic to COME ON, AND GET A MOVE ON! Woops! As the line of traffic accelerated due to his urgent beckoning, all of a sudden, Ben spotted a felony: an expired inspection sticker on the #6 vehicle, a junker towing a fishing skiff with a tilted up 25 horsepower Evinrude outboard motor mounted on its stern. Ben jumped in front of it (like he did a lot of things), and the vehicle screeched to a halt. Guess what vehicle #7 did. You got it. "BOOM-YOW," as Magistrate Carlton Perry (December 23, 1937 to November 4, 2017) would say. The 25-horse bounced up then came down through the hood of #7, a brand-new Cadillac. As #6 lurched forward, the skeg of that motor made an impressive wound in the hood of that jet-black Cadi. Like I mentioned earlier, Ben created a little bit of excitement every chance he got (and that was often).

Michael J. McArthur

The Sunday Matinees

It seems like a lot of "stuff" happened on Sundays in Chowan County. One bright Sunday morning, a summer retreat river beach cottage resident arrived to spend the day, and found that the back door was kicked in, and LOTS of stuff stolen from inside. Well, being of the curious nature that Ben was, when the call went out to the Deputy Sheriff to investigate, Ben met him at the crime scene at Kelly's Beach off Wingfield Road up by the Chowanoke (People of the South) Indian burial mounds. After milling around, surveying the damage, and admiring the Navy memorabilia still inside, suddenly the Deputy and Ben were called to a shooting in "Honey Pig" Tripp's yard, about two miles downriver. It seems that Mr. Tripp had been standing shirtless, rippin' and rarin' in his front yard, and been shot with a shotgun from the adjoining woods. The half nude body was peppered in every square inch with what appeared to be #6 birdshot. Nonetheless, Honey Pig was Graveyard Dead, or DRT (dead right there). The single shot, Stevens twelve gauge sawed off shotgun was buried in the yard right near the body under about one inch of sand. I recovered it, and still have it. Before Ben left the river cottage break-in to go to the murder scene, another off-duty officer was called to "stand by" until the Sheriff could get there. When told of that, the homeowner/victim agonized to Ben, "Please don't leave <u>him</u> here. I've already been robbed once!"

By now, evening was upon us, and we headed South on Dillard's Mill Road by the Blue-Backed Herring processing plant run by lucky (another story) Ed Ward where 97-year-old Walter Lane ground, on his Dillard's Creek water powered gristmill, white and yellow Dillard's Mill Corn Meal (fish breader). Wouldn't you know it! We met a blue clunker: a blue '63 Chevy Nova with a busted windshield and two blinkin' blue lights mounted just under the front bumper. Lo an' behold, it just wouldn't do for Ben to pass up such a golden opportunity to spread his brand of good will among the populace. We "slood around," right in the middle of that bad curve where alleged bootlegger Eugene Dean Keene met his final fate. We saw a cloud of bluish white smoke pour out the tailpipe of that Nova. He must have blown the engine trying to put distance between us and him, because about one mile up the road, where Ben cajoled him, there was a black oily substance running out the bottom of what used to be "the getaway car." Now, for the reason of this sidesplitting "enforcement contact" / scratch in the column: the blue lights "not sealed in the manufacturer's original package," and "operated by use of the vehicle's battery." N.C.G.S. §20-130.1 (a).

When necessary, and only when necessary, Ben's mind was like a steel trap as it came to the laws and regulations promulgated by the Great State of North Carolina. MOST of the time he "adapted" things to where he liked them. Well, contained inside the Nova were Joe Boy Johnson (Ruby Kaye's common law husband) and his brother (perhaps), Joe Johnson. Ruby Kaye was Angus Earl's BEST girlfriend (he had a wife and three other girlfriends). Anyway, Joe Boy was the "pilot" and **just a little too drunk**. Unfortunately, a local furniture store owner, Pete Townsend ran over and killed him the next week, about midnight, lying drunk in the middle of the southbound lane of NC-32, wearing black pants and a dark blue shirt (I've got the cloth samples to prove it as evidence). Joe Boy's blood alcohol was only 0.12% because due to cirrhosis of his liver, it no longer took as many Colt forty-five oz.s to get him "knee walkin', fallin' down drunk."

Back to the Nova: On this evening excursion, Joe Boy was under the wheel, and Joe was in the passenger seat with blue and red wires running up under his holey plaid shirt with the buttons not aligned in the proper buttonholes. Ben Asked, "Joe Boy, is this your car?" Joe Boy mumbled something about his "appendage." You know Ben, he had to ask, "What appendage?" It turned out that Joe Boy had aggravated the starch out of his "craps" buddy over in the Punch Bowl section of Gates County, and after a knock down- drag out brawl, Joe Boy's buddy got a ten inch, single shot, twelve gauge shotgun from under the front seat of his truck, pointed it at Joe Boy, Joe Boy grabbed the four inch barrel, the shooter released the ladies' dress belt induced backpressure on the trigger, and the gun blasted a crater in Joe Boy's midsection, about two inches below his belly button. This should have killed him, but it did not. Joe Boy developed a ten-inch in girth and ten-inch-long "appendage" / growth, from this wound, and he would take it out and shake it at people who bothered him. He said he was "casting a spell on 'em." I've still got that shotgun, and one hot summer day in the 1767 Courthouse parking lot, I called Joe Boy over to my air-conditioned patrol car, he staggered over after having just left his DWI trial inside, I reached under the seat, lifted out and displayed to him the "modified" shotgun, and he backed up so hard that he fell down, rolling backward. Neither did it kill him when the tractor trailer mirror caught Clyde in the back o' the head and knocked him unconscious into the ditch for two days, as he walked along "Drinkin' Hole Road" over in Perquiman's County, Neither did it kill Joe Boy when Lenny Perry of Perry -Wynn Fisheries, tried to drown Joe Boy in the salt brine of Ed Ward's Fishery on Cannon's Ferry Road, after Joe Boy reached into his pants, and pulled a fourteen inch "Old Hickory" butcher knife on Lenny for "gittin' in the way" of Joe Boy trying to kill Ruby Kaye who worked at the fishery (again, I've got the rusty knife as evidence.

Again, back to the Nova and those two blue lights (I've got both of 'em). We learned a lot about Joe Boy's anatomy that day, whether we wanted to or not! Joe Boy told us that the car was his, but that Joe had "warred them thangs up," and Joe has a switchblade knife under his leg." To quote Rocky Hock Baptist Church Deacon D. C. Forehand (December 7, 1920 to April 29, 1991), a good friend of mine, one of my farmer buddies, "That brought on more talk." We got both men out of the car and made them sit across the ditch on the ditch bank because they were "**just too drunk**" to be standing anywhere near the paved portion, or us. Besides, they were beginning to have just a little too much mouth. Imagine that! Poor planning on their part. Well, we got the switchblade knife from Joe (sure, I've got it), and arrested him for carrying a concealed weapon. We asked Joe Boy for a pair of pliers to unbolt the two blue light fixtures from the vehicle's bumper. Guess what! No tools! Oh, well. Ben had some tools. Well, Ben had A TOOL: his SHP issued, black and silver painted "Plumb" AX. You know it! Ben laid down sideways on the pavement, put both hands on the handle of that ax, and with one lick each, severed each of those lights right out from under that Nova. We arrested Joe Boy for DWI, again, and operating the Nova with no insurance or valid inspection. We discovered that the license plates were revoked on it, too. After watching Ben surgically remove the blue lights, when we told them that we were gonna take the license plate off next, Joe said, "Hey! Y'all can use my switchblade for a screwdriver," and you know we did. We also arrested Joe and charged him with operating the blue lights with an "on-off" switch that was found connected to the taped-up ends of those two wires that ran up under his shirt. We already had more than a child's share of commotion, so we let the Aiding and Abetting DWI fall by the wayside. I don't think we could have ever really determined whose Nova that was, anyway.

Ben Chappell's Harley Davidson

You may remember that Anita and Ben seemed to enjoy riding his Harley Davidson. Supposedly they put over 8000 miles on it during their honeymoon. Along that line of thought, one of the worst threats/promises I ever heard delivered to Ben (and there were several) concerned the removal and confiscation of "the front wheel off that G D motorcycle." Not to fold up under pressure, the Harley and its companion El Camino pickup mysteriously vanished under the veil of darkness... that night! It turned up over in Hertford behind Jimmy Stallings's house, right up next to the back door. This was the same fully dressed Harley Davidson that thundered throughout northeastern North Carolina under the watchful guidance of a State Highway Patrolman (Ben Chappell) having investigated wrecks (or wrecked) in most all of those counties: Tyrrell, Washington, Hyde, Dare, Perquimans, Camden, Pasquotank, Currituck, Gates, Hertford, Bertie, and Chowan. The pipes on that motorcycle defied the laws of physics, as MOST of the good ol' farm boy thunder merchant pickups couldn't hold a candle to Ben's Harley.

One day while on duty, patrolling inside the famous Mrs. Boswell's Restaurant on Queen Street in Edenton, Ben was conniving with about 12 or 14 (not thirteen though) friends and acquaintances. Had there been 13 at the table, Tugboat Captain Emmett Wiggins (died September 30, 1995) or novelty inventor Charles O. Tysor (November 5, 1914 to January 23, 1994) would have gotten up and left. Not that they were superstitious, but it was a known fact that Charlie did put a "dark cloud double whammy hex" on Ben with his "Goat's Eye" ring that he wore on his right-hand middle "communicating" finger. Electric wheelchair sidewalk terrorist Henry Layden, Edenton Police Chief J. D. Parrish (November 15, 1938 to March 27, 2018), Juvenile Probation Officer Robert Hendrix (September 18, 1927 to

May 29, 2021), Edenton Fire Chief Luther Parks (July 8, 1923 to February 2, 1997), Wildlife Supervisor Ray Elks (December 16, 1942 to January 29, 1988), Magistrate Raymond Tarkington (January 31, 1911 to June 10, 1997), Sheriff Troy Toppin (February 17, 1920 to October 8, 1985), Edenton Town Manager Bill Gardner (Dece3mber 9, 1934 to December 28, 1983), UNC basketball fan John Muriel Phillips (November 4, 1929 to November 19, 2001), Pilot Life Insurance Agent Ralph Outlaw (November 27, 1922 to May 24, 2001), "Captain Wallace" Goodwin (September 22, 1903 to August 29, 1999), Probation-Parole Officers Bob Roberson (February 21, 1930 to April 1, 2000) and Mike Thomas, and other sordid souls were huddled up in the center of the dining room, drinking free hot coffee and enjoying Ben's stories and other half-truths and bald faced lies from one another. In walked N.C. DMV Inspector Harold Babb (November 6, 1931 to December 8, 1997) (his son, Jeff Babb is now retired as an SHP Major). Harold Babb told Ben, right in front of all his cronies, that his Harley Davidson looked like "a Guzooki been run through Warren Hibbard's (died February 22,1999) Western Auto and everything in the store stuck to it." Ben got red in the face, speechless for once in his life, and stomped out, much to the glee of his buddies. After Harold spooked Ben, he turned his attention to "short story made long" Emmett Wiggins. Harold asked him what progress was being made on President Gerald Ford and Chief Justice Warren Burger returning to Emmett, ownership of the "King's Grant Galberry Plantation" in Rocky Hock. With such an <u>agonizingly</u> long argument soon to follow such prompt, most of us except poor ol' Henry, plopped a quarter on the table, got up and ran for the exit, Harold leading the pack, and laughing out loud.

Trooper Chappell's Colt "Trooper"

Ben had a Colt "Trooper" model .357 Magnum issued sidearm. I, being the rookie, was issued a nickel-plated S&W Model 19 .357 Magnum that outshined (and out shot) his stainless-steel pistol (just one of several _____contests we got into). Not to be outdone, Ben contacted a clandestine autobody chop shop friend of his in New Bern, N C, and this gentleman CHROME PLATED Ben's "Trooper." Once again, he beat me out, until we went to Little Washington for firearms qualification among the yellow flies and mosquitoes down by the Tar River. The fearsome SHP armorer John Rowe (July 11, 1926 to February 15, 2017) stormed onto the scene after having been beckoned by Sgt. Billy Apple, the range master. It seems that the sear in Ben's "Trooper" had been filled in by that chrome which would not allow what Ben called his hogleg, to be "cocked." A hasty trip to Edenton's gunsmith, Deputy Sheriff Buddy Bunch, and Ben's quandary was rectified. He was back "10-8."

Factory Defects Galore

Ben drove a black and silver 1974 Plymouth with what he reported to the Sergeant as a "factory defect." One fine Sunday afternoon, he chased seven four wheelers from the Icaria Road in Chowan County all the way up to the Jehu Road. The bikers jumped a ditch to get around a steel cable across the muddy field path, and in the nick of time, Ben skidded to a stop. Of course that "Trooper" came into play, and it is alleged that some controversial "warning shots" were released into the air. Somehow, one of those "Law Enforcement Only" 158 grain, JHP projectiles "creased" the ridge that ran right down the centerline of the shiny hood of his muddy patrol car; thus the "factory defect." Another "factory defect" became apparent inside the passenger compartment of that same patrol car. Back then patrol cars had only AM/FM radios (Up from AM only just a few years prior). Ben wanted a cassette tape player/AM/FM "Sound System." Well "Tonto," "Kojak," Milton Jordan had one still mounted in the dash of a freshly totaled Dodge Ram truck sittin' on the lot, that would fit nicely into Ben's car, we thought. After a midnight requisition, and the not so painstaking removal of the padded dash of that '74 Plymouth Patrol Vehicle, somehow the "unit" was installed, and it looked and played "good." Now all we had to do was wedge the padded dash back into place. Not so fast there, ol' buddy. It didn't QUITE fit. Thus another "factory defect." It only rattled a little bit especially at speeds over 100mph in the rain with the windshield wiper blades standing straight out, having been lifted off the windshield by excessive turbulence.

Michael J. McArthur

The Infamous "Machine-Gun Search" of the Micro Minibus

One of Ben's least favorite things in life was a "long haired hippie," driving a yellow psychedelic painted Volkswagen micro minibus, with anti-Viet Nam slogans and Peace Signs prominently displayed thereupon. Upon sighting such, Ben became incensed. Right there in the middle of the US-17 Perquimans River Bridge, which was only two skinny lanes back in the early '70s, Ben turned that land yacht, '74 Plymouth around, and gave hot pursuit. The inhabitants of such vehicle were no match to the keen investigative techniques and skills soon to be inflicted upon them by Master Trooper Benjamin Franklin Chappell. Upon his approach to the busted-out driver's door window, Ben detected a cloud of white smoke rolling out of the portal. Lo and behold, what happened next.... well, you just would have had to have been there to fully appreciate the truly amazing things that happened next, as if choreographed straight from Saturday Night Live (premiered October 11, 1975).

The driver ("floater" as Ben called him) asked Ben, "What's happenin', Man?" And from that point of the encounter, things went downhill like the slope of the Perquimans River Bridge behind us. Next came what Defense Attorney Keith Teague named "The Famous Ben Chappell 'Consent Search' for Machine Guns." Ben inquired, as though a marriage proposal, "Do y'all have any machine guns in there?" Of course asking for a driver's license and registration was the last thing on Ben's fever pitched mind. The hesitant answer was, "No, Man." Next, as nice as he could muster, "Well do you mind if I take a look/see for myself?" Again the answer was, "No, Man." Gentle Ben rolled up the worn sleeves of his too tight uniform shirt on its fourth day. Slammed his faded Highway Patrol "flat hat" on the top of the "hoochmobile", and believe you me, IT WAS ON!!

We called him Gentle Ben because his favorite "cabbage patch" for catching drunks was a roadside drinkin' hole about two miles up the road named Gentle Ben's, along with E. J.s, and "There is no rest at the Crest - Hillcrest Gardens Bar and Grille." Back to the "Consent Search." After inquiring about the machine guns, the first thing Ben did was "invite" all four barefooted hippies out of the van. The first place he looked for those machine guns was inside the overflowing ash tray. EVIDENCE! The next thing he did was lean in and place his right fist near the back and in the middle of the floater's seat. With all of his lean and mean 185 pounds he pushed down, baring the crack of the seat, and watched more EVIDENCE roll out toward his fist. Ben was left-handed, and he snatched up those little pellet sized marijuana seeds like a duck on a June bug. Needless to say, now all four occupants were placed under arrest. Next came the vehicle search, the baggage search, the engine compartment search, and glove box search. I can barely relate to you how extensive and hilarious that became. Guess who got to drive the ransacked, to put it mildly, minibus to the Perquimans County Magistrate's Office, to appear before The Honorable Broughton Dail. An exposed broken seat spring snagged my uniform pants, and punctured my... leg. We had a 14-year-old Sheriff's Department Dispatcher, Todd Tilley working the radio. He was of the impressionable age, and couldn't quite fathom the events that were unfolding before his very eyes. Maybe that episode is what got him hooked on judicial procedures (such as they were with Ben at the helm). He is now The Honorable Todd Tilley, the elected Clerk of Superior Court for the County of Perquimans.

Two months later in court, immediately after convicting the defendants, Ben was surprised when legally blind District Court Judge Fentress Horner suspended the 14-month active sentences. Unwisely, but highly predictably, Ben sprang up from his worn pew, shot up beside High Sheriff Julian "Little Man" Broughton, and asked, "Well, Judge Horner, Your Honor, do you want me to give back to those hippies their two grocery bags full of 'dope'?" That was not a pretty sight, but what entertainment! You just cannot make this stuff up.

Warning Shots and Face Plants

One COOOOLD January night, Sheriff Troy Toppin, Ben's neighbor/landlord called for assistance from the on-duty Chowan County Highway Patrolman - Ben Chappell. There was an on-going break-in at

Tiny Boy Perry's Store on NC-32 at Cannon's Ferry Road. Ben didn't get the word to meet the posse in "blackout" at Robert Hendrix's house. My best friend Robert Hendrix passed away on May 29, 2021 at age 93. Ben slid to a stop right in front of the busted-out store front, quickly joined by Sheriff Toppin and Juvenile Probation Officer Robert Hendrix. Out the front door dashed suspect #1. Ben, with his buckshot loaded Ithaca pump riot shotgun let loose another one of those alleged, controversial but highly effective "warning shots." Now we already know that Ben's aim and intentions can become "clouded." Well, suspect #1 face planted right into (not onto) the concrete driveway, right beside the $0.74 per gallon, Sinclair gas pump. He was quickly scooped up by Deputy Sheriff Joseph Byrum and "escorted" off-site. Suspect #2 bolted into the shroud of darkness. Suspect #3 was not to be accounted for until just after daybreak. When snatched out from underneath the kerosene tanks in back of the store below the broken-out bathroom window, the first words out of #3's mouth were, "Did y'all kill them other two boys?" That was a good question. He must have known Ben, for when the sun came up it was apparent that the full load of 00 buckshot had blown the sign off the stoop, just above the streaking head of now scraped up suspect #1. I learned right then and there that warning shots can be hazardous for your health.

Paradise Road and All Its Glory

Working alongside Ben Chappell was truly a life changing phenomenon. Ben could "generate" thoughts and ideas within your soul that you had never acknowledged, much less employed. One hot Sunday morning in May of 1975, Ben and I were what he called, "Patrolling our beat in a military manner." The yellow flies were ferocious out there on RPR 1317, Paradise Road in central Chowan County. Paradise was one of the favorite illegal drag strips in eastern North Carolina, known far and wide for its dangerous, to put it mildly, road racing. Occasionally, "rollbacks" would drop fuel dragsters and "crotch rockets" in front of the plumber Sid White's cow barn over near the "Big Woods" in Bear Swamp. The races ran for thousands of dollars, and when we would mysteriously drive up among them, the racers, the cars, and the money would "scatter like roaches when the light comes on," according to Ben.

On one occasion, Ben had devised a scheme: imagine that! He had developed a notorious stoolpigeon commonly known as, "Big Bud." Big Bud had told "Boss" (Ben) about the Sunday morning race involving a white '66 convertible Oldsmobile 442 driven by Hoochie Thompson, now deceased having been shot to death and then run over by a responding Edenton police officer as he lay unconscious in the front yard of his "trailer house" as Ben called it. The alleged race would take place right out in front of the cow barn where all us "Patroleums" could hide and watch the almighty spectacle. Swag Chesson would be driving a blue over black racing stripes, '65 SS 396 Chevelle. Big Bud, in all his radiant glory would be wearing a floppy white hat so that when all the hoodlums (Ben's 'roaches') hauled butt, us "Patroleums" would somehow allow Big Bud freedom to high-tail-it for another day. Wouldn't you know it? Sunday morning came, Ben and I were itchin' up in the hay loft of the barn with our military surplus, Sheriff issued binoculars.

The Gray Ghost Posse and all the black and silvers were secluded elsewhere. Here came the convoy of race fans and a blue Chevelle and a white 442. Everybody pulled onto the shoulder, and about eight folks got out of each of the 6 or 8 cars. How many white hats do you reckon we counted? About twenty! Somehow, one of the crooks spotted "that pointy headed Ben Chappell" up in the loft. They all scrambled back into their rides, and "oozed" – Ben's word, on back to "The Stop and Rob" in town. They couldn't run on foot on account of the fact that monstrous rattlesnakes are rampant on Paradise. A side note: about a week later, on a hot Sunday afternoon, Ben and I got a call that the "roaches" were racing out on Drummond's Point Road. I had our Magistrate, Carlton Perry with me. Ben came in from the south end and Carlton and I came in from the north end. Rattlesnakes (big ones) abound on Drummond's Point Road, also. When we got to the site, the roadside visitation/spectacle/encounter/enforcement contact became intense. Those same six carloads with at least forty runners were on the scene. Ben got out with his shotgun (same one). I made all the drivers get into their vehicles and "fire 'em up." Then Ben and I commenced to checking licenses of these "operators." Ben and that shotgun had "convinced" all those spectators to re-enter their vehicles while we conducted our in-depth investigations. We checked the mufflers (or NOT), the catalytic converters (or NOT), the turn signals, the running lights, the light lenses, the inspection stickers (1975 remember), the "signed" (or NOT) N C Registration cards listing the owner, the high beams, the low beams, the tires, the backup lights, and anything else that Ben could come up with, legal or illegal, searches incident to arrest or just for the heckuvit.

By the way, did I forget to mention that with no breeze, it was at least "a 'hunerd' degrees" in the bearing down sun? As we sat in our air-conditioned patrol cars, how long do you think it took us to write those six drivers their umpteen tickets? Oh, yeah! The registered owners got tagged for "aidin' and abbettin' " their drivers. We "made our week," right there on the East side of Drummond's Point Road beside the Yeopim River. As I recall it, "hot" was an understatement; it was more like "scorching" in more ways than one!

Back to Paradise Road: We were conscientiously "patrolling our beat in a military manner, when out on the road there arose such a clatter." Between Pat Flanagan's (March 18, 1917 to December 3, 2013) contemporary AM Radio Station WCDJ and Dottie Lillibridge's FM country music station WBXB, Ben spied an old blue and white, '57 Buick Roadmaster "oozin'" toward the Town of Edenton by the Iron Gate to The Big Woods. After it crossed the centerline about, well maybe one time, Ben jumped into action: "Why there's David and Davis Taylor!" We exercised our "felony stop" on the tank Buick right in front of Dr. Dees house. After checking the ditch for rattlesnakes, I got out of the passenger side while Ben was already buttonholing David. Swatting yellow flies as I approached the open, alcohol aromatic passenger window, I heard Davis ask, "David, do you want me to kill them two fellers?" Huh? Well, to quote Master Trooper Eddie Blowe, "My blood pressure went straight to .357!" I hit Davis in the back of the head, right behind his ear with that S&W .357 Magnum revolver (the shiny one, remember), and Davis took his hand right off the wooden grips of his rusty old Colt.38 six-shooter loaded with 4, stuck in his waistband. Davis had already pulled time on a Johnston County chain gang, and just gotten out on parole for drivin' drunk down Granville Street, stabbing his drinking buddy in the heart, and giving him a rolling shove out the door right beside Vine Oak Cemetery alongside Filbert's Creek. David hollered, "LORD, GOD, DAVIS. DON'T DO IT!" When the dust settled, David went to jail, Davis went to the house, and

Ben and I went to lunch at The Chicken Kitchen on North Broad Street. Davis's .38 went to Cisco, but ultimately it ended up on Cowpen Neck Road.

Fruit Loops and Looney Toons

Ben was a magnanimous kind of guy, and would do anything to help anybody. At that point in his life, Ben had no "curtain climbin' crumb snatchers," as he called children. He would help everybody else's children attain whatever goals they sought, but he really, just didn't have time for kids. Once after Ben had transferred to Boone, and had been subpoenaed back to Chowan County for court on Tuesday, he was asked by Trooper Y Z Newberry, if he would bring Y Z and Elizabeth's daughter, Kathy, home to Hertford during spring break from Appalachian State University. Of course he would. Well, at daybreak Kathy hopped onto the back of that Harley Davidson, and East they went. Back then, US-64 ran through Wilson, N. C., and Kathy and Ben stopped for lunch at Parker's Barbecue on Old US-301 between the Tobacco Trail Motel and the American Legion Fairgrounds, across from Raper's Store beside the N. C. DOT Weigh Station. In the parking lot, upon Ben and Kathy dismounting the Harley, an elderly woman sitting in her Mercedes Benz, rolled down her window and bristled to Kathy: "Young lady, aren't you afraid to ride that thing?" Before you could blink your eye, Ben shot back, "Why Ma'am. I would have you to know that that child is just as safe perched up there on the back of this here Harley Davidson motorcycle, as she would be if she was asittin' on the parlor rug in her Daddy's livin' room, eatin' Froot Loops and watchin' the Looney Toons on color television."

Bless His Heart, Ben Goes Home

By now, it was time for ol' Ben to get a little SHP Geography 101 lesson at the hands of Captain Carl Gilchrist in Greenville, N.C. It seems

Ben had been "invited" to return to his old stomping grounds, the Blue Ridge Mountains, the County of Watauga, and the hamlet of Boone. He took what he called his red Congo Cruiser and went west. I lost track of Ben for about fifteen years until he magically appeared at my dorm room late one night. During that time period, I was temporarily assigned to run the 89th Basic School, and serve as a High-Speed Pursuit Driving Instructor at the Highway Patrol Training Center on Old Garner Road in Raleigh. In its infinite wisdom, the SHP had decided to do some "remedial training" in the field of pursuit driving and "run-off-road, lane re-entry." I was fortunate enough, having sufficiently wrecked my fair share of patrol cars, thereby earning the right to go and assist my fellow "Troopers" as they were now called.

Ben wanted to know what to expect the next morning on the track, so that he could be "ready for 'em." I tried to look out for the "old heads," and make them look good in front of the younger and faster Troopers. Over on Tryon Road, across from the Highway Patrol Helicopter Pad (Flight Pilot Sergeants Chuck Boyd's and Ken Thompson's hideout), when we gathered at the track the next day, I noticed Ben's car sat a little higher, no, MUCH HIGHER than any of the cars around it. When I looked underneath his car, I saw two, yellow, heavy duty, Gabrielle Hi-Jacker air shocks. "Ben, what are those?" I asked (knowing full well what he had done). Turns out, Ben had gone into the hills, bought some land right next to the Blue Ridge Parkway, and built a house so far off the road that it was out of sight. He had to put those Hi-Jackers on his car so that he could get back and forth. Having built where he did "prevented those nosey 'Lyin' Sergeants from snoopin' around in his driveway, and spyin' on him," on account of because their cars couldn't navigate the treacherous ravine. Speaking of building his house, somehow his property lines became muddled as he used the United States Park Service motor graders and log skidders and excavators to "appropriate" building timbers and landscape boulders from "OVER YONDER" to "RIGHTCHERE."

Our friend, Ben died Monday, April 24, 2016 at about 1:00 p.m., doing what he loved, as the small Piper aircraft crashed onto the fairway of one of his favorite golf courses, The Boone Golf Club.

May Benjamin Franklin Chappell rest in peace. May all involved find solace in the fact that death is a part of life, and that, thanks be to God, there is a better place awaiting us all, without pain or suffering, among those with whom we share love.

May 30, 2016 Veterans Day

Michael J. McArthur

Clerk of Superior Court

County of Chowan

101 S. Broad Street

Post Office Box 588

Edenton, NC 27932

Phone- 252-368-5000

Fax- 252-368-5001

Michael J. McArthur

SECOND BOOK

The Peerless, Fearless Sidekick Extraordinaire

Doesn't everybody have a sidekick?

Well, if you don't, you should!

GET ONE!

God knows, I was blessed with "The Best."

My sidekick, **Robert Hendrix** was truly one of a kind when it came to the

BOY SCOUT LAW:

TRUSTWORTHY: Robert was as "solid as a rock," and that "rock" in his case was The Hope Diamond. Nothing rattled Robert. He was always prepared for whatever presented itself. He was as honest as the day was long, and together we pulled some extremely long days: airplane crashes, manhunts, jailbreaks, shootouts, missing persons, drownings, barricaded suspects, wrecked vehicles, and wrecked lives.

LOYAL: Robert considered his mission in life to be an enabler, orchestrator, provider, and stabilizer. His vast knowledge of "all things worldly," served me, him, and everyone else around us well: and with distinction, I might add.

HELPFUL: Robert always had good ideas and was highly sought after by the law enforcement and the legal communities. One of the best things about Robert was that he was ALWAYS THERE! It didn't matter what time of the day or night of this week or next week: he was always on site and ready to help proceed toward peaceful resolution.

FRIENDLY: Robert, up until his dying day, presented a cheerful countenance with a wry smile upon his wrinkled face. You could almost see the wheels turning behind those sparkling blue eyes. Even in the darkest moments, Robert was an uplifting soul who always saw the good in everybody, while consoling the bad!

COURTEOUS: Robert treated all with respect, regardless of race, color, creed, religion, sexual orientation, or national origin. Often Robert demonstrated that, "Silence is golden."

KIND: Robert never met a stranger, and gave everyone his best when it came to the kindness of acceptance. His philosophy of refraining from parlaying in misfortune earned him many accolades from those who probably didn't deserve his many kindnesses.

OBEDIENT: Robert followed God's law, the law of the land, common law, and statutory law. No one ever questioned where Robert stood when it came to doing the right thing, the first time, for the right reason. He was always "on time," or early.

CHEERFUL: Even during the darkest moments, Robert found a less difficult path toward resolution through cheerfully lifting up those of us in the trenches with whom he served. Amid pain and suffering, often his own, Robert never let anything "get him down."

THRIFTY: While having come up somewhat privileged, he was always mindful of the plight of others without the benefits of financial comfort and security. He would pinch a penny, and then give the resulting dollar to someone less fortunate.

BRAVE: Robert stood in the face of death many times as a member of the U. S. Navy. He shared his veracity and lust for life with his family who developed character traits of their own, based upon Robert's tenacity. As my sidekick, he and I survived countless harrowing escapades in the shadow of death, about which he never spoke.

CLEAN: Robert was a shining light in the darkness when it came time to stand up and be counted. His internal fortitude and his external shining armor shined forth with endearing quality. Everybody wanted to be "like Robert."

REVERENT: Through the splendor of his faith in God, Robert led his family in the paths of righteousness, for His name's sake. Robert's "green stick" persona never allowed him to fail, as he pressed on to the greater achievements of the future.

Highway Patrolman Michael John McArthur Meets Julian Robert Hendrix

As a "State Man," North Carolina State Highway Patrolman, my new wife and I reported for duty in the smallest county in the State: Chowan County on September 11, 1974. People compete as they traverse our small county from west to east: "Can I hold my breath that long?" There have been those who succeeded, with practice.

Following our arrival, and after finding an apartment on Broad Street in Edenton, Becky and I began the arduous task of acclimating to a less hectic lifestyle than Raleigh had afforded us. The more we acclimated, the more we liked our new lives. We were able to focus on important things like core values, projected paths of accomplishment, and building our futures. We were accepted by nearly all with whom we interacted. Thankfully, "The Law" was well respected in our little slice of Heaven. "The Law" was personified by many good men and women who worked hard to make the living worthwhile.

Our children were born within a few years, and we became more ingrained in the sandy soil surrounded by the Albemarle Sound, Edenton Bay, The Chowan River, Catherine's Creek, and The Yeopim River. The terrain is relatively flat, and allows for few banked curves or hilltop crossings. For those of us assigned the duty of traffic law enforcement, Chowan County is a "Hunter's Paradise." The terrain coupled with support from the community made our entire existence, "just what the doctor ordered."

Chowan County is blessed with one incorporated town and about nine communities with a total population of about 14,000, and fading! So many of the younger generation seem to seek the bright lights and the city nights of Tidewater Virginia or Piedmont North Carolina. Without decent career paths, Chowan County is not attractive for bright futures with family and friends. UNLESS OF COURSE a young family has a healthcare profession, boat building proficiency, government salary, or family farm upon which to rely.

Little did I know that our community would wrap its arms around Becky and me and welcome us into "the fold." We have now lived here for forty-seven years, but that makes us neither local nor native." In order to be a local, you must have lived here for at least 120 years. But that's OK, we're headed that way. Our children are locals <u>and</u> natives, so we trade upon their blessings and good fortune.

Friends are a valuable asset, and a resource never to be denied nor taken for granted. Our yard became a gathering spot for neighborhood kids as they hiked the Wilderness Trail, climbed the towers, painted the castle, biked the ramps, slid the slides, rocked the swings, climbed the rock wall, built the fires, rang the bells, sailed the Pirate Ship, slid the fireman pole, rappelled the Tower, roped the knotted lines, washed the bicycles, cooked the hot dogs, flew the kites, shot the doves, navigated the Ninja Courses, jumped the ditches, flew the flags, threw the axes, shot the BBs, knocked the arrows, chopped the trees, marked the treasure hunts, hid the eggs, sucked the Honey-suckle, built the birdhouses, "handed" the concrete, chased the butterflies, filled the bird feeders, walked the dogs, got stung by wasps, got bitten by snakes, splashed in mudholes, shot hoops, jumped ropes, tied knots, shot marbles, scooped poop, rolled the tunnel, picked the flowers, etc.

Back to MY Sidekick, J. Robert Hendrix

(September 18, 1927 - May 29, 2021)

How many of you remember that Robert was affectionately known and characterized as "The Lone Ranger?" His neighbor and best boyhood friend "Tonto" (alias "Kojak" but birthed Milton Jordan, June 19, 1928 to December 11, 2019), and The Lone Ranger won many battles for the betterment of the neighborhood and the improvement of the world.

Robert was a consummate ballroom dancer as he could flip the lapels of his tuxedo with the best of 'em. Marvis and he could "really cut a rug!"

Robert could out-cook Betty Crocker and outperform Martha Stewart when it came to making a house a home for his beautiful and talented family: Marvis and Robin and Jill and his dogs and cats.

Once when I stopped a speeder in front of the Hendrix home, out bounded King, their full-grown German Shepherd. He immediately jumped up and almost into the young woman's window. The driver took off toward Virginia, and I just figured that she had gotten enough punishment. I let her go. After all, I had to undeputize King, and get him back in his yard.

Michael J. McArthur

"Is That a Bullet Hole in Your Car?"

How many of you remember that he did not take kindly to three midnight marauders trying to steal Marvis's blue '73 Gran Prix Pontiac, and the resultant bullet hole that somehow appeared in the driver's door? That always embarrassed Marvis at the Crossroads gas pump when the attendant would ask, "Mrs. Marvis! Is that a bullet hole in your car?"

Robert was my sidekick on roughly seven hundred-fifty night shifts of fighting crime here in Northeastern North Carolina. When I would get into a roadside fistfight, he was there to even the playing field. No telling how many fights were discouraged or prevented.

When drivers would run from the scene of my traffic stop, Robert was my central communications specialist, coordinating the calling out of the cavalry, and pinpointing our exact location (Jehu Road near Blackjack White's liquor still).

In the dark of night, Robert was my light station in that he would hold the spotlight upon the prescribed next lick from my nightstick.

Robert once was afflicted with a "stiff neck" as he entered my patrol car. After a five-mile chase at a speeds in excess of 140mph, and then totaling three cars at that breakneck speed, from then on Robert called me Dr. Mike for having cured his affliction.

.38 Special to the Rescue

Robert once intervened upon an active, ongoing, blazing gunfight immediately following a brazen midday bank robbery with Edenton Police Officer Billy Spruill having been tragically shot twice. Robert saved Billy's life by his blued steel Smith and Wesson .38 Special's intervention. The robber ended up with four "through and through" bullet holes, and the death was ruled a suicide by the UNC-Chapel Hill Medical Examiner!

After a daring armed robbery of Hollowell and Blount's Pharmacy in Edenton on a Sunday afternoon, Robert responded and met "The Milkshake Bandit's" car traveling north on NC-32 at Valhalla. He of course gave hot pursuit until Deputy Sheriff Joseph Byrum (August 16, 1927 to September 9, 2001) (Steve and Randy's Daddy) took over, thereby capturing the suspect because of Robert's vigilance and diligence. Back at Herbert and Jim's Pharmacy, teenaged cashiers Sheila Cherry and Janet Hollowell were still lying on the floor saying, "Don't talk to me! Don't talk to me! He told us not to talk!" NEXT!

Robert was an early proponent and aficionado of trendy electronic devices. He had the first bag phone I ever saw. He had at least three police radio band scanners. He had a high intensity flashlight that was better than any I ever owned or was issued by the Highway Patrol.

Robert was well known and respected by the ENTIRE law enforcement, legal, and judicial communities, from Raleigh to the northeastern coast, especially in Dare County where he maintained a satellite office.

When frustrated, Marvis once (well maybe more often than once) called Robert (and several others) a "Rooster" for his dogged pursuit of doing the right thing for the right reason, the first time, and trying to hold others to that high standard.

"Wolfpacking"

We were "Wolfpacking" NC-32 up near Baker's Hog Market one Saturday night when a drunk driver ran us off the road, head on. They weren't going but about 35 mph, I bootlegged my patrol car, and I got them stopped in front of Robert's house.

When I walked up to the window, Thomas Adolph was driving, and he took off spinning tires. Throwing rocks onto the hood of my new Crown Victoria.

One of Thomas Adolph's three brothers, Roland Mark (Mike) was seated beside him. I overtook them again and they would not stop as I pulled alongside them at about 15 mph. Robert leaned out the window, and yelled, "MIKE, PULL OVER." Apparently, after the first stop, at about 30 mph they had switched drivers, and Rowland Mark (commonly known as Mike) – <u>the owner of the car</u> – had gotten under the wheel. Thus, the confusion about whether he or I was supposed to "pull over" when Robert yelled. Finally I told Robert to roll his window up and put his seat belt on. We bull-dogged them into the ditch in front of Ballard's Bridge Baptist Church (circa. 1781). After "dynamically extricating them," I ended up arresting BOTH brothers, charging each with driving drunk, and Rowland Mark for allowing Thomas Adolph to drive drunk. That was three drunks out of one car with two occupants. Robert ALWAYS got the distinct honor and privilege of driving the drunk's car over into a parking lot somewhere, or following me into town to safeguard the contents. After all, there were thieves out there who might steal that half case of Schlitz if we left it on the side of the road.

About two weeks later, Robert rode up on me in a roadside brawl with (Mike) Rowland Mark. I had already smoked him pretty good with Sheriff Little Man Broughton's five D cell Kel Light, and "Mike's" head was "bleeding like a stuck hog." I had Thomas Adolph at my favorite point of disadvantage: .357 Magnum, "high-noon-gunpoint," trying to keep him off me, prepared but not really wanting to kill him. He was actually trying to hit "Mike" with a six-foot bean pole he had snatched up out of Country Music Legend Vince Gill's drummer, Martin Parker's (June 1, 1952 to September 10, 2015) garden. Robert saw the gleaming reflection off that nickel Smith and Wesson, and figured he better get out and help me, which of course he did. Everybody but Robert and I had to go to jail that night. The following Monday morning, Mike went to work for Milton and Murray Tynch at Valhalla. His whole head was wrapped in white gauze, and Murray told him, "Good Grief, Mike. All you need now is a flute and a Cobra in a basket."

You really can NOT make this stuff up! And it sure was fun.

Getting "Rolled" at Choke's Grill

The very next night, Rowland Mark's, and Thomas Adolph's brother Eddie got "rolled" over at Choke's Grill on Oakum Street. That is the honky-tonk with about fifteen or twenty bullet holes through the walls, just above head height, around the pool table and craps arena. Eddie was a little bit scrawny, and didn't go out much without his two older brothers (now incarcerated from the night before), because they protected him from what they called, "The Bad Asses."

But on this night Eddie, in all his radiant glory, flashed too much of his " 'backer croppin' " wages in front of the wrong people. In his drunken stupor, from his RIGHT front pocket, his cash had "gotten away from him." Or so he thought.

He staggered about four blocks over to my house on Carteret Street, and started banging on the screen door: "MACATHER, COME HELP ME!"

Becky and my newborn daughter, Jenny were already asleep, but awakened by the commotion. Becky dialed 335-4300, Williamston SHP Communication Center, and got Richard Alexander on the line.

Eddie finally kicked in both the screen door and the main door, still yelling, "MACATHER, COME HELP ME!" Richard could hear him yelling through the telephone, and got busy sending the cavalry to my house.

Robert Hendrix and I were the first ones there, found Eddie crawling up the steps, and snatched his little drunk self right out onto the brick patio. By now Eddie was blubbering like a baby. We found almost all of his money in his LEFT front pocket. I let the other responding Edenton Police Officers go on about their business, and Robert and I sat on the porch, trying to figure out what to do with Eddie. We couldn't put him in jail, because his brothers would have beaten his butt a second and third time for his having lost his cash with which he would buy them beer. FINAL ANSWER: I wrote a note and put it in Eddie's pocket: "Eddie, you kicked in my front door. I have kept $50.00 of your money to fix the door." We then took Eddie over to his mother's house at Valhalla. The next day, Eddie was out on Rocky Hock Road trying to hitch a ride to town to bond out his two sorry brothers with what little cash he had left.

"GO GITTUM, MACATHER! GO GITTUM!"

Valhalla seemed to be a hotbed of activity when Robert and I were working. We had just left our dutifully ritualistic cleaning off the grass and dirt on Trooper Robert Allen's gravestone (November 6, 1940 – July 12, 1976), and we met a drunk driver just pulling back onto the roadway from having "cleaned out" the ditch in front of HER Rocky Hock Baptist Church. I arrested Henrietta, and Robert got to drive HER old Pontiac up to The Tynch Family's Valhalla Trucking lot. Before I could get that mile and a half, I met not one, but two cars running 87 and 91 mph respectively. When I bootlegged my Patrol Car in front of Tommy and Jean Leary's Green Leaf Plant Farm, I threw the unbelted drunk woman slam up under the dashboard. When she crawled back up onto the seat, Henrietta took her boney little fist, slammed my dashboard, and yelled, "Go gittum, MacAther! G. D. it! Go Gittum!" Of course I did. The first car was a favorite son in Rocky Hock, NC, and the second car was Chowan County Sheriff Troy Toppin chasing him. Sheriff Toppin's dash mounted blue light had fallen into the floorboard, and he couldn't drive that fast and remount it. In quick order, we cleared up that "little misunderstanding", I went back to Valhalla, picked up Robert, and we took the drunk to the breathalyzer where she blew .31%. She and Robert had been childhood friends, and from then on, she didn't ever have much to say to Robert.

Once when we were chasing an "absent parent" kidnapper, the speeding car skidded through the T-intersection, jumped the ditch, cleared the yard, struck a tree, and ran into Robert's brother, Mack Hendrix's house on Cannons Ferry Road. The car was wedged sideways between a pine Tree and the chimney. Turns out that Mack was asleep in bed, and upon the horrific crash, ran out the back door: "Running Bare." Not knowing what we might find, Robert and I ran up to the smoking wreck with its wheels still spinning. The kidnapper handed Robert the baby out the now perpendicular car's window. He was too "injured" to climb out on his own. Indomitable Robert recognized his tenant neighbor and told him, "Junior, if you don't climb out of your daddy's car RIGHT NOW, on your own, I am gonna send Trooper McArthur in here to drag you out." Guess what! Out popped Junior, with a sheepish grin.

Tonto and his Hook Truck

About 3:00 one morning, we chased a '55 totally restored Chevrolet 210, 2 door Post, 454 CID, up a woods path. The occupants jumped and ran into the darkness and cloud of dust. We never saw them, but we knew they were hemmed in by snake infested swamps. I sat down on a stump and waited, while Robert drove my patrol car back out onto Wildcat Road and radioed SHP Telecommunicator Gay Pearce to call "Tonto" to bring his "hook truck" and to come get the cherry red feast for your eyes out from the woods. Upon arrival at the scene, Tonto observed a grizzled old white-haired man wearing a black leather jacket and a baseball cap driving Mike's car. That was not good. Tonto took off back down Wildcat Road toward town. Robert had to run him down and Blue Light him. When Robert approached Tonto, what Tonto had in his hand was not a bow and arrow. Eventually that night, not only did I charge the driver, but the owner also, with LOTS of "good stuff!"

We stopped a car that ran the stop sign one night at Valhalla. The young nurse told us that she had been called in to the hospital to assist some bad wreck victims. Well, me and my high and mighty self said, "Well, LuAnn, if there was a bad wreck, Robert and I would certainly know about it." Her response knocked both of us off our feet: "I suppose that they call the important ones first!"

Mr. and Mrs. Do No Wrong

As Robert and I "stationary patrolled" the Cisco Community one night, sitting in the parking lot of Joe Hoggard's Place, we observed two vehicles rapidly approaching a T-intersection controlled by a duly erected stop sign. We could tell by their rapid rate of approach, that they did not intend to "come to a full and complete stop." There was actually, adequate visibility to the left and right for it to be determined safe to proceed, but how about if "the coast had not been clear?" You know what happened next! SWOOSH! The white Cadillac swerved right through the intersection, nearly in a broadside slide to the right, as if they were fleeing from the pursuing vehicle behind them. Not to be outdone, lo and behold, the second vehicle, a pickup truck blew through the intersection in nearly the same manner. In this mini-residential community, it was best not to spook the neighborhood. Since it was obvious that these two vehicles were coupled on a mission, rather than to throw caution to the wind, and take off after them like a bat out of hell, we eased out of the gravel lot and I nailed that '78 Plymouth. Northbound by Tim White's pecan orchard toward Tyner we went. I could see the offenders still ahead of me, but at my speed in excess of 100mph, I was gaining on them. Apparently, the driver of the Cadillac saw me coming up behind at a rate of speed greater than hers, which was significant in its own right. I saw brake lights come on and then the truck's lights lit up. Right in front of Center Hill Baptist Church, Robert and I made our move. I activated my blue lights and pulled alongside the Cadillac. My "modified high performance blue light" spun so fast that it illuminated the driver's face as she "wide eyed" to her left. She pulled onto the right shoulder at the Tyner Post

Office. I stayed in the roadway, and motioned with my flashlight for the pickup driver pull in behind the Cadillac. I circled into the Post Office lot and shined my halogen headlights into the two vehicles, and onto their single occupant drivers. I approached the Cadillac driver, and she characteristically asked, "Mike, where did you come from?" She was unsure whether I was gonna blister her butt for speeding, running the stop sign, reckless driving, or all of it. I responded, "Anne, you were running in excess of eighty in this forty-five zone, and what about my stop sign back in Cisco?" She shot back, "Mike, if I had stopped at that sign, Joe would have hit me so hard from behind that it would have knocked me into next week. Besides, we always run that stop sign on the way home from the basketball games at Rocky Hock Academy." By now Joe was out of his truck. He had heard what she had just told me, and raised his hands, palms up, shaking his head in total surrender! What did I do? As Robert joined in the melee, I knew that he was related by marriage to Anne, and she was so embarrassed. I wrote them both for reckless driving. In court Assistant District Attorney Dick Parker let them plead to fifty-four in a 45, and wished them, "Happy Motoring." We all still laugh about this episode when we meet at the July 4th events, Fall Festivals, or the grocery store.

Everybody liked Robert and respected him even more so. I admired him a lot because he made everything he did look easy.

Robert's love for his two daughters, Robin and Jill, and wife, Marvis (July 24, 1929 to October 1, 2018) showed through in all that he did. He always was a gentleman, and considered the feelings of others before his own (even some of my arrestees benefited from Robert's compassion and empathy).

"Marine! Ten-Hut!"

One morning about 4am, Robert on his way home, ran up on a passed out drunk driver in the middle of NC-32 in front of Chowan County Commissioner Wayne Goodwin's (July 14, 1947 to October 25, 2006) "Convenient Center." He called me on Perquimans County Sheriff Little Man Broughton's two-way radio to, "Come get this drunk out of my way." I arrived at the fairly well-lit section of storefront roadway, and could tell that this driver was a military man from his many bumper stickers. His FM radio "sub-woofer" was blaring obscene "so-called music." **I never touched him**. I reached over his "head-bobbing to the music" body, shifted the car into PARK, turned his ignition off, and removed the keys. I yelled. I blew my siren. I shined Robert's bright flashlight on his face. I beat on his white vinyl topped, blue Buick Riviera boat-tail cruiser, - 455 cubic inch, 260 horsepower. I hit his back bumper with my patrol car front bumper – twice. Nothing seemed to faze "Mr. Cool."

And then along came a cooler head: Marvis Hendrix boss and Chowan High School Principal, Gil Underwood. At the top of his lungs, he commanded, **"Marine! TEN-HUT!"** That Marine lurched forward, sprang from his vehicle, and performed a low crawl combat maneuver, right there on the centerline of NC-32. He was unsure of his location, and his PTSD reaction was not a pretty sight.

In his red fedora and pin striped Zoot Suit, this Marine was sharp as a tack. We frisked him and poured him into the back seat of my Black and Silver. Robert drove the Riviera onto the store lot. After blowing a .24% breath alcohol, off to the Magistrate's Office we went. Carlton Perry was summoned to find Probable Cause, the warrants were issued and served, and we "Perp walked" him over to the Chowan County Detention Center. He made several phone calls, and family members were on their way to bond him out quickly so that Jailer Jim would not have to "stripe" him.

Finally, as the sun was rising, we were headed home when Jim Aylesworth (April 30, 1939 to December 28, 2020) at the jail called us back to town. When Jailer Jim searched the Zoot Suited inmate, he found a loaded .32 caliber, Harrington & Richardson blued revolver, strategically dangling at an angle in front of his dangle, on a clothes hanger wire, attached inside his belt buckle. He was **just too drunk** to shoot any of about eight of us with whom he had been in much too close contact.

Living Out Loud with Grace, Grit, and Gratitude

Sheriff "Little Man" Broughton Invades the Bear's Den

Julian H. "Little Man" Broughton (January 23, 1926 – July 13, 2005) served as "The High Sheriff" of Perquimans County from 1966 through 1986. He was a friend to all and stranger to none. Robert had grown up with him. Everybody knew or "knew of" Sheriff Broughton. Particularly his driving repertoire. When nothing seemed to work, "Little Man" found a way to fix it. He provided Perquimans County police radios and five-D cell KEL lights to all of us who worked in HIS COUNTY, just in case he needed us. And he needed us, a lot!

His neighbors complained about the traffic and drunks that hung out at "The Bear's Den" on US-17. That Saturday night he put on one of Catfish Hunter's New York Yankees baseball caps and a leather flight jacket. He pulled the cap down over his eyes, paraded right past the front door bouncer, up to the bar, and ordered a Long Island Iced Tea. Within minutes, he was "made." On his radio he called for help, and Robert and I were standing by. Upon our arrival, the parking lot was so jammed with cars, that we had to park across US-17. Little Man's Deputy "Cracker" was standing in the lot with his drawn .38 pointed up to the sky, "scanning" the situation. I handed Robert a sawed-off double barrel 12-gauge shotgun ("ESCOPETA" scratched on the stock- Spanish) I had confiscated up at Ike's Place on Millpond Road in Gates County back in 1975.

We now had one man inside the honky-tonk. Two men were covering the parking lot into which there was not room to squeeze even a single moped, and my entrance made the second man inside. As I passed "Stickum," the bouncer at the front door, I snatched his .25 semi-auto out of his right hip pocket which was where I had been told it would be. When Little Man pulled out his Smith & Wesson .45, the game was on! Everybody in the house scurried for cover, "Like cockroaches when the light is turned on." (Lingo from Trooper Benjamin Franklin Chappell, my SHP Field Training Officer). The main function that Sheriff Broughton and I managed to accomplish (somehow), was to see that neither of us got shoved, shot, kicked, spit on, or run over. Partiers went through the attic.

They went out the bathroom window. There was only room for so many to get through that narrow front door at one time, and Stickum had been the frontrunner. The two-inch galvanized pipe still had the back door barricaded with a lock on it. The illegal tax-paid liquor was abandoned on, under, and around the bar. "Green, leafy, vegetable matter" was scattered everywhere.

The dust cleared. Robert and Cracker came inside and joined Sheriff Broughton and me. We all determined that on this night, a miracle had taken place, right under our noses: nobody got shot, nobody left bloody, and everybody was GONE. Not one single wreck in that jammed up parking lot, though we did find several strips of chrome side molding that had been scrubbed off somebody's Oldsmobile. Throughout the bar we began to collect "evidence:" two .32 Long Colt revolvers, four billy-clubs, a short piece of half-inch chain, several razor blades, a sawed off pool cue, half a pair of dice, the equivalent of six or eight decks of playing cards, two switch blade knives, three pairs of ladies' panties, one bra, forty plus marijuana "roaches," one nickel-plated set of brass knuckles, an Old Hickory Butcher Knife, four box-cutters, a partridge in a pear tree, and a screw driver. There was a stainless steel, Charter Arms, "Bulldog" .44 Special revolver underwater, inside the toilet tank in the ladies' bathroom. There were enough fedoras, scarves, studded canes, pin-striped vests, one black eye-patch, and fake diamond rings to have a heckuva yard sale.

We took a few minutes to celebrate Cracker's last day of employment: "Boy, am I glad y'all didn't get me kilt on my last day!"

"I Stobbed Him to Death!"

As we headed back to Edenton, we decided to swing by the "Blue Eagle Night Club" down by the Perquimans County line on the Yeopim River. As we rounded the curve, we could see headlight beams flashing across the tree line behind the club. So many cars were trying to get out onto the pavement that they had effectively "stopped up" the single lane exit. A pickup diagonally traversed the shallow ditch, and was gone in a cloud of blue smoke.

And there she was!

A partially clad woman was standing on the centerline waving her arms for somebody to stop and pick her up and take her away. Carlton Perry (riding shotgun), Robert Hendrix (backseat driver's side), and I obliged her. She seemed oblivious to her misfortune: she climbed right into a marked, black and silver North Carolina State Highway Patrol car. Even with the blue light flashing on the top of the car, she opened the door and rolled herself into the darkened back seat. Did I mention that she was only partially clad when she jumped into the back seat? Also, did I mention that she jumped right into Robert's lap? Robert, while scrambling for relief, and I wondered aloud what the big deal was that had driven her to such erroneous distraction.

She had just stabbed her husband, Clyde to death with a pair of barber's scissors.

In the last twenty minutes.

Her words: "I stobbed him to death!"

She had very little blood on her, but both hands were covered when she grabbed my headrest. We pulled onto the narrow shoulder, out of the way of the outflow melee/evacuation. I am sure that one or more of the forty cars contained either witnesses or evidence, but there were only three of "us," and hundreds of "them." Robert and Carlton monitored the killer, while I got the traffic straightened out. We summoned SBI Special Agent William Earl Godley to the scene. He always brought his own version of "taking care of business."

Agent Godley quickly summed up the nature of the behest, put Aretha in handcuffs and into the back of his brown Dodge. He went into "the back room" at the club, took pictures of the body, checked the multiple stab wounds, came back to the roadside, and off to town they went. In the interrogation room, Bill determined several very interesting facts:

- Aretha was "Toe up from the flo up," drunk.
- Aretha had, in fact stabbed Clyde over 40 times.
- Aretha had choked Clyde to death with a red wool sweater that was the only piece of clothing anywhere near the naked victim's body.
- The reason behind her rage was that Clyde would not, could not "perform" his usual abilities in a satisfactory manner. SO SHE KILLED HIM!

- Aretha was nearly uncontrollable, in that she weighed about two-hundred pounds, her too little clothing was in shambles, and there were really no "handles" by which to grab her.
- Aretha was placed into the holding cell at the Edenton Police Department to "rest."

Robert and Carlton and I were, by now growing weary of the rubber-neckers and the flatulent inquiries, "Did anybody get killed?" Ed Taylor brought the Rescue Squad ambulance to the scene, scooped up Clyde, and took him to the Chowan Hospital Emergency Room for examination by the Chowan County Chief Medical Examiner, Dr. Liebert E. DeVine (May 21, 1947 to December 7, 2011).

Dr. DeVine was not an unassuming entity. He told it like it was! His first words upon our arrival were, "Well, I can tell you that he did not die from those scissor pocks, in that they are only about a centimeter deep. SEE! The sweater around his neck is not sufficient for his having been strangled. His heart blood/alcohol reading is .52%. He drank himself to death!" "Alcohol Poisoning!"

He was right, and Aretha lived to party another day.

"Talkin'"

It was cold that Christmas Eve. Robert and I were winding down our "wish lists" for the night as we headed to the Edenton Police Department where Robert had left his car. We were traveling south on NC-32, and approached The White Oak School intersection where both my children, Jenny (11) and John (6) were students. An old blue Chevrolet Nova pulled right out in front of us, and I had to slam on brakes and go into the northbound lane to keep him from killing us all! I blocked his path, and his world immediately lit up!

The Nova stopped dead in its tracks in the middle of the Highway Patrol car blocked, southbound lane. When I got to the driver's locked door, he would not roll down the window. There was a female voice raising a ruckus from inside the car, but I could not see inside the car at all. I told Robert, "Watch this!" I took out my trusty, beat up blackjack and prepared to knock out the glass, but it began to slowly recede into the door panel. There sat Toot Stanley in all his radiant glory, buck naked. His female acquaintance had already missed several good chances to shut up.

Somehow Toot got his drunk self out, grabbed his pants and shirt, and dressed himself, still right there in the middle of the road on Christmas Eve. Thank goodness there was absolutely no other traffic then traveling on NC-32.

I told you that I could not see through the rolled-up window into the car. The windshield was also occluded, as was every single window on the Nova. All except for a peephole the size of a cantaloupe on the driver's side of the windshield. Don't you know that all that <u>heavy condensation</u> on the interior of those crystal-coated windows created a mystical, supernatural experience for those therein when I lit up my blue light serenade.

I arrested Toot, and put him in the back seat of my patrol car. I went back up to the Nova, and told Zula (She worked in the lunchroom at White Oak School), to sit tight and shut up for just a little while. Under the interior lights of my black and silver, I began to question ol' Toot. We had known each other for at least ten years through working together at the Chowan County Fair and helping out our neighbors during hurricane relief efforts.

When I asked him what in the world he was doing out this late on Christmas Eve, he had a great response, "I went to the shop at White Oak to get my Christmas presents, hidden there from my six children." Good GRIEF! He was right. There were about three boxes of wrapped presents, a BB gun, and a tricycle in his back seat. When I asked him about the windows being all fogged up, he didn't have much to say. So I asked him again, "Toot, how did those windows get so fogged up that you could not see through any of them while you were trying to get home?" His response was, "Me and Zula been "talkin'." "Talking?" I asked.

Robert and I rolled our eyes at each other, and I lit back into him. "Toot, Mr. Hendrix and I have been riding around all night, and we've been talking too. But our windows are not all fogged up!" "Well Cap'm Mac! I reckon y'all probly ain't been talkin' about the same thing that me and Zula been talkin' about."

'Nuf said!

We pushed the Christmas presents over onto one side, and loaded Zula into the back seat of the Nova. We all headed to town. Robert was sitting on my SHP issued, disposable thermal blanket, and driving the Nova. He dropped Zula off at her daddy's house at Valhalla. We went to the Edenton Police Department where Sergeant Jim Farmer administered a Breathalyzer test:.24%. We called Toot's wife, and she sent her two brothers to pick up the Nova and Toot to bring him home so that he could be there on Christmas morning.

Merry Christmas! Right?

Hootie to the Rescue

Before we left Edenton one Saturday night to go work traffic after the Chowan Middle School basketball game, we stopped by Allen Swanner's Edenton SHELL gasoline station and filled up with fuel. We heard four shots! They sounded like firecrackers to a novice, but I knew them to be at least .45 caliber slugs being let loose. AND THEY WERE CLOSE, TOO. The deeply echoing reverberations indicated to me that they had come from Choke's Grille on Oakum Street. We jumped into the car, did not activate my blue light, sped south on Broad Street, and turned left onto East Albemarle Street.

THERE HE WENT!

A tall skinny black man wearing a white short sleeved unbuttoned shirt with a large pistol in his left hand, ran from between two houses, right across (right to left) in front of my patrol car. I don't mean he "ran!" I mean he nearly flew! I slammed on brakes, jumped from my car, drew my own .357 Magnum pistol, and the chase was on. We ran between houses all the way across the block toward East Carteret Street. He tripped on a rusty discarded set of box springs, got up and continued his flight. Not having seen the box springs, I too tripped across them. He ran back toward Blair Funeral Home and cut across a weeded vacant lot where he climbed a chain link fence. I holstered my .357, and climbed the fence. When I landed on the other side, somehow I heard a "thump." My forward momentum was up, but I stopped and realized that my pistol had just fallen from the holster into the knee-high weeds. I still had my .22 Magnum Derringer in my hip pocket, so I continued the chase.

About this time, Edenton Police Officers Sonny Jones (November 8, 1942 to May 12, 2010) and Jeff Knox had arrived. They effectively "cut off" and tackled the exhausted shooter. The shooter's gun had fallen into the box springs back behind Carteret Street. My gun was over behind Blair Funeral Home near Oakum Street. What a predicament!

I placed that .22 Magnum into my too large holster, covered it with my right forearm, and returned to where I thought I had lost my .357. With my flashlight I was milling around in the weeds near the fence line, when here came one of my friendly local drunks to whom I had loaned five dollars the week before. "Can I help you, Cap'm Mac?" Sure he could help me, but did I want his help? No! We were attracting entirely too much attention. I wandered 100 feet toward Oakum street, and continued my search for "my handcuffs." I took my handcuffs and put them in my pants pocket, thereby showing Hootie that my handcuffs were no longer strapped and snapped onto my Sam Browne belt.

I thanked Hootie for his help, and returned to my patrol car where Robert was standing guard as was standard procedure. He had radioed my location and my flight pattern to the Edenton Police Department, Senior Dispatcher William A. "Bill" Elliott, Jr. Bill was a good friend of mine, and he took a personal interest in all the shenanigans that involved his "Good Friend, Trooper McArthur." Always the gentleman, was Bill, and we all loved him dearly for his resourcefulness in always getting us what we needed on the other end of the radio signal.

Without adequate firepower, Robert and I went to my house and got a Browning, Hi-Power 9mm, semi-automatic pistol that would fit into my holster. We finished out the night, but at Sunday daybreak I was back over on Carteret Street, looking for my issued .357, nickel plated, Smith & Wesson Model 19 Revolver. I really did not want to have to tell Sergeant Deans or First Sergeant John T. Rowe, that I had lost "his" weapon.

I walked and I circled. I backtracked. I kicked weeds. I pulled weeds. I walked and I circled some more. Here came Hootie. He walked and he circled. He backtracked. He kicked weeds. And then he kicked some more weeds. And then he kicked some more weeds, kinda in the same spot. I watched him as he kicked some more weeds. By the time I could get over to his location, he had effectively covered up my pistol, and stood on the weeds in an effort to suppress its mound. I reached down, picked up my pistol, thanked Hootie for finding my pistol, gave him $10, and off we both went.

All's well that ends well. Right?

Location, Location, Location

Location #1, The Plane Crash

So many jurisdictional (LOCATION) dilemmas permeate law enforcement strategies, but many can get "manhandled" if approached and begun in a timely manner. County lines or city limits are usually the territorial jurisdiction delineators, but deep in the swamps it becomes difficult to decipher just where that "line" is. Once when I was in Greenville, N.C. getting my oil changed, I was notified of a small Piper J-3 Cub, high-wing aircraft having disappeared from the Edenton Airport's radar, and presumably crashed in "The Big Woods" section of Chowan County. From the racks at Troop A Garage, I asked SHP Telecommunicator Lenward Cowan, Jr. to contact The Chowan County Sheriff's Office.

A great friend of mine, Chowan County Magistrate Carlton Nixon Perry (December 23, 1937 - November 4, 2017) hunted and knew those woods like the back of his cancer scarred hand. Telecommunicator Cowan called Carlton off his blue Ford 2000 Tractor, who immediately responded to The Iron Gate entrance into the vast Poccosin and swampland of the famous "Big Woods." A United States Coast Guard Helicopter had been dispatched and arrived at the crash site at about the same time that Carlton arrived. As the Sikorsky HH-60J "Jayhawk" helicopter hovered over the towering pines of the forest, Carlton directed first responders to travel to Davenport Lane and enter the woods from that location as being more appropriate and less daunting to get to the site. The pilot from the helicopter advised Sheriff Troy Toppin and his deputies that there were no survivors, and that the plane had partially burned on impact. There was no pattern or trail of gradual descent, but that it appeared to be a straight down, vertical crash trajectory. Paul Edsel Waff, Jr. (January 31, 1953 to April 29, 2018) of Waff Brothers, Inc. arrived with his Allis Chalmers HD-11 tracked bulldozer, and bulldozed a path to the crash site. We lost Paul way too early, and his children, Stephanie and Cam continue his legacy of unselfish giving and magnanimous generosity to his country. Robert Hendrix wondered aloud whether the crash site was in Chowan County or Perquimans County, but was naysaid. Sheriff Toppin and his men were doing the heavy lifting, and therefore the crash was in Chowan.

First responders, the North Carolina Forestry Service, and half of Chowan and Perquimans County residents braved the Timber Rattlers, and traipsed through the thick Poison Ivy and Cat Briars. Investigators from the Federal Aviation Administration (FAA) arrived and took control of the scene. Two pilots' bodies were recovered. The plane was painstakingly extracted by Paul Waff, an experienced pilot himself. The FAA team of investigators reassembled it inside a hangar at the Edenton Airport. Sheriff Toppin and his team of professionals reported and documented the procedures with a fine-toothed comb. The burgeoning paperwork was completed and submitted to the Federal Aviation Administration (FAA), and to all the dozens of agencies requesting such.

Guess what: The "LOCATION" was Perquimans County.

Location #2, The Floater

There was another LOCATION issue that surfaced up on US-17 at the Chowan – Perquimans County Line. SHP Line Sergeant Jim Farmer was traveling to the Pizza Hut in Edenton to take a dinner hour with several of us (too many in one LOCATION according to our First Sergeant D. G. Dail). He was late, so his speed MIGHT have been a little excessive, but roadside motorists flagged him down. There in the headwaters of the Yeopim River was the fully clothed body of a dead man, floating face down. This "ditch" was the county line delineator between Chowan and Perquimans. About the same time as Sergeant Farmer got there, so did Perquimans County Sheriff Julian H. "Little Man" Broughton.

As Sergeant Farmer summonsed Trooper Y Z Newberry, Trooper Mike McArthur and Robert Hendrix, and Chowan County Sheriff Troy Toppin, Little Man clawed his way down to the floater, took a broken off reed, and pushed the body over onto the Chowan County side of the delineator ditch. There you go! Another LOCATION/jurisdiction issue solved.

Location #3, Fishing/Driving Drunk

As Robert and I were patrolling our beat in a military manner over in Arrowhead Beach beside Dillard's Creek in Rocky Hock, SHP Telecommunicator Alec Jones radioed in. He had received a report that over in Belvidere in front of Wolfman Jack's house there was a party goin' on at the N. C. Wildlife Resources Commission's Boating Access Area. Supposedly there was some underaged drinking and driving going on; and fist fighting, too. Well there was nothing to do, but to head on over there and see how we could "help 'em." We shot north on NC-32, turned right at Teeny Boy Perry's Store across from Robert's house, rocketed through Ryland, NC, crossed through Bessie's Bottom at the County Line, and onto Drinking Hole Road which dumped out onto NC-37 whereupon the melee was situated (Imagine that).

As we passed Hunter's Fork Pentecostal Holiness Church and approached The Belvidere Fire Department, lo and behold we nearly collided head-on with a pickup truck, fully in our lane. Fortunately there was enough shoulder to avoid the collision, but not enough to avoid a severe case of hostility on Robert's and my parts. The driver of the truck apparently seized in the moment, realized his error in judgment, and accelerated toward Bessie's Bottom at the County Line.

As I overtook him, Robert noticed something flopping off the back of the truck. With only about 100 yards before the intersection, and both the truck and I still in Perquimans County, I decided to let him enter into Chowan County before I activated my blue light. There again, LOCATION/jurisdiction came into focus. Of course the young driver tried to run on foot, but I captured him. He probably didn't weigh much more than 120 pounds, but he was just a little slow, and stumbled onto the ditch bank covered with "Cockleburs." Obviously, this was not his night, and wouldn't be for about the next two hours before he was placed into the Chowan County Jail. He only blew a .11%, but in an inexperienced, lightweight driver, that was enough for him to have fallen into a heap of trouble, not to mention having to pick about twenty cockleburs out of his hair, and off his clothing. Inexperienced driver, inexperienced drinker, inexperienced speeder/runaway, and trying to do it all at one time.

Oh, yeah! What was that flopping off the back of his truck? On each side of his truck bed, at the rear of the siderails, there is a square hole suitable for anchoring 2x2 posts to erect a canopy over the truck. This boy had inserted a fishing rod and a Zebco 404 closed faced spinning reel into each of the two holes. Flailing haphazardly from each rod tip was about thirty feet of fifty-pound test, green monofilament fishing line. One was affixed with a yellow tailed Arbogast Hula Popper, Largemouth Bass lure, and the other was fitted with a black Arbogast Jitterbug. The driver/fisherman wished he had never cast his lot onto Drinking Hole Road.

Don't Rob Your Neighbor in the Snow

One snowy afternoon, Robert and I had positioned our cars door to door in the center of Chowan County so that WHEN, not IF a wreck happened we could get there in a reasonable amount of time. Response times were much more significant "back in the day," than they are now. SHP Telecommunicator Tommy Tolson radioed to us that an armed robbery had just occurred at one of Chowan County's last "country stores," just about a mile up the road from Valhalla, across from the N C Forestry Service Fire Watch Tower. Mrs. White, Tim's Mom was the operator of this store, and was like a "Mom" to all of us who frequented her store for the free coffee and Apple Fritters for which she was famous.

One of the local hooligans, in a drugged craze, decided that he would use his stolen .38 revolver, and rob Mrs.White of the thirty or forty dollars that she might have had in the old timey crank style cash register. He pulled a Virginia Fork Produce Grain Dealership cap over his face, pulled up his T-shirt over his nose and entered the store. He knew that Mrs. White would recognize him, so he took these extra precautions.

He scooted around the end of the counter, cocked his pistol, and demanded her money, "All of it!" When he turned around and grabbed a burned, red, hot dog off the rotisserie grill, that was where things went further south, quickly. Mrs. White took the four-foot-tall box of wafer ice-cream cones, and whacked him over the head with all of her might, and with its three pounds of rigidity. She knocked his hat off, and his T-shirt came down. His OODA LOOP (Observe, Orient, Decide, Act) was totally shattered. She yelled, "Poor Dog," what are you doing?" With that, rather than squeeze back by the cone box wielding, "mad as a hatter" storekeep, he bounded over the counter, and fell in the floor, right beside the telephone mounted on the wall. He took out his hawkbill knife and cut the cord - - - to the Budweiser sign, not the telephone. (I've still got that nicked blade hawkbill).

In his haste, he dropped his knife, and ran out of the store, turning left right by Rufus (August 13, 1919 to August 23, 1986) and Bert (July 13, 1922 to October 31, 2010) White's house, toward Gary Farmer's (October 24, 1947 to September 26, 2018) Automobile Repair Shop. In the three-inch snow, we tracked him east on the Cofield Road to the Union Camp Papermill logwoods path that ran parallel to NC-32, behind the store. We tracked him about a quarter of a mile, and found where he left the path, ran over to a downed White Pine stump, and stuffed the gun, and a white, four- pound paper sack stuffed with $63.00 in it. He returned to the logwoods path, and continued his flight. Robert and I looked at the length of his stride. That armed robber was covering some ground, er, snow.

About a mile north, the path dumped out onto the Greenhall Road right beside the Wallace B. "Cowboy" White (died September 6, 2011) Family Graveyard. Just as "Poor Dog" broke out of the tree line, up pulled Chowan County Deputy Sheriff Glenn Perry (October 5, 1924 to December 23, 2016). "Poor Dog" skidded to a stop, and yielded to that pointed and aimed .38 revolver that Deputy Perry drew down on him. Ol' Robert quoted the A-Team (1983), Lieutenant Colonel Hannibal Smith, and said, "I love it when a plan comes together!"

Sneaky Snakes X 9

To put it mildly, Robert did not like snakes. Occasionally when our paths crossed with a Copperhead, Timber Rattler, Black Snake, or even just a little Green Snake, Robert's demeanor became defensive, almost to the point of hostile. He just really didn't like them. BUT I DID. When William Fleming killed a monstrous Canebrake (Timber Rattler), he called Chowan County Dispatch for me to come get the five-foot torso. Robert and I were at Mrs. Boswell's Restaurant on Queen Street, drinking coffee (Cokes) with the locals, and listening to their yarns. Robert had ridden to the nationally famous restaurant beside Filbert's Creek with me, but he told me that he would "Catch a ride" back to his car. I was not surprised. I went out to Indian Trail with a Toe-sack and got the snake, skinned and tanned the hide, and mounted it on a Cypress "lap" cut from a monstrous, centuries old specimen that had been harvested by Ray Bateman's Logging Company. My daughter Jenny and son, John entered it in the "Miscellaneous Category" at the Chowan County Fair and won a blue ribbon for "Best in Show." It now hangs on the wall at the Chowan Edenton Optimist Club Building at 147 Old Hertford Road, Edenton, North Carolina.

#1. "The Flying Black Snake"

You know that snakes really seem to begin their nightly scavenger hunts in the somewhat cooler, late evenings. One September evening a little after dusk, four of us were holding a very productive "driver's license checking station" in front of Chowan High School Principal Gil Underwood's apple orchard on Jody Dail's Curve on U S -17 in Hertford, N.C. As darkness was upon us, the decision was made to "call it off." Apparently, each of us had met our "Reasonable Level of Production," spelled Q.U.O.T.A.

Robert, ever wary, somehow spied a six-foot Black Snake climbing the cinder block wall onto a rental storage unit about seventy-five yards off the road. The wall angled underneath a mercury vapor security light mounted above the doorway entrance. It seems that the "bug light" attracted moths,

Mayflies, gnats, and other insects which provided a smorgasbord of dining delights for American Toads, Blue Tailed Skinks, and Bullfrogs. As the bugs increased, so did the four-legged amphibians.

As the frogs and toads multiplied, guess what came looking for an easy meal. Well all four of us drove our marked Black and Silver patrol cars up the gravel path to get a better look at this huge snake, and Robert was not excited … yet. The snake propelled itself from the wall and onto the parking lot, coiled up, and got ready to do battle. Charlie Mims (April 12, 1938 – September 18, 2017) peeled out his SHP issued Ithaca Pump Model 37, 12-gauge shotgun, declaring, "I'm gonna kill that so and so."

I could stand it no longer. I said, "Wait Charlie! Don't shoot that thing. I will kill it for you." With that being said, I walked behind the snake which was focused on the other Troopers. I reached down, grabbed it by the tail, and raised my hand gripping the snake so as to "crack the whip" with the snake. "SLIPS." The weight of the flailing snake going skyward was great enough, that when I came down with my arm, the serpent continued on up into the darkness.

Wouldn't you know it! It was not skyborne but just a very few seconds before it magically re-entered Charlie Mims atmosphere, falling right at the spot where he used to be standing. You know that I could not have orchestrated a better/worse outcome. Greater fun hath no Trooper than to "get over" on one of his friends. I might have gotten a leg up on Charlie that night, but he never let me forget that he owed me a killing like the one he gave that poor ol' Black Snake that night. He led me to believe that I had been, "spared," "for a reason that only God knew!"

#2. Who Put That Snake In The Telephone Booth?

Hubert was the Senior Jailer who worked the "Booking Desk" at the Chatham County Jail on "The Circle" amid US-64 in Pittsboro, North Carolina. We all liked Hubert, but understood (and appreciated) that he took no "junk" from anybody. Therefore he consummately qualified himself for some of us ingenious young (and old) law enforcement officers to try to "get his goat." And we did! Regularly! It was learned that he disliked snakes. Uh, Oh!

One hot Monday afternoon in July, as a Wildlife Enforcement Officer (Game Warden), I was "checking" fishing licenses of some fishermen on the Haw River up near Bynum, just south of Chapel Hill, North Carolina. University of North Carolina at Chapel Hill college kids were notorious for fishing without licenses, keeping too many <u>and</u> undersized Largemouth Bass, smoking marijuana, and generally "frolicking" along the cooler secluded areas of the river's banks. Naturally this was a "target rich environment" for those of us with inquiring minds, and a job to do.

As I approached a group of two boys and a girl optimistically casting what appeared to be Mirrolure silver spoons into the river, a pit-bull mix bulldog silently ran up and bit me on my "buttocks," to quote Forrest Gump. It turned out to only be a slight nip, but enough for me to lose my element of surprise (and my patience) with the fishermen. The scantily clad yankee girl told me that I had gotten what I deserved, trying to sneak up on them like that. She was probably right.

I could not believe what they had in a five-gallon bucket: a very dead, four-foot Red Bellied Water Snake. Can you see the writing on the wall yet? I cajoled them out of their snake, put him in a burlap sack in the trunk of my car. Off to see Hubert I went.

This was the first day of a two-week-long session of Criminal Superior Court for Chatham County. Famous U S Army World War II Captain James Hinton "Pou" Bailey (August 14, 1917 - January 20, 2004) was the Senior Resident Superior Court Judge, and was still "on the bench," trying a pair of Ku Klux Klansman for "innocently" planting a shovel, late one night, into the front yard of a black man's house over in Siler City. Earlier that day, due to the controversial nature of the case, there had been a lot of commotion in town, but not as much as there would be a short while later. For such occasions as this, Judge Bailey was known to come to court "armed" with two Colt .45 Revolvers: one underneath his black robe, and the other emphatically slammed upon the Black Walnut bench, right beside the worn King James Version of God's Holy Bible. At the time the Chatham County Sheriff J. A. Farrell, Jr. (May 2, 1921 – October 8, 1994) opened court "for the dispatch of the State's business," His Honor, Judge Bailey instructed "his officers" to remain inside the courtroom for the protection of the citizenry, "I have my protection."

On this day, since there were many pleas of Guilty resulting in much activity into and out of the jail across the street from the courtroom, old Hubert and his staff of one, were getting a workout. This played right into Master Trooper Coy Daniel Blackman's, Deputy John Henry Tripp's, and my hands. We had a golden opportunity to make a difference that day, and we did. Glaringly so!

I took that dead four-foot snake and tied him by his tail to the top hinge of the bi-folding glass door of the Bell Telephone Booth. This was on "The Circle" just outside on the sidewalk beside the steel door to the jail. Hubert was known to receive incoming whispered telephone calls from "Precious" upon that phone. None of us or anybody else was allowed to answer those calls on that phone! Coy and I went over to the courthouse, planted ourselves in Chatham County Sheriff J. A. Farrell's office beside the southeast window toward the jail, and dialed the number to the payphone. You will see for yourselves why we distanced ourselves.

Even though he was "busy," on about the tenth ring, Hubert nearly broke his neck exiting the jail, and grabbing the cabled receiver to the telephone handset. He simultaneously slammed the door, and guess what slung itself out of the corner, like a prize fighter, and wrapped itself around Hubert's shoulder. Now, at that point in my life, having grown up in Wilson, North Carolina around the likes of Henry, Ralph, and Graham Parker, <u>and my father John William McArthur</u> (February 7, 1921 – January 24, 1990), I THOUGHT I had seen a mad man! But I had not!

Hubert was a mad man. Everybody on the block became aware of that. Everybody inside the jail became aware of that. Slowly but surely, everybody inside the Courthouse became aware of that. Before the aftershocks diminished, everybody in Pittsboro became aware that Hubert had had an unfortunate experience and an awakening of the worst sort on a hot July afternoon in downtown Pittsboro, North Carolina.

Somehow, by the grace of God, we all lived to prank another day!

#3. Snakes in General

Snakes were nearly "tools of the trade" for young boys back in the '50s, '60s, and 70s. We were always on the lookout for them. We found snake eggs. We found snake skins. We found snake holes. We found big snakes, small snakes, poisonous snakes, non-poisonous snakes, live snakes, and dead snakes. My father's opinion and that of my best friend Robert's was that they only disliked two kinds of snakes: live ones and dead ones. Jimmy Stallings constantly liked making bad snakes (live ones) into good snakes (dead ones). Once when I made my son John thrust his arm into a five- gallon bucket containing a green snake so that he could be bitten, Jimmy threatened to call the police and the Child Protective Services Division of the Chowan County Department of Social Services. Even so, at the card game one night, I saw a snake fall from the ceiling of Jimmy's mancave. I caught it before it got into his wife's red leather E-Z Boy recliner, thereby avoiding Jimmy's golden opportunity to NEVER have Pam visit inside the holy grail of mancaves, for any reason.

#4 Snake Mail

Back in 1968, I lived as a second year Freshman at North Carolina State University in the basement of Owen Dormitory in room #51 – streetside. My roommate was Jerry Davis (WEE WINK) of Kitty Hawk, North Carolina. To put it mildly, Jerry had a vivid imagination and a lot of money. He parked a scooter behind the Belltower Restaurant on Hillsborough Street, just around the corner from Player's Retreat (PR) and The Jolly Knave (The Knave) nightspots at which he was "a regular." Upon this scooter we would go downtown into the bowels of Raleigh's nightlife to The Embers Club where he lit the place up, and I was totally out of my comfort zone. But I learned who Jackie Gore was!

One night we found a two-foot Black Snake in the gutter as we walked the half-mile back to our dorm room. I caught the snake, and let him coil around my short-sleeved forearm. Upon arrival at our dorm, Jerry's imagination caught fire. He took that black snake, opened our Post Office Box #51, and tied the snake to the interior locking mechanism. We then closed our 3"x5" postal portal. The next morning, a strange thing happened. The United States Postal Service Mail Carrier was a very small woman of Asian descent. In her crisp blue uniform, with her "Master Key," she opened the large panel consisting of about eighty mailboxes, ours included. You know what happened next! That poor ol' sneaky snake got snatched out of our mailbox, and began wildly flailing itself all about her head and shoulders. Jerry and I were too "sleepy" to have gotten up to watch this, but you can believe that we heard about it. Thank goodness that when our snake made its hasty withdrawal, it had caused the string to become unattached from the #51 lock. However heavily suspected, the powers that were, never could place the blame, even though we really wanted to own it!

Like I said, Jerry had a vivid imagination. Back in those days, each dormitory had a housekeeping staff, and our "main man" was Sam. Jerry and I shared our wealth of "souvenirs" with Sam: liquor, fireworks, cigarettes, and "magazines." Sam liked us, and we liked him. Not once did he ever report us to the RA (Resident Adviser) Ralph Birkhead for having contraband inside our room. Yes, we had two shotguns for duck hunting out at Lake Johnson. Yes, we had a Mason Jar of White Lightnin' that Doug Champion had gotten us from one of his rum-runner buddies in Johnston County (Jerry dated Becky Flowers for a short time when he had that '68 cream-colored Road Runner). Yes, we had a snakeskin draped over the doorway on the heating pipes. And yes, there was a loaded .38 pistol under Jerry's mattress. Remember I said he had a lot of money? And he intended to keep it from midnight marauders or sorry poker players.

When we decided to come (and when they would let us) back to school one Sunday night in April, there was a message taped on #51 Door, that we should contact Ralph, immediately upon our return. We knew why. Before we had left, Sam had told us that he was gonna be in Queens, New York for the next month with his new granddaughter. In his absence, we would have a substitute housekeeper. "Link" had "interfered" with us previously over Christmas Break when he confiscated our blinking Budweiser Sign just because of the extreme static it caused throughout the building's electrical system. With this in mind, we decided to try to prevent Link from entering our lair. Over on the bike rack beside Carmichael Gymnasium was an abandoned SCHWINN Mountain Bike that looked like it had been run over. We went over and cut the inner tubes away from the warped rims. After tying them together, we tied one end to the inside doorknob of #51 Owen Dorm. With some NCSU Engineering, we stretched and tied the other end to the radiator across the room, under the window, our escape hatch. Sometime over the weekend, Link attempted to enter our room with his master key attached by a chain to his belt loop. YEP! When he turned his key, the door flew open, and launched his 30 keys all over the room, plus tore his belt loop off. Like I said, NCSU Engineering.

As a Game Warden I encountered A LOT of snakes. One little bitty two-foot Eastern Hognose Snake (Puff Adder), I tied to the underside of my trunk lid of my patrol car on a two-foot string. When I needed my binoculars, I asked my training officer Don Augustine to retrieve them from my trunk. He got the surprise of his life, right on his kisser. Later he threw a water snake at me at Buckhorn Dam near Avent's Ferry on the Cape Fear River in Lee County, but he missed! I returned the favor, and didn't miss. On the way to a District Meeting at the Arrowhead Restaurant in Mebane, I found a dead snake in the parking lot. I rested the limp little critter on my chrome bumper, and drove forward, slamming on the brakes as I approached the feet of my Supervisor, Cuckleberry Jones. He was not impressed!

#5. Whose road is this, anyway?

One afternoon, I was patrolling up near the Icaria Road, and had just picked up Robert to go to town and meet with Trooper Billy Long and new Trooper Butch Whitley. We were planning our strategies for when Governor James B. Hunt, Jr. would bring the North Carolina Legislature to hold their session in our Historic 1767 Chowan County Courthouse a few weeks away. Traveling south on NC-32 as I came through Small's Crossroads, SHP Telecommunication Center Supervisor Thurman Perry sent me to a wreck in front of the N C Forestry Service's Fire Watch Tower on NC-32. We rolled up on the scene before Thurman got the words across the airwaves. There was no wreck, but there was a commotion on the roadway. A three- foot Timber Rattler (Canebrake), had been nicked as it crossed the road. It was currently coiled on the centerline, and violently striking out at passing vehicles. About thirty people were watching the show, and wondering what was gonna happen next. Robert chose to stay inside my patrol car rather than get out and run the risk of too much exposure to an injured, very much alive Rattlesnake.

Several of "the locals" were prognosticating as to how to best handle this bristling scenario. You know me, I hatched a plan. As I blocked vehicular travel then upon NC-32 with my patrol car, I stepped out and drew my nickel plated .357 Magnum pistol. "MacAther, you ain't gonna shoot that thang are you? You know you can't hit him twisting like that." Now, you also know that I like a challenge! I squatted down about three feet from "my friend," held the revolver about two inches off and parallel with the pavement, pointed the trajectory toward Bennett's Millpond, and pulled the trigger. That blasted snake never knew what hit him. That hollow point 157 grain bullet nearly cut him into three pieces with his head turned inside out. Robert was maintaining a cautious vigilance, still seated "shotgun."

Now, you have to know that on the spur of the moment, occasionally things become less satisfying than if you had waited and planned your maneuver just a little bit better. As the old cliché goes, "Hindsight is 20 - 20." Right there on that centerline, in front of many of my future "customers," at that early stage of my Highway Patrol career, and not yet "proven," I REALLY should have stalked around and challenged that pit viper – face to face. Then I should have uttered the Apache Proverb, "It is better to have less thunder in the mouth, and more lightning in the hand." Then I should have grabbed those seven rattles and "coachwhip" cracked the neck of that serpent; then thrown him into the ditch, re-entered my patrol car, and driven off into the sunset. Think about it! (I still have those rattles in the console of my truck, just in case!)

Had I perfectly performed that maneuver, the word would have traveled across the land: "Don't mess with McArthur!"

Fire in the Hole, Almost

Up in the Puzzletown and Chappell Hill sections of Perquimans and Chowan Counties, there has always existed a, "Live and let live" way of thinking. In this tight knit, suppressed den of iniquity, when things went right, things went right. When things went wrong, still things went right; or so it was made to appear from the outside looking in! Many times during routine patrol, I found where a horrible car wreck had left hundreds of feet of scuffs, yaws, skid marks, gouges, and motor parts strewn along the highway rights of ways. Not having been there the day before, but lo and behold, in plain view today, meant that the accident had happened during the previous night. "The locals" had completely cleaned up the scene and removed the evidence. The cars were nowhere to be found. And no injuries were reported or taken to any of the local hospitals. "Tight-lipped" was an understatement when it came time for questions of the scofflaws.

Once when a local Quaker girl was "violated" by the son of a locally famous bootlegger, word came down that the girl's father, uncles, and four brothers were gonna kill the horses, poison the well, and burn down the house and barns of the bootlegger. Sheriff Little Man Broughton enlisted the help of the local Revenuers, game wardens, and highway patrolmen. Robert and I were two of the lucky ones to get "stationed" inside the plantation house to "lookout for the property and its owners." A banged-up Ford Mustang rode by the house one too many times, and Little Man got after him. As they rounded the curve the other side of Wolfman Jack's mansion, the Mustang flipped twice and skidded, sparks flying, to rest upside down with the teenaged driver still buckled in. He was hanging upside down with gasoline dripping onto the console and running out onto the pavement. Little Man ran (walked fast) up, crawled into the car as the young boy regained consciousness and began to flail his gasoline-soaked self around in a frenzied effort to escape. Little man was overheard to yell, "Calm down, boy! This thing is liable to catch fire!" Do you reckon that statement soothed the frantic driver one iota? I doubt it!

These two "Almost" fires were quelled by the seamless effectuation of Sheriff Julian H. Broughton's planning, and his having the right people in the right places with the right forces to ensure the safety and well-being of all concerned. HOWEVER, there was a "rumored" fire of mysterious origin that erupted some months later inside a Perquimans River "distillery" of undetermined ownership! But we all knew the deal!

Michael J. McArthur

Puzzletown

About a week later, Robert and I were patrolling back up in Puzzletown when Trooper Y Z Newberry "jumped" a duded-up black Cadillac adorned with sail panel mounted lanterns, headed north from Sandy Cross. This was unmistakably Wolfman Jack's Cadillac, and was traveling in excess of eighty miles per hour. It skidded to its right into Wolfman's and Wolfwoman's (Lucy Lamb Smith's) yard, went across the imported rose bushes, hit a yard ornament, sideswiped a Cypress Tree, and came to rest underneath the Scuppernong Grape arbor in Wolfman's back yard. Y Z overshot the driveway, just as I turned in behind the Cadi. The driver jumped to run, but was just a little too slow when I tackled him, right up against an old, unmarked tombstone. There was little or no fight in this young hooligan, and when Y Z arrived on the scene, he pulled me off Junior, and took credit for the capture by taking him straight to the Perquimans County Magistrate, The Honorable Broughton Dail (April 16, 1927 – April 5, 2020) (Assistant Clerk of Superior Court, {Harriette Dail's 1928 – June 19, 2010} husband).

Maybe two months later, Robert Weston Smith a.k.a. Wolfman Jack died of a massive heart attack in his lair in Belvidere, N.C. (January 21, 1938 to July 1, 1995 57 years old). Wolfman and Lucy were talented and generous souls known worldwide, but still "down home folks" in our neck of the woods. Their legacy of benevolence and charitable giving lives on in the Belvidere Community, and his Wolfman groupies still visit his homesite and gravesite. The superlatively distinctive howl of Wolfman Jack resonates up and down the Perquimans River at all times of the day and night. Admirers <u>Howl</u> as they pass his mansion. He and his lovely daughter "Joy Jack" Smith are buried side by side, right on the Smith Family Estate.

I worked part time for Chris Evans Funeral Home in 1995, and was enlisted by Funeral Director Chris Evans and his florist wife, Lisa to assist with the massive wake and funeral services for the infamous entertainer, Wolfman Jack. I was blessed to be able to work closely with Wolfman's family who could NOT have loved him more! His loving nature spread throughout the community which came together to honor and respect THEIR Wolfman. Famed Televangelist, Dr. Robert H. Schuller (September 16, 1926 to April 2, 2015) of the Chrystal Cathedral in Garden Grove,

California graciously accepted the invitation to bring his Hour of Power regalia to Belvidere, North Carolina and pay reverent homage to his longtime friends. As he arrived in his white Cadillac. His flashy yet respectful attire caught the attention of local folks who were unaccustomed to the lavish entertainment normalities: Lavender and Purple vestments. On the day of the funeral, there were hundreds of "foreign" automobiles swarming Chowan, Perquimans, Gates, and Pasquotank backroads. "Where's Belvidere?"

As the hour of the service approached, Perquimans County, Gates County, and Chowan County Deputy Sheriffs came together and manned traffic posts throughout Puzzletown, Piney Woods, Joppa, Gliden, Whiteston, Craney Island, Sandy Cross, Bear Swamp, Rocky Hock, Small's Crossroads, Nixonton, Bessie's Corner, and Chappell Hill. Golf carts, jacked up pickup thunder merchants, and local farm vehicles were utilized to transport the cadre of mourners from offsite parking lots and dormant cotton fields to the funeral services at 1602 Belvidere Road, Belvidere, N.C. 27919. Right down the road in downtown Belvidere (population 87), Layden's Country Store (since 1948) has provided all of Northeastern North Carolina and Tidewater Virginia with fresh meats, hard candy, garden vegetables, fatback, the best "Sharp" hoop cheese, the friendliest atmosphere, and the fabled Big Orange Crush Soda (Think Andy Griffith's "What it was, was Football (1954) comedy routine). You can find NEHI Peach Soda (1924), pig's feet and chicken feet to your liking. There is also available a fabled concoction known as Pinee® Oil. This is "An unmixed oil of the Long Leaf Pine," and dates back to 1928. There is a human dosage, but the livestock preparation has always been stuff of which legends were made: ask your friendly hog farmer!

During Dr. Schuller's eulogy for Wolfman, occasionally mourners would alternate from sobs to wails to howls. There were, by my count, just over 800 mourners plus attendants, drivers, concessionaires, and service providers. Dress (or undress) for the day ranged from diamond studded evening gowns and elaborate gold jewelry, to shorts and flip-flops. Entertainer Alice Cooper, "The Godfather of Shock Rock" brought his menagerie to the funeral, and set up an honorary shrine for Wolfman's memorabilia. Rocker Johnny Angel and The Halos, wearing purple outfits performed small acts of respect as they harmonized their condolences. Mary Hart of "ENTERTAINMENT TONIGHT" graced us with her radiant splendor, as did many other lesser and better-known celebrities. Lisa Evans miraculously and flawlessly provided floral arrangements to complement each of the entertainers, and a beautiful corsage to match Mary Hart's gown.

As the three-hour funeral service began to wane, so did the fervor begin to diminish. Lisa Evans had created a six-foot cross elegantly adorned with hundreds of white roses. The urn was beautifully displayed amid six stages of white roses gracing the altar. As the afternoon wore on, the multitude of mourners/revelers became exhausted and/or too drunk to carry on the celebration any longer. Gradually the yard became visible again, even though littered with all forms of "stuff." Funeral Director Evans summonsed me to his side and asked for a count of attendees, and inquired as to the wellbeing of the house, the recording studio, and the surroundings. I reported that I had found no one stealing, desecrating, or vandalizing any of the host of honorarium displays. The gold records, the plaques, the banners, the champagne bottles, the wine glasses were, for the most part, still in place. The crowd had conducted themselves in solemn revelry as they honored Wolfman's legacy.

"Leave It Go, Mama, Leave It Go"

Somehow, the Chappell Hill Community and Puzzletown were magnets for good times, amusing personalities, and logic defying experiences. In one of the clusters of family oriented, fun-loving, native communities a pickup truck got stolen. Not just any pickup, but one that had been awarded to Jimmy "Catfish" Hunter, the famous New York Yankee "fast ball" pitcher, for his having broken all kinds of records on the mound. During his baseball career, he had made many friends, helped many people, and been helped by many people. One of his best friends was the ultimate recipient of this "special" truck, as a gift from "Catfish." Branch and Hazel had helped Helen, Jimmy, and the whole Hunter family for many years while Jimmy was away. On this particular evening, Hazel's truck was taken from her yard by Boogie, a friend of her stepson. Boogie was a troublesome young lad who had not yet learned that fire burned. Hazel called the Perquimans County Dispatcher, Todd Tilley who broadcasted a B.O.L.O (be on the lookout) for the red Dodge. Next,

Living Out Loud with Grace, Grit, and Gratitude

Dispatcher Tilley got a report that a red Dodge pickup had just sideswiped a car in front of Jiggs White's Barbecue. Sheriff Broughton lived right up the street, found the Dodge, and gave pursuit. Boogie went straight to Branch and Hazel's yard, and pulled across the ditch into the driveway. Hazel came out, and got between Sheriff Broughton and Boogie, more concerned for her truck than the joyriding teenager.

Robert and I pulled onto the shoulder of Belvidere Road, and approached what had now become a full-blown cuss fight. Little Man wanted Boogie, Hazel wanted her truck, and I wanted both of them. Sheriff Broughton wanted me to have both of them, too. Hazel did not! Boogie was handcuffed to the door handle of Sheriff Broughton's patrol car. Hazel was hunched up and locked onto the side panel of the bed of the pickup, and the wrecker was on its way. Hazel would not give up her position as she tried to keep the truck from being towed away as evidence of a reportedly stolen truck, having been involved in some level of a hit and run over on Edenton Street. Hazel's family was yelling, "Leave it go, Mama. Leave it go!" She wouldn't.

Robert tried to "prize" her death grip from the truck's sidewalls. He couldn't. He and I together tried to pry her hands off the truck. We couldn't. Family shouts of, "Leave it go, Mama. Leave it go," were having little or no effect on Mama. Sheriff Broughton came over and whacked Mama's right hand with his five D-cell Kel Light. Mama "leaved go" with one hand, tightly still gripping the truck with her other hand, and then the other again. Robert grabbed the broken hand, and Mama chomped down on his right forearm, through his leather jacket, ultimately causing a huge blood blister and broad-based welp and contusion of his forearm. Robert "leaved go!" The scene became much less procedurally correct from that point on.

SHP First Sergeant Walter P. Upright arrived on the scene in his shiny black, unmarked SHP Patrol Car. He was a big man who just died last week (May 16, 1935 – July 6, 2021). As he descended upon the scene, the "Leave it go, Mama"s, became, "LOOK OUT, MAMA"s. For some reason, when Mama saw this giant of a man bearing down on her, she knew her time was up. She "leaved go," and collapsed onto the rutted, broken cinder-block strewn driveway. Thank goodness the First Shirt had not seen (or so he said) some of the fracas leading up to the arrest.

277

Little Man took Boogie to Magistrate Dail in the Perquimans County Courthouse. Hollowell Chevrolet wrecker driver Pete Owens took the red Dodge to the Dealership for careful inspection later that night. Robert and I scooped up Mama, and found that she was bleeding from her knees and elbows. We encapsulated her in my SHP issued, silver foil, thermal space blanket. Her broken hand had swollen to about the size of a cantaloupe, but her countenance and demeanor had taken a turn for the better. We took her over to the Perquimans County Doctor's Office of Dr. Robert Earl Lane. He quickly and professionally dressed her wounds. His main and unmistakable concern was the broken hand. Husband Branch was called to the doctor's office, and was allowed to take the newly "<u>unarrested</u>" Mama over to the Emergency Room at Chowan Hospital. Only two of her five metacarpals were "green stick" cracked, but the pain was apparently intense.

Upon breathing a sigh of relief after the strenuous and tenuous evening's events, it was discovered that Robert's blue uniform style dress pants had been ripped open, right down the front through the zipper. We all surmised how that could have happened, but never really figured it out. But between having been bitten, having his glasses and hat knocked off into the darkness, and his pants ripped open, Robert, too, had had a bad night. We made a solemn pact not to tell anyone any of this, but that pact lasted about forty-five minutes until Trooper Ray Potts arrived at the late-night coffee shop. We all, (those of us still living) still laugh about that harrowing engagement.

When the court date came, Boogie pleaded guilty to hit and run driving. The Dodge was returned to Branch and Mama. Mama's Resisting Arrest case was given a Prayer for Judgment upon the payment of the Cost of Court ($46.00). All's well that ends well. Jimmy Hunter had appeared as a character witness for his friends, and was able to negotiate a great outcome for all concerned.

Bessie's Bottom

As I related earlier, Chappell Hill, situated on the Chowan – Perquimans County line experienced more than its fair share of memorable events. One of the most horrible motor vehicle accidents that I ever investigated occurred at the intersection of County Line Road and

Drinking Hole Road, just north from Chappell Hill at Bessie's Bottom. Having just arrested a Pasquotank County High School English teacher for drunk driving on Liver Lips Road in the Punch Bowl section of Gates County, I received a radio dispatch from SHP Telecommunicator Burrus Taylor: "A-346, 10-50 multiple F-Frank, Road Blocked, intersection of County Line Road and Drinking Hole Road. 10-52 (Rescue) 10-17 (En-Route). A-311 (First Sergeant Pete Eure) and Chowan 205 (Deputy Glenn Perry) standing by."

It was June 4, 1977, a very sad day.

With the drunk teacher handcuffed and belted in the back seat, Robert and I rocketed across the north end of Chowan County, and arrived at one of the most horrific accident scenes imaginable. A demolished Ford Mustang – driver deceased, pinned inside, a young motionless female passenger, splayed on the grassy shoulder of the intersection, an exploded pickup truck, and complete chaos and pandemonium engulfing the entire ghastly site. Deputy Perry was administering CPR on the passenger without success. Graduation gowns were bloody and still hanging inside the mangled Mustang. I will not, out of respect for the families, go into any more unpleasant details, other than to say that the Mustang driver was drunk, traveling at a high rate of speed, ran the stop sign on Drinking Hole Road, exploded the northbound pickup truck into three pieces, and killed himself and his graduating senior girlfriend. The driver of the Morris and Hinton pickup truck walked away, unscathed.

I had been on the scene of the accident for about an hour and a half. Upon his arrival, I relinquished the accident investigation responsibilities to Trooper Y Z Newberry since it had occurred on the eastern – Perquimans half of the County Line Road. The poor old drunk in my backseat had completely sobered up (He blew .08%..10% was the presumptive level of alcohol impairment in 1977). Sadly for him, he knew of both students from his position as a tenured Pasquotank educator but did not teach at their Northeastern Academy. If he ever drank another drop and ever got behind the wheel of a car again, I would be surprised. If this night ever sent a message to anyone, he got it: DON'T DRINK AND DRIVE!

Together Robert and I stopped a lot of cars and would carefully analyze what the best approach might be: Arrest? Warning? Citation? Once

I told the arrested drunk driver in the back seat, that I really wanted to let him go, but that Robert had said, "Take him on down!" We all were friends: Robert, me, and the drunk, so we all laughed about it.

Some of Robert's juvenile offenders aged out of the jurisdiction of Juvenile Services Division of Crime Control and Public Safety, and graduated into my arrestees. When they entered the lighted interior of my Black and Silver Highway Patrol car, they would sometimes say, "Oh, I am so sorry Mr. Hendrix, I have let you down."

Many times, I could depend on Robert to point me in a better direction when my adrenaline surge had me headed in a more difficult direction, and for that I am eternally grateful.

Robert on many occasions was my "front sight" as I plied the highways and byways. That carried over into my personal family life with Becky and Jenny and John as well. He and Marvis kind of adopted our whole family.

I already miss him more than words can say.

CHAPTER THREE

The Good Life

"Trash Ducks" to Treasure Trove

"The Best Day Ever"

These were the excited words of my 5-year-old grandson, Nolan on a cold January 12 morning, just after shooting hours. Nolan, his father John, and I had made plans a week in advance, to meet at Bennett's Millpond on Rocky Hock Creek in Chowan County for our first duck hunt of the 2018-2019 Migratory Waterfowl season. Little did we know that the edges of the swamp at the boat launch would be 1" thick, frozen ice. Little did we know that the day would go down in our family's history, as Nolan called it, "The best day, ever!"

Emptying out of two pickup trucks, with a 14-foot jon boat, three paddles, three PFDs, two shotguns, a vittles bag, a grass bag of decoys, and one too many flashlights, we shoved off into the darkness. After carefully loading our gear and our bulky selves into the black, tannin-stained water topped with duckweed and milfoil, and after carefully cautioning our youngest duck hunting team member to "stay low" in the boat, it was time to paddle out into the darkness. Already we had heard the barnyard roosters beckoning sunrise over at Valhalla. Already the Canada and Snow Geese were flying toward the Smith brothers' Turkey Neck Farm on Paradise Road where we would fill our Tundra Swan Permit the following Saturday (along with about forty others). The log trucks were already blistering NC-32 south toward the Weyerhaeuser/Domtar paper mills in Plymouth. The day was off to a great start, destined to become an even better "best day, ever."

We had the millpond to ourselves. The first quarter of the moon was waxing toward the Super Blood Wolf Full Moon appearing the next week on the 20th, and cast a radiant glow over the Bald Cypress trees and Water Tupelos, allowing us to chart our course. The swoosh of low, rapid wingbeats broke what silence there was above the scrape of the sculling paddle on Nolan's starboard side. Not a word about being cold, yet.

It seemed just a short paddle to the sixteen-foot stake we had driven in the run of the creek for our Mojo electronic decoy. Slowly we plopped two dozen decoys onto the ripples: some were homemade from instructions in the <u>Wildlife in North Carolina Magazine</u> article entitled, "*Trash Ducks.*" Later in the morning, not surprisingly, two of the dekes were seen to be upside down at first light. Nolan said they were, "sleeping."

All the decoys except one with a missing weighted keel had emptied the burlap toe sack. Carefully we paddled over to the base of a midstream Cypress Tree with a massive trunk. Encircling but now split apart by annual tree growth, was a small platform for hunters too skittish to hunt from above. There were no surprises such as once before in 2002 when that rattled raccoon torpedoed from the darkness onto our backs and into our boat. There was no nutria scat matted on the 2x12 planks this go 'round. No partial Belted Kingfisher skeleton dignified the crevices. We used to have to sweep it off so as not to track detritus onto the ladder, the steps, or the blind floor. Also the "boat hide" didn't seem as wide as when constructed, which made for a tight fit into the slip. The water level was low also, making for a tight fit. Nolan bounded out of the boat, jumping onto one of the Cypress "knees" at the water's edge. Was it slippery? Who knows! He wasn't on it long enough to find out!

This duck blind "The Castle" was built in 2001, 20 years ago by my son John, Jimmy Stallings, me, and a now deceased fellow hunter and conservationist. Ol' Carlton Perry from Chambers Ferry was known to sit along the top rail of this blind, feet on the seat, casually smoking his Marlboro, right while the ducks were flying. He also had two or more lit cans of "Sterno" heating-fuel on the seat over which he hunkered from time to time. His Daddy's antique beat up Belgian Browning with a gold trigger, to Carlton was like a Steinway Grand Piano to a concert pianist. He could make shots with that "piece" that defied description. On many occasions he killed Mourning doves at sixty yards. One snowy morning he shot a cannonballing Ringneck so close to us that the cardboard wadding was embedded in the side of the hollowed-out carcass. He had replaced the burnished walnut stock due to it splintering from the four ounces of #5 lead shot and the four drams of gunpowder reloads that he and his buddy

Wildlife Enforcement Captain Ray Elks had concocted. Once, when the "damp reload didn't shoot," he had dumped the entire load of lead out of his sawed off 26" barrel into the hollow tree trunk rather than allowing it to invade the workings of his Browning. Before he was "sternly warned" by that same Wildlife Enforcement Captain to "cease and desist," Carlton would bring Bristo's 1934 Winchester Model 67, .22 caliber bolt action single shot rifle, and would use it to rain "rifle balls" into the water or ice beside a dead bull Pintail floating below. This was to prevent the Red-eared Slider turtles as big in diameter as basketballs, from eating the dead duck carcass as it lay in the water, thereby ruining it for appearance's sake. Supposedly, Carlton had been "reported" for using that .22 rifle to shoot migratory waterfowl on the wing! Imagine that! No! Don't imagine that!! Just take it "for what it's worth!"

Among other nuggets, Carlton taught me to "ring" a shotgun shell with my Case "Sodbuster" pocketknife to effectively make it into a slug. When that slug hit trees over on the field side of the swamp, the sitting ducks would fly toward us due to the slug having hit beyond their hole in the Duck Weed. Midmorning, Carlton would skillfully J-stroke his seventeen-foot Grumman canoe into the headwaters and return with two squirrels, four doves, a rabbit, and two wood ducks. Truly a sportsman's sportsman.

Back to the duck blind. It is nestled ten ladder rungs up the side of the lightning split trunk. Then thirteen solid stairwell steps twist around the trunk, dumping out onto the floor of the four-foot by eight-foot Christmas tree bushed blind. Nolan's grandmother, Becky helped camouflage the insides and the "wings" of the blind because I am colorblind, and chartreuse might blend into the color scheme of my rods and cones, but not a sharp-eyed Mallard's. I honestly think that this reinforced structure has allowed the tree to survive Hurricanes Floyd, Isabel, and Florence. At 25-feet up in the air, lots of the shooting is "straight out," or below your feet, especially with Hooded Mergansers. Almost always, this is disastrous for the floating decoys below, but puts the hunter "right up there wid 'em. Eyeball to eyeball." No kiddin'. And, yes, we do eat everything we kill. We used to have a half inch rope suspended from the blind, down to the boat to pull up our shotguns (unloaded). And, yes, in our haste, the rope broke on at least two occasions, sending our guns to the muddy bottom. Luckily, the floating rope end was used to retrieve them. We dumped out the water, and got down to business. Joe Hill, our friendly local gunsmith, upon receipt of our shotguns for "take-down" cleaning, accused us of having dropped the guns overboard to avoid capture by the Wildlife Officers. Wrong!

That weathered platform at the base of the tree by the boat blind has Cedar and Pine bushing around the perimeter, and is suitable for "lo, I be with you," hunters. I don't know whether it is the climb itself, the shade tree engineering, or the sky-high altitude that humbles some who refuse to go, "up top." Also, when John was Nolan's age, it was a good hide for his Chocolate Labrador Retriever, Molly to sit, bristling in anticipation.

The water surrounding the tree is only about six-feet-deep. Many times, due to whatever agricultural field runoff has occurred during the summer, thick green vegetation covers much of the water's surface throughout Bennett's Millpond. Some of it we call "Duck Weed," or Hydrilla, and some of it is Milfoil. It stands about a foot above the waterline, with its massive root ball extending about a foot below. In years past we have taken half-sheets of plywood, and thrown them onto the vegetation, to facilitate the weight of a hunter behind a toppled Cypress. On one particular January morning, Tommy Jeffries, <u>John's and my mentor</u>, was hunting with us from above. His massive Black Labrador Retriever, Boone was manning the platform at the base of the tree, waiting to perform his retriever duties. Five shots from above, and three Wood Ducks hit the water, about twenty yards out front in the open space among the two-dozen decoys. Boone launched himself onto the Duck weed, and he immediately became 100% submerged below the thick mass. Tommy and I could see his enormous hulk trying to push up through the thick vegetation, but with no luck. We raced down from our blind, but out popped Boone, about fifteen yards toward the downed Woodies. Even in his dire predicament, he had swum underwater in the direction of his quarry, and popped up in the clearing, about fifteen feet from the three "graveyard dead" ducks. Boone brought two at once, and then returned to get the last one. He had tried to get all three in his massive mouth, but just couldn't manage it.

In years past, out of the kindness of their avian hearts, several broods of Osprey chicks have fledged in a four-foot wide nest skillfully woven by the parents into the hog fence wire framework of the blind. Hatched out, craggy, sun bleached eggshells and Hickory Shad skeletons littered the floor of the blind and the nest itself. What great natural blind bushing! And our not having had to haul it up the ladder and steps was an additional bonus. Of course, Nolan wanted to throw the sticks over the side where he dropped his cup of milk later that morning.

As we impatiently awaited "shootin' time," Nolan spied two boatloads of hunters electronically motoring toward our location. I guess they were startled to see his now dimmed flashlight shine out from the treetop blind, because they immediately altered their course toward Minnow Point, another good duck blind site on the far side of the swamp. Since nobody in our blind had the Northeast Hunt Zone – Canada Goose permit, we had to pass up two Canada Geese, both falling victim to the interlopers.

It was now about an hour into legal hunting time, and Nolan was becoming restless and dangerously navigating, where else, the fringes of the blind, 25-feet up. John gently admonished, "Son, get away from those steps! And stop stepping over the stock of my shotgun." We both shoot Remington 870s, John's blued and mine black. Somehow, two miniature dinosaur trucks and two "Hot Hands" hand warmers had been smuggled up the tree in camouflage cargo pant pockets. As we enjoyed the fresh cold breeze, we should have easily, but didn't hear any shooting out on the confluence of the Chowan River and Salmon Creek where the Bertie County Sage farmers hunt Bluebills and Blackheads. That site is currently thought to be the newest proposed site of Sir Walter Raleigh's Lost Colony's final resting place, right up Rocky Hock Creek from my house where the "Dare Stone" was discovered on the Ed Goodwin farm. The Albemarle Sound's westernmost point is sandy and shallow enough that the hunters must only wear chest waders while using gigantic, overblown Cypress tree roots for concealment. Not once had the prevailing southwest wind relayed the unmistakably characteristic, "ka-ta-PLOOM!" of their 10-gauges as the blasts echoed out across the mouth of Salmon Creek and up the Chowan River. Those crafty hunters used open faced spinning reels to retrieve their downed ducks for two reasons: sometimes the ducks fell or drifted into deeper channels, and the hunters didn't want to expose themselves and flare incoming flocks of 15 to 25 Lesser Scaup (bluebills).

Just in the nick of time, Nolan first spied the flock of six Ringnecks, highballing against the North wind toward our "Trash Duck" decoys. Nolan "got down" as well as a five-year-old standing in a chair could be expected. As the tight knot of winged rockets banked away, John called them back. We were just below them when we could see their heads turn and their golden eyes look at the J-rig of decoys. "BOOOH-yow!" Lunch hit the water! Quickly, after John told Nolan to cover his ears (we forgot his hearing protection), a well-placed shot from John's 870 settled the duck's escape.

On this fresh morning, it was time for John and Nolan to retrieve the quarry. It seemed like Nolan went DOWN the tree much more quickly than he went up. Anyway, he was in the bow of the boat with his Daddy, paddling for all he was worth. I heard Nolan ask, "Daddy, where is he? Is he gonna get away?" 'long about that time Nolan spotted the dark form lying motionless on the water. Without hesitation he scooped up the drake Ringneck, and held it up for his father to take the picture. Now, back to the Cypress. Back up the tree. Back into the blind, and no longer the least bit cold. But hungry!

Scrambled Eggs and Spanish Moss Sausage

As luck would have it, contained in the vittles bag was a cache of sausage balls, four patty sausages (uncooked) and six scrambled eggs (uncooked), milk for Nolan, and soft drinks for the older "kids." John's Eagle Scout, weather-beaten, Coleman propane stove with double burners, fired up on the first strike. Suddenly, here came two "big ducks," just below the stratosphere. John's "Y'all come back!" Lohman calling didn't work this time. That was OK because we were BUSY. Four sausages will not "flip" themselves, but Nolan became proficient, nearly flipping more than one more than once onto the floor. By now the two dozen sausage balls were history. The Neese's sausage patties are ready. Scrambling cheddar cheese eggs (with just a dab of Spanish Moss and a pinch of lichen) in a duck blind requires patience and practice: neither of which was abundant, but constituted a work of art. The wind caused the "seasoned" iron skillet to heat unevenly due to the low flame, but all's well that ends well! That red "Spider Man" (teasingly chided 'Spitter Man') ace cap, jauntily atop Nolan's noggin was a sight to behold. A great breakfast with great buddies in a great location is a hard combination to beat.

Later, John pointed out some more "big ducks" flying up the creek. I asked Nolan which direction they were flying: "That way," he pointed. I pulled open my coat and retrieved a BSA compass doubling as a zipper pull. Why I now carry two compasses is another whole story, BUT: "Nolan, you are a Cub Scout. Use this compass and tell me which way is North." He pointed straight up, and I showed him the red arrow pointing up the creek and he understood. Later as we loaded the gear into the trucks, a flock of Tundra Swans flew low over the far side treetops where Wild Turkeys sometimes roost. Nolan, at five years old, volunteered, "Granddaddy, those Swans are flying South." That's my boy!

Now it was time to go on to the next adventure. After descending the Cypress tree, stowing our gear in the jon boat, and precariously settling in with an inch of water in the floor, from the upwind position, we paddled around and drifted down through the icy water, picking up decoys and winding weighted cords by hand. The wind carried us South through the set, and we all got wet while realizing we had missed one all the way back at the top. And of course, with 870s unloaded and encased, here came the five remaining Ringnecks, low enough to shoot! Isn't that the way it always works? Either unload your gun, or especially take it apart, and here comes the monster buck or the whole gaggle of geese.

Paddling back to the dock was uneventful as we passed under Walter Noneman's (November 24, 1932 to October 6, 2003) now dilapidated "Eagle One" treetop blind, once highly productive, from decades past. Along the way, several fairly well-maintained Cypress Wood Duck nesting boxes were erected by Boy Scout Troop 164 years ago, and they seemed to be standing the test of time. A murder of crows seemed to be "telling the news" to all of Terrapin Hill. Dragging the boat out was less difficult than launching it. We left it unplugged and stern down on the bank for the next Thursday's hunt if Nolan can play hooky. The tilled cotton field where we were parked had lots of Whitetail Deer tracks, and Nolan did his best to follow the biggest track. Next, we had to, "Come on Granddaddy. Let's race!" back to the truck." He won!

Jutting from the shoreline toward Minnow Point, over beside two propped up jon boats covered by Spanish Moss, stands a hundred-foot fishing pier. Time has taken its toll on some of the planks, so we had to (HAD TO) walk out on it carefully, stepping along the railing where the stringers seemed to be solid enough, maybe. Upon the return to safety, Nolan shouted, "Daddy, let's do that again!" Before we left, we prayed to God for having allowed us to safely experience a successful hunt, and thanked Him for the meat we had harvested from His bountiful kingdom.

Grandmother's House

Now, "Over the river and through the woods" to "Grandmother's House," as Nolan calls it. Upon arrival, as he ran into the house he yelled, "Grandmother, we caught a duck!" Cleaning the duck for consumption fell upon John as he deftly removed the edible parts of the drake Ringneck. The heart was of particular interest to Nolan as John explained its function. As is common knowledge, severed wings are always desirable with children, and two went home with Nolan. Our team of successful duck hunters now participated in a ritual from the days of the Chowanoke Indian Tribe which lives in our part of the State as evidenced by their names, their families, their festivals, their tribal burial grounds, and the arrowheads found in the surrounding countryside. As evidence of Nolan's first successful duck hunt, we smeared blood from our quarry across each other's cheekbones. This symbolically represented God's grace for having provided us a successful hunt, and to reduce glare into, and reflection from the sunlight falling upon the hunters' cheekbones. Think, "Duck Dynasty." Believe it or not, Nolan was not particularly excited about that part!

Sunday lunch will never quite be the same. Always a favorite delicacy, Grandmother's Southern fried chicken had to share the platter with "duck meat." Enjoyed by all, the dark brown fried duck breast was delicious; something like sweet roast beef. We all shared parts of the heart which was REALLY good tasting. The mashed potatoes, green peas, dark sweet iced tea, and jellied loaf bread satisfied everyone. Nolan had great pride in having helped provide Sunday lunch.

Hindsight hints at other things that we could have done, and opportunities explored, but does not minimize in any way, the huge significance of life's lessons we shared as a family during those two days.

To exemplify just one of the many teachings was the taking of wild game over recycled *"Trash Duck"* decoys touted by the Wildlife in North Carolina Magazine published by The North Carolina Wildlife Resources Commission, written by Keith Hendrickson, photographed by Melissa McGaw, and appearing in the November – December, 2018 edition.

Mayhem on the Millpond: Another History Making Hunt

Sometime in mid- December 1991, with the too soon sunsets and freezing sunrises, the urge to go duck hunting became overwhelming. My fourth grader, John (10) (Nolan's Daddy) was out of school the next day, the weather appeared to be cooperating, and we all had our licenses, duck stamps, decoys, shotguns, and plenty of Winchester, Super-X, Mark-V, Steel Magnum #4s. For John when he was born, his Mother and I purchased a "Lifetime Sportsman's" hunting and fishing license from the N C Wildlife Resources Commission for one hundred dollars (a lot of money from a Highway Patrolman's salary). Never, upon the approach of an N C Wildlife Enforcement Officer, would John have to quickly wonder, "What was the expiration date of my license?"

Somehow, probably with help from grandparents, we had found $1500.00 for John to "purchase with 'his own money' - $3.00," "his first pickup truck" from family friend, future BSA Scoutmaster Hardy Gilliam. It was a well-used 1976 Chevrolet Scottsdale 1500, known by John and his friends as, "the multicolored green panel van," for a number of reasons: maybe all the paint didn't match; maybe green primer was visible; maybe it would lead three young men on immeasurable "learning opportunities." On one of our first outings, as we barreled over Beaver Dam Creek on Chamber's Ferry Road, lo and behold, the left rear "may-pop" did so. This was a learning experience for John, just as when he buried it in Duck Cowand's Wildcat Road sandpit: deeper than axle deep, deeper than chassis deep, "near 'bout sunk." We were checking our three Cypress

Wood Duck nesting boxes in the center of the pit, but we got sidelined. Thank goodness we had a shovel. Who sank it? John sank it. Who dug us out? John dug us out.

This glorious morning, the grass at the boat launch had a frozen sheen of ice from the heavy frost. As we pulled the jon boat from the bed of the truck, we could already hear Canada Geese both in flight, and over by the slough below the N C Forestry Service's Fire Watchtower on NC-32. We loaded the paddles, life vests, decoys, and shotguns. As we paddled to the duck blind, John made sure he had his own duck call. In the bow of the boat, with his sculling paddle, a little scrape here and there was quite all right. We were hunting from Steve Taylor's four-foot-off-the-water, plywood duck blind, with a duck dog boardwalk sloping underneath to the water. After John moored the boat, and after climbing into the blind, we could not have imagined what lay ahead. The pine bushed railings of the blind were taller than John's head. As he looked up through the dense fog, he saw ducks, lots of 'em, circling the decoys. Plop! Plop – plop! About fifteen landed right out in front of the blind, about thirty yards out.

Jimmy Nixon, in his treetop blind (that he eventually gave to John – henceforward "the castle"), was calling (NOT ON HIS SMART PHONE, on his **P.S. Olt** duck call). Gary Smith (September 12, 1956 to July 27, 2009) and Mark Bass were in their blind at Minnow Point, and successfully calling. Small flocks of ducks continued to land in their decoys and, more importantly, ours. By now it was ALMOST shootin' time. The fog was lifting. I told John that the statutory "30 minutes prior to sunrise" was about two minutes away. He decided to climb up onto the frosty 2x8 plank bench, and rest the barrel of his worn twenty gauge, single shot Winchester, loaded with one yellow Winchester, Super-X, Mark V, Magnum cartridge of #4 steel shot, level, on the railing. At the exact legal shootin' time, I reached over and laid the "hog's ear" back for him. I told him, "Now when the boys down the pond shoot, all these feeding ducks are 'gonna git up' off the water. Shoot 'em!"

One Shot = Five Ducks

"BOOH-yow!" One shot!

You would have had to have been there to believe what happened next. I WAS there, and I had never before nor since seen such mayhem! It truly defied belief. What follows is the absolute, gospel truth. Go ask John!

At the very moment that John heard Gary, Mark, and Jimmy shoot, the puddle ducks in our decoys sprang from the water, John pulled the trigger, then slipped on the frosty seat. I caught his mighty weapon. I call it a "mighty weapon," because of what it had just done! When the smoke cleared, John grabbed the rail and looked out. FIVE DUCKS LAY ON THE WATER! Well, one lay on the water, while the other four were swimming toward the swamp. "Come on, Daddy. Let's go gittum," John yelled as he slid down the boardwalk into his 10-foot jon boat too loosely tied below. "Oh no!" I spoke. "You shot 'em. You go get 'em." As it turned out, I probably would have had to jump straight from the blind, over the rail, into the boat anyway, because ol' John was already "in gear" toward his heyday. I can tell you this: I was as proud of that boy as if he had just been elected Sheriff of Chowan County.

John was paddling that boat so hard that Goliath could have surfed on the wake it was throwing. He had to get with it because the swimming ducks were rapidly making their getaway. He paddled after a Green-Winged Teal which "dove" as the boat approached. Gone forever! The two Widgeons were both headed down Rocky Hock Creek toward Cypress Point and the Chowan River. The Wood Duck was slowly making its way toward the far shoreline, and the other unknown waterfowl was swimming toward the head of the millpond. It was a sight to behold. A young boy, trying to make good on having shot game that he could not catch, paddling as hard as he could, not knowing which duck to go after next, and WAIT! What was that noise? More ducks flying into the millpond, right in front of a grandstand full of amused hunters.

One of the other hunters yelled at John, "Hurry up. Get back in the blind. The ducks ain't coming in with you beating the water like that." This is the "edited" version of what he REALLY yelled, but John probably didn't hear a word of it anyway. More shooting from the Minnow Point boys dropped more ducks onto the water. Now Gary was in his boat paddling after his ducks.

Michael J. McArthur

"Sneak" on Wiggins Millpond
Wilson, North Carolina

As I stood watching the hullabaloo unfolding before my eyes, I recalled similar days from my childhood in Wilson, North Carolina. Back in the early '60s. Wiggins Mill on Contentnea Creek at the third bridge, just below world famous Bill's Drive In Barbecue on unpaved Lovers' Lane was always good for a couple of black water Wood Ducks, but it was hard to retrieve them. My Charles L. Coon, seventh grade teacher's husband, Game Warden Elmo Walls (November 20, 1917 to July 4, 1991) was kinda' known to slip out from behind a tree, right in front of you, much too often! My father and I built a light weight, one-man sneak ("Sneak") boat out of a single sheet of half inch plywood to solve the retrieval problem. Once, as the sun was setting ☺, in my undisciplined haste, for some unknown reason I left my split Beaver Tail paddle stuck in the mud underneath the 6-foot-high blind, and didn't have time to go get it! It was hard paddling ol' Sneak with the stock of my Sears and Roebuck, J.C. Higgins Pump Shotgun; too scared to stay on the creek, and much too scared to return to the dock. More on that later.

Out in the melee, John's twenty gauge barked twice, and he now had the two Widgeons and a Wood duck on the bow of his boat. What was that other "big duck" that he could not seem to overtake? BOOH-yow. Now four of the five were in the boat. As I looked over toward C. T. Dixon's (March 3, 1934 to April 4, 2019) and Marsha's (June 22, 1953-January 3, 2022) horse pasture, I noticed a slight ripple in the water. All I could see was the tip of the bill on that Green-Winged Teal as he was making his way toward the clump of duckweed on the shoreline. Since I was "boatless," all I could do was yell and point for John to go "atter'im." Had the cripple made it to the duckweed, never would he have been able to be recovered due to the thick underwater vegetation.

Booh-yow! After all that work, all that frantic paddling, all that young boy decision making, and all that ruckus, John finally had retrieved his limit: five ducks. The Teal was a fine-looking drake. The two Widgeons (Baldpates to some) were really fat. The Wood Duck drake (Gentleman Duck or Summer Duck to some) was as striking as always. That fifth duck was still a question mark. Never before had I seen, much less killed one like it (still haven't). It was a drake Redhead, fit for the taxidermist. John McArthur was a proud young'un! If only I had had a camera!

Word traveled far and wide, that John McArthur had, at the age of ten, mastered duck hunting. His dead-eye marksmanship was exceeded only by his ability to work hard, and his willingness to overcome the diversities and acquire the acumen associated with hunting wild game. We had had a good hunt, and later several good meals. My statement concerning that incredible day was/is, "You know what? I taught him everything he knows." ☺

Michael J. McArthur

Mourning and White-winged Dove Hunt

Opening Day 2019

It started out innocently enough. Due to the increased familial pressures from all directions and incoming rounds from totally unreliable sources, I had decided to forgo the opening day of North Carolina's 2019 Mourning Dove Season for maybe the second time in over half a century. Yes, I was backsliding! Maybe even back-tumbling. What? Not go on opening day? Mike McArthur? You gotta be kidding! Whine, whine, whine. It's too hot! Yes, I believe in global warming and climate sabotage. I gotta get ready for that Cat five Hurricane Dorian camped out on top of the Grand Bahamas. My grandchildren are not quite old enough to go hunting, and they will be in town. Did I mention that I am nearing seventy years old? My knee(s) are not up to it! On and ON and ON! But guess what!

As I drove around Chowan County, up through Terrapin Hill and Rocky Hock for the two weeks prior to opening day, there were not nearly as many doves perched on lightlines as had been sighted in previous years. Maybe it was because of those two big rains we had last spring: one lasted thirty days and the other, forty days. Maybe the nesting doves had experienced too much rain for the chicks to survive. Maybe we haven't planted as much corn. Maybe that extreme drought last month had prevented the tassling ears from developing during the prescribed time period, according to the agronomists over at N C State University's Agriculture Institute in Raleigh.

While I was still contemplating whether I would go hunting on opening day, I was building a 48-inch, seven-foot-tall ax throwing target in my back yard (age 69 remember). BOOM! BOOM! BOOM! Yep! Somebody over by the Seine Ground on Rocky Hock Creek was A L R E A D Y dove hunting. Brave Soul!!! I went over to the shop and got my camouflage hunting vest off the upside-down bicycle handlebars, and found where a crafty Metallic-blue Dirt Dauber had built her nest right square on the zipper. That vest is over 30 years old, and I have to sew it up along the pocket seams every year. Seems like I always try to put two boxes of shells into a one box pocket. Wait a minute! TWO boxes of shells? I thought the limit was fifteen birds, and you have to take two two5 shell boxes into the field with you? You know the deal: I take some extras in case my son John runs out! YEAH! RIGHT!

The opening day of dove season is usually the first Saturday in September, within a week of when most mule corn is cut (harvested) in northeastern North Carolina. A cutover cornfield is the most utilized "target rich environment" for dove hunting because there are more acres available to hunt. Up on Turkey Neck Farm, the Adrian J. Smith (September 12, 1944 to February 4, 1977) family in years past hosted a massive opening day dove hunt. Nearly everybody killed their limit which was twelve back then. There were so many spent cardboard hulls left in the field that the first big rain washed them all down the ditch and clogged up the drainpipe.

Some of the absolute best dove hunts I have made have been over a partially harvested yellow, seven-foot Sunflower field down by the mouth of the Yeopim River on Drummond's Point. During one of those hunts, while I was looking for a downed dove, Molly, Jenny and John's Chocolate Lab was playing in the ditch, chasing dragonflies. Really? She came out muddy and froze in her tracks. Not a whisper of movement. Coiled right between her front legs was a thirty-inch Canebrake Rattlesnake (Timber Rattler). My hunting buddy Richard Jackson was hunting across the ditch, saw my predicament, came over and shot the snake (seven rattles and a button) sideways with his double barrel L. C. Smith twelve gauge from between Molly's legs, knocking it out into the field still thrashing.

Up in Rocky Hock, N. C., another great enticement for early season doves is a plowed under cantaloupe or watermelon field. Seems like those seeds make for good eatin' by the doves. This early in the fall, milo has not been harvested, but by the time the winter season arrives, and the migratory big fat dark gray doves get down here, it is just right for "shootin' a mess of doves."

This year's hunt, Labor Day, 2019 was going to be a hit or miss in many more ways than just one. The weather was unpredictable to say the least. There were WAY too few doves on the power lines in Chowan County. Not much corn had been cut because of the late rains after the drought after the two big rains I mentioned earlier. And not to mention there was a Category 5 Hurricane (DORIAN) churning off the Florida Coast with its sights set on Edenton. One of our best hunting buddies was unable to attend due to recent back surgery. But our other best hunting buddy had five other guys loaded into two NEW Dodge Ram Hemis, headed our way for the hunt down on Pungo River Farm, Tim Powell's massive acreage on the Washington/Beaufort County line, Pantego, NC on Railroad Bed Road. If you know anything about "peat soil," you can imagine what those new Raleigh trucks looked like after traveling over a mile through the black dirt bogs, dust flying, and then just a light dusting of huge rain pellets. I had checked with the landowner, Tim Powell and he had plenty of cut corn, and more importantly, plenty of "slow flying doves." That "slow flying" is a joke of course, but those gray feathered rockets had additional momentum from the outer bands of Hurricane Dorian's breezes: up, down, and sideways.

Four o'clock (Zero: four hundred) as in a.m. came early. The concrete driveway at my house was wet, and the fog was thick. What I used to call "heat lightning" was busting across the southern horizon every few minutes: right where we were headed. My son, John and my grandson, Nolan were not worried in the least. After all, this was opening day. As we crossed the Chowan River at about 4:45am, we noticed that we were experiencing the calm before the storm. The river was slick as glass with reflections of the shoreline security lights flickering in the purple/black darkness. Four hot sausage and egg biscuits were quickly becoming history. Almost anything, especially big, fat, greasy biscuits taste delicious at that time of the morning. The lightning was becoming more intense, but when we left Plymouth and crossed into the tree shrouded country roads down through the vast farmland once proposed for a U. S. Navy Jet OLF (Outlying Landing Field), we lost sight of any lightning for the rest of our hunt.

Have you ever noticed how landmarks in the dark of night, shrouded in dog tick fog, and rearranged since last year, become a little difficult to make out? Well that was our predicament. We had left in plenty of time to accommodate any inconsistencies, and this was but a very small "bump in the road." We crossed Fixed Bridge Creek, turned right, and blew right past the field path that we thought would be lit up with pick-ups preparing to hunt Tim Powell's PUNGO RIVER FARM. As we crossed the Washington / Beaufort County Line, here came a "convoy" of pickups with dog boxes. We executed a three-point turn, and followed two loaded down pickups into the path that we now recognized. Isn't that the way it usually works? Who needs a Garmin?

Landowner Tim was glad to see his old friends and the new one sitting in his child safety seat behind his daddy. We paid our fee, got directions to the "honey hole," and hastened down the path, right past the combine parked in the middle of the path, right past the bean field, and turned left at the crossover. John dumped out our "stuff," Nolan and I started kicking husks of corn to find unpicked ears, and waited for John to go back to the highway and lead in our compadres. Nolan's strong little thumbs shucked one-golden kernel at a time off about five full sized unharvested ears by the time his Dad got back.

Now was the time to realize just how beautiful God's world is, but from the perspective of nine hunters eagerly awaiting "shootin' time." While we waited, Nolan broke sweetgum branches from the tree line and wrapped up the shiny white plastic lid of the cooler. He replied, when asked why we do this, "Because we don't want the doves to see that hunters are in the field."

It is now 6:00am. Almost all of the hunters, our nine plus at least seventy-five others, are hunkered down, spaced out around a 300-acre field. From the flashing light mayhem, I know that every hunter must have brought a handheld flashlight plus a cap visor mounted LED. The overcast skies and the misting fog have caused it to remain pretty dark, even though it is now shooting time: 6:08am, thirty minutes before sunrise. At exactly 6:08am, somebody from the far irrigation ditch fires his shotgun, and we can see the fire belch from his gun. Surely it must have been an "AD," accidental discharge. I know that he or she who pulled that trigger could not have seen a dove in this murky piece of Heaven.

Game On

We all fought for our turn at missing doves for the first thirty minutes, some more than others. Hunters on one side were continuously raining shot down upon those of us across the field. More than likely, we were returning the favor! Sometimes, John said, "It hurts." Y'all didn't' know that, did you? By now the Snowy Egrets were crossing the field, and I

Michael J. McArthur

hoped that nobody would shoot one. They didn't, thank goodness. Not so lucky for the barn swallows. Honestly, they do slightly resemble a dove, but much smaller. They fly differently, too, gliding and darting instead of pumping and flaring. I saw at least two swallows hit the ground, whether they came out of the field at the end of the day is anybody's guess. My guess is that they were stomped down into the bottom of a muddy ditch. Right in the thick of the gunfire, here came Johnny-long legs, a Goolagong, a gawk bird. Actually, the correct name for this stately gentleman is a Great Blue Heron. Somehow, he made it through the gauntlet unscathed.

Not having fired at flying birds since last year's quail season, believe it or not, shotgun marksmanship is a "perishable skill." After a while, most of us "hit our stride," and began making up for some of the easy shots we had missed earlier. Jeff Mullen, right down from John McArthur was the exception, as he usually is. Due to work related (Raleigh Fire Captain) injuries and other "mess," he had not hunted for ten years. This day, for starters, he fired four times and put four doves in his game bag. He was shooting a black Remington 870 three-inch magnum with which I have seen him perform miraculous feats of skill. BUT He does not hold a candle to his son, Dusty who routinely and consistently kills doves at sixty yards, and makes it look easy. Dusty and his son Westley soon had their limits, and come out of the field for the return trip to Raleigh. I heard him exclaim as he drove out of sight, "This truck will be clean at sunset tonight."

John and Nolan and I gather under the lonesome pine on the edge of the field to count birds, and place them into Ziplock bags before placing them into the cooler for healthy keeping. John has 14, I have 8 (there were more than that under our backyard bird feeder the day before), and Nolan has ONE: "Fluffy." Seems like John wounded a dove that hit the ground running, but no match for the determined, booted six-year-old retriever (Nolan). Now it became apparent: "Houston, we have a problem." Nolan has become attached to Fluffy, even though the bird has succumbed to his #8 shot injury. After some pretty intense conversation, Nolan agrees to place Fluffy into the Ziplock, but on top so that he can retrieve him when he gets home.

Speaking of those nine doves on the ground under my bird feeder the day before, there was a clear indicator of future weather conditions in their presence. In years past, immediately prior to some of the really bad storms that have ripped through Chowan County, the birdfeeder would be "wrapped up" in a feeding frenzy by multitudes of songbirds, especially English Sparrows, Tufted Titmice, and Northern Cardinals. No such indicator this year as Hurricane Dorian approached.

While on this trip, John had entrusted Nolan with a plastic double-barrel shotgun plus a wooden single barrel with golden Sacajawea dollars inside the trigger guard. Hopefully he would learn and demonstrate safe gun handling and respect for the toy guns. For the most part, he did: pointing the gun toward the ground while walking, placing it on the ground when not holding it, and making sure it was not loaded. When it came time to end the hunt, John and Nolan had to return to the tree line from their makeshift blind over along the four-foot-wide drainage ditch. John laid his blued Remington 870 Wingmaster among the weeds and straddled the ditch. Nolan, still looking for doves, walked over, chunked his shotgun across the ditch like a tomahawk, and jumped into John's hands. Oh well. It has been a long day, and maybe some of that gun safety stuff had been just more than the little guy could bear. We picked up all the spent shotgun shells on the ground around us. Way too many for too few birds.

As I recall, this was the same ditch that my hunting buddy Joseph had "jumped," but fallen into a few years back. When I turned to look, all I could see was his right wrist holding his shotgun above the ditch bank. I didn't acknowledge it. When he came shuffling up to the truck, we loaded his pick-up, and he asked me to drive home. "All right Joseph, I saw those acrobatics over by the ditch." By now his pulse was racing, and his face was flushed. Three broken ribs later, he is now fit as a fiddle – an old fiddle! UPDATE: Right here in 2021 Joseph finally has successfully completed back surgery, with an inserted steel rod, at Duke University Medical Hospital in Durham, North Carolina.

That black Labrador Retriever puppy from across the way has now gotten restless (again). He is running all over the field, and did I tell you it was a 300-acre field? His handler is hollerin' at the top of his lungs: most of it printable. Other hunters are now joining the raucous tirade, others mumbling under their breath. The dog picked up one of John's doves, mauled it really good, spit it out, and ran on "to fight another day." GREAT entertainment value. Before we leave, we take one more trek through the woods which were "wrapped up with poison ivy," looking for one or two doves that we had lost. No luck again.

John walked half a mile and retrieved the Toyota, driving past hunters not too thrilled with the interloper, but understanding the plight of a young man with a six-year-old boy and 69-year-old father, waiting in the shade under the pine at the other end of the field. That black dirt I talked about was in every nook and cranny of everything that was on site: the guns, the cooler, the camouflage five-gallon bucket/seats, the bottom of our boots, and the seats of our pants. Nasal passages and ear canals were not exempt, either! We cleaned up as best we could, loaded into the Toyota, drove back past the die-hard hunters that put us in the same category as that Labrador, pulled onto the main path, and lo and behold! There stood body armored, Lt. Mark Cagle with the North Carolina Wildlife Resources Commission's Law Enforcement Division. For probably the obvious reasons, he had a couple of red-faced hunters moping around over beside his patrol truck (lucky guy!). Having been a Wildlife Enforcement Officer in my previous life, I kinda sorta knew what their immediate future was gonna look like.

Lt. Cagle was most amicable and skillful during our interview with him. He spoke to Nolan who told him what a great time we had had. He went about his job, kindly gave one of us (initials MJM) the professional courtesy of trusting that I was in fact licensed, but not in immediate possession of the card. He asked John, "Do you have three hours to bring your Daddy and meet me at the jail in the Washington County Courthouse?" Thank goodness he opted to discuss our "good luck," checked what he could, and waved us on our way, as other hunters were beginning to gather in our rear-view mirror. He probably checked 200 sportsmen that day. That field was what law enforcement officers refer to as, "A target rich environment."

Hardison's Carolina Barbecue in Jamesville, N.C.

Now, at 11:30 it was time for lunch. We decided to go to a new (to us) Hardison's Carolina Barbecue Restaurant over in Jamesville, about ten miles toward home, the long way. Light rain fell on us, making the black dirt on the silver Toyota look like Dalmatian, or a bad case of the measles. Nolan was sound asleep, probably dreaming about his new best friend, Fluffy. We bounced into the gravel lot, unloaded, went in, ordered our meal at the counter (like any good barbecue hut), and went to wash our blackened/bloody hands – really not making much difference. Nolan ordered his standard "plain cheeseburger, fries, and a glass of milk." John and I got barbecue and commented on three things: how good the service was, and how good the barbecue was, and how reasonable the price was. Nolan had heard talk of banana pudding while we thought he was asleep, and reminded us, "Hey! How about that banana pudding?" My lunch cohorts and I are authorized to tell you that that little half-pint Styrofoam cup full of homemade banana pudding is so good that, "It'll make you write bad checks!" I handed Nolan a twenty-dollar bill, and he raised his little hand, just like he did in first grade. The transplanted yankee waitress came over, and Nolan asked, "Can we order three banana puddings, please?", handing her the money to cover the $4.50 expense. We commented how he had managed to treat the lady with the same courtesy and kindness as if we had been dining in the Waldorf Astoria, New York. The pudding came along with $15.50 change. Guess where the two quarters vanished: right into Nolan's camouflaged hunting pants pocket. On the way out, the gumball machine became the new owner of those two quarters, and Nolan shared his reap. Nolan had learned that trick (among others) from his grandmother on numerous occasions. As we headed for the door, seated at "the family table," along with the restaurant owners, Nancy and Jerry Hardison was State Trooper Chris Moore. When Nolan shuffled by, Trooper Moore said, "Now there goes a dove hunter."

We left the restaurant, drove through Williamston and out onto what the locals call, "The Williamston Field." It is a stretch of, straight as an arrow, tree lined, elevated four lane US-13 / US-17 that runs parallel with the Roanoke River across Conine Creek through the U. S. Fish and Wildlife, Roanoke River National Wildlife Refuge in Bertie County. I tell my colleagues from afar, as they travel to and from Edenton, that, "If you don't get a speeding ticket along that 'cabbage patch,' you are just not trying."

When we arrived at John's house, we gave Fluffy to Nolan, and cleaned the rest. As we were finishing up, with the saddest little face, Nolan came over and offered up Fluffy for preparation for dinner that night. We cleaned Fluffy, marked the meat as "Fluffy," and placed the harvest in a brine solution for soaking over night until we ate them several days later. Life goes on, and Nolan has grown up a little bit more, much to his father's and my disdain. All's well that ends well.

Just think of the life lessons learned during this adventure. By all of us!

Watermen are Survivors

"Listen Close"

During these increasingly challenged and harrowing times, one way that I "decompress" is to give in to one of my many indiscretions. After a rough start at the office, I go out, get in my black cherry Chevrolet pickup truck my sister Kathy gave me, and go see Lina and Doug at Westover General Store. I pick up a "hi-test" Coca-Cola, a Snickers Bar, a big Honey Bun, a big yellow bag of Lay's Potato Chips, and a new *"COASTAL FISHING"* magazine. Then I go down to The Rocky Hock Creek Boat Ramp at Buck Bond's Cypress Point Marina near the Chowan River. I try to time it just right for the morning float of licensed commercial fishermen, and let them help me get "caught up" on **what's important and what ain't!**

The Real Issues in Life

- "Enough" and "guns" do not belong in the same sentence

- "Limits" What's that? Jus' jokin'

- "Size" only matters to commercial fishermen and fish cops, not sport fishermen, and certainly not poachers

- "Quota" equates most closely with infinity, but not really, Officer Long

- "DMV Operator's License" is optional, sometimes use it to unlock the back door, block out the "check engine" dashboard light, or "jimmy" the boathouse lock

- "Fishing License" is to be revered, but not necessarily mandatory. (Ask the mate without a license who cost his Captain the million buck grand prize in the Morehead City "Big Rock Blue Marlin Tournament" a few years back.)

- "Boat License" is absolutely essential since it can be read from a great distance with a pair of cheap binoculars

- "Plan" basic but flexible, K.I.S.S. (Keep It Simple, Stupid)

- "Vessel" Commercially licensed 36-footer was Grandpaw's legacy, now mine

- "Rough seas" hazardous travel conditions, also occasionally present at the house

- "Flats" too shallow estuarian water, or what I found on my boat trailer this morning, right at 4am

- "Bar" too shallow water, Gilley's honky tonk in Pasadena, the snout on Bubba's McCulloch chainsaw, that monster she-bar bruin with two cubs in the swamp behind the house

- "Breaker" a rolling wave, or the opening lingo during CB channel nineteen chat

- "Time" means nothing unless it's Miller Time

- "Social Distancing" six inches, to six feet, to sixty miles, depending on the nature of the varmint, and whether you saw it comin'

- "Pistols" always at least one, pocket rockets for varmints and critters: two legged, four legged, furred, feathered, finned, or scaled

- "Blade" "nife" "noife" interesting only if razor sharp, not too many nicks, occasionally used as screwdriver, look at the point

- "White Knee Boots" trick of the trade; keep your feet dry, also known as Wanchese Wingtips or Wanchese Re-Boks.

- "Yamaha or Honda Outboards" the only way to go

- "Friends" can never have too many, but sometimes one is too many

- "First Mate" only if honest, sober, and dependable (which may be an oxymoron)

- "Deck Hand" most often recognizable in the Captain's mirror while shaving (if at all)

- "Bait" tactical maneuver, diversionary, mummichogs, chum, fatbacks (menhaden), killifish, mud minnows

- " 'backer" breakfast of champions, dessert always, what cancer?

- "Good Wife" can back a 32-foot boat trailer down a crooked woods path while singing Loretta, Patsy, or Tammy to "the baby" at the top of her lungs

- "Mama" by God's grace, she's the mother of my young'uns and the wind beneath my wings. She's got my back, and she's got my heart. Bless her

- "Young'uns" make life worth livin', most of the time, but always near and dear to their heart, pictures on dashboard and boat windshield

- "Dawg" man's best friend – <u>no cell phone</u>, can't talk to "nobody but his owner," cleans up after his master, fights to his death anyone who fights with his master, rides "shotgun" on front seat and does NOT adjust the heat, the seat, the radio, or the sun-visor, and cares not where you turn or where you get your potted meat

- "Banker," Grandmaw and Grandpaw, our ancestors and our heritage. Who needs a banker / teller when you got $1000 cash under your seat?

- "Bearings" directional intuition from landmarks or the constellations – not electronics

- "Bearings" greased (hopefully) small metal roller pins within the wheel hubs – ALWAYS looked "atter"

- "Pain" settled with "cold beers" or white bootleg "likker," sometimes referred to as "Apple Brandy" out of a Mason fruit jar

- "Skin Cancers" occupational hazards most often cut out by the wearer, or their 'coon dog's veterinarian (been there – seen it done)

- "Lies" 5/95 some do / most don't

- "Scars" badges of honor, sometimes hidden, but always present ("Chainsaw slipped!", damn a dull knife, truck fell off blocks, safety musta been "off")

- "Broken bones" badges of honor, ever'body's got 'em, load shifted, underwater stump collision, winch cable broke, slipped on dock

- "Missing Appendages" more common than not – most often from falls, gunshots, mechanical failures, fish "pizen," caught cheating at cards, caught messin' with another fisherman's "baby", borned that way

- "Three sisters" aptly named, three consecutive waves that will sink you, quick

- "Hell's Kitchen" beware of storms borned over there

- "Vision" failing, but good enough to work fourteen hours a day, play poker 'til dawn, and spot a yankee messing with his nets

- "Future" uncertain, but we're bettin' on it

- "Blow" certainly not cocaine, but much more of a challenge, it tends to shift causing lost time, time is money

- "Bail" what you do to get the fish out of the pound, what you do to keep "Miss Ella" from sinkin', what you do to keep you from drownin', or what somebody does to get yourself or your brother out of jail. Also, the rewind mechanism on an open-faced Shakespeare spinning reel

- "Dirty Politics" is there really any other kind?

- "Hunting" anywhere, anytime, long as the fish ain't bitin'

- "Fish Cop" your best friend and your worst enemy, all at the same time

- "Five-O" Fish Cop at a bad moment

- "September 11, 2001" "First Blood" declaration of war

- "Congress" who needs 'em?

- "Fish Camp" the beach house settin' on four cinder blocks up the creek

- "Endangered species" he who gawks at Mama, fishes my pots, kicks my dawg, blocks my driveway, or steals my gear

- "Rustlers" those who fish your pound nets during the dark of night, subject to a .30 -'06 rifle ball being strategically placed in proximity, immediately before chaos erupts, equipment lost (with thief's initials branded onto handle), and erratic flight is taken. I've seen it happen.

Life's Lessons

These are just a few of "life's lessons" you can pick up if you are willing to sit and listen. One of the things that I find amazing: many of these professional watermen "cain't swim a lick." Due to governmental regulations, or aging, or double toil, and triple trouble, many of the old reliables are "hangin' it up." They can go days without sleep, overcome "arthur," read the stars at night, find the birds at daybreak, fix the unfixable, fight anything and everything that moves (or won't), and greet the Preacher-man while tithing in church on Sunday morning with Mama, the kids, and a starched long sleeved white shirt.

Life on the open waters of eastern North Carolina is never easy. The weather is a HUGE variable, and can not only keep fishermen at the dock, but cause lost gear, lost product, lost income, lost time (time is money), lost homes, and lost lives. I am not sure where commercial fishing ranks in the National Registry of most dangerous professions, but I know where it belongs. Some surveys rank Fishery Workers right between Loggers and Roofers and above Firefighters, and Police Officers. I understand that, and I admire all who directly or indirectly place their lives in danger on a daily basis, just so I can eat a soft-shell crab sandwich. Most veterans cannot see well, have lost their sense of smell, and none of them can hear worth a tinker's damn.

Illnesses further sideline our fishermen. Cancers of all kinds seem to saturate the industry, while today's regulations do little to ward off such destructive forces. Skin cancers, lung cancers, pancreatic cancers, liver cancers, and other forms of cancer are prevalent due to the inherent risks associated with the profession. Hazardous material exposures result from crab pot construction, line treatments, motor exhaust, chemical treatments, fuel vapors, chemical spills, and every other environmental contaminant imaginable to man. Gum disease is rampant, and dental care is way down on their list of priorities. "Fish pizen" is a common malady that, if you have never had it, you don't know what you are missing.

I cannot begin to list the injury causing factors that our watermen endure. Just getting out of a warm bed and out onto the water is a challenge. Launching the boat with that worn out winch, and nighttime navigating the slick ramshackle docks is challenging. Pouring gasoline into the truck's carburetor has "swinged" many a mate. Spraying ether into the air filter of the outboard is another explosive risk. Once you are "out," then the navigation risks pose their glut of dilemmas. Collisions with underwater snags, with other vessels, with fishing gear, and other unknowns cause lots of injuries. Handling the fishing apparatus is treacherous at the angles necessary to successfully land the catch. Poles break. Knives slip. Lines snap. Rusty steel breaks. Aluminum joints crumble. Churning gears catch clothing and extremities. Gunwales and decks collapse. Sterns separate. Shelves disintegrate. Seats topple. And the bows split. But you gotta go, because it is "now or never" when the "bite" is running.

Chowan County's Bounty

Here in Chowan County, we are blessed with a bountiful fishery. We have Striped Bass sport fishing derbies. We have Largemouth Bass tournaments. We have the palate delicacy, Speckled Perch. We are blessed with tons of White Perch. We have every kind of catfish. And yes, we have Blueback Herrings. Occasionally a sturgeon will venture this far inland as will flounder and dolphin. Blue Crabs are also a highly fished industry in these parts.

Most of my exposure to commercial fishermen and their trade has been my occasionally being asked to assist while some of the local lifers fish their pound nets or pull their crab pots in the Chowan River, Edenton Bay, and the Albemarle Sound. I am authorized to tell you that I am not much help, maybe just a tad better than no help. I have learned to do what I'm told, not do what I'm told not to, when to get out of the way, and how to stay out of the way. These are valuable lessons for not only fishing but for living a productive life, in general. Not to mention that it can make your life less difficult. More than likely, these lessons can save your life and that of others. So, **"Listen Close!"**

A 5:00am FISHING OPPORTUNITY

At about 5:00 am one Thursday morning in April, I heard (how could I not?) an unmufflered thunder merchant pickup truck pull into my driveway. As a veteran North Carolina State Highway Patrolman, the sky is the limit when it comes to people dropping by the house, but at 5am? I immediately wondered whether someone needed help, was lost, or had come to surrender.

Boozey Forehand needed a deckhand. He was a small fisherman by volume, but a large fisherman by stature. Over the years, I had probably written him and his family "a whole book of tickets" (25) for everything from speeding, to operating a vehicle with blue lights mounted on the front bumper, to drunk driving. I caught him one night up in Tynch Town at White's Landing, driving so drunk that he couldn't walk. He was "**just too drunk**!" He had just gotten off his brother's boat, and had "borrowed" a twenty-six-inch rockfish (closed season I might add) for dinner. He knew from past experience that he was gonna spend the night in jail, but didn't want to leave that rock where somebody else might steal it for the second time. So, wrapped up in my aluminum foil State Highway Patrol emergency blanket, into the trunk of my black and silver, went the rockfish.

However, on this Thursday morning at 5am, Boozey wanted my help in a far less oppressive way. Could I please go help him fish his single pound net in the mouth of Rocky Hock Creek near Cypress Point. After I determined that he would probably not blow ten hundredths of one percent breath alcohol, I consented. But I drove myself the quarter mile down to Buck Bond's Marina. He told me to get a five-gallon-bucket, and bring it along for some fresh Herrings.

Somebody's "piece o' boat" was moored right beside the ramp, and had two, rickety white plastic folding chairs in it. A broken paddle was holding the barnacled foot of the 25 hp Mercury out of the water. A long stick (20 foot) with a bolt through the end (gaff fashion) was stowed along the starboard gunwale. He had a small net, about two feet across, on a long handle, stowed along the port gunwale. Boozey eased his clumsy self off the dock, and plopped into one of the folding chairs. It collapsed. He let out a blue streak of cuss words, grabbed the other chair, and took the wheel. I unleashed the boat (that's right, a dog's leash), and got in. I got the prop into the water, and he fired it up. The red-green bow light was dangling outside the cleat, and there was not a stern light to be found. After the smoke cleared, and we could once again see our surroundings, I shoved the bow away from the dock toward the mouth of the creek.

Of course, the motor sputtered to a halt. Another epic blue streak of profanity was turnt loose. But, somehow, once again in a cloud of blue smoke, that antique Mercury fired up, and we were off toward the river.

As a rule, most fishermen take their time going past the other folks' boats moored in the marina. Evidently, we were in a hurry as dawn was breaking, and visibility improving. As we rounded the last green channel marker, it became obvious that we were in a hurry. He nailed it, and I grabbed holt to the rail!

We went more or less straight to the nearest of about seven or eight pound nets, just offshore. He killed the motor, and plowed right across the leader that extends up to the pound. Boozey took that gaff, and hooked the perimeter of the net, cinched the net rope that closed the purse, and said, "Let's fish!" He grabbed the net and started "shoveling" Herrings into the bottom of the boat, right on top of my new Converse All-Star Tennis shoes. He dumped two of the netfuls into my bucket, and said, "Let's go." Now I understood the urgency of high-tailing-it out there and back to the dock before the rising sun could shine too much light on our clandestine operation.

We released the purse string, unhooked from the fouled net, cranked the Mercury, and back to the dock we went. I asked him, "Whose net was that?" His answer did not surprise me. **"Listen Close!"** "Damned if I know!"

William "Dossey" Pruden, V
"The Salt of the Earth" Mathew 5:13

Another of my friends is a "crabber." He has had a crabbing business since Moses was a baby, and his Merchant Seaman Captain's license since he himself was a baby (about fifty years). He is at least a fifth-generation waterman, with an interesting family and a colorful history. His given name is William Dossey Pruden, V, and his son is blessed to come along as William Dossey Pruden VI. I met V in 1974 when he invited me to come and hunt Snow Geese and Canada Geese on his sound front property, "anytime, day or night," and laughed. But he did give me, right on the shoulder of Soundside Road, right underneath my spinning blue light, written permission to hunt his farm with its waterfowl infested shoreline.

One day my wife Becky and I bumped into him at Westover General Store where we were all getting bowls of homemade New England Style Clam Chowder. He was planning to fish his two- hundred-and-fifty crab pots the next morning and asked if I would like to help him. Never having done that before, I was quick to take him up on his offer.

At 9am the next morning I climbed aboard his 24 foot Carolina skiff, "EZ Money." Another of his friends, a retired CIA Agent called "Spook," was piloting the work vessel while Dossey and I prepared for our mission. Again, I did what I was told to, didn't do what I was told not to, and stayed out of the way. I could tell that The Captain appreciated that.

We shoved off from Edenton's Waterfront Park/Docks and proceeded toward The Bell Buoy. On top of two of the United States Coast Guard maintained channel markers, magnificent Ospreys had built nests. There were two fuzzy chicks in each, peering over the edge, as their mothers circled protectively above.

I watched as "Spook" maneuvered the boat up to, and immediately skirted and circled the first buoy marking the first of fifty crab pots in a zig-zagged line toward Mackey's Ferry. I am color blind, so I reckon Dossey knew which pots were his by the buoy coloration, or the location. As we slowed to a stop at each buoy, Dossey hooked the line with a gaff, strung the line onto his motorized "crab pot puller," and waited just a few seconds until out of the water came the three-foot, cube shaped, fish baited, chicken wired, crab pot. It was deftly manhandled by Dossey's gloved mitts, before resting it on the starboard gunwale.

He unhooked the opening, raised the pot containing three to ten crabs, "Larges, 6" to 6 ½ between the points," and then slammed the pot down onto the open top of the wooden bushel basket/box until all the crabs were jostled out of the mesh enclosure and into Dossey's basket/box. When necessary, he shoved a fish or shrimp-soaked Styrofoam fingerling sized pellets into the bait well. Back over the gunwale the pot went, unharnessed from the "puller." On to the next pot, maybe 50 yards distant. And so it went.

"Crabbing is an Acquired Skill"

We pulled those pots in a short while, and motored west, over toward John's Island where another line of pots needed fishing. By now I wanted to try my hand at crabbing. Dossey explained to me that "crabbing" was an acquired skill, and more than a knack, and that it could prove dangerous for novices. I got out of his way!

In a little less than an hour, we fished the second line of pots, and Captain Pruden declared that it was lunchtime. We set about eating our ham sandwiches and our potato chips, right out there in Edenton Bay. The bottled water was good, and welcome. All during the morning I had taken pictures with my Fujifilm disposable camera. Later on, after the pictures came back from CVS Pharmacy, I gave them to Dossey. His 60th birthday party came and went, and Carlette had baked him a cake with a likeness of one of my pictures carefully embedded onto the icing.

Along about 1:00, Dossey determined that he had had about all the fun he could stand from a novice on his boat. He wheeled me back to town, dropped me off, and again headed out to The Bell Buoy. This time he steered East, back toward his Blue Heron Hunting Lodge. Later that day, when he took his catch to Beech Springs Seafood up in Belvidere, NC, he got the best price per pound that he had ever gotten. I told him that I had been his lucky rabbit's foot.

"Listen Close!" This was one of those times when "The harder you work, the luckier you get!"

H L and Sharon Bond, Vintage Americana

Defying the Odds and Cheating the Grim Reaper

During my time here in Chowan County, my family and I have been blessed in many ways when it comes to the rich tapestry that abounds. Strangers are usually friends whose acquaintance we have not yet made. Such was the case with a local notorious personality. Whatever "notorious" might mean to you, when it comes to licensed commercial fisherman Henry Luther Bond, DOUBLE IT!

H L, as he prefers to be called made his first pass into my life as an unsung hero of the highest magnitude. H L accomplished a feat of skill and daring (one of many), that I will defy anyone else to duplicate. H L and his neighbor were fishing their pound nets in the mouth of the Chowan River on the Chowan County side near the mile-and-a-half, US-17 bridge. This area is right across the river from what was then, The R. J. Reynolds Tobacco Company's Laboratory and Product Development Facility. Due to the heavy marine construction of Waff Marine Contractors in that area of the river shore, there is a deep and wide channel that seems to attract all manner and schools of migratory fish: White Perch, Flounder, Striped Bass, Blue-backed Herrings, Alewife, American Shad, and Sturgeon. H L is a fifth-generation commercial fisherman and has forgotten more about the skills and tribulations of commercial fishing than most of his cronies will ever learn. And he knows when, where, why, and how to catch fish and Blue Crabs.

It was a bright sunny morning, about 8:00am. The shifts had just changed over in Bertie County at R. J. Reynolds on Salmon Creek, and the night shift workers were headed north on the US-17 Bridge, returning to their homes, many in Chowan County. As H L fished his pound nets, when their horn blew, he could see his friends waving as they were traversing the bridge. H L, being everybody's friend would wave back to them as they passed overhead. This morning, one of his neighbors DID NOT honk his horn and DID NOT wave to H L.

The red pickup truck's driver was watching the fisherman on the river below. The truck crossed the broken white lines of the narrow two-lane Chowan River Bridge, and collided, head-on with a blue 1972 Ford Maverick being operated by a Methodist minister on his way to Windsor to preach his Sunday morning sermon. Also inside the Maverick was his wife wearing her Sunday best, and their eighteen-month-old son. Smoke was already rising from the Maverick and the pickup truck.

Without hesitation, H L skillfully maneuvered his 16-foot River Ox— loaded with 2200 pounds of blue-black herring— up to the spot directly below the wreck scene. He tied the boat to the creosote splintered piling that was about 22-inches in diameter and stretched twenty-five feet straight up to the underside of the bridge's crossmember support beams. H L kicked off his white rubber boots, and climbed that splintered piling up to its union with a four-foot overhang below the concrete slab of the bridge. Somehow, while dangling twenty-five-feet above his boat, which the current had pushed around to a position directly underneath him, he managed to "hand-over-hand" out to the edge of the bridge railing foundation.

Now came the truly death-defying part of his rescue efforts: he did a chin-up and hooked his chin over the 6X12 crossbeam and brought his foot up and wrapped it over the top of the beam. Next, he pulled his upper torso along the vertical outer edge of the two-foot-high, extremely course concrete bridge railing. This in itself caused extreme pain and suffering from the scrapes and cuts he received. With all his might, he launched his barefooted self over the railing and onto the glass strewn bridge surface.

Oil and gasoline and water were all mixed together, and ponded up around the two totaled vehicles. The pickup driver was unconscious under his steering wheel, and the preacher was very dead. The Maverick erupted in flames! The baby was crying, and the mother in the front passenger seat was dazed and in shock. The flames were gaining momentum, when H L reached into the back seat, grabbed the baby boy, yanked him out of the busted back driver's side window, and carried him like a football under his left arm.

H L ran around to the passenger side, and was somehow able to pull the mother from inside her smoke-filled confinement. He picked up her tiny bloody torso, and carried her and the baby away from the flames, and placed them next to the railing, well away from the Maverick which was now fully engulfed in twenty-foot flames and black oily smoke. This is when I arrived on the scene. As I exited my patrol car, the mother was wrapping her now fatherless baby in the flowing blue fabric of her full-length Sunday dress.

As I was hovering over the mother and baby, a thunderous roar passed overhead. F-15N Sea Eagles from the United States Navy's Oceana Naval Air Station in Virginia Beach regularly train over the Chowan River, using the Center Swing Span Bridgetender's Shack as their simulated coordinate. After the passing of the first southbound fighter jet (world's fastest at the time), here came two more at what seemed to be a slower speed than their usual Mach 2.5 (1650 mph). These next two jets passed so very low and perpendicular to the roadway, that I could see the rivets in the fuselages and the helmeted heads of the two single pilots turned toward our spectacular scene.

Immediately I scooped the mother and son up and put them inside my patrol car. I went and roused the driver of the pickup truck who spontaneously told me that he was "So sorry." And that he, "Must have fallen asleep after working all night."

Danger began to decrease, and things became less intense as more help arrived.

"Little did I know, but dog-gone if H L didn't climb back over that three-foot rail 45 feet above the water, swing himself over onto the A-frame, and then shinny down that splintered piling. He hooked the bow line with his foot and floated the fish laden River Ox up under him. Then he dropped his "swinged" and bleeding self onto the fish box he used for a seat. And off he went!"Murray Ashley (August 1, 1919 to September 1986), Gil Johnson (January 3, 1924 to August 4, 2016), and Bill Underkofler (February 2, 1936 to April 26, 1986) with Unit One of the Edenton Chowan Rescue Squad transported all three survivors to Chowan Hospital to unite with supporting family members.

The Chowan County Coroner, Dr. James N. Slade (September 7, 1930 to August 14, 20014) came to the wreck scene and "pronounced" the driver of the Maverick. Wrecker Drivers Felix Chambers (March 24, 42 to August 7, 2017) and Pruden Forehand (August 3, 1917 to December 23, 1978) hauled away the destroyed vehicles. The Fire Chief Luther Parks (July 8, 1923 to February 2, 1997), Junius Britton (May 31, 1933 to May 15, 2011), and Bertram Byrum (January 18, 1917 to August 4, 2006) with the Edenton Fire Department extinguished the inferno and hosed the debris onto the side of the bridge to be scooped up. And the paperwork began.

While reading the photo-laden accounting of the wreck in the next edition of our local weekly newspaper, *The Chowan Herald,* I got a call from the Highway Patrol Telecommunicator Shift Supervisor, Alex Jones in Williamston to 10-21 (telephone) H L Bond at his residence. Since, as the crow flies, I live only half a mile from him, I drove over to his fishing operation on Macedonia Road, and pulled into his driveway. H L had two Boxer dogs before one of them got struck by a giant bolt of lightning, and knocked out of the bed of H L's Ford pickup while motoring down the highway. The other Boxer met me at my patrol car door. Apparently, the color and shape of my Black and Silver were not to his liking. When I spoke kindly to him, he ran on off to play.

Sharon, H L's wife of many years came out on the porch and said, "Mike, you are in deep trouble." She laughed and called H L to come outside. H L is a burly kind of guy, and can present himself as rough and tough; but he's really just a big ol' teddy bear (now I am really in trouble). H L, still scuffed up, came over, shook my hand, and we talked for a minute about the horrible wreck, and how badly our friend felt about all the heartache he had caused. We both were friends with the pickup driver and could adequately commiserate.

The real reason that I was asked to stop by, and the real reason that I was in such big trouble was probably well justified. On that Wednesday morning, when all of H L's friends got their weekly copy of *The Chowan Herald*, there on the front page was the really well written article about the horrendous motor vehicle accident having occurred on the Chowan River Bridge the previous Sunday morning. The pictures were graphic, and the factual accounting was even more so. And then came the clincher: I had given newspaper Owner/Reporter Bud Amburn facts that caused dismay with H L. I had referred to the homegrown hero as, "Henry Luther." Well, you would have thought that I had kicked his last Boxer dog. Or slapped his horse! "DON'T NEVER TELL NOBODY THAT MY NAME IS HENRY LUTHER. AND DON'T NEVER PUT THAT IN THE NEWSPAPER, AGAIN. NOW ALL MY FRIENDS ARE GIVING ME A RATION OF YOU KNOW WHAT!" Whew! Was that it? "The only people who have ever called me Henry Luther were my teachers in grade school when I brought a little snake to school, skipped class, or cheated on a spelling test!" You just cannot make this stuff up!

What a Benevolent Soul

On Sundays, even though his many nets and more crab pots needed fishing, H L took time to bring his big old fishing boat down to Captain Wallace Goodwin's (July 6, 1929 to June 30, 1997) Beach or Bond's Fishing Center and Trailer Park on Rocky Hock Creek at Cypress Point for the enjoyment of the neighborhood kids. He would spend all of his Sunday afternoon and countless dollars of gasoline, pulling skiers. (Every local family had kids and at least one water ski). H L would take his time to teach young watermen and water women how to ski, how to fish, how to catch "speckles" and "yellowbellies," how to paddle a canoe, how to catch a snake, how to shoot a BB gun, and just about anything else that a young person needed to know. Now, go find someone today who has that level of dedication and the patience to accomplish such good for his fellow watermen and neighbors.

Bambi, Buck, and H L

Deer became a tantalizing attraction for H L at a very young age. All his uncles and most of his aunts were hunters. All his friends hunted deer, and he only hung out with those who also enjoyed, "the hunt." Hunting Season for H L sometimes stretched a little beyond what was written in the Digest of Game Laws produced by the North Carolina Wildlife Resources Commission. That occasionally put H L at odds with his neighbors and game wardens. Nighttime shots at raccoons or coyotes or wild dogs had a tendency to upset some of what he called "tree huggers."

H L "creatively" managed all sorts of wild game resources from Northern Bobwhite Quail to Turkeys, from Flathead Catfish to Largemouth Bass, and from American Mink to Black Bears. He knew most all the animals in his kingdom <u>by name</u>, knew where they lived, and knew what times and where they were most likely to be found grazing, grinding, chipping, or chewing. One night about 8:00 he and Sharon stopped by our newly built house on what he referred to as, "The Rattlesnake Crossing," beside Beaver Dam Creek. He invited me and Becky (from downtown Raleigh, N C), to go "look at some deer." Off we went, four abreast in a single seat Ford pickup truck with only one headlight on dim, but both on high.

First, we went to Grover (January 28, 1911 to July 20, 1971) and Mrs. Effie Cale's (February 14, 1909 to July 7, 1995) Store get some Red Man Chewing Tobacco. He offered me a chew, like the gentleman he was, but I declined like the geek that I am. He was drinking water from a canteen. We went straight to the Chowan Country Club near the old World War II, MCAS Edenton (1942 to 1946) on Soundside Drive. There were four sets of eyes over on #4 green, appearing to know that they could not be shot during nighttime hours. A big Whitetail buck, a sagging doe, and two little spotted fawns were out for their evening meal. Not only did H L know that deer would be there, but he knew how many would be there. Next, we went to Richard Jackson's Plantation over on the Albemarle Sound beside the Sound Bridge. There were a buck and two does, one of them obviously pregnant. H L said that she would probably deliver twins in the next day or two.

"I'll Stop Twice Next Time"

Back out onto Base Road, we went toward the winery, Deerfield Vineyards, owned and operated by Frank Williams (November 11, 1918 to February 24, 1982) Paul Williams (January 26, 1950 to May 28, 1994), and Ben Wood (1936 to August 13, 2007). Sure enough, right there in the parking lot, it must have been a deer convention: seven deer scattered when they heard the sliding tires on the gravel roadside. There is a great big S T O P sign at that intersection which seemingly H L missed. As a freshly minted N C State Highway Patrolman, I was shocked! His response to Becky and me: "Oh well. I'll stop at it twice next time."

That is not the only time that H L failed to honor a S T O P sign. One night I was parked on the shoulder of Chamber's Ferry Road at its intersection with Cowpen Neck Road. I looked back toward my house and Macedonia Road beside Grover Cale's Store, and here came a one-eyed, loud pickup truck at a higher than usual rate of speed. ZOOM! Right past my house. Out went the one headlight! ZOOM! Right through the intersection (What about that S T O P sign?). I already knew who I was after, but at eighty-five miles per hour, I probably was gonna have to do some fancy driving to overtake him on those crooked Rocky Hock roads that he grew up on, and knew like the back of his hand. As luck would have it, I didn't have to go but about a half a mile before I saw a thick cloud of dust in the air where H L had turned left, into his Uncle Buck's (Murray P. Bond March 30, 1924 to January 20, 2004) Marina and fur buying station.

H L was already out of his truck and running toward the sliding glass door to the dimly lit arcade/store. Little did I know it, but the second and fourth Tuesday nights of the month were the only nights when H L could sell his Mink, Otter, Beaver, Raccoon, Opossum, Bobcat, and Coyote pelts to the grizzled old fur buyer from Waycross, Georgia. And he had to be there before the buyer left at 8:00, or hold and freeze his pelts for the next two weeks.

I figured that ol' H L had come up with an original reason/excuse for violating N. C. General Statutes 20-141 and 20-158. Before I got too deeply ensnared, I went and got back into my patrol car, and went back out on patrol. You understand, don't you, that he had cut out his headlight(s) as he approached the intersection to assist his night vision as to whether there was an approaching vehicle from either his left or his right. But at eighty-five miles-per-hour?

Returning a Favor

85 miles-an-hour must have been his favorite cruising speed (except when Becky and I were seated on the front seat beside him and Sharon). On patrol one Sunday night when I was returning to Edenton from turning in my weekly reports in Elizabeth City, out on US-17, I was operating my brand-new MR-7, moving radar unit. I always "primed" my next week's totals by writing a few citations on Sunday night, and "carrying them over" onto next week's "reasonable level of production," spelled Q U O T A.

Look out! Here came a one-eyed pickup at eighty-five miles-an-hour, over the crest of the Perquimans River Bridge. As I was not traveling but about 45mph, I pulled over, executed a power-spin, and fell right in behind the violator. Lo and behold, it was H L and Sharon. H L jumped out of the truck and ran back at me before I could exit my patrol car. I stepped out and asked him, "H L, what is the emergency?" He had one! He told me that he and Sharon were going to the Riverside Movie House in Elizabeth City. Next, he told me, "Mike, I've got to go!" I thought he meant to the bathroom. Nope. "Me and Sharon are trying to go see the new movie "JAWS." And? "If we don't get there during the very first minute and a half, there won't be any more naked women in the whole damned movie!" I let him go. Again he was original.

H L to the Rescue

I was working a 3 p.m. to 11 p.m. shift that same Sunday night. About 10:30 I met one of my local terrors, Amos Andy in his bronze 428 cu. in. Ford Cobra G. T. "Snake." Little did he know it, but I had been "lying in wait" for him for months due to his growing reputation for lawlessness on the backroads around the Punch Bowl and Rocky Hock, N.C. This night, he was running 104 mph on Base Road, headed toward town. Again, I power spun right around behind him, and the chase was on! He cut his lights off as we approached the T-intersection with NC-32, while he glanced to his left and right for approaching wreck victims. There were none. He slid sideways right in front of Fred Keeter's (September 14, 1929 to September 30, 2014) house, cleaned out the ditch, and powered west into town past Carter's Ink. I was on his tail by now. I had not had a chance to radio in a chase, and no "help" was on its way. We blew past Wesley Chesson's (March 2, 1927 to August 5, 2008) John Deere Tractor Company at about 75 mph, and I thought surely, when he entered that curve and hit the steel, raised railroad tracks he would/did go airborne.

As a N. C. Certified High-Speed Pursuit Driving Instructor, I learned and taught for many years: "Do not let the rabbit drive your patrol car." I was in a controlled skid, braking maneuver when I crossed the tracks, and could see the sparks flying from under "The Snake" as parts of it tumbled toward Leslie Kirby's (December 17, 1934 to November 13, 2015) lamp store. He blew through the stoplight at Oakum Street, and turned left onto Broad Street which was then US-17, before the Edenton bypass. He blew past Ed and Steve Taylor's Bridgeturn Exxon, past Taylor Theater, and blew through the stoplight at King Street. Three wet miles of Edenton Bay lay ahead! I always wanted to live this scenario, but Amos Andy also knew what lay ahead of him, so he skidded left, up onto the sidewalk at Kermit Layton's Edenton Office Supply. I thought I had him, but he squalled tires right past Frances Drane Inglis' 'Homestead,' and abruptly stopped on Water Street, right in front of the three mounted cannon on the 1767 Courthouse Green. Smoke was pouring out from both our cars, but his was the worst.

Wouldn't you know it, now he ran on foot. During a nighttime foot chase, the fleeing suspect will usually look back over his or her dominant side's shoulder. On this night I performed the maneuver that Trooper Pete Peterson taught me in the 58th Basic Highway Patrol Basic Training School: I shined my five cell Kel Light right in the middle of his back, thereby casting a shadow directly in his path. Amos Andy ran right past Hood and Anne Ellis's house, up past Bob, and Mary Ann Thomas's house, and up to the steps of the 1767 Historic Chowan County Courthouse at which he would most certainly appear in just a few short weeks. Having paced myself, I was dead on his heels. As he tripped on the elevated, shadowed curbing, I tackled him. He did not hit his head on the sandstone steps and die as did former Chowan County Game Protector John W. Hollowell (1886 to August 30, 1930).

We rolled around on the ground for a few minutes until I could get my blackjack out of my right hip pocket and chill him out! It worked. During the fight, my SHP issued handcuffs had become unattached from my belt, and fallen out of sight. I thought about hitting him again to knock him out cold like I had on several previous occasions on several other ne'er-do-wells. No, he really didn't need that, YET! I twisted his arm right up behind his back, and we staggered together down through the giant American Sycamores on the Courthouse Green toward my patrol car. When I yanked him around to the passenger side door, IT WAS LOCKED! Thank goodness, there stood H L Bond and Sharon. Amos Andy was a neighbor of Sharon's, and she started fussing at him. "Are you carazy? Can't NOBODY outrun McArthur. He teaches that stuff!"

I said, "Here, H. L. Hold this S.O.B." He grabbed the Amos Andy around the neck and grabbed his left wrist which was about half-way up the middle of his spinal cord. I thought that I had had a good hold on Amos Andy. When I heard H L tighten up on him, and heard that crack, I knew that my troubles with Amos Andy were over. And they were!

After a "search incident to arrest," and the discovery of an illegal switchblade knife, I gave Amos Andy two options: be charged with carrying a concealed weapon (a switchblade knife), or throw that thing as hard as he could out into Edenton Bay beside the Cypress Trees where Blackbeard the Pirate (Edward Teach) had hidden his looted treasures and bootleg rum. Amos Andy would have made a good pitcher!

I took Amos Andy to the Chowan Hospital Emergency Room and got his head sewed up and his arm looked at. Milton Jordan (Kojak / Tonto) came and hauled off "The Snake." H L and Sharon lived to tell the stories of their eventful evening for years, and until this day. Every time that someone relates to me what H L or Sharon told, it becomes more glorified. That is OK with me!

Big Snakes, Little Snakes, Live Snakes, Dead Snakes

Good Snakes, Bad Snakes

Speaking of snakes, H L liked them. In fact, he liked them a lot! They were kinda like his calling cards. If you could give him an hour, he could bring you ten snakes, all shapes and sizes, all species, and all very much alive.

Down at Joseph Goodwin's one afternoon, H L swam up underneath a four-foot poisonous Cottonmouth Water Moccasin, grabbed it, pulled it underwater "so that it couldn't bite him," came up and slammed it against Mrs. Hilda Rae Goodwin's (October 13, 1933 to February 3, 2018) pier, killing it graveyard dead right at her feet.

Once H L took just one, small little snake to school in his zippered coat pocket. All was well until the Hognose Snake hognosed his way out of there, and fell onto the floor of his fifth-grade classroom. So why was I not surprised to see H L and Sharon pull into my driveway with the admonition, "Becky. Mike. Come here, I want to show y'all something." First, he had a crate of Silver Queen Corn for us, "So y'all won't starve to death." Then he had a bushel of Blue Crabs that he wanted to give us, but we didn't have a clue what to do with them. Next, he had a wooden crate with a three-foot Canebrake (Timber) Rattlesnake in it which was not very "sociable." H L would shake the box, and the snake would coil, and those eight rattles would "sing." "Hear that?" H L said. "Stop. Look. Listen. And slowly back away. You cannot really tell from which direction these sounds are coming." He then baited the snake to strike at him, and deftly grabbed him by the "no-neck." He then grabbed the snake's tail right above the rattles. As much of a man as H L was at that time, he could not prevent the snake from flexing and coiling himself into a knot. H L threw him back into the crate and wired it shut. The "singing" was ear-piercing.

Wallace "Cowboy" White (January 19, 1928 to September 6, 2011) called H L to come over toward Paradise and get a H U G E six-foot Canebrake out from under his barn. H L was swift in his actions, and the snake ended up inside a 55-gallon barrel. That snake nearly was long and strong enough to climb out the top of it, before H L reached in and after several enticements, caught the viper right behind his pits. He placed the snake into an Igloo fifty-four Quart Cooler and rode off into the sunset. Who knows what happened over the next several hours? I can only imagine.

H L was, at times, a multi-talented and tireless and unrestrained and intemperate incorrigible. He could do anything, anytime, anywhere, with or without provocation. He was as solid as a rock in his preferences, and thank goodness they ran toward helping folks. He recognized danger, but he never really ran from it. Many times, he was found to "test the waters!" He was a courageous entrepreneur and rarely was beaten. He could make a dollar when nobody else seemed to be having much luck. It seemed that luck was always on his side.

Lucky, Lucky

Speaking of luck, how about the time he and Pee Wee Campbell were cutting firewood off a hurricane downed White Oak Tree over on Bowens Road. As H L stood on the limb under duress, Pee Wee chain sawed the tree's trunk which fell onto that very limb, thereby catapulting H L over thirty feet into the evening air. H L lived to cuss him out. During the eight-month recovery process and amid all the physical therapy rehabilitation sessions, H L would go up to Murray Nixon's (March 20, 1934 to August 14, 2009) Fishery in Rocky Hock, and visit with his Commercial Fishermen friends, Murray's young'uns: Ricky Nixon, Louis Nixon, Leon Nixon, Jimmy Nixon, and Lynda Harrell. As he sat on the tailgate of his truck, somehow he got knocked off onto the concrete platform, flat on his already broken back. Somebody else toted a cussin.' LUCKY, LUCKY!

How about the time he and Bald Eagle (David Goodwin (April 18, 1923 to April 24, 1990)) were "scouting deer" in a field over on Terrapin Hill, and while H L "carefully maneuvered" through the field at about 75 mph, that cow horn buck ran up to and wrapped himself around that Ford's front right tire, causing the truck to roll over onto its top. When Bald Eagle couldn't disentangle his large self from inside that truck out into the field, he made a mistake. Eagle told H L, "Help me get out of here you S.O.B., I'm gonna kill you!" H L responded, "I ain't that stupid!" LUCKY, LUCKY!

How about when he had promised Sharon that he would cook her dinner, and have it ready when she got off work over at the Tyrrell Prison Work Farm on Snell Road in Columbia, NC? The pan of grease caught fire on the stove, and H L picked it up by the handle, walked to the back porch, opened the screen door, and pushed rather than threw it out. That fire raced out of the pan, up the handle, and all the way up H L's gun arm onto his neck. Yep! Third degree burns. Get him to show you the scars. Still he was lucky in that the fiery grease didn't reach his eyes or burn his nice brick home to the ground. LUCKY, LUCKY!

How about when he and Pee Wee (his brother-in-law, Gloria's brother) were trapping muskrats over on John's Island in the mouth of Pembroke Creek beside Emmett Wiggins' sunken, bottomed-out, bulldozer laden, flatbed barges? My buddy, Game Warden Dave Dowdy and I were called to go over there, and find H L and Pee Wee because, it seems like they had trapped a Red-Tailed Hawk, and "somebody" had thrown it in the air, and the "other" somebody had shot it down. When we arrived at the Edenton Marina which was where Pee Wee's car was parked, a conversation ensued. Nobody really wanted to talk about trapping, or shooting, or dead hawks, or really anything else. Finally I asked Pee Wee, "Pee Wee, what do you have in your trunk?" "Nuthin' boss man. Why?" Dowdy said, "We heard that H L killed a hawk, and you put it in your trunk." Well, a hush fell over the crowd. I asked Pee Wee to look inside his trunk. As we walked over to the Chevrolet, Dowdy said, "Pee Wee, maybe that dead hawk has gotten out!" Pee Wee moaned, "If he's got out, he's a gittin' out bitch." You'da had to been there to get the whole picture as we raised that trunk lid! Pee Wee took the whole rap, and H L dodged another bullet. LUCKY, LUCKY!

One blustery winter day, H L was fishing his crab pots in his River Ox, all by himself, which was not unusual. It was a day when there were no other boats plying the Albemarle Sound between Mackey's Ferry and

Edenton Bay. But there was H L. Somehow, one of "Three Sisters" raced across from Hell's kitchen, and launched H L's boat sideways into a thirty-foot concrete piling in the middle of the Sound. This series of pilings formed the structural support for a Dominion Powerline cable stretched across the three and a half mile wide Albemarle Sound.

At about twenty-five miles-per-hour, H L was knocked conscious, but completely out of this boat without a life saving device. The boat continued about three miles on its way toward Scotch Hall Golf Course on Salmon Creek, made a big loop through Batchelor's Bay, crossed the mouths of the Cashie River, The Middle River, the Roanoke River, and H L watched it coming back after him. It crossed within fifty yards of where H L was precariously perched on the cusp of the slanted concrete piling. H L continued yelling for help.

H L watched as his 16-foot River Ox careened toward the northern shoreline of the Albemarle Sound, right beside the Chowan Golf and Country Club. At twenty-five miles-per-hour the boat perpendicularly ran ashore and head-on into a creosote wooden bulkhead at the home of Jon and Nancy Nicholls. Gear flew everywhere as the bow of the fiberglass vessel embedded itself four feet through the 4" X 10" pilings, and arched up into their manicured lawn.

As H L continued to yell, a friend of some friends of his miraculously heard his pleas. Three friends, Melissa Halsey's Uncle Jim Whitaker (June 11, 1933 to February 3, 2021, Jack Held (May 23, 1935 died eight years later November 17, 2018 in the Albemarle Sound), and Tony Hughes, all three fishing buddies, went out and scooped up H L off that piling and saved his life. North Carolina Governor Pat McCrory later awarded all three men North Carolina's highest honor by awarding them "THE ORDER OF THE LONG LEAF PINE." This award recognized the men for their courage and compassion under extraordinary circumstances, by saving the life of another person.

Again: LUCKY LUCKY!

"Watch 'Em Get Up" and a Remington .30-06 Rifle

About a year later, Game Warden Dave Dowdy was watching H L and Pee Wee fishing their pound nets in the mouth of Rocky Hock Creek.

There was a flock of about 200 Tundra Swans rafted up over by Cypress Point near Dr. Blakemore's mansion. H L had a .30 -'06 Remington semi-automatic rifle in the boat in case he got the chance to shoot a deer. Instead, he fired a shot in the direction of the placid Swans, "Watch 'em get up." That was all it took for Dowdy to spring into action. "Taking" Tundra Swan with a rifle, and without a Federal $20.00 Duck Stamp was not only a violation of North Carolina Migratory Waterfowl Regulations, it was a Federal Offense.

Having grown up on Currituck Sound, Dave Dowdy was an expert boatswain while operating his Wildlife Resources Commission issued 16-foot, tri-hull Glassmaster, seventy horsepower, outboard motorboat. The chase was on! As both boats planed out, they both were able to navigate the shallow waters of The Seine Ground along the shoreline of Rocky Hock Creek which made for a more direct path as an escape route for H L and Pee Wee to get "up the creek without a paddle."

There in front of Buck Bond's Marina on Rocky Hock Creek Road beside Meredith Lowe's (June 8, 1911 to October 22, 1999) Spanish Moss laden acreage, was a relatively low creosote crosstie bridge across Rocky Hock Creek. Are you beginning to get the picture? Sure enough, safe haven ahead for H L and Pee Wee. The motor and gunwales of H L's Privateer were low enough to the water at idle speed to allow passage of the vessel under the bridge. How about Dowdy's Glassmaster? Not so lucky! As Dowdy approached the bridge, he down shifted his throttle to allow the front of the boat to dip and clear the lowest horizontal support beam. That worked, but the tri-paneled windshield was not so lucky. Dowdy ducked down, sheared off his windshield on the bridge's trusses, and the full body of the boat made it through the passage.

Again, the chase was on. Northbound up by Dick Lowe's (August 28, 1938 to September 12, 2019) field and Boatyard Landing. Up through the Hairpin Cuts and the downed Red Maple Tree overhangs. H L ran his boat aground, and stepped out onto the bank. Dowdy was right on his case. As trained, Dowdy searched H L, and confiscated his sheath knife. H L was offended, "Dowdy, you know I ain't gonna cut you!"

Dowdy lived. Pee Wee lived. The Swans lived. And H L lived to fight another day. All in a day's work for both H L the waterman, and Dave Dowdy, The Game Warden. That story and many others live on, and will be retold and embellished for decades to come. There was no evil intent on anybody's part. It was just another day of, "Livin' the Life!" LUCKY, LUCKY!

Four Units of Blood and a Remington .30-06 Rifle

Occasionally, North Carolina State Troopers are tasked with relaying blood, body parts, personnel, and other emergency apparatus for medical transplants. When the aeronautical transfers are weatherbound, Troopers are not. EVER! During my time of sixteen years as a Highway Patrolman, maybe thirty times I "ran blood," relayed transplant patients for organ harvests, transported corneas for transplant, and relayed medical operating procedure apparatus (intubation apparatus, antivenin, prosthetics, and medical personnel).

Speed determinations were based upon the critical need of the immediate circumstance. Blood and platelets always necessitated the highest speed and time sensitive considerations.

Never would it be considered reasonable for a Trooper to be found N O T at breakneck speed when responsible for three units of Type B-Negative blood, when the patient was dying on the operating table RIGHT THEN for insufficient blood supply.

Trooper Ray Potts hit some debris in the roadway and wrecked right here in Edenton relaying blood for a teenaged girl, right then dying on the Emergency Room stretcher. She lived, thanks to Trooper Raymond M. Potts skillful delivery of critically needed blood from Tidewater Blood Bank in Virginia Beach, Virginia.

I once delivered an infant sized trachea windpipe intubation apparatus to an infant boy, then dying as a result of anaphylactic shock from a wasp sting. He lived to currently work with me as a Chowan County Magistrate. I bought Georgia Peaches from his son, Grant this morning up at Wilbur Ray's (September 17, 1934 to October 13, 2005) Produce Stand on Rocky Hock Road, just north from Dana Balance's Deli at the Crossroads, toward Terri Lynn's and W.E. Nixon's Welding and Hardware Store.

As I stated earlier, foul weather prevented aerial transport of supplies, personnel, equipment, and human tissue. But the North Carolina State Highway Patrol filled in where others fell short, ALWAYS. One night about 3:30am, I was sent to the Virginia State border to pick up four units of A-Positive blood. An SBI Agent had been shot in the back of his head in Greenville while sitting at his kitchen table reviewing evidence.

At the State Line on US-17 the Virginia State Trooper rolled up from Tidewater Blood Bank at the same time that I rolled up from Edenton. We hurriedly transferred the insulated cargo and belted it into my back seat. Southbound through Morgan's Corner. Blew through all those stoplights in Elizabeth City. Topped the Perquimans River Bridge at about 4:30am and headed toward Edenton.

I was driving my 1978 Plymouth Gran Fury, 440 magnum. I had taken it to a speed shop in Rocky Hock, North Carolina and had it "tuned up." Magnum carburetor jets replaced the standard issued jets, thereby increasing my top speed to about 152 mph, but decreasing my gas consumption mileage to about eight mpg. Felix Chambers was responsible for this prohibited SHP policy modification and did it "unbeknownst to me." He also installed a Plymouth racing steering wheel, chrome accessories, and halogen headlights. These headlights would prove invaluable during subsequent high-speed chases, manhunts, and just general highway patrolling procedures.

During this "blood run" from the state line to Greenville, I was prepared to meet the challenge. My gas tank was full. I was alone at the wheel. The night air was crisp. And the roads were open. I rounded "The Five-Mile-Y" at about 100mph, and hammered down toward Greenville. The Edenton US-17 Bypass was newly paved with a "tater grater" rock surface, and traction at almost any speed was guaranteed. I opened up that Plymouth, and the speedometer needle buried itself (past the 140mph marker) in the telemetric facade. My console mounted VASCAR (**V**isual **A**verage **S**peed **C**omputer **A**nd **R**ecorder) speed timing device indicated that I was traveling at 147 mph. As I approached the high-rise, railroad overpass bridge over the Chesapeake and Albemarle Railroad tracks, I released the pressure on my accelerator in preparation for the ever so slight "lift" from the crest. It is a good thing that I did!

As I topped the bridge, right there in my lane was a crusty old Ford Pickup Truck with a homemade dog box on its bed. It was 45 degree angled with its front two wheels dropped down onto the shoulder, and the rear end on <u>my pavement</u>. This positioning effectively shined the light from his high beams down onto a soybean field below. Whitetail Deer are abundant in that field, just off Paradise Road. A bib-overalled big overweight hunter was sprawled across the massive hood, with his butt in the air and his .30 – '06 rifle spitting fire out the muzzle. I recognized the truck, and the profile of the shooter. BUSTED!

I safely (luckily) maneuvered around him at about 140 mph. I didn't have time to stop and whip his butt, but I wanted to. Duty was calling. I went on toward The Chowan River Bridge at the Bertie County Line. 195-foot barges from the Alcoa Aluminum Plant in Winton commonly travel that river, and have been known to break loose from their moorings up the river in Winton, N.C. One of these 1400 ton, loaded barges could slice through a section of that old wooden bridge in the dark of night, and leave a gap too large to jump, even at 150 mph.

I went on through Windsor, and out onto "Williamston Field" which is what the locals call that stretch of elevated US-17 above the roadside swamps of Roquist Creek, Conine Creek, and the Roanoke River. I found myself having to place my right hand on my right knee to force my accelerator foot to remain "pedal to the metal." I slid into the lot, and met Trooper Reid Roberts by the gas pumps in Williamston at the Troop A Telecommunication Center on US-64. SHP Telecommunicator Chuck Rogerson spurred us on, and would later save my life in the midst of my ferocious, half-hour gun battle against two armed robbers from Plymouth, NC. Trooper Roberts took over the flight with that blood from Williamston to Pitt Memorial Hospital (now Vidant) in Greenville. As I stood in the cool, still night air, Chuck told me that I was averaging over 110 mph from the time he logged me in at the state line until I arrived at his Communication Center. Both my kneecaps were uncontrollably jumping up and down within their range of motion. I was physically and emotionally drained.

Do you remember the story about Bald Eagle and H L getting tangled up with a cow horn buck inside the front wheel-well of a Ford pickup truck? And the .30 – '06 rifle that was inside that truck? Well guess what!

That was the very same Bald Eagle, the very same .30 – '06 rifle, and the very same truck that was blocking my lane of travel with that blood at 140 mph on the railroad bridge earlier that night. About two weeks later, my wife Becky, daughter Jenny, son John, dog Molly, and I were at Grover Cale's Store in the Advance Community, buying a loaf of bread. Who walks in? Bald Eagle! I said, "David, was that you sprawled across the hood of that pickup truck on US-17 the other night?" He growled back, "Were you that crazy son-of-a-bitch that came by me?" Again. LUCKY, LUCKY.

AND THE BEAT GOES ON

Waterman H L Bond and Sharon and their children and their grandchildren live on, wrapped in their own exceptional, exciting, and blessed accoutrement. The world is a better place for this family. It has been an honor to know them and learn from them. Take time in your busy schedule to meet up with someone you might not know well! It might serve you well! They have certainly enriched my family.

Michael J. McArthur

Fishing and Funning the Old-Fashioned Way

The Early Years

During the early 1950s, Becky Beckler and Mike McArthur independently began their legacy of love in all ways imaginable within and through their families: Becky's in Raleigh and Wood, N. C., and Mike's in Wilson, N. C. While there was never much financial wealth or security, there was always deep, abiding love and respect which fostered unbridled wealth and security from our humble births. The intrinsic value of such warmth and affection provided a host of opportunities for development through internal strengths taught at the knees of our strong family matriarchs and patriarchs.

Becky's families were hard working farmers and coal miners. Mike's much smaller families were independent small business owners. This blend of self-made American backgrounds laid the solid foundations upon which we began our marriage, and built our family in Edenton, North Carolina along the banks of the Albemarle Sound, the Chowan River, and Rocky Hock Creek in the Advance/Macedonia Community.

Fortunately for Becky, Chowan High School needed a Secretary not long after I was assigned as a North Carolina State Highway Patrolman to Edenton, N. C. As a young couple, we rented an apartment on Broad Street and became witnesses to all that transpired on US-17, Edenton's main drag. During our first two Christmases, money was tight, and we went out into Carlton and Alice Perry's woods and cut down "Charlie Brown" pine trees. In fact, there was a Charlie Brown Christmas tree in our living room when we brought our first baby home from Albemarle Hospital in Elizabeth City, January 2, 1976. These were some very enlightening and extremely happy times as we began to learn to love our community, and our community began to learn to love us.

At Chowan High School, while working with Principal Gil Underwood, Becky developed many deep and long-lasting friendships. Mrs. Dorothy Cooke (September 2, 1930 to December 129, 2019) invited the young couple to visit and become members of Ballard's Bridge Baptist

Church (circa. 1781). This wonderful church family immediately took us under their wing, and made us feel like we belonged. They loved us. They taught us. They fed us. And fifty years later they still love us, and teach us, and feed us.

Becky had grown up with membership in Longview Baptist Church, just down Milburnie Road from her family's home in Raleigh. I was still a member of the 1st Presbyterian Church in Wilson. At Ballard's Bridge, Reverend George Cooke (April 26, 1926 to November 7, 1992) was like a father to both of us, but had a reservation: Mike had to give his heart to Jesus Christ and become baptized in the name of The Father before membership could be bestowed. After counseling and much consideration, the decision was made that come springtime, I would meet with other believers on the banks of the Chowan River, and be baptized by full immersion.

Down at the sandy landing of The Dallie White Road was a community of Ballard's Bridge Baptist Church members' homes. There was a sandy beach that gradually proceeded down into the Chowan River which was, at the time pocked with pound nets. These commercial marvels of science produced Blueback Herrings BY THE TON for harvest. Preacher Cooke, in his white robe was waiting. I waded into the water alongside eight others who were "candidates" for baptism.

Preacher Cooke, at his turn took me by my folded arms, and said, "In the name of The Father, The Son, and The Holy Ghost, I hereby baptize you my brother in Christ." At which time he laid me back into the water. I regained my upright position and, together we all walked back into the arms of our waiting families, fully united as members in Christ with our Ballard's Bridge Baptist Church family.

There were blessings aplenty in those early years in Chowan County. Lo and behold Becky gifted birth to our firstborn: a tiny blond-haired, green-eyed angel we named Jennifer Dianne McArthur. She was born on January first, 1976, the year our nation celebrated the bicentennial of its Independence.

And our Jenny became its charm.

While she had five years as an only child, she learned to play the piano, sing her heart out, keep us overjoyed, and make our lives more beautiful every day. She was everything that we had ever hoped for, and we cherished her every moment. School was her oyster. She never met a book she didn't like. Here in Edenton, while she is now a resident of Raleigh, we still have boxes and boxes of her books that she still cherishes.

There were days during her childhood that she donned camouflage clothing, and went duck hunting with her daddy. While paddling the boat, occasionally she hit the gunwales, but she apologized. When she accidentally dropped her paddle overboard, somehow she thought it was hilarious. That is our Jenny: fun loving and full of life. And inquisitive! She was a master of the swing set, and maintained the uncanny ability to fall off her bicycle at almost anytime, anywhere. Once she stepped over a smoldering fire, but just inside the ring of ashes which taught her a life lesson: fire burns!

Her tall slim self was "poetry in motion" while slalom waterskiing on Edenton Bay behind our blue and white, 1990 sixteen-foot Bayliner Bowrider. She and her brother John literally wore that boat out. Jenny was crossing in front of Dr. Blakemore's mansion when the boat hit an underwater stump and broke the stern and two of the seats out of it. We all limped to shore, got it fixed, and just a week later were back on the water.

As the John A. Holmes Senior Class Valedictorian, she was an acclaimed John Motley Morehead Scholar, and earned full scholarship with summer enrichment programs to The University of North Carolina at Chapel Hill. During her junior year she hydroplaned her red Chevrolet Lumina, catapulted over a four-foot bridge railing, and landed upside down in a foot of water beside Rocky Mount's, Stoney Creek Rescue Squad below. Somehow, we all lived through those years, and she now is a successful UNC-CH, School of Law practicing attorney.

Up there in Raleigh Jenny and my perfect grandson Jay and perfect granddaughter Leela are "living the life!" They run Ninja courses, build playhouses, raise dogs, house hamsters, and chase rabbits. Their neighborhood is their extreme bike course, and the neighbors have learned to "look out." Schooling is all-consuming, and there just doesn't seem to be enough hours in a day to accomplish all that needs doing! Together all of our mutual families plan adventures and retreats. Sometimes they work out, and sometimes they don't but Jenny is always right in the middle of whatever is on fire, and fanning the flame.

Our Cape Fear River Caper

When Jenny was a first-year law student at UNC-CH, she decided that she and her roommate would take a canoe trip down the mighty Cape Fear River. Sounded like a good idea with adequate opportunities for learning. Jenny is all about "learning!" Well, as the date approached, the roommate backed out. Undeterred, Jenny decided she would go-it alone. You know I could not let that happen. As an Enforcement Officer with The N. C. Wildlife Resources Commission back in the early '70s, I was too much aware of the inherent risks that dwell in the low country along river basins and watersheds. This little jaunt would involve twenty-six-miles, twelve hours of canoeing, with a thirty-two-foot drop in elevation.

Our mapped course would begin at US-1 near Buckhorn Dam and end at the US-401 / NC-210 high rise bridge over the Cape Fear River in Lillington, North Carolina at David Averette's Barbecue Restaurant. Jenny's Grandmother, Josephine Wood Harper and her husband L. J. Harper cinched our 16-foot Old Town, fiberglass Canadienne canoe into my 8-foot bed pickup truck, and off to Moncure we went. The banks of the river were as slick as eel fish. Jenny and the rest of us literally had to hold onto each other <u>and the canoe</u> as we loaded gear into it. We then slid it down to the rivershore, jumped in and off we went.

"Josephine shouted, as we paddled out of sight:

You forgot your ax. You'll need it tonight!"

There was no way, with the swift current from recent rains, that we could reverse course, and paddle back up-river to retrieve our ax. We pressed on. Buckhorn Dam was not raging at full capacity, but the water coming over was throwing an eerie mist. With Buckhorn Falls now behind us, Jenny figured that we had better get going if we were to make it to Raven Rock State Park, and our overnight campsite.

Michael J. McArthur

Jenny, Would You Please Sit Down!

A couple of hours into the adventure, we approached an obviously centuries old "boulder stacked" dam site. Having been rendered at some point, there were obvious "channels" that we could safely navigate, IF JENNY WOULD PLEASE, JUST SIT DOWN! Somehow, we made it through the rapids, and had smooth paddling and gliding for the next five miles of beautiful shorelines. Often, there would be a Volkswagen sized boulder within our path, and the water was coursing around each side. As I paddled to avoid colliding with it, Jenny would paddle toward it. Jenny was not afraid of it, and certainly didn't try to avoid whatever it brought.

Remember how I implied that Jenny has an inquiring mind? For reasons only known to her, she wanted to look closely at the powerful hydraulics that encircled those boulders. As she stood in the bow, leaning over the gunwale to get a good look, I asked her to, "Jenny, would you please sit down." Blasting right past her rock, she turned to me and said, "Daddy, I am not going to sit down, and don't ask me to again!" Did I say, "inquisitive AND independent?"

While she was imagining what was occurring right there at the rocks, I was imagining how I would try to recover our mountain of gear that was carefully stowed along the beam of our tandem canoe. Going overboard, it would certainly go floating down the river ahead of us more quickly than we could overtake it. All's well that ends well: we did not capsize, we learned some physics, and became more savvy in the ways of hydraulics (while wearing our PFDs -Personal Flotation Devices).

Occasionally we would run up on a band of partiers, floating along in tractor tire innertubes for relaxation and sunbathing. They usually were "mellow" for having gotten too deeply into their Mint Juleps and Falstaff-Lites. But they offered to share. Crusty old bearded fishermen in dilapidated old wooden skiffs were tied up to branches along the shore, or anchored in the middle of the forty- yard wide river. Using twenty-foot cane poles and crickets for bait, they seemed to be VERY content, but intensely interested on these two interlopers. As we inquired (Jenny, of course), they would hoist up their stringers of catfish, bream, bass, and other sunfish. They too, were "heavily hydrating" from Mason fruit jars, and spitting tobacco juice. There appeared to be no ice cubes in those jars.

They seemed a little stingy or uninterested in sharing their libations. The term "lookout" comes to mind!

Moonshiners and Trotliners

Just a short distance down the river an unmistakable aroma wafted across the approaching late afternoon cacophony. Again, having been a State Game Warden and assisted in the destruction of several clandestine bootleg liquor stills in Chatham County, I immediately recognized and could name the aroma as a yeast/sugar/mash laden concoction that could easily draw attention from The United States Bureau of Alcohol, Tobacco, Firearms, and Explosives. I was thankful to possess, tied to the canoe's yoke, a fifteen shot Remington, Nylon 66 semi-automatic .22 caliber rifle. You know, varmints come in all sizes and shapes. We paddled on! Albeit, a little more quickly.

Gliding along and idly chatting, Jenny "not to miss a thing," asked, "What is that rope across the river?" As we approached the "rope," it became obvious what it was. It was an illegally set trotline fishing apparatus. Appropriately, this contraption was "set" right in the jaws of a section of the river known as "The Fishtraps." Having used a trotline to fish in Contentnea Creek as a boy, I knew exactly what lay ahead. Jenny and I put on the brakes. A trotline is a heavy rope with twelve-inch "droplines" spaced three-feet apart, all the way across the river. Each dropline is terminated with a large Snelled number 4/0 baited hook with cut bait like pork rind or chicken gizzards. These hooked lines are weighted down with heavy homemade lead weights, or other scrap metal to keep the current from raising the baited hooks to the surface: keeping them down where the Bullhead and Flathead Catfish can find them.

I could see where the rope was tied to an overhanging Sycamore tree on the west bank. We paddled over to the knot, and under the rope. While there, we lifted about six hooks out of the water and could see the heads of two catfish that would have weighed probably eight pounds apiece, hooked and waiting for the return of the poachers. Again, we paddled on, quickly.

Another hour down the river we flushed a flock of seven Turkeys from their roost, high up in the Oaks along the shoreline. The huge birds would launch off their perches, and glide toward their destination, rounding the bend into the mouth of a slough. We had now circumnavigated numerous, old bridges, fjords, bridges, locks, and dams: none functional. To our right, on the starboard side of our canoe, the steep banks were now rising "clifflike." This was the outer perimeter of Raven Rock State Park. Of course, Jenny had done her research, and knew that about half a mile ahead, lay our State Park Campsite. This campsite is not accessible by vehicle, so you can imagine the amenities and facilities that were not available.

Jenny's brother, and Becky's and my son John had just turned 18 (1999), and boldly purchased his own neon red, Blackberry flip phone. We had borrowed it and brought it along in a Ziplock bag for emergencies. Neither Jenny nor I knew how to use it. Sure it rang. Could we answer it? Heck no. Could we call out for help if the need arose? Heck no! We might as well have left it with John. But just having it in our possession, made us feel a little less isolated. Sorta like a fire inside a 55-gallon barrel a hundred yards away: at least you could go over and warm yourself if you wanted to. As we off-loaded our gear, Jenny studied the phone to see what it would take to "call out." Probably without a signal, we could not "call out," had we wanted to.

Raven Rock State Park

Our campsite was a grassy plot in the midst of a rock formation. It accommodated our tent pegs, but barely. With our tent erected, and our gear stowed, we went exploring. We found the bat cave under the winding stairway to the top of the cliff. A summer thunderstorm rolled through, and we were able to wait it out in the cave under the outcrop. We climbed the thousand or more wooden and steel steps, and took in the breathtaking view "from the top." Then we had to go back down which was a little more challenging than going up. When we got back to our tent, we decided to unpack our food: steak and canned baked beans. Coca-Cola, a half-loaf of Sunbeam Bread, and Snickers Bars rounded out our meal.

We "set" our fire "lay" from a double handful of dried grass that I had stuffed into my cargo pants from inside the bat cave. Around the edges of the campsite we gathered "kindling." There was a lot of it lying around, but most of it was wet from the thunderstorm. We commenced to breaking off "squaw wood" from the Maples and Poplars. (Squaw wood consists of the bottom two or three dead branches, low down on the trunk of a tree. The subsequent bark has overgrown their base, and cut off nourishment, thereby starving it of sustenance: dry as a bone and brittle.)

There was a rhododendron thicket near the trailhead, and it had midsized branches that were dead. And then of course, there were the lower larger limbs that had died last year, and not been taken to burn by previous campers. Since we were without an ax, we had to break them over rocks to make them usable. We tufted up the grass with a hole in the middle. We "set the lay," gradually enlarging the stock. Jenny leaned over, with a piece of flint in her left hand and a small steel file in her right. She scraped the flint about three times before her spark ignited the "rat's nest" dried grass. With just a couple of puffs, voilà! We had a cook fire. We laid the opened can of beans up next to the flames. We had brought a steel grill upon which we placed the steaks. Campfire food always tastes great, and this was no exception. As the smokey aroma drifted across the campsite, we figured that the raccoons and Chipmunks would soon drop by.

All our gear had to be put inside the tent for protection, but we made sure to leave all food outside. We climbed into our tent, and crawled into our sleeping bags. It didn't take twenty minutes. Those raccoons were camper acclimated. And noisy. I got up and put all our trash inside a Food Lion plastic garbage bag, tied it to a rope, and slung it over a Live Oak limb over on the other side of the campsite. It worked, and we finally got some sleep.

We listened to Whip-Poor-Wills and Owls all night long. What a peaceful sound as we drifted off to sleep. Crows (or hopefully, Ravens) woke us up the next morning with their raucous calls. We poked our head out into the morning chill, and found that a heavy dew had soaked everything but our fire. We cooked and ate our eggs and sausage, ate our grape jellied bread, drank our Cokes, cleaned up our site, poured water on the dwindling fire, and packed our gear. We followed the signage, and hiked up to the Ranger Station. We picked up a couple of finger sized quartz rocks and saved them as mementos. As we were studying the topographical map of where we were, up walked Park Ranger Charlie

Green. He greeted us, and thanked us for checking in with him for statistical purposes. We thanked him for our overnight lodging, and hiked back to the campsite. We loaded the canoe, and shoved off toward Lillington, two hours away.

The following eight miles were relatively uneventful, except for the beautiful riverside homes built along the shorelines. At one point, Jenny and I had to crawl out of the canoe and "manhandle" it through narrow passageways which also produced forceful currents. After successfully getting the craft leveled off, and the scrambled gear re-arranged, as we prepared to re-mount, I placed my hand over my heart in thanks. Jenny immediately freaked out, thinking I was having a heart attack. Funny, but not funny.

Gradually we began to hear the distant drone of tractor trailer trucks out on US-401, running parallel and then crossing "our river." We navigated the narrow passageways through "the rock garden" that cluttered the shallows. We were thankful that the river had granted us safe passage, with relatively few "snares." All along the shoreline were teenagers with Zebco casting rods and reels. There was a Harnett County 4-H "fishing camp" being conducted that morning, and we pulled over under a Sycamore along the bank and watched the organized chaos. I am not sure whether they were fishing or playing, but they appeared to be having a good time. Jenny surmised that the fish were in no danger.

We could see barbecue smoke, and smell bacon cooking. Always a good thing. David Averette's Barbecue Restaurant was teeming with business as we pulled our canoe onto the grassy shore right beside his restaurant. Two "older" men came down and asked us, "Did y'all have any luck?" Jenny, never having met a stranger, launched into the retelling of our Cape Fear adventure. To me it had been enjoyable, but relatively mild. To Jenny, never having quite done anything like it, it had been "life changing." And YES, we had had some luck.

Chatty Kathy "Loose Lips Sink Ships

Since it was lunchtime, we went into the spacious restaurant, and sat at a table beside the window so that we could watch our canoe. The nicest waitress came over and asked us, "Is that y'all's canoe down thar?" When we affirmed that it was, Kathy asked, "Whur'd y'all put in at?" We told her Buckhorn Dam, and she launched into how much fun she had had on the river two weeks earlier, but that the water had been so deep and fast that she and her sister had capsized twice. She had lost her watch and both earrings, but her sister had broken a toe. We told her that we had not found any jewelry, or broken any bones. That our trip had included mid-river chats with several "erratic inconsistents," but that we had come away relatively unscathed. She pulled her chair closer, and whispered that her Uncle Frank and Granddaddy had a liquor still, and made "good Likker" up near "The Fishtraps." We told her that we had smelled it when we went by there, and she said, "Don't tell nobody."

We asked her about the forty-yard trotline, and she said that her OTHER uncle put that up, and that he made a ton of money selling those fish to local restaurants as "wild catfish." She told us "Don't tell nobody 'bout that, neither!"

After this refreshing visit, we told her that we had a slight dilemma, and needed her help. Of course she asked, "What'ch'all need, Honey?" We told her that we had borrowed a cell phone to take with us on our trip, but that we didn't know how to use it. Jenny took John's Blackberry phone out of her pocket and showed it to the waitress. Immediately, Kathy reached into her own pocket and pulled out a yellow Blackberry cell phone. We knew right away that we were in good hands.

Kathy took our order, and we ate some of the best chopped barbecue and fried shrimp known to exist. We managed to call Jenny's Grandmother and L.J. to come to David Averette's Restaurant in Lillington and pick us up for our return trip to Angier. All the way back to town, Jenny shared stories about our trip as we sat four abreast in a one bench seated Chevrolet Silverado, 1500. As the years have worn on, Jenny and I have shared many recollections and thought good thoughts about our adventure. I wish we could do it all over again.

Michael J. McArthur

Fishing Poles, Fishing Holes, Fishing Frenzy and "Jump over Grandmother"

On Wednesday, July 29th, 2020, a 98 DEGREE day, it was Grandmother, Becky's and my golden privilege to amuse and entertain our four grandchildren, ages 7, 8, 9, and ten. The children and I strung, hooked, and corked six American Native Bamboo, ten foot cane fishing poles (like Opie used on The Andy Griffith Show). Together we cut and crafted these unique, personalized fishing poles from standing green stock gathered at the A. J. Smith and Sons, Turkey Neck Farm on Paradise Road. The massive half acre of bamboo is growing so rapidly, and taking up valuable farmland, that the owner says, "Come get all you want." It ranges from one inch in diameter and fourteen feet tall, to a mighty two inches in diameter and thirty feet tall. Lots of possibilities!!!

The six of us, Becky – Mike – Nakayla – Jay – Leela – and Nolan, went down to Pembroke Creek which empties out into Edenton Bay beside the restored Roanoke River Lighthouse (1887 to 1941) on Edenton's waterfront park. The U. S. Fish and Wildlife Service has a <u>SHADED</u> scenic overlook platform (snake free) from which we fished. The Service calls this "their newly expanded fishing access at Edenton National Fish Hatchery (NC) (1898)." One of the Project Coordinators, Fisheries Specialist Sam Pollock assisted us in using their bountiful resources, and made our day truly amazing.

From Westover General Store, Doug Baird had sold me two "tin cans" of big, fat earthworms and off to the creek we went. With children's excitement building, I double-baited five of the six hooks, set the depth of the yellow cork at about 36", and dropped them five feet down into the tea-colored, slow-moving Pembroke Creek. Each of the four kids immediately caught their first of many, 1½ pound Channel catfish. All four fishermen had fish "on" at the same time, and were scared to death of the "frisky" flailing flopping fish frantically flying (tongue twister) haphazardly through the air, landing on each other, and flopping onto the deck, (Think about three nasty spikes per catfish). Jay was independently fishing in the more open part of the water, and the other three were fishing next to bushes growing out of the water's edge. Jay caught about five bream and yellowbellies, plus his share of catfish. I honestly could not keep the hooks baited because of so many fish coming over the rail.

Either the fish were too big, or the boys too impatient, or the poles too puny. Both boys somehow broke their fishing poles and Nolan and Jay resorted to "hand lining" the fish up over the rails. We cut off the broken sections, retied the "spider wire" braided line that Brent Layton had given us, to the broken pole, and they were back in business. In the meantime both Leela and Nakayla were catching bigger catfish. Nakayla caught one so big that it broke her hook (The big one that got away). Leela patiently waited for her hook to be re-baited, yelling "I caught another one!" within seconds. About that time, Becky's unmanned fishing pole #5, which had been propped up along the rail was yanked over the deck, and last seen bobbling along and being pulled southward toward the mouth of the creek. Gone!

During the hour-long fishing frenzy, we had caught at least thirty fish. We kept most of them in a bucket, except some of the smaller ones. Wouldn't you know it! Just as the first "tin can" of worms gave out, so did the kids. So we spiraled the lines around the poles, poked the barbs of the hooks into the corks, gathered our gear, and headed out to the next adventure.

We went up the hill to a mound of Texas Gulf Phosphate Mine ore: small shells, coral, rocks, and sharks' teeth. Each of the kids found sharks' teeth, but they were of little interest to Leela. She said, "I don't do sharks." The area was shaded, and the kids had a lot of fun digging and exploring. The U. S. Fish and Wildlife Service (1956) in Edenton, North Carolina provides a great service to our entire region of eastern North Carolina. They host fishing derbies with the Chowan Edenton Optimist Club (1980). The biologists give guided tours of their facility. "Look and learn" exhibits are present throughout their facility. And they host a Disabled Veterans fishing event for fifty or more wounded warriors. They have big aquariums full of live fish. And an alligator. The uniformed staff and all the workers are great folks with a real interest in promoting their conservation agenda while patiently teaching children the value of respect for the resources so abundant in our area of North Carolina.

Suddenly, all the children were hungry. Grandmother took them to get some lunch at Westover General Store, and Granddaddy went home to clean the fish. I cleaned (Cut my thumb on a gill plate) about ten of the biggest, and returned the rest to nature beside my house along Beaver Dam Creek. I am sure the raccoons, Opossums, and Coyotes enjoyed their free meal that night. Peanut oil from Hal Burns and Paul Britton at Jimbo's Jumbos got hot. I battered and fried those fish filets. I took them down to the banks of the Chowan River at the mouth of Rocky Hock Creek where the kids were swimming, and "Jumping over Grandmother," off the end of the pier. As I left the house, one of my "good buddy" courthouse "clients" pulled up and blocked me at the Chamber's Ferry intersection with Cowpen Neck Road. "My brother ain't treatin' me right. He's mean! What can you do about it?"

Fish and Chips

With still hot fish, fried golden brown, and a big yellow bag of Lay's Potato Chips, I arrived at the river and each grandchild came up and devoured some of their fish they had caught that morning. What a feast. The lessons that these children learned on this day will carry them throughout their lives: how to cut and string a fishing pole, how to bait a hook, how to manhandle their equipment to make it work, how to use caution around the water, how to watch for the fish to "bite," how to bring the fish ashore, how to remove the hook from the fish's mouth, how to release the smaller fish, how to conserve our natural resources, how to store the fish in the buckets, how to rebait and continue their fishing extravaganza. A large helping of successful socialization was also accomplished.

After their "fish and chips," they returned to the dock and continued "Jumping over Grandmother." Not yet having gotten either scratched, scraped, skint, snake bit, or worn out, they got busy running and jumping off the pier into and onto the scorching hot black rubber tractor tire innertube that I had gotten from our friend Charlie Creighton at Colony Tire. They took turns standing on that tube. They rolled onto and off that tube. They spun around on that tube. I remember as kids, my brother and sister and I had tons of fun on innertubes in the swimming pool with our Mother and Daddy on hot summer days at the Tobacco Trail Motel (1947 TO 1989).

Living Out Loud with Grace, Grit, and Gratitude

This was a Wednesday, and seven-year-old Nolan told Pastor Chris Gravning at Macedonia Baptist Church during Family Fun Night, "My arms are tired. I caught at least a million fish today."

There might not have been "at least a million fish" caught that day, but there were "at least a million" memories made.

Having shared this story with the entire U. S. Fish and Wildlife Service through their nationwide newsletter, many inquiries have been made as to, "How can I bring my grandchildren and 'go fishing' down there?" Also, Colony Tire Corporation, President Charlie Creighton shared with his thousands of employees their part in making this story interesting. Hal Burns and Paul Britton at Jimbo's Jumbos, Inc. shared their part of the story with their hundreds of employees, many of whom have fished the very waters mentioned. Anyone who is anybody who has ever visited Edenton, N. C. should have developed fond memories of the great big "adult sized" sandwiches offered for lunch at Westover General Store with Lina and Doug, and Dougie, and Kelsey Baird.

Again, this is just one small example of what a great community we have here in northeastern North Carolina, and the wonderful people who let us be a part of their lives.

Michael J. McArthur

An Elected Clerk of Superior Court in Chowan County, NC

As the elected (8 terms) Clerk of Superior Court for the County of Chowan, in northeastern North Carolina, I have had the good fortune to work with and help many people through some bright days and some dark days in their lives. I have had the honor of assisting my constituents through thick and thin, through good times and bad, and always trying to achieve my personal goals of enabling others to achieve success while making their lives more meaningful and less difficult.

Jury service, competency determinations, land divisions, adoption adjudications, civil arbitration, criminal and civil courtroom recording, cash receipting, estate probate, child support records, juvenile case management, foreclosures, domestic violence intervention, Magistrate selection and empowerment, technology and information dissemination, personnel administration, social media management, employee safety and courthouse security creativity, re-election political strategies, and many other aspects of my job necessitate that I surround myself with the most competent and congenial Assistant and Deputy Clerks of Superior Court that I can find. I am blessed to have such a team of professionals, that I need not worry or fret over the performance of their duties and my duties. They are the wind beneath my wings!

Highly acclaimed promotional speaker, "His Biz," Trey Baker, during his personality typing exercise (think Meyers – Briggs), once asked all of North Carolina's one-hundred elected Clerks of Superior Court for a characterization of "The Perfect Clerk." Through the elimination of character flaws (many of which I myself tend to exhibit – but not my teammates), this is the best that I could come up with:

"The Perfect Clerk"

Isn't it funny how one clerk is always 1 or 2 minutes late for work, one clerk starts getting ready to go home at 3:30, one clerk spends a questionable amount of time on personal phone calls, one clerk cooks smelly food in the microwave, one clerk visits throughout the building too much, one clerk is always just a little sick, one clerk has children and a husband/significant other who cannot change the television channel without checking with Mom, one clerk has too much education, one clerk has not enough education, one clerk uses poor grammar, one clerk talks over everybody's head, one clerk wears her dresses a little too short, one clerk wears too much perfume, one clerk walks too fast, one clerk doesn't walk fast enough, one clerk has "inconsistent" friends, one clerk has too many friends, one clerk has no friends, one clerk has too much time on her hands, one clerk can't find time, one clerk is too loud, one clerk cannot handle but three things at once, one clerk leads a mystery life after 5, one clerk leads a mystery life 8 to 5, one clerk wears too much expensive jewelry at the front counter, one clerk is a work in progress, one clerk is a wreck in progress, one clerk is too much of a cowgirl, one clerk just wears the hat, one clerk doesn't know where she's headed, one clerk doesn't know where her head is, one clerk likes men too much, one clerk likes women too much, one clerk can't read minds, one clerk apparently can't read at all, one clerk plays with fire, one clerk IS fire, one clerk wears a dark cloud over her head, one clerk IS a dark cloud, one clerk comes from the wrong side of the tracks, one clerk has the wrong side of the tracks come to her, one clerk drives a wreck, one clerk wrecks the drive, one clerk eats "healthy" ONLY, one clerk eats junk ONLY, one clerk can't tell time, one clerk-bless her heart-time tells on her, one clerk thinks she's entitled, one clerk knows she's entitled, one clerk is always out of the loop, one clerk doesn't understand the loop, one clerk can't hear, one clerk can't see, one clerk listens to too much Rush Limbaugh (January 12, 1951 to February 17, 2021), one clerk listens to too much Lynard Skynard, one clerk talks too much, one clerk is afraid of her own shadow, one clerk is too trusting, one clerk is not trustworthy, one clerk is too crude, one clerk is too goody-goody, one clerk is too goofy, one clerk is overly confident and projects it, one clerk has no confidence and projects it, one clerk has all the answers, one clerk doesn't know what the questions are, one clerk assumes too much, one clerk hasn't got a clue, one clerk helps too much, one clerk helps too little, one clerk needs help, one clerk drives too fast, one clerk gambles too much, one clerk tries too hard, one clerk doesn't try hard enough, one clerk operates too deeply "inside the box," one clerk doesn't know where she left the box, and believe it or not, one clerk is perfect – by my definition, NOT HERS - and which clerk that is, changes from day to day!

I am blessed to work with five perfect clerks; it just depends on which day you are asking!

I must soon replace one of them who is marrying a United States Navy S.E.A.L. and moving to Hawaii. Wish me luck!

Just What Does It Take To Be An Elected Clerk of the Superior Court?

There was once an occasion when everybody's best friend Joan G. Brannon (UNC-CH, School of Government 1971 to 2010) asked all 100 elected Clerks of Superior Court in The Great State of North Carolina:

"What does it take to be an elected Clerk of Superior Court?"

Professor Brannon served honorably as a revered and beloved Assistant Professor of Public Law and Government within the University of North Carolina at Chapel Hill, School of Government.

She, along with former Director of The Administrative Office of the Courts, James C. Drennan (Jim), served as the "go to" operatives for the entire State of North Carolina when it came to Constitutional law and responsibilities and procedures within the one-hundred offices of the elected Clerks.

Living Out Loud with Grace, Grit, and Gratitude

Let me begin my response by saying,

"I LOVE A CHALLENGE!"

In response to Professor Brannon's question, I began an in-depth, soul-searching quest to determine, just what it takes. I found that her question was posed, not so much as an assignment, but meant to stir the thought processes of those with whom she engaged.

Immediately I admonished her to, "Be careful what you ask for!"

Here I go!

These are but fifty of the millions of attributes that constitute a successful **North Carolina Clerk of Superior Court:**

Trust in God

Respect for humanity

Good luck from which to prosper

Bad luck from which to learn

Blind luck to ensure fairness and impartiality

Good sense to know when to duck

Patience of Job

Stamina of Atlas

Teamwork mindset

Exhaustive humility

Integrity above reproach

Kindness of acceptance

Compassion and empathy

Genuine sincerity

Empowering countenance

Michael J. McArthur

Inquiring mind

Suspicious nature

Broad vision

Focused vision

Reasonable tolerance

Eagerly generous

Courage to change things that must be changed

Serenity to accept what cannot be helped

Good sleep habits

Intense bravery

Intestinal fortitude

A keen sense of humor

A big heart

Thick skin

A long "fuse"

An optimistic attitude

Leadership willingness

Passionate enthusiasm

Analytical acumen

United front

Friends in high places

Friends in low places

Solid references

Questionable references

Solid family support

Good educational foundation

Good memory capabilities

Mathematical proficiency

Psychological understanding

Legible handwriting

De-escalation/defensive tactic skillset

Proficiency with weapons

A trustworthy vehicle

A driver so that you can work from your vehicle

More than twenty-four hours in a day

North Carolina Administrative Office of the Courts

Legal Quagmire!

Blessed be the "small counties,"

For they don't suffer much "stuff."

Blessed be the larger counties,

For they shall have to bluff!

Blessed be the senior Clerks,

For they have led the way.

Blessed be the newer Clerks,

For they must learn to play.

Blessed be the **Eastern** Clerks,

For they are out of the way.

Blessed be the rest of the Clerks,

Who seek the light of day.

Blessed be the **Piedmont** Clerks,

For they are "where it's at."

Blessed be the rest of the Clerks,

For they are yet to bat.

Blessed be the **Mountain** Clerks,

Well you already know why.

Blessed be the rest of the Clerks,

For they still seem to get by.

Blessed be our faithful staff,

Preening every feather.

Blessed be our Judicial team.

We're all working together.

Blessed be the job we do,

We know it is a calling.

Blessed be rewards we get,

And let us not forget!

Blessed be the Clerks' Conference,

> In all its radiant splendor.
>
> Blessed be our lovely staff,
>
> For all the help they render.

Blessed be the elected Clerk who works through his or her lunch so that staff members, during their regularly scheduled lunch hour can go to the grocery store, get their hair done, call their mother, check on their grandfather, take their child's coat to school, walk the dog, go pick up four prescriptions, pay the water bill, wash two loads of clothes, stoke the crockpot, and paint the bathroom ceiling. Oh, yeah, and grab an apple and a PBJ.

Honor and Cherish Them, For They are the Wings Beneath our Wings

Michael J. McArthur

The Raucous Caucus Pushes Its Luck

One of my up-state, high-brow buddies asked me about our friendly, Down East "games of chance." This is about as close as I could come!

You Ready?

On a rotational basis, about twenty of us play about thirty-five different "games of chance" from 7 p.m. until 10 p.m., once or twice a month.

We don't gamble. We don't play our cards. We don't even play "Lady Luck." <u>We play each other!</u>

Braggin' rights are highly coveted, often embellished, and always expected. The weight of our cash box fluctuates very little, and has very little significance. Sometimes, one or more of the braggards requests assistance from a 30" 2x4, to "prop up" his "coin-laden" side of the table. Next he asks one of us to summons a Brink's Armored Car service to swing by upon his departure. Before we deal the first hand, one or more of us serves dinner: filet mignon, lasagna, fried chicken, Low Country Boil, Fried Speckled Trout from Swan Quarter, half-pound cheeseburgers, or some other delectable dish, followed by Little Debbie Cakes or Brownies. Seems like it always costs each of us $7.00, or if somebody is trying to make amends for some errant misdeed, he might feed the crowd for free! Once I overcharged the guys by $2.00 apiece ($9 instead of $7) for their pregame Low Country Boil. They didn't care, but I did. The next day, I went across the street to Southern Bank, and Bank President Charles Britton found me six, two-dollar bills. I took them home, shot a gaping, .44 magnum hole through one end of each bill, and mailed each player his "overcharge." I will probably hear about that at my retirement dinner, if and when I ever retire, two weeks after I die!

We play a smorgasbord of games: Black Jack (21), Texas Hold-'em, Acey-Deucy (in-between), Four Quarters, Three Card Molly, High-Guts (69 wins all with the pregnant lady), Low-Guts, 3-5-7, Low Pair Wild-High-Low, Up and Down the River, Waldo Wins, High Chicago, Low Chicago, Chicago Royale, 2-22, 7-27, Bertie, Criss-Cross, Straight Five Card Stud, Seven Card Stud – one-eyed Jacks and Deuces wild, Typewriter, Buy Two – Fifty and a Dollar, Anaconda, Mexican Sweat (no-peak), Mount Addie,

Five Piles of BS, Jacks or Better-Trips to Win - Progressive, Follow the Queen (with and without the wrinkle), 23 Skidoo, Baseball, Midnight Baseball, Fleets, Dr. Pepper, Woolworths, Walmart, Spit, Showdown, and several more that I cannot think of right now. We rotate the deal clockwise to the left, so that everybody gets to play his favorite game. Oddly, it seems that the dealer more often than not, wins his own dealt game (If you won't deal yourself a winner, who will? Right?). If by chance, you misdeal, drop the deck, or commit some other egregious error, you are profoundly admonished to, "Get control, McArthur!" Some dealers have a proclivity to "flash" the dealt cards of their opponents. Of course, when that happens, none of us "look", and we immediately relegate ourselves into forgetting that Deems Cole just got that fifth spade that he needed for his King high flush.

There is a really fun game called, "Four Quarters." If you are one of the six sore losers, it costs you four quarters, but, if you are shrewd, and/or lucky, you might win the other <u>six guys'</u> four quarters, and it takes about twenty minutes to play it. Some of the "purists" do not like it (hate it), but we who shoot from the hip, love it! How can it be, that the same good people get so many sorry cards, and then innocently, and without so much as a smirk, slide them along to their good next-door buddies? Great fun!

One unique characteristic of one group of seven card players, is that each participant places one green dollar bill upon the pool table that sits directly behind the card table. Usually that cache of $7.00 quietly sits there the entire evening. However, should some lucky card player get dealt a "natural" (with no wild cards) Straight Flush or a "natural" Four of a kind, he reaps the benefit of the $7.00. If no one gets lucky that night, then the $7.00 gets dumped into "the last hand" for the evening.

The last hand for the evening is a variation of Mexican Sweat. The pot consists of a collection of a little over two dollars from each of the seven players, plus the pool table $7.00. The total number of dollars is divided into two sizable stacks, with "the best hand" winning half the pot, and "the worst hand" winning half the pot. Each of the seven participants is dealt seven cards, face down, and they cannot be looked at. Even when we absent-mindedly pick them up and look at them, we ultimately cannot remember what we saw anyway! One of the three remaining "deck" cards is rolled over to expose say, the seven of diamonds. The player to the left of the dealer must, one by one, roll his first, second, and third cards in front of him, until his hand beats that neighboring hand that bested the seven of diamonds. There is no betting. Next, the player seated two positions to the left of the dealer begins to roll his cards until his hand beats his neighbor's hand to his right. And the procedure goes around the table until all seven players have rolled all seven of their cards. That is when the "team poker" begins. The cards "speak for themselves." It has been known to happen, that when a particularly good hand appears early in the ritual, that the holder will sell his "likely winner" hand to the highest bidder, who is perhaps "down on his luck, and having a bad night." That is called "gambling." I have only done that once to my extreme dismay at the conclusion of the game.

We have two guys who can "count cards" with the best of 'em. The rest of us do all we can to defeat their self-proclaimed, uncanny abilities, and get great pleasure while doing so. Some enthusiasts require help and advice, whether they want it or not! Phone calls during the game are highly disruptive, and generally discouraged! Believe it or not, on any given night, as thick as some folks' skin might appear from the outside, there is always a "chink in their armor," and they take some level of offense to good-natured ribbing! Those who concentrate too hard, or take too long to make their move, or fall asleep, get penalized for delay of game. We chide them with, "Think long, think wrong." Cheating is frowned upon, unless it becomes necessary. Team poker is allowable, to a point! We are all CCH (Concealed Carry Handgun) certified, and ours is an extremely polite card game!!

"THE POT'S LIGHT!" is a favorite exclamation, and the offender is always severely chastised! "Light" means that he has not placed his obligatory "ante" of one singular dollar onto the middle of the table to "build the pot." We find ourselves in total agreement, or in total disagreement on any number of topics during the course of the evening, and we occasionally impart bits of wisdom, some fact – some fiction. When dividing "the pot," occasionally there develops a bit of confusion – over a stupid nickel! There is generally a piece or two of US Coin and greenback Currency with a hole (or six) in it. Some appears to have had a bullet hole shot through it. Some appears to have had holes drilled through it (Swiss coins). Some appears to have been run over by a Mack Truck. Some appears to have come from the bottom of a wishing well. Some appears to have been gnawed on. Some appears to have been used by a tractor machinist / mechanic and placed in the jaws of a 5/8ths open end wrench to reduce it to a 9/16ths wrench opening. Some appears to be "swinged" or scorched. Some appears to be counterfeit. Some is counterfeit. Some appears to be bedraggled (as on a sander or an anvil). One of the guys claims that <u>all of his money</u> has been "marked" so that he knows with whom it has absconded, and in whose possession it currently stands. The originator no longer owns it, but can readily spot who does!

Betting is more of a skill than first meets the eye. It is extremely difficult to bluff somebody out of the game when the bet is only a dime, but it happens. Occasionally, someone will hastily bet out of turn, and the rest of us automatically assume that he is so proud of his hand, that he jumped out of line. Bluffing is not only expected, it is a strategically sound tactic, and takes on many forms. Sandbagging is another stratagem that is somewhat aggravating, but usually highly effective. After all, why not let somebody else "bet your hand," and build the pot (that you end up winning)?

One night during a rollicking game of Mexican Sweat (No Peak), when the bet was a quarter, one of our miscreants launched into the pot, a silver colored New Orleans Mardi Gras "trade" coin about the size of a Morgan Silver Dollar, and had the nerve to draw back three quarters. Not, NO, but H NO! A little while later when Goofy went into the kitchen, I took his coin outside, placed it on the ground, shot a hole right through the center of it, and placed it back into my dwindling "stash" in my coin tray. A few minutes later, during a heated exchange of raises and double raises, when the bet was again a quarter, I "called" his bet with that "holey" bogey. The original owner snapped it up, examined it, and whined, "That coin belonged to my daughter, Anna. What happened to it?" When told what, Goofy asked how! I told him that while he was zoned out, I had taken it outside, thrown it up into the pitch black darkness, shot a hole through it with my .22 Magnum pocket rocket, and then had a heckuva time finding it in the knee high grass over in his neighbor's yard. His response was, "You mean you have a gun?" My response was, "You mean you don't?"

As a young man, Goofy had been to Las Vegas, Reno, and Atlantic City, New Jersey, and played for big money. Back home here, up in Jerry's "man-cave," when he tried to deal his souped-up version of Blackjack, he always had to find his blue Crowne Royal bag, break out his stash of still rolled quarters to pay out his excessive losses. He could never figure out why, but the rest of were elated.

Occasionally during the evening, four or five cards get "misplaced." Imagine that! Invariably, purely by accident, lo and behold, some aficionado has dropped two Aces into his clearly visible money tray (or into his bill stuffed shirt pocket in plain sight)!!! These atrocities are just part of the organized chaos. Newcomers or "substitute" players are completely dumbfounded by this chicanery. Occasionally when seven of us are vigorously playing Seven Card Stud, after the last round of seven cards are dealt, rightfully there should be three cards (52 minus 49) left "in the deck," on the table. This night, there were only two. Wouldn't you know it: we found the "one-eyed jack of hearts", still in the red bicycle, tax stamped, cardboard, cellophane wrapped box. Now you tell me: just how much did that affect our chances of winning (or losing)?

We might (we do) gossip just a little. We might (we do) tell a few "small white" or "big fat" lies. We might (we do) disagree on sports outcomes. We might (we do) share good (and bad) jokes (repeats are allowed up to four times). We might (we always) talk about women. We might (we do) talk about cars and trucks. We might (we do) talk about hunting and fishing. We always talk about guns and game wardens. And lately we have even allowed partisan politics to creep into the mix, but only briefly. Most of us have become disgusted with, and no longer watch "the news." There is never a shortage of good humor! Hypocrisy is always "front and center." Clearly, shame and couth have not seats at our table. And, "The beat goes on!"

Liar's Poker

One of the characteristically routine games of chance that Highway Patrolmen and Game Wardens used to play was called, Liar's Poker. During mid-week pit-cooked barbecue dinners at Donnie Murray's Barbecue Lodge (1979 to 2017) up on Capital Boulevard in Raleigh, each of us (usually 4 or 5, but sometimes 12 to 20) would each pull out a one-dollar bill and hand it to the sergeant-at-arms. He would randomly distribute them, and we would then examine the eight-digit serial number we now held on the face of our assigned bill. We would then, on a clockwise rotational basis, try to guess how many aggregate 3s or 7s or 8s were incorporated into ALL THE DOLLAR BILLS in the hands of all the fellow officers. The guessing game would rotate clockwise throughout the circle. "I've got six 3s. I've got six 7s. I've got seven 3s. I've got seven 9s. I've got eight nines. I've got nine sevens (after all, he had four on his own dollar bill). I've got nine aces (1s). I call you. I call you. I call you. I call you." Now, four of us had just "called" the optimist who had jumped out front with "nine aces." In the likelihood that he did not, among all five serial numbers, have a total of nine aces, well the "liar" had to pay each one of us a dollar apiece. If, in fact he DID have as many as nine aces, then he collected a dollar from each of us. Just a little twisted, but still, great fun.

Slap the Table

Another fairly common challenge at the Knightdale Barbecue Lodge, was to determine who would be responsible for leaving the 15% gratuity (tip) for the entire meal expense. A bunch of Game Wardens or Highway Patrolmen would be seated around the dinner table back in the private dining room, waiting for our meal.

Before dinner, Lt. R. I. Weathersbee told us one night out there, that he owned nine Boa Constrictors, two Anacondas, and a Brazilian Salmon Pink Bird-Eating Tarantula, and that he kept them all in his house. He went on to say that he had to be careful with whom he shared that diabolical information because, "People will steal your snakes."

Willis Peachey slumped over "dozing," came to, jumped up, and blurted out, "That is where I draw the G D line. I WILL NOT steal another man's snakes."

Moving on, Lt. Weathersbee said, "All right, now we are gonna determine who will leave the tip for the waitresses tonight. We are gonna scientifically make this determination by seeing who is fast and who is slow. Everybody, right now place your left fist upon the white papered tabletop. Now place the open palm of your right hand upon the top of this fist, like this. Now remove your fist, leaving your hand suspended about four inches above the tabletop. On my count of "three," you slap the table!" He would then count, "One, two, three!" and everyone would slap the table.

As you can imagine, it was next to impossible to honestly determine who was the last one to slap the table. So, nothing else would do, but that we had to do it all over again. All of we senior officers knew the deal: this time, on the count of three, none of us would slap the table at all, and leave the poor ol' rookie, "high and dry." He was not only the LAST person to slap the table, he was the ONLY one to slap the table. After the gnashing of teeth, the verbal clashes, and the raucous laughter subsided, we would kindly let him off the hook.

"Odd Man Out"

Do you know how to play, "Odd Man Out?" Well, just let me tell you! A bunch of idle law enforcement officers with spare time on their hands, can come up with all sorts of deviant variations of almost any endeavor, whether or not the need arises.

Down in Lumberton, North Carolina at the Holiday Inn just off I-95, we were sitting around in #201, playing cards, watching substandard, grainy "training films," and waiting for the Domino's "Meat Lovers" pizza to arrive. We heard slidin' tires, bustin' glass, lots of yelling, and a loud crash. A drunk driver wielding a blue Cadillac had careened off the highway, jumped the bushes, sideswiped the neon signpost, nosedived into our parking lot, and collided with two, T W O marked, black and silver North Carolina State Highway Patrol, high-speed pursuit, training cars, parked under our second floor balcony.

Of course, we all bounded out onto the balcony where we watched the commotion of sordid events unfold. Sgt. John Taylor (died October 18, 2011) was our supervisor, and he handled the disaster with pizzazz. The Lumberton Police came over, measured the skid marks, took pictures, and handcuffed the New Jersey driver. As they led him away, Willis Peachey yelled out to the drunk, "Hey, fella! When you bond out, come on back over here and play poker with us. With your luck, we'll be glad to "spot" you."

Back to the "Odd Man Out," scenario. After the drunk hit our cars, and before the pizza arrived, Charlie Greene (November 20, 1952 to March 15, 2020) got us goin'. "Men!" he said. "Who knows how <u>WE PLAY</u> "Odd Man Out?" Everyone mumbled, "Oh no. Here we go." It seems that in order to play Charlie's version, we all (6 or 8 of us) stood around John Atwater's queen-sized bed, and we would each throw a crisp (hard to come by) hundred-dollar bill onto the middle of the bedspread. If the rookie didn't have a hundred-dollar bill, well he would just "sit out" this theatrical production and watch in awe.

Next came the coin-toss. Each of us flipped a Morgan or a Liberty silver dollar onto the bedspread in front of us. The "odd man" was "OUT." We did this until only two brave souls remained. At that point, one or the other would call, "Just like you," which meant "even." If the two Morgans, BOTH landed heads "up," or tails "up," whoever had called "Just like you," won ALL the hundred-dollar bills. Normally, we conducted this ghastly phenomenon about three or four times before somebody would finally say, "Man, I can't stand any more of this fun."

The pizza came, and all bets were off! Time to eat. Later that night, we returned all "marked" hundreds to their rightful owner, and the charade lived on!

"Is It Ten O'clock Yet?"

One of our former "card sharks," for unknown reasons, just couldn't manage to get to the game on time. He never had any change, just twenty-dollar bills. He told long-winded, boring stories, numerous times, in an effort to curtail his losses. He attempted to "deal" games which he neither understood the rules, nor the card count. He constantly forgot to throw in his ante. He never trusted his half of "the high/low split." He parked his car where it blocked others from leaving, and was always the last one to come outside to leave. He didn't like and wouldn't play certain "stupid games." If it became his rotation to deal, he would always switch the Blue Bicycles for the Red Bicycles in a misguided attempt to change his luck. He would shuffle, and shuffle, and shuffle to burn time while he exclaimed, "Is it Ten O'clock yet? That clock must be broken." And he always eagerly encouraged "the opossum to walk," supposedly changing his luck. Occasionally, he would stand up and twice walk around his chair as a last-ditch effort to adversely affect our luck and improve his own luck. He would sally out the following banter: "Winners deal cards slowly. Losers yell, 'For God's sake, hurry up and deal the cards'." He just didn't appreciate "the journey." His main objective was to "win our money." And it became an integral part of our evenings for the rest of us to good-naturedly "push/punch all his buttons." He finally aged out.

For some reason, in all our infinite wisdom, we have not yet found a way to develop a simple strategy to incorporate into our evenings, "Rock, Paper, Scissors," or coin tossing to the line. One night we did, however, throw axes at thirty-five-inch, bull's eye targets. I am convinced that at some point, some resourceful, enterprising newcomer will knock us out of our comfort zone, and get us up to speed. None of us are smart enough to understand "dice." Most of us don't even understand or play "The North Carolina Education Lottery!" Who knows! If it happens, we will find something to blame, like the COVID-19 pandemic, or just like everybody else, blame former Republican President Donald Trump.

One of the good things about our group is that we are diversified in many ways, on many things, and pretty much inconsistent throughout! This week one or more of us might be devout N C State fans or UNC-Carolina fans or Duke fans or Wake Forest fans or ECU fans. Next week, ain't nuthin' none of 'em's got worth five cents. We have just about all gotten to the point that there is relatively little or no drinkin' during the card games on account of because we have to keep what little wits we've got left, as sharp as possible. Dalton's fervent hope is that when, not if, when we all end up in the same nursing home, that we probably won't even know it!

One thing that we are pretty consistent on is whether Ford Motor Company or General Motors truck manufacturers turn out the better product. One of our Chevy guys told his Ford buddy, while riding across the 3.5 mile Albemarle Sound Bridge in a veritable monsoon, a. don't let me get killed in a Ford, and b. since I am sitting right behind you, you're the one who's gonna get killed first. The Ford guys cite the NASCAR victories, "number one bestselling pickup truck in America" ads, and the fact that the presidential limousine, "THE BEAST" is a Ford product.

Another fairly consistent deplorable/debatable insight is the socio-economic condition of "our world." "It's going to Hell in a handbasket," is the fairly common, long-faced lament. "I dread it for our grandchildren." And also, "THEY" (the wretcheds, the deplorables, and the worthless) are not <u>taking</u> it from those of us who work for a living, "We are <u>handing</u> it to them, hand over fist." Uh, oh! I've gone to meddlin'.

We all have friends in low places, but all of us also have friends in high places, from Rocky Hock, NC to Washington, DC. How else would you think that,... well, I will stop right there!!!!!

It just might be that we could be classified as rednecks, but we have all been called, and guilty of much worse. Some of us are better at being a redneck than others, so we try to bring those with upbringings down to our level!

Wish us luck!

Michael J. McArthur

Dove Hunt Opening Day 2020, and other Trivia

September of 2020 began as one of the hottest Septembers on record with the National Oceanic and Atmospheric Administration's National Weather Service.

Not only was it hot all day and all night, but it was humid and muggy, all day and all night. Approaching Autumn, the days were becoming shorter, which meant that, in order to do much hunting, scouting, blind building, etc., you had to get up early in the morning, or stay out later in the evening.

This was the prime time for mosquitoes and snakes, mind you. Not the normal mosquitoes but the little, tiny ones that you could not feel before the bite, and the big ones that effectively bit you upon landing.

Sweaty and using a trimmer or swinging a machete is not a good time to swat mosquitoes or dodge yellow flies which were on the wane.

Apparently ground bees, yellow jackets, machetes, and weed eaters are not compatible. Have you ever been enshrouded by yellow jackets or ground bees?

My friend Rudolph Walston says that not only do the insects sting, but they bite at the same time. Having been afforded the wrath of the ill-natured critters on more than one occasion, I can assure you that I never watched and waited to see if they were biting or stinging: I ran.

Once at Bennett's Millpond, where in 2001, my son John McArthur, Jimmy Stallings, and I built our famous **four-man upstairs and six-man downstairs**, 30-foot tall Castle Tower Duck Blind in the top of a centuries old Bald Cypress tree, I had the extreme misfortune of crossing paths with yellow jackets. The path to our "solid as a rock" boat dock/pier had become overgrown with webs from Yellow Garden Spiders commonly called writing spiders, catbriers, Sweetgum trees, poison ivy, wild grape vines, and Cypress "knees." Unfortunately, in early Fall when their food supply begins drying up, yellow jackets become "ill-tempered," and more aggressive. Wouldn't you? I had waited until the hot sun had ebbed below the western tree line, and cranked up that Echo, straight shaft Weed Eater that Don Bass at Dixie Outdoor Equipment had sold me with his guarantee: "This thing will cut down anything." Deceptively, "anything" did not include clouds of yellow jackets. As I finished mowing the three-foot-tall outer perimeter of the undergrowth, I reached the point that the previously hidden Cypress knees were impeding the effectiveness of the "Black Diamond" weed-eater cord. Time to swing the machete. Cypress knees protruding from the peat earth are extremely porous and soft, making them easy work to cut off at ground level. "Easy," until the bees enter the equation.

I guess I disturbed the giant colony of yellow jackets, just under the leading edge of the sloping dock entrance. I remember watching swarms of honeybees get after Yogi Bear and Boo-Boo when they pilfered kettles full of golden honey from Yosemite's beehives and "pic-a-nic" baskets from unsuspecting campers. Yep! That is what these yellow jackets looked like, but the swarm wasn't looking for Yogi. Or Boo-Boo. They were looking for me, and at me. The bolo style machete was good for cutting underbrush, but not much good at swatting yellow jackets. Somehow, I made it to the truck without getting stung. All my lucky stars must have been aligned perfectly is the only excuse I can offer up for not having gotten "eaten up."

Let's talk about **opening day of the 2020 Mourning Dove – White Winged Dove season**: Saturday, September 5, 2020. Like I said: "It was hot." Supposedly (and it did), a weather cold front was approaching from the west. That proved to launch two things: cooler temperatures, and an occasional "fresh breeze" (19-24mph) which stirred mini dust-devils and set the doves to caterwauling. We arrived at Pungo Farms on Railroad Bed Road at about 5:20am and got in line to pay our $60.00 ($30 X 2) to Tim Powell, the hunt organizer. He remembered us from the previous ten years' opening day hunts, and directed us to this year's "honey hole." The 200-acre field where we usually hunted in years past was a soybean field this year. His recommendation was to go past the grain combine, past the tree lined canal, and turn left at the "Y."

We thanked Tim, and drove into the pitch black with what looked like a lighted mini-city on the far horizon. All those early arrival trucks had congregated at what looked like miles away through the dust filled ground-fog. In fact, it was miles away, almost two miles. Upon arrival at the burned-over cornfield, a hunter from Kill Devil Hills told us that some hunters had gone "this away," but that most hunters had gone "that away." You really would have had to been there to try to interpret that "Banker's" brogue through the darkness and a camouflage mask (COVID-19, remember?)

John and I looked across the still pitch-black expanse with "first light" breaking over the horizon. Barely could we make out a hedgerow (soybean field) that we drove along down into the darkness. We and our five-truck caravan drove about ¾ of a mile down the edge of the field, pulled over into the weeds, and stepped out into the fresh, cool night air. We had a total of twelve hunters with us, and we spread out along the edge of the field, squatting on our camouflage five-gallon buckets in the weeds. This is the same pattern that I have followed on about six opening days with my friends gathering for the first day of dove season. My Highway Patrol mentor Tommy Jeffries and our "can do anything" friend, Jeff Mullen have watched sunrises and killed our limits of doves at this very location on many occasions.

Sunrise this morning was at 6:42 am, with shooting hours thirty minutes prior to: 6:12am. John, Jay, and Nolan were overheard counting down the last twenty seconds on John's Apple Watch. 6:12 came and went with "nary a shot." We looked out into the middle of "our field," and there were three camouflaged hunters, previously unseen, too close for comfort. We and our fellow hunters moved down a little farther, not knowing that it would prove to be good fortune for us.

All of a sudden, at about 6:22am, from behind us to the East, barely above the soybeans, came a crashing cadre of doves: little ones and big ones, all "arcing" at Mach II with afterburners on overdrive. Even I could hear them. They swarmed over us, all 150 of us surrounding the thousand-acre BURNED CORN field. IMMEDIATELY, there was difficulty evident in our hunters' responses: How do you pick/shoot one of twenty-five birds, rocking-rolling, zigging-zagging, rising-falling, darting-dropping, zipping and zooming? Simple answer: You couldn't! I had dropped to one knee, and somehow as I twisted in the direction of the flight pattern, I rolled flat onto my back, not having fired a shot. Now THAT was "a first!" Call it "buck fever!" Call it "Awe struck." Call it "Unbelievable!" Call it whatever you will, here I lay flat on my back, hundreds of doves darting everywhere, J.C. Higgins, Ted Williams pump-shotgun pointed straight up in the air, and still unable to make heads or tails of how to do whatever lay ahead.

Gunfire was exploding in every direction. Every imaginable level of firepower: a red headed "Banker" from Kitty Hawk with a double-barreled Stevens 12-gauge, an older man with what appeared to be a model 19 Smith & Wesson .357 Magnum revolver loaded with "snake shot," a young girl with a superposed twenty gauge, and two little twin boys with Winchester single shot .410s (now that was scary). The war was waging. Fast and furious from "First Blood." Extreme care was taken NOT to get too close to anyone you didn't know (think boys with .410s). It quickly became our responsibility to assist our fellow hunters "mark" and retrieve downed doves, "as you would have them do unto you." Retrieving the downed doves of others took on new meaning when those young boys were close by. Any dove that "took a dirt nap" was a result of their, "I got him." They were much quicker afoot than we "more seasoned" hunters. John and I each lost at least three stolen birds to their bag-limits. Our opinion was, "Good for them. Maybe they were right!"

Doves were not the only thing that got shot that morning. My Magistrate/hunting buddy, Greg Dail watched himself get shot by a fellow "hunter" who didn't observe good firearm safety and hunting skills. Granted, the doves were flying fast and extremely LOW. This was unusual based upon my 58 years of hunting experience. By "LOW," I mean three feet off the burned stalks. By the time a hunter spotted the bird, drew-down on him, lead him, and pulled the trigger, the bird had traveled a good forty yards: right about the effective kill range of a "high brass" Super-X Mark V, number 9 shotshell in a 12-gauge, modified choke, 3" chambered shotgun. Greg got hit solid on his arm, thankfully without penetration. I can almost guarantee you that there was not a hunter afield who was not peppered with "rained down" shotgun pellets. I was rained on at least fifteen times, and learned to move to another spot when the "rain" became too intense.

When I was a Wildlife Enforcement Officer "Game Warden" with the North Carolina Wildlife Resources Commission, Enforcement Division, it was a common occurrence for our hunters to "inadvertently" and/or "mistakenly" rain shot down upon us. Ours was a tough lot: approaching "sportsmen," all of whom had a weapon or weapons. Hunters had long guns and usually pistols, and always knives. Fishermen usually had pistols "for snakes," and knives. Boaters usually had pistols and always had knives. These men and women were usually on the backside of deep woods, on the other side of the ridge, up the hidden hollow, or way, way up the creek. Few of them wanted to be "bothered." The dark of night always threw an additional element of risk into the equation. On two occasions while "checking" deer hunters in their stands, I observed the high-powered rifled hunters "scope" Sergeant Cuckleberry Jones across the cut-over.

The Wary Woodcock and the Sly Sleuth

The most complimentary "complaint" ever lodged against me was by an N. C. State University Professor of Forestry, made to his neighbor, the Chief of the Enforcement Division, C. J. Overton at the Ivory Tower in Raleigh. I had tracked the professor while he and his 14-year-old son and Boykin Spaniel were Woodcock hunting in the Haw River basin near Lystra Chapel Church, deep in the "bottom" with Tulip Poplars, White Oaks, and Red Maples.

Little did my N. C. Wildlife or my State Highway Patrol entrance screeners, applicant processors, training officers, or supervisors know it, but I am "red-green" color blind. With all the hindrances therewith associated, there are several advantages. I could spot "Real-Tree" camouflage patterns from a great distance. It just didn't "blend in" as the wearer hoped. The lawfully worn "hunter orange" did blend in, particularly in the early fall before the leaves began to turn from green (orange to me) to scarlet (?) to brown. Our Wildlife game biologists were right: game animals are color blind, too.

This professor and his son were methodically coursing a path from East to West, into the Autumn sun. I was able to see them from above, circle ahead of them, and was waiting as they emerged from the woods into a Duke Power Company, heavy electric transmission line, bush hogged right of way.

I can still see the startled smile on dad's face when I asked from the shadows, "Son, have y'all had any luck?"

Now, you know? A well-educated college professor and son, wearing Filson hunting vests over Mackinaw flannel shirts, LaCrosse Boots, and carrying .28 gauge Browning over and unders, and having a $5000 Boykin Spaniel "heeled" at their side, these guys are SURE to have their lawfully required hunting licenses.

Yep! They did.

Both had Lifetime Sportsmen licenses. That night they telephoned Chief Overton that their sport required a lot of scouting and a lot of stealth in deep woods, far from "the beaten path." Never had they been "checked," nor expected to be "checked" by a "Game Warden." They were impressed at having been outwitted and snagged by a ROOKIE Game Warden at that!

Poachers and Bootleggers

Back in those days, few sportsmen afield respected the resource, the law, or the officer. Respect for all three has come a long way since 1971 when I was trying to apprehend year-round turkey poacher Hubert Davis near the forty-foot-wide Devil's Tramping Grounds beside Harper's Crossroads in southwest Chatham County, NC. Hubert hated game wardens. Hubert hated revenuers (for the obvious reason). Hubert hated Highway Patrolmen who hated him. Hubert hated "hippies" and college kids who trespassed on his property in Bynum, NC alongside the Haw River. Hubert hated tax collectors from which he drew his "check" each month. The only folks who could get along with Hubert were the local sheriff's deputies. Two of them had caught him with the "worm workin'" at his liquor still on Wilkinson Creek up near Mann's Chapel. Of course he ran, or in his case, he moseyed. Of course John Henry Tripp captured him. Of course his whole week's load was somewhat at risk of being railroad pickaxed. Of course he got arrested. Of course he was taken to the Chatham County jail in Pittsboro. Of course Big Ed, the jailer, unwisely or by plan gave him his "one phone call." Of course he bonded out. Of course the eighty cases of bootleg, stump-hole, white ligtnin' were gone by the time the revenuers got to the site. Also "gone" were all the lead soldered boilers, vats, cookers, and copper tubings, including "the worm." I went up there a week or so later while checking for fish traps and rabbit gums along the Haw River near Chicken Bridge. I walked around the now barren site littered with punctured 55-gallon barrel lids, charred oakwood, broken brickbats from the brickyard over in Lee County, and crumpled cardboard boxes. I found a loaded Harrington and Richardson, Owl's Head, five-shot, revolver hanging on a nail on the backside of a River Birch tree. Still got it.

Shooting Doves in Self Defense

Back to opening day, 2020. There were so many doves flying before intermission, that a hunter could not keep a constant focus on one bird. Like Santa Claus: "They're everywhere! They're everywhere." I killed two doves that fell across a four-foot-deep irrigation ditch separating me from the larger, more heavily used, harvested and burned-over cornfield. In an effort to claim my birds before the twins did, I decided to "jump" that water filled ditch. Both sides of the ditch bank were sloped at about sixty degrees. From top to top, the ditch was about seven feet wide. I handed my unloaded shotgun to John, backed up, and ran four steps before the leap. I cleared about 9/10ths of that thing. Both feet slipped on the muddy slope into the water below, BUT THAT WAS OK. My hands had a firm grip on the golden-rod weeds and dog-fennels on the far bank. I scrambled myself up, not willing to admit that I did not do it that way on purpose. I wiped my hands on my Carhart work pants, adjusted my DU camouflage cap, and John threw me my shotgun. I loaded up and was back in business.

I looked over my shoulder, and saw John walking to the trucks. I wondered had he filled his limit. Also, another hunter, David Parker was walking toward John. Apparently, David had gotten that black silt/peat dirt inside the firing mechanism of his Franchi semi-automatic shotgun, and rendered it "out of service." David was now hunting with John's shotgun while John disassembled David's gun, cleaned it out, test fired it, and returned it to David. David and his whole hunting party were soon to fill their limits of birds, and John and I were equally close. David exclaimed to John, "In all my born days, I have never had to shoot doves in self-defense."

About that time, I heard Greg Dail's shotgun bark twice, and then a thud and splash. One of his sons, Brody had backed up, taken a run to jump the ditch, got hung up in the brambles on the leading edge, and cleared about 60% of the width. Undaunted, not missing a beat, he climbed up the bank and retrieved his Daddy's quarry. Later that morning I was at the truck when Brody ambled up there, muddy from the waist down, grinning from ear to ear. He told me the story, of which I was quite aware, and with which I could easily identify.

For the next twenty minutes, John, Nolan, and Jay, just up from Greg and his two sons, were busy waylaying doves on both sides of the ditch. I killed the next four for four, had twelve doves in my game bag, and killed two more that fell about seventy-five yards up the ditch. After I picked up 4 of John's, I had exceeded my bag limit. I went over to the ditch and threw his 4 across to Jay and Nolan who "Olympic Torch" ran 'em to John. It was time to "lay down the kill," and get an accurate count. I jumped the ditch, and two dead doves went unnoticed as they fell out of my game bag. The count came to 26, four shy of our limit. As I now slowly walked back to my field blind, I found the two doves along the ditch bank (28). While my back was turned, John's Remington 870 barked twice. As I hunkered down to blast another dove, John yelled, "Hey! Hold on. I think we have our limit."

Again, it was time for an accurate count. John, Nolan, Jay, and I placed the doves on the ground at Jay and Nolan's feet. The boys carefully placed the birds in piles of five, except for one that, upon re-examination only had six. Now we had thirty-one dead doves. When you get right down to it, we also had <u>four</u> North Carolina Wildlife Resources Commission Lifetime Sportsman licensed hunters. Whether we could have convinced the Wildlife Officer that one of the boys had killed that extra dove with his Granddaddy-made wooden shotgun was highly improbable. Jay said, "Let's count 'em again." Upon recount, we in fact had thirty dead birds. I put 15 in my game bag and John put 15 in his. We all hanker for the day when both grandsons will actually "hunt" with us and make their own memories.

We unloaded our shotguns, picked up our 5-gallon lunch-bucket seats, knocked the dirt off and out of our clothes and boots, and loaded into the 2006 Toyota 4-Runner. It was 7:55am: we had killed our limit in just under ninety minutes, and before 8am. John put the Toyota in 4-wheel-drive, U-turned, and drove us out of the field. As we drove the mile and a half back to the pavement, we noticed hunters with black Labrador Retrievers just entering the field. Many of the earlier arrivals were also leaving the fields, and the birds were still flying like I had never seen them at that time of the morning. One hunter dropped his camouflaged bucket, fired his 20 gauge, and his Lab streaked over, retrieved the dove, and they proceeded on down into the organized chaos.

Tim Powell, the hunt organizer who I think owns the farm, was sitting in his truck at the steel bridge over the roadside canal. We stopped and shared our good news with him. He was glad that we had had a good hunt, and that he was able to provide such a memorable outing. Nolan and Jay told him about their exploits, and thanked him, also. Evidently, they were not as tired as John and I were. They ran around, climbing on the huge bales of hay along the roadside, and throwing corncobs at each other. We asked Tim for the location of a country store where we could get some snacks. Tim offered us water, but John said he was hankering for his characteristic, "Honey Bun and a Coke." "Go out to the road, turn right, cross the Hyde County line, and Pungo General Store will be on your left at Indian Run Road. They have a gun store in there, too!" That settled it, we were headed that way.

Pungo County Store and the Memories

When we got to the store, all the "locals" were "ponded up" in the gravel parking lot, sharing "the truth; the whole truth; and nothing but the truth." Our two boys waded their way through the trucks, people, and bicycle racks, right up to the front door, and went in. Long guns were leaned up everywhere. A retired U. S. Navy S.E.A.L. who had served on President Trump's Security Detail in Afghanistan was the gun shop proprietor and spokesman. He was good at putting five pounds of "baloney" into a two-pound sack. We talked about the preponderance and lack thereof of firearms in today's world of civil and criminal unrest. He said that due to demand, that he could not keep handguns on the shelf, and he had not a single box of handgun ammunition for sale. On the wall was a flier for a Concealed Carry Handgun (**CCH**) certification class to be held the next week at Poccosin Lakes National Wildlife Refuge at Pungo Lake, but that he thought it was already booked solid.

I asked how often he found a Remington Nylon-66 .22 caliber, semi-automatic rifle for sale. He told me that they were what he called *"scace."* Hard to find, and even harder to buy: some going for $600 to $1000.00. It seems that they are the "guns of choice" for what he called "Preppers." Survivalist extremists who are "prepared" for the next holocaust, and or world/civil war. He admitted that he collects them, and only had five. John and I have given away five, and still have "a few."

Concealed Carry Handgun (CCH) Permit

One of the locals was overheard asking, "What are the pros and cons of applying for and getting a Concealed Carry Handgun (**CCH**) Permit?" Of course, I could not resist the open invitation:

"To me there are more pros than cons, but my philosophy could be deemed radical by liberal pacifists.

Pros:

> *1. For the safety of yourself and those you love, become familiar with a firearm and the associated responsibilities and legal aspects of gun ownership so that, in the event of an incident, you can make an informed decision based upon training instilled observation and techniques. Combine that with your trained ability to, "articulate.".*
>
> *2. In the event of an incident where a firearm is your best choice for surviving, as a **CCH** permitted citizen, you can more readily survive not only the incident, but the ensuing legal ramifications.*
>
> *3. As a **CCH** permitted citizen, you are more likely to feel comfortable being armed on more occasions, thereby following the Boy Scout motto: "Be prepared."*

4. Rather than illegally carrying a pistol for your protection and that of your wife's, <u>make it legal.</u>

5. If physically and mentally capable, why wouldn't you carry?

6. Get your **CCH** permit, carry a gun, and if you aren't comfortable in a crunch, "Gimme that thing! I'll shoot him!"

Cons:

A. Once you have become **CCH** permitted, you are then assumed to have had training that would preclude reckless operation of a handgun.

B. Once you have become **CCH** permitted, you are then assumed to have had training that would prevent you from unlawfully using a handgun.

C. The single biggest "risk" if you want to call it that, is that, if you are legally armed, and if you are suddenly immersed into a 'situation,' are you mentally prepared to shoot and kill someone: <u>are you of the 'warrior' mindset</u>?

D. There are specific requirements and procedures that you must follow, once **CCH** permitted, upon the approach of a law enforcement officer: 'I have a **CCH** permit and a pistol in my right pants pocket.' The officer already knows that you have the **CCH** designation as displayed upon his "in-car" computer. Lawfully, you must tell him right away, upon his approach.

Once you take the course, you are not <u>required</u> to go and become **CCH** permitted. It is a good day's training in either event!"

Jay and Nolan were by now on the other side of the creaky wooden floored store in the candy bar section. They had each found their snack and a drink. They wanted quarters to play the pinball machines, but there was just too much going on. John and my grandsons headed for the cash register. I quickly grabbed my snack and headed to the register. John and I had each independently gotten a Coke and a Honey Bun. The store had an iced down, open topped, galvanized metal cooler filled full of Salisbury originated (1917) Cheerwine soft drinks, Dr. Peppers, Sun Drops, and Sunkist Oranges "Big Orange Dranks" like Andy Griffith carried into "The Football Game" (little orange punkin – remember?) during tent revival. The 2' X 2' galvanized drink box was squeezed in between the North Carolina Education Lottery ticket display and six Bubble Gum machines. Those glass bottle drinks had compressed metal "caps" that were caught in a shallow box below the opener fastened to the front of the cooler. The cashier told me I could have them – about twenty of them. I plan to make "badges" out of them by inserting a cardboard disc inside the t-shirts of the Cub Scouts, and then forcing the cardboard through the t-shirt and into the smaller back of the bottle cap. Remember? The boys went back through the gun store, and outside to the well-worn picnic table where they were plopped down in the shade and eating their snacks. We went out, gathered them up, loaded back into the 4-Runner and headed north. For the next half hour, there was no U S Cellular tower available for a cell phone signal. NICE! Both boys wanted to call their mothers to tell them of their success. Couldn't happen.

As we bounced along uneven NC-99 and crossed back into Washington County along NC-45/99, the site of the "never-happened" U. S. Navy Jet Outlying Landing Field (OLF), we looked in the back and both boys were asleep.

We went through Plymouth, crossed the Roanoke, Cashie, Middle, and Chowan Rivers, and got back to Edenton. It was time for the children to all get together and try to wear out the newly installed "NINJA" rope course strung from the White Oak in the backyard to the Pin Oak on the property line. And try they did.

John and I got busy and popped the breasts out of thirty doves. Becky and Jenny heated up the peanut oil, battered the doves, cooked some mashed potatoes, field peas, and "mac and cheese," dipped some applesauce, and lunch was served. What a feast! Good fellowship, highlighted by plenty of Becky's dark and sweet iced tea.

"Life don't get no better!"

BONUS!

January 15, 2022

The Benevolence of an Eight-Year-Old:

Swan Hunting– 101

It was cold. 35 degrees at 5:30am, but as dawn began to break on the eastern horizon, the temperature dipped to below freezing, 31 degrees. <u>Hunters know this</u>. Tundra Swan season was winding down for another year, so an element of urgency became a factor to the 30+ hunters. We all began to realize that this might be our last chance to fill our 2021 – 2022, "luck of the draw," North Carolina Wildlife Resources Commission's Tundra Swan Permit. The Commission had only issued just under 5000 permits this year, and in order to be considered eligible for issuance, all hunters young and old, were required to be fully licensed with HIP Certification (Harvest Information Program), and a U S Fish and Wildlife Service, $25.00 Federal Duck Stamp.

On this cold morning, John McArthur and I had each independently awakened at about 4:30am, prior to our 5am, wake up buzzers. We loaded our gear and our children/grandchildren into our trucks and drove to RPR 1316, Greenhall Road in Chowan County, North Carolina, and the A. J. Smith and Sons, Inc. massive agricultural operation near the now inexistent community of Barber, N.C. We could barely make out the silhouettes of the towering grain bins and the heavy equipment as we pulled onto "the lot." This farming operation encompasses thousands of acres and mile long rows of soybeans, watermelons, corn, and again this year, jack-o-lantern pumpkins.

Radio station WRAL, 101.5 FM in Raleigh was reporting light snow with their roads already sheets of ice. Thank goodness (and geography), that stuff was predicted to stay west of the "I-95 Corridor." Here in Edenton, N. C. the thermometer read 35 degrees, but dropping just as it always does. The wind was not as brisk as it would be around lunchtime, as a huge winter storm had already dropped over a foot of snow in

Waynesville from which fellow hunter Tucker Smith had narrowly escaped.

Retired Wildlife Enforcement Captain Mark Rich dutifully assisted each hunter (parent or guardian) in completion of their "written permission" slip, ".. . to hunt Swan on land belonging to A. J. Smith & Sons, Inc. located on Greenhall Road in Edenton, NC on January 15, 2022. The hunter agrees to hold harmless A. J. Smith & Sons, Inc., and its owners, any liability associated or derived from Hunting activities."

Signed: *Jeffery A. Smith* Authorized signature for A. J. Smith & Sons, Inc.

A light breeze was already carrying a cacophony of Swan feeding calls over the one-mile distance from their encampment on a flooded pond in the center of this farm. As we air-activated and stuffed "GRABBER®" ten-hour hand-warmers into our shirt pockets over our hearts, our chest waders, and insulated gloves, we hurriedly pulled the wader straps over our heads. Next came ear-flapped hats, and lastly our "Quad-IV" hooded parkas. We grabbed our shotguns, our shells, and it was

TIME TO GO!

Traditionally, six hunters ride in the crew cabs with eight to ten hunters and dogs riding in the open, extended beds of the now cleaned out, 4-wheel-drive, white Chevrolet farm pick-up trucks. At 31 degrees, with a north wind and a 40 mile an hour speedometer reading, the NOAA charted chill factor made our two-mile jaunt feel like 12 degrees. As we passed George Holmes' 31-foot-tall Bamboo patch, a deer stood motionless, just across the canal. Through evolution or genetic mutation, and maybe due to COVID-19, for some reason most of the greenhorn hunters chose to drive themselves and their entourages in their own trucks, over to a field path beside Earl Davenport's plantation. This also was nearly within walking distance from our reserved, site ready "ditch."

On this morning, with the sun just cresting over the now defunct WBXB Country Music Radio tower, all eight trucks emptied their excited hunters, dogs, and equipment. Now we had about 29 hunters, each bundled up like the Pillsbury Dough Boy, and each without the foggiest idea of where we were headed. We gathered the seven children into our midst, and John McArthur, upon Fred Smith's signal, welcomed us all with encouragement and enthusiasm in his voice. He thanked and commended Doris' and Adrien Smith's sons, wives, and grandchildren for inviting us to hunt on their Turkey Neck Farm along Paradise Road. John explained that due to health and COVID-19 Pandemic safety concerns, Fred would be uncomfortable mixing and being his usual cordial self. Fred did however later, share with us his wisdom of what to expect from the Swans, how to "HIDE" in the ditch, and how to shoot the wounded Swan two or three times to prevent his suffering or escape. Also he told us that if a grounded Swan began escaping toward the woods, for the children to circle ahead, and, "Run that Swan back toward us."

Preaching

With the hunters now becoming restless, John McArthur kindly encouraged everyone to exercise extreme gun safety measures as taught in the National Rifle Association's "EDDIE EAGLE GUN SAFETY COURSE." "Rule number 1. Always point the gun in a safe direction." Next, John offered a prayer for safety to Our Lord and Savior, thanking Him for His gracious privilege of allowing us to venture into His beautiful world on such a magnificent morning, and sharing His rich bounty of game for our tables.

The Decoy Set

Kaitlyn Smith (Chowan County's wonderfully talented, 2022 NCCAT Teacher of the Year), Walker Rich and Paul Ward assisted Fred Smith as they had previously "set" forty of Dale Davis' JUMBO stackable decoys, half on each side of the ditch from which we would shoot. For maximum visibility, these white decoys were positioned broadside to the hundreds of roosting birds, almost a mile away. No longer, due to the wisened-up Swans, would white trash bag "wind-socks" on sticks achieve the desired deception. Some decoys characterized resting birds with their heads tucked beneath their wings. Some decoys appeared to be feeding on the Winter Wheat shoots. Only a few appeared to serve as sentries, their vigilant heads raised high. About half of the fifty-inch decoys were fitted with grey necks instead of the characteristic bright white. Grey necks indicate younger, maybe yearling birds and therefore, much better table fare.

The Ditch

Twenty-two hunters (Four Eagle Scouts), their seven children, and Uncle Kevin Briggs' Yellow Labrador Retriever, Sally approached and slid over the deactivated electric fence, and into the bottom of the three-foot deep and three-foot wide ditch. On the north end of the hundred-yard stretch of "our" ditch, frozen water was about ankle deep. John (Permitted), his eleven-year-old daughter Nakayla, his eight-year-old son Nolan (Permitted), and their seventy-two-year-old Granddaddy Mike (Permitted) walked <u>south</u> toward a slight rise along the ditch bank.

We walked southward, away from the main group of hunters for THREE REASONS:

We had the youngest hunters, and there were four folks in our group. Children, dogs, mud, Swans, and GUNS demand a lot of extra care and parental guidance. Safety is paramount.

The slightly elevated portion of the ditch was almost dry with no standing water, ice, or mud. Weeds were growing in clumps there with which to cover up the gun-shell bags, the cooler full of snacks, two zippered leather gun cases, TWO RESTLESS CHILDREN, two 12-gauge shotguns, and two "John Wayne 'lil Duke,".177 caliber BB guns. Those John Wayne, Lever Action BB Guns were great training tools, and were 2020 Christmas presents from Grandmother and Granddaddy McArthur. Though the lever action was difficult to operate, both Nakayla and Nolan quickly mastered the function. We are ALL still working on keeping those muzzles pointed in a safe direction.

Now for the real reason that we commandeered the south end of the ditch: Prevailing winds, however slight <u>always</u> dictate from which direction birds in flight will descend before pitching their wings and extending their feet to land, especially big birds like Tundra Swans. If the current wind is blowing from the North to the South, this is called a "North Wind." That is what we were experiencing on this cold January 15, 2022, morning.

So this is a test:

If several flocks of eight to ten Tundra Swans lift off from their roost site ¾ of a mile away, they spot fellow feeding Swans across the wide-open expanse, and they wing their way to join those decoys for breakfast,

FROM WHICH DIRECTION WILL THEY APPROACH THE DITCH FULL OF HUNTERS?

YOU GOT IT! THE SOUTH END! RIGHT WHERE WE WERE HUNTING!

CYGNUS COLUMBIANUS

Now it was time to get serious about harvesting a *cygnus columbianus*. Bwana Fred Smith had instructed 30 hunters and one dog to, "step over" the single strand of deactivated electric fence, and slide up against the frosty ditch bank. We would spend the next three hours, sprawled out in this location, and thankfully out of the building wind. The heavy frost gradually melted, and the wind dried out the grasses.

Before settling into the ditch with Nakayla, Nolan, and me, John made a hasty trip to his truck to retrieve his box of 3½ inch, Winchester, Super X, Mark V, Magnum, BB Steel shotshells. Ultimately, he would need only one of those shells to claim his permitted limit. He subscribed to the motto of The American Sniper, Silver Star and Bronze Star medalist, U.S. Navy SEAL Kris Kyle: "Slow is smooth, and smooth is fast." "One shot. One kill."

As we hunkered down, Nolan thought he could smell a country ham, egg, and cheese biscuit from Joe Boles' Chicken Kitchen about three miles away. He settled for several of Nakayla's famous Rice Krispy Treats. Looking across the center pivot irrigation system, John spotted two Bald Eagles as they soared toward their usual perch in the top of the dead Oak Tree over by the horse barn. When the Swans started flying, we never saw the Eagles again. As we waited for the first flight of Swans to come our way, Nakayla and Nolan sighted in their BB guns, shooting holes in the iced over side ditch. Nolan took a sharp stick and poked holes in his handwarmers, marveling at the "dirt" inside them. Evidently his hands were not as cold as ours.

Just after I said, "John, I don't have a lot of faith in those Swans coming over here," Nakayla heard Swan noise. As you know, Tundra Swans (Whistling Swans) are great big, almost twenty pounds, with over seven-foot wingspans. They appear to fly slowly, but that is a misconception fueled by their uncanny, in-flight prowess and their huge size. In fact, they appear to fly and glide effortlessly while approaching documented speeds of up to 100 miles per hour. They are strikingly bright white which makes them easy to spot, and appear much closer than they actually are. They appear to be easily "within range," when they can more easily be seventy yards out. On top of their size, their brilliance, and their *faux* slow-motion flight, they "holler" their approach from the time they lift off the water. From a distance, their high-pitched squeals imitate an ankle-biter Fice dog as he yips and yaps. Their shrill "whistle like" squeals are unmistakable. As they approach their landing site, sometimes within twenty yards of the hunters, they utter a guttural trill that indicates that, "All is not well." That is just before a 10-gauge, 1¾ ounce load of steel BBs cut them short.

THOSE JUMBOS DID THE TRICK

We looked southwest and saw a flock of nine swans eyeballing our spread of forty "JUMBO," fifty inch long, three-foot-high decoys. As the Swans slowly made their way, Nakayla and Nolan began "calling them." Their little voices became unnaturally loud and convincing. Those Swans bee-lined it for our location. John was to my left and Tucker Smith was to my right. I told John, "You shoot left, and I'll shoot right." At about 30 yards out, the Swans set their wings for landing, then flared.

We let the first three birds fly past us, right into Tucker Smith's kill zone. BOO-YOW! I peeled one out. Tucker killed his, and someone up the ditch killed theirs. John had graciously and successfully allowed his Daddy and others their glorious first opportunity. He had not fired at all.

The moment the gunfire stopped, Nakayla and Nolan sprang from the ditch like rockets. Within twenty seconds they had captured their Granddaddy's dying Swan. BUT WAIT, the Swan was not quite dead! Nakayla jumped back and yelled, "That Swan growled at me! GRRRRRR!" Nolan was undeterred. He pounced on the Swan's bloody head and the swan became lifeless.

Together Nakayla and Nolan skidded the twenty-pound bird across the frosty grass. They stopped just short of the ditch and positioned the carcass as if it were a decoy. As the left wing suddenly flapped and the grey neck lifted, Nolan made sure it was dead before he jumped back into the ditch.

There was a twenty-minute lull in the action. Nolan took my spent shotgun shell and stuck it out front on the third weed stalk after he broke the first two. He and Nakayla honed their marksmanship skills as they took turns aiming at and shooting the red, high-brass shell off its branch.

All of a sudden, right out in front of us appeared a flock of eleven low flying Swans. Uncharacteristically, they had not hollered their approach. We all, "GOT DOWN," like Fred Smith had told the group, and did the, "DON'T LOOK UP," as instructed. John deliberately raised his Remington 870 Wingmaster as the flock crossed our ditch. One shot! One kill! Nolan yelled, "You got him, Daddy." John's Swan had taken a "dirt nap" about twenty yards in front of us.

"I'LL SEND MY TWO DOGS AFTER HIM."

Down the way a little bit, somebody's wounded Swan was running for cover, straight out and away from us. John told the older gentleman, "I'll send my two dogs after him." Nakayla and Nolan again shot out of the ditch toward the loose Swan that was at least one-hundred yards away. As they closed in on the bird, Nakayla went high, and Nolan went low. The overtaken Swan turned back toward the hunters, and was quickly dispatched.

By now, more Swans had lifted into the air from their flooded roost. There were still hunters in the ditch waiting to fill their permits. As a small flock turned toward our spread, John yelled, "GET DOWN!" Nakayla and Nolan hit the dirt, motionless, face down. The flock of Swans turned back toward Paradise Road, and Nakayla told her Daddy, "These people need to learn how to be quiet and GET DOWN."

After another lull in the action, and Nakayla and Nolan had finished off the Rice Krispy Treats, many of the successful hunters loaded up and were hauled away in Phil Smith's "bus." Everybody was grinning as they held their tagged Swan, put them in the back of the truck, and climbed in.

John, Nakayla, and Nolan had stayed the course. I had walked "out" a little earlier, and had asked Nolan to attach the Wildlife Commission tag to my Swan. Nakayla, with her Daddy's help, had fired at a Swan, but missed, causing her ears to ring. It next became Nolan's turn to shoot that 870 Wingmaster. He nestled under his Daddy's right arm with the stock of the shotgun rising just above his own right shoulder. Nolan's right hand, trigger finger rested horizontally along the receiver, just above the gun's safety.

THE BENEVOLENCE OF AN EIGHT-YEAR-OLD

As expected, a new flight of about seven Swans came flying right down the ditch line. Nolan swung that 12-gauge barrel toward the lead Swan and pulled the trigger. He hit the Swan solidly in the body, causing it to fall. It unsuccessfully tried to gain altitude, and another youth hunter fired at the Swan, but missed. The trophy Swan fell to the ground, right in front of the other hunter. The parent of that hunter exclaimed, "You got him, son!"

Nolan and John were at a loss for what to do. They could go and claim the bird from the other hunter who was all aglow about, "Not having to go very far to get their bird." You know what Nolan and John did? They graciously allowed the other hunter to enjoy the fruits of their hunt. Nolan was a little disappointed, but John shared some wisdom about God's grace and other rational thoughts. They figured that, "There will be another day." (Gone With The Wind, 1936)

On this day, thirty hunters had gone into the ditch to hunt Tundra Swans. Three did not have NCWRC Permits, so they were unarmed. Twenty-six Tundra Swans were harvested. One permittee shot almost a box of shells, and could not make the connection.

After they left the field, Nolan called his Grandmother and me and told us of his good luck, and having successfully bagged his first Tundra Swan at age eight, Saturday morning, January 15, 2022. He shared that there would be another "Youth Hunt" later in the month, and that he and his Daddy would try their luck again. He invited us to come to dinner on Sunday: Tundra Swan and Black Cherry casserole. Fit for a king.

The never faltering, always faithful Benevolence of an 8-year-old.

Living Out Loud with Grace, Grit, and Gratitude

AMEN

Youth Tundra Swan Hunt - 2022

February 12, 2022

On February 12, 2022, Turkey Neck Farm along Paradise Road in Chowan County became the site of a truly magnificent event. Doris and Adrien Smith's children, grandchildren, and great-grandchildren hosted a special day of hunting, designed for and limited to a special group of hunters: youth under the age of 18, United States Military veterans, and active-duty soldiers. The North Carolina Wildlife Resources Commission once again displayed its compassion, understanding, and appreciation for those who deserve special attention.

A. J. Smith & Sons, Inc. is a huge farming operation from which many Chowan County residents earn a living producing food for America's tables. And they make it look easy! Their extensive holdings cover much of our county, and support all of the good things of which we can all be proud, here in the smallest County in the Great State of North Carolina. Corn, soybeans, and winter wheat are what attract thousands of Tundra Swans and other migratory waterfowl every year for the past three decades.

Since 1789, the emblem of our nation (beating out Benjamin Franklin's advocacy for the American Turkey), the indigenous American Bald Eagle nests along the edges of this storied farmland. Several of the magnificent birds can be seen way up high, soaring nearly out of sight, almost every day. Occasionally they are seen perched in the old Oak by the horse barn, and occasionally they can be seen devouring carrion in the fields and roadkill along Paradise Road.

Speaking of roadkill, along Wildcat Road, as I was driving my Toyota 4-Runner over to the hunt, an Eastern Screech Owl flew across and collided with my front right headlight. It collapsed into a small pile of horned feathers on the shoulder beside Tom Drew's house. I stopped, turned around, picked it up and continued on over to Paradise Road. Later in the day I suspended the beautiful creature on a wire, as if in flight. I will take it to Nolan and John's Cub Scout Pack 164 meeting on Monday evening. This will allow 16 Cub Scouts and their parents the opportunity to learn and appreciate the beauty of nature, and the chilling effects that a raptor, a bird of prey utilizes during their hunt for food, just like our skills are used while hunting Swans. Razor sharp talons, piercing eyes, spiked bill, and brushed feathers to allow silent flight while in pursuit of field mice, insects, and lizards.

On this glorious morning, the temperatures were a little less brutal than during the regular season hunt back on January 15, 2022. You might not think so, but there is a huge difference between 31 degrees and 41 degrees, especially when you factor in a cold front's 20 miles per hour, North wind. The traditional ride from the staging area to the hunting spot was not nearly as bone chilling cold, especially since the sun was just rising over Joseph Goodwin's Loblolly Pine woods to the East.

Fred Smith, Mark Rich, and Walker Rich (having just aged out of the "youth" category at age 18 on February 6), had loaded eighty-one bright white Tundra Swan and Snow Goose decoys into the back of Fred's truck for the ride to the field. Several of us rode in the back of the truck for the two-mile trip, and bailed out onto the still frozen sandy-loam soil beside "our ditch" for the next hour and a half. A good sign: large, webbed footprints imbedded in the frozen ditch bank. Also, there were right many white feathers hooked in the grass, blowing along the edge of the ditch.

Six adults: Fred Smith, Mark Rich, Steve Evans, Sam Evans, John McArthur, and Mike McArthur marveled at the energy of one 6-year-old – Ty Evans; one 8-year-old – Nolan McArthur; and one 11-year- old – Nakayla McArthur. They ran. They jumped the ditch. They threw dirt clods. They rolled in the grass. They pushed, they pulled, and they dragged those 81 decoys across the ditch and two fields to where THEY thought they should be "set." We adults were proud to let them make those decisions with very few modifications. And then came the arduous task of attaching heads with long necks to each of the shell decoys. That took a little more time, but it was fun to watch.

The Swans had not yet left their flooded pond about a mile away. They were becoming noisy, and could be seen lifting up and then settling back into their family groups. Swans, in the early morning, will not leave the roost until the frost has melted off the wheat. Apparently, they don't like the icy shoots, or the slippery landings. No longer, now in 2022, could we see "neck bands" having been attached to the Swans' necks by the U. S. Fish and Wildlife Service. John killed a neck banded with leg banded also, Tundra Swan when he was about 10 years old hunting with Tom Miller over on Tyson Farms Hog Operation in Washington County. The shot he made was about 70 yards out in the pouring down rain. He was shooting 2¾ inch steel, Winchester, Super-X, Mark V, Magnum T-shot out of his semi-automatic, Winchester 12 gauge that I had sawed off the stock to fit him. At the end of the hunt we all waded into the swift flowing canal and washed out our shotguns and boots to remove the black silt mud.

On this morning, Nolan was shooting his Daddy's Remington, 870 Wingmaster 12-gauge, 3½ inch, shotgun with Winchester, Super-X, Mark V, Magnum #2 steel shot. And it worked!

About 7:00am, after all 81 shell decoys were "set," and after huddling up to get "our plan" together, we were all filled with excitement and anticipation. Hunt master Fred asked John to open the hunt with a prayer. John prayerfully thanked God for the opportunity to come into His beautiful world on such a spectacular morning. He thanked the Smith family for allowing our invasion of their rich and bountiful resource. He prayed for extreme safety and good luck during the morning's hunt. He thanked God for friends and family.

Little did any of us know that there was a youth duck hunt underway at Lake Mattamuskeet, just a few miles south from our hunt. Their waterfowl outing would end in the catastrophic loss of eight lives during their flight home from Engelhard to Sealevel, Cedar Island, Atlantic, and Harker's Island, North Carolina. Four teenaged duck hunters, two of their fathers, the pilot/Hunting Guide, and his girlfriend crashed their single engine Pilatus PC-12, into the turbulent, 55-foot-deep waters off Drum Inlet in Carteret County, just east from the Ferry Dock toward Portsmouth Island. Sadly these "down-easters" were all from the small commercial fishing communities within six miles of the crash site.

I have chosen to list these victims to honor their passion for life and give testament to the tight-knit communities from which they hailed.

Jonathan Kole McInnis, (15) Sealevel

Michael Daily Shepard, (15) Atlantic

Noah Lee Styron, (15) Cedar Island

Jacob Nolan Taylor, (16) Atlantic

Stephanie Ann McInnis Sealevel

Douglas Hunter Parks Sealevel

Ernest Durwood Rawls, Pilot, Greenville

Jeffrey Worthington Rawls Greenville

Kendra Lewis of the Atlantic community organized a prayer vigil in the parking lot of a shuttered Red & White Grocery store, and said, "We're just an old fishing community. We're used to banding together and taking care of one another." Those boys, "are the definition of 'Down East' people. They hunted. They loved each other. They were just a part of the community. We're all just a big family." Now go tell that!

The United States Coast Guard, Carteret County law enforcement, Carteret County Emergency Services, N C Marine Fisheries, N C Wildlife, Down East Volunteer Fire and Rescue, Morehead City Fire Department, United States Marine Corps Air Station Cherry Point, five other agencies, and of course the locals searched a 2014 square mile area of Core Sound and Atlantic Ocean for the recovery of their friends and neighbors. Three days later, on Tuesday, when the fuselage was located containing seven of the eight passengers (the eight passenger had been recovered on Monday), much of the recovery effort was relegated to the "locals." As you well know, there will be pleasure boaters, commercial fishermen, sport fishermen, dive teams, and family members from all over eastern United States searching those waters and pausing to remember, for years to come. So sad!

Here in Chowan County, nine of us spread out along the ditch, while we waited for Mark Rich to give us last minute instructions. He told us that the wind was from the Southeast, and that the Swans would most likely swing around behind us, approaching the decoys from over toward the timberline. He was right. Here they came. First there were about six who wanted badly to land in the decoys but flared to return to the safety of their roost. These birds were about ten yards up in the air, and every single one of the hunters courteously "waited" for one of the other hunters to shoot first. This was truly a "gentleman's hunt." And the Swans benefitted from the hunters' kindnesses.

Needless to say, the next round of incoming birds was met with much more intensity, in that the very first Swan, the LEAD Swan "did not survive the encounter," to quote Steven Seagal. As the small flock of four Swans crossed just to Nolan's left, he pulled up that 870, swung to his right, and gave the lead bird a "dirt nap," right out in front of us. Graveyard dead, I mean! The first Swan of the day. He hit the Swan with the first shot and turned him a flip with the second shot. No need to chase that bird down. Just go prop him up to look like a decoy!

Now we were becoming besieged with Swans. They were coming from behind us. They were coming straight in at us. Somehow, they were getting past us. As we kept our heads down, not "looking up," we watched what appeared to be a swarm of Swans, circling above us. We could see their reflections in the water in the bottom of the ditch. Nakayla was sprawled stock-still on the leading ditch bank and her camouflage outfit appeared to have been poured out of a pitcher. She was the epitome of "motionless." The Swans' extremely powerful wings were pushing forced air maybe 15 feet above our heads with nearly deafening, "whoosh, whoosh, whoosh, whoosh," noises. This is a phenomenon that defies written description. You truly would have had to have been there to fully understand and appreciate this incredibly unbelievable marvel of powerful winged flight.

And then, down the ditch, the next shot rang out from that .410 shotgun that Ty Evans was shooting with close supervision from Sam, his Daddy and Steve, his Granddaddy. That Swan rolled over in the air, and glided away from us. When he hit the ground, he was running. But he was no match for Ty, Nolan, or Nakayla. That little six-year-old boy was outdone by the size of his bird's seven-foot wingspan which had been displayed upon the approach of the hunters. However, when three children pounced on him, the Swan succumbed and was brought back to the ditch, propped up, and the hunters returned to the ditch for the third hunter to bag his Swan.

Our United States Air Force Veteran / waterfowl hunting guide Mark Rich had patiently watched the young sportsmen claim their trophies. Now it was his turn. He waited for a good clean shot, and took it. The bird flinched, hit second gear, and flew straight away. Feathers from the injured bird drifted slowly in the breeze toward the ground. Mark's comment: "Well, those two Bald Eagles have to eat, too!"

There was absolutely no break in the action. The next flock of Swans crossed low, right over Nolan and John and Nakayla, and one broke loose. It entered into Mark's line of sight, and met its demise, we all thought. Mark's Swan hit the ground running, and I do mean running. About that time, Ty's Swan took off running, too. Now we had two of the three Swans on the lam. Ty's Swan was easily captured, while Mark's ran on to cross the ditch into the next "cut." And it was at least 200 yards ahead of three booted children, in "hot pursuit.". Mark, with his pocket technology, called his son Walker who, with binoculars on us, was laughing with Fred up at the barn.

Walker carefully drove out into the melee, snagged his Daddy's Swan, and brought him to us about 20 minutes later. Just enough time for us to have begun to gather up the decoys. Nolan mentioned that he needed "an energy boost from the Chicken Kitchen."

Underneath individual shell, stackable decoys, each of the three children scrunched-up and hid, undetectable by approaching Swans. In years past, Swans have landed amongst the decoys, only to be startled when the children emerged, more afraid of the Swan than the Swan was of them.

I picked up some Swan wing feathers and Nolan's spent 3½ inch Winchester shotshell and will mount them with his name and date onto a piece of Chowan River driftwood. Small things can mean a lot to an old man, and I qualify.

81 decoys were quickly stacked and bagged for next year's hunt. This year, not having been used excessively or during a rainy hunt, they would not need to be individually washed as has been the case previously. That black ditch mud gets into every nook and cranny of all things with

crevices: guns, boots, bags, decoys, ears, gloves, and more. The children dutifully raced around collecting the heads of the decoys, while the adults stacked the montage of size-specific bodies. Local crop-duster Carey Parrish flew his specialized yellow plane over us at about 500 feet up, and rocked his wings as we waved at our pilot friend. Fred said that three days earlier, Carey had sowed liquid fertilizer onto the field next to ours, and the Swans had not even budged. We loaded the decoys into Fred's truck, and Sam, Mark, and I rode with Walker out of the field, and back to the staging area up by Earl Davenport's homestead. Walker's truck, with the children and their Swans was following us, when lo and behold, Ty's Swan decided that he had had all that bumpy truck ride he could stand. Over the side rail he jumped and again ran about 50 yards before the children corralled him again.

While sorting out our equipment for the ride home, Fred thanked us for having made his day and his hunt so successful, in many ways. Fred has always enjoyed providing the venue for young kids to enjoy the thrill of the hunt and build confidence hunting with their parents. Tundra Swan hunting is almost like the last frontier of waterfowl hunting. The conundrums and logistics of a migratory waterfowl hunt are things that must be learned through experience, and that experience must be adaptable to the then present, "tides of change." Just like in today's world. What, if anything, stays the same for any period of time? These young hunters face a multitude of challenges, and a complex life of adjusting their approaches as life throws them curve balls. Think pandemic, think war, think recession, think aging, think immigration, think prejudices, think climate change, think fuel, think food insecurities. The list is endless.

These renditions of taking to the field to harvest game for the table and looking out for your fellow man have illustrated just a small snapshot of what our youth are facing and will face in the future!

LET'S HELP THEM EVERY CHANCE WE GET!

About the Author

Michael John McArthur, at age 72 is the oldest of three children. As such, his Merchant Marine father would supplement the family's income by, "going to sea," and leaving Mike with the ominous admonition, "While I am gone, you are the man of the house. Take good care of your mother and brother and sister." Mike has been taking care of his mothers, brothers, and sisters ever since!

Having lived, learned, loved, and been loved all his life, he has developed a keen sense for knowing right from wrong, and doing the right thing, for the right reason, the first time: as painful as it occasionally turned out to be.

Through his years growing up in Wilson, North Carolina and while working at his family business, The Tobacco Trail Motel, and by helping the tourist customers, he honed his invaluable "People Skills." As an after-school and weekend table waiter at Parker's Barbecue on US-301, he earned a decent income and supplemented his family's income. He paid $250 for a 1955 Pontiac Star Chief which spawned a driving force for his diverse career path.

At North Carolina State University he learned that with his new-found freedom came a boatload of responsibility. To survive during this time period, he worked four different part time construction jobs by day, and shot high-dollar pool at night. He played poker with his country cronies from Johnston County when they weren't running moonshine for a famous bootlegger. He even managed to attend Psychology, Ecology, and Forestry classes on the brickyard. In an English 202 – Journalism class he found a calling. He wrote stories about his Boy Scout Troop 222, and hunting trips for Canada Geese on Dr. Stotesbury's farm beside Lake Mattamuskeet in Hyde County. The first and only A+ he ever got!

He became a "Game Warden" during his second Junior year and moved to Pittsboro in Chatham County where he first encountered politics: good politics, bad politics, and worse politics. He transferred into the North Carolina State Highway Patrol where he and Becky built a home and raised their family in Chowan County, Edenton. Jenny and John grew into successful and productive adults with families of their own. Mike's final five years as a Trooper were devoted to fine-tuning over twelve hundred, knuckleheaded "Road Warriors," and transforming over two-hundred SHP Cadets into high performing Troopers at the North Carolina State Highway Patrol Training Academy in Garner.

After surviving way too many car wrecks, a nearly fatal gunfight with two armed thugs, and then a disastrous political gunfight with the Colonel on the Highway Patrol, Mike persevered and retired as a Master Trooper.

He spent the next five celebrated years working throughout Chowan County assisting his friends as a licensed North Carolina Farm Bureau Insurance Agent with his mentor and good friend, Jimmy Stallings. In 1994, local attorneys encouraged Mike to file for election, and to fulfill the unexpired term of the sitting Clerk of Superior Court. He won election and has since served twenty-eight years as the elected Clerk of Superior Court for Chowan County and the State of North Carolina.

Throughout his fifty plus years as a public servant and as a gun totin' law enforcement officer, he has reached out, and been reached out to. Through heavy involvement in his family life, his church life, and his civic life he has strived to, "BE PREPARED" as his Eagle Scout motto, "Press on to the greater achievements of the future," as an Optimist, and, "Make his community a better place in which to live," as a Ruritan.

He and his family have worked to live a good clean life and have been richly blessed.

Michael J. McArthur

Index and Page References

LEGEND: letter at end of page numbers

E = Edenton related

R = Raleigh related

W = Wilson related

CSO = Chowan Sheriff related

EPD = Edenton Police related

SBI = State Bureau of Investigation related

SHP = State Highway Patrol related

WRC = Wildlife Resources Commission related

Adams, Bill   57, 85, 86 E

Adams, Bozie   185 E

Alexander, Chuck   185 E

Alexander, Richard   248 E

Allen, Robert, Margie   148, 166, 189, 218, 249 SHP

Amburn, Bud   318 E

Anderson, Hamp   57, 86 W

Anderson, Dr. Kent   76 W

Apple, Capt. Bill   230 SHP

Ashley, Murray   317 E

Atlantic Beach   46, 47, 48 W

Atwater, Sergeant John   148, 362 SHP

Aurora, N C   68 – 73 W

Aylesworth, Jim   253 E

Babb, Inspector Harold   229 E

Babb, Major Jeff   229 SHP

Bailey, Judge "Pou"   268 E

Baker, Trey   347 R

Barefoot, Colonel Bob   183 SHP

Barefoot, E. B. and Elizabeth   38 SHP

Barnes, Warren, Bill, Anne   45 – 78 W

Basnight, Senator Marc   116, 117 E

Bass, Don   366 E

Bass, Mark   291, 292 E

Bateman, Ray   266 E

Bill's Drive In   29, 66, 91, 206-208, 293 W

Blackman, Colonel Coy   269 SHP

Blakemore, Dr. William   328 E

Blount's Mutual Drugs   246 E

Bond, Buck Marina   304, 311, 320 E

Bond, H. L.   111, 314 – 332 E

Boswell's Restaurant   228, 266 E

Boyd, Flight Sergeant Chuck   175 SHP

Boykin, Dennis   57 W

Brakefield, Mike   201 R

Brannon, Joan UNC-SOG   349 E

Briggs, Sergeant Kevin   381 SHP

Britton, Charles   355 E

Britton, Junius   317 E

Britton, Paul   345 E

Britton, Terri Lynn Nixon's Welding   329 E

Brooks, Pam   87 W

Brothers, Louis   189 E

Broughton, Sheriff Julian "Little Man"   110, 133, 134, 180, 232, 254 – 255, 263, 274, 275, 278 E

Browder, Preacher Ashby   148 E

Browning, Raymond   36 W

Bunch, Sergeant Buddy   230 CSO

Bunch, Harold Lloyd   127, 134 E

Bunch, Wilbur Ray – Keith – Teresa   329 E

Burke Bros. Hdwe.   215 R

Burns, Hal   345 E

Burroughs, Gil   326 E

Butler, Gerald   52, 59 W

Bynum, Donkey Ray   12, 42, 43, 44 W

Byrum, Bertram   317 E

Byrum, Deputy Joseph   110, 246 CSO

Byrum, Fahey, Butch, Joey, Joe Carroll   121 E

Cagle, Sergeant Mark WRC

Cale, Effie   319 E

Camp Meeting   65 W

Campbell, Ronnie "Pee Wee"   325 E

Casino @ Nags Head   60, 61 W

Chambers, Felix   166, 317, 330 E

Champion Doug   52, 54, 57, 58, 66, 85, 271 W

Chappell, Ben & Anita   228 SHP

Chappell, Benjamin Franklin   110, 189, 217 – 238   255 SHP

Cherry, Sheila   246 E

Chesson, Wes   322 E

Chicken Kitchen   382 E

Chowan Herald   318 E

Clark, Captain Bobby   97, 102, 103, 171 SHP

Claus, Santa   371 E

Cole, Deems   356 E

Connor, Attorney Pinky   29, 73 W

Cooke, Dorothy, George   333 E

Cooper, Alice   277 E

Cowan, Lenward 261 SHP

Cowand, "Duck"   291 E

Cox, Pete   107, 180 SHP

Creighton, Charlie   345, 346 E

Cummings, Tony   190 SBI

Dail, Broughton & Harriet   232, 275 E

Dail, Greg & Brody   368 E

Dail, Sergeant D. G.   263 SHP

Daniel, Coy   52 W

Davenport, Earl   392 E

Davis, Jerry "Wee Wink"   60, 61, 270 W

Davis, Tommy   38, 41 W

Deans, Sergeant J. R.   192, 193, 223, 224, 261 SHP

DeVine, Dr. Leibert E.   155, 257 E

Dick's Hot Dog Stand   74, 86 W

Dixon, C. T.   293 E

Doughtie, Sheriff Doug   131 DARE

Dowdy, Dave 62, 326 WRC

Drennan, Jim UNC-SOG 349 R

DRUM INLET PLANE CRASH VICTIMS 389 CARTERET

Duvall, C. C. 131 DARE

Edmiston, Atty. Gen. Rufus 194, 202 E

Eley, Sid 133 E

Elks, Captain Ray 229, 284 WRC

Elliott, Dispatcher Bill 260 EPD

Ellis, Attorney Hood & Ann 323 E

El Ramey, Ralph, Gwen, Terri 95 W

Embers Club 49, 50, 51 E

Etheridge, Major Bill 146 SHP

Evans, Chris & Lisa 276 E

Evans, Deputy Melvin 154 CSO

Evans, Steve, Sam, Ty 387, 390, 391 E

Fajer, Delois 185 E

Farmer, Gary 265 E

Farmer, Sergeant Jim 159, 263 SHP

Fike, Ralph L. High School Forward, 6, 21, 23, 36, 39, 45, 53, 54, 95, 143 W

Flanagan, Pat 235 E

Fleming, Lou, Wray 55 W

Flowers, Becky 271 W

Flowers, Percy 22, 57, 205, 206 W

Forehand, Pruden 317 E

Formo, Arnold 94 W

Furlough, Dalton 363 E

Gardner, Bill 229 E

George, Nick 166 E

Gilchrist, Captain Carl 106, 180, 182, 193 SHP

Gilchrist, Colonel Mike 182, 183 SHP

Gillette, Bert 86 W

Goard, Tommy 57, 68, 85, 86, 200 W

"Goat Man" Ches McCartney 14, 26, 27, 28 W

Godfrey, Lin 121 – 124 SHP

Godley, Bill 192, 194, 222, 256 SBI

Goliath 292 E

Goodwin, Captain Wallace 229, 318 E

Goodwin, Carl Cason 311, 312 E

Goodwin, David "Bald Eagle" 325 E

Goodwin, Joseph 300, 387 E

Goodwin, Representative Ed 286 E

Goodwin, Wayne 253 E

Graves, John 57 W

Gravning, Preacher Chris 346 E

Greene, Sergeant Charlie 362 SHP

Gregory, Marsha 293 E

Griffith, Andy, Opie 276, 343, 376 E

Haigler, Mary Scott Perry 139 E

Hammond, Carol Ann 45 W

Hardison's Barbecue 301 E

Harper, Josephine & L.J. 336, 342 E

Harrison, Donnie 170 SHP

Hart, Mary 277 E

Hawkins, Hawkshaw 4 W

Hayes, Sergeant Ray 46, 86, 87 W

Held, Jack 327 E

Hendrix, Mac 250 E

Hendrix, Robert 104, 106, 107, 187, 188, 229, 233, 239 – 262, 280, 281 E

396

Hendrix, Robert, Marvis, Robin, Jill   244, 245, 252, 246 E

Hester, Bob   46, 57, 76, 77 W

Hester, Dr. Mac   76 W

Hibbard, Warren   229 E

Highsmith, Lew   45, 52, 57, 59, 86W

Holley Brothers   247 E

Hollowell, Officer John   323 WRC

Holmes, George   379 E

Horner, Judge Fentress   232 E

Hughes, Tony   327 E

Hunter, Jimmy & Helen   278 E

Hunter, Jimmy "Catfish"   221 E

Inglis, Frances   322 E

Jackson, Richard   295, 320 E

Janet Hollowell   246 E

Jeffries, Lieutenant Tommy   97, 102, 104, 161, 169, 178, 218, 285, 367 SHP

Jenkins, Colonel John T.   100 SHP

Johnson, Gil   317 E

Jones, Alec   180, 263, 317 SHP

Jones, Colonel E. W.   189, 219 SHP

Jones, Sonny   260 EPD

Jones, Sup. "Cuckleberry"   161, 272, 369 WRC

Jordan, Calhoun   130, 131 E

Jordan, Lucy   167 E

Jordan, Milton   122, 230, 243, 250 E

Kemp, Delores   181 SHP

Kirby, Leslie   322 E

KKK   10, 114, 199 W

Knox, Jeff   187, 260 EPD

Lane, Carl   159 E

Lane, Donnie   220 SHP

Lane, Dr. Robert Earl   279 E

Lane, Sergeant "Pinky"   180, 223 SHP

Lane, Walter   225 E

Layden, Henry   229 E

Layden's Store   276 E

Layton, Kermit   322 E

Leary, Tommy & Jean   249 E

Lee, Harold "Polecat"   124 SHP

Lillibridge, Dottie 235E

Liner, Harry   57 W

Long, Sergeant Billy   272 SHP

Lowe, Dick   328 E

Lowe, Meredith   328 E

Madrey, Patty   162, 163 E

Marines   47, 48, 49 W

Martin, Bill   124, 125 SHP

Maurice's Grill   Red Walston & Sue   11, 12, 72 W

McArthur, Nathan Jenny, Jay, Leela   1, 195, 248, 266, 334, 335, 336-342, 343-346, 365-377 E

McArthur, Becky   Dedication, 1, 189, 195, 205, 242, 243, 248, 289, 313, 319, 324, 332, 333, 343-346, 376, 385, 393, Back Cover E

McArthur, John, Nastacia, Nakayla, Nolan   1, 266, 332, 339, 248, 282-303, 343-346,   365-377 E

McArthur, Kathy & Waldo Floyd   1, 27, 39, 87, 143, 355 W

McArthur, Mac, Betty   13, 18, 19, 20, 21, 78, 80, 88 W

McArthur, Pat – Debbie   1, 39, 76, 878, 143, 210 W

McCall, Mac   52, 59 W

397

McCloud, Sergeant Billy Ray   124 SHP

McLaughlin, James   201 R

Meeks, Leonard   161 SHP

Mims, Charlie   144, 145, 267 SHP

Minton, Sergeant Jim   104, 105, 108 SHP

Mitchell, Trooper Pat   153 SHP

Moore, Trooper Chris   302 SHP

Morris Family   58, 59, 60, 85 E

Mullen, Dusty, Westley   299 E

Mullen, Jeff   367 E

Mullen, Jeff, Dusty   145 E

Murray, Don - Barbecue   8 W

Newberry, Sergeant Y Z   72, 106, 107, 123, 162, 180, 220, 223, 236, 275 SHP

Nicholls, Jon & Nancy   327 E

Nixon, Grant, Keith   329 E

Nixon, Jimmy   291, 292 E

Nixon, Josephine   188 E

Nixon, Murray, Leon, Ricky, Louis, Lynda, Jimmy   325 E

Noneman, Walter   288 E

Oakes, Cliven   25 W

Ober, David   113, 127 E

Onley, Lieutenant Aubrey   132, 134 E

Outlaw, Ralph   229 E

Overton, J. C. Chief   369 WRC

Overton, Mike   69 WRC

Owens, J. E.   68 - 75 W

Owens, Pete   279 E

Parker, David   371 E

Parker, Judge Dick   252 E

Parker, Loretta Forward,   55 W

Parker, Martin   248 E

Parker's Barbecue Restaurant   1, 2, 11, 17, 29, 31, 32, 38-44, 85, 212, 269 W

Parks, Fire Chief Luther   188, 229, 317 E

Parks, Jerry   358 E

Parrish, Carey   392 E

Parrish, Chief J. D.   229 EPD

Pate, Elaine   60 W

Patterson, Pat   201 R

Patton, Major Fred   102, 107 SHP

Peachey, Sergeant Willis   360, 361 SHP

Peal, Jimmy, David   158, 159 E

Peal, Walter, Molly, Lori, Regina, Crystal   155 - 160 E

Pearce, Gay   250 SHP

Peebles, Mearpelene   185 E

Peeping Tom   79 - 94 W

Perry, Carlton & Alice   159, 186, 224, 234, 253, 256, 261, 283, 284 E

Perry, Lenny   227 E

Perry, Sheriff Glenn   266 CSO

Perry, Sup. Thurman   273 SHP

Perry, Teeny Boy's Store   154 E

Peterson, "Pete"   51, 132, 170, 322 SHP

Phillips, John   229 E

Plummer, Ken   57, 59, 66 W

Potts, Sergeant Ray   142, 190, 329 SHP

Powell, Tim   297, 298, 366, 373 E

Price, Lieutenant B. G. 104 - 108 SHP

Pridgen, Sheriff Robin 11, 21, 79, 84, 88, 92, 207 W

Princess Anne 115 - 118 E

Pruden, Dossey V, VI 312 - 314 E

Rand, Senator Tony 208 R

Ransome, Dwight 131, 132, 133, 135 SBI

Redd, Trooper Brenda 183 SHP

Rich, Captain Mark 379, 387, 390, 391 WRC

Rich, Walker 387 E

Riddick, Harold 166, 219 SHP

Roberson, Bob 229 E

Roberts, Trooper Reid 331 SHP

Rogers, Dennis 201 R

Rogerson, Chuck 131, 331 SHP

Rowe, Sergeant John 100, 229, 261 SHP

Ruffin, Patty 86 E

Sawyer, David (Amos) 322 E

Sawyer, Robert 166 E

Schuller, Christian Evangelist Robert 276 E

Scott, William Earl 220 SHP

Self Kicking Machine 47 W

Shepard, Tom 189 E

Shingleton, Aubrey 58 W

Siles, Sergeant Joel 110, 112, 113, 110 - 121, 164 SHP

Slade, Dr. James 317 E

Small, Sergeant Shack 122 SHP

Smith, A. J. & Doris 378, 386 E

Smith, A.J. Farms 343 E

Smith, Adrian 295 E

Smith, Carroll 140, 158 E

Smith, Earl 223 E

Smith, Fred 380, 382, 384, 388 E

Smith, Gary 291, 292 E

Smith, Jeffery 379 E

Smith, Kaitlyn, 380 E

Smith, Phil 384 E

Smith, Tucker 379, 383 E

Spruill, Sergeant Billy, Peggy, Amy, Melanie 185-194, 246 EPD

Stallings, Lieutenant Ronnie 131 HERTRORD

Stallings, Mayor Jimmy 220, 221, 228, 270, 283, 365 E

Stallings, Sergeant Ricky 128, 129, 131 SHP

Stamper, Arthur 52 W

Stephens Hardware 34 W

Stillman, J. C. 193 E

Stotesbury, Dr. Goose Lodge 75, 78 E

Stutts, Glenn 21 W

Tarkington, Raymond 229 E

Taylor, Burrus 166, 280 SHP

Taylor, Ronnie, Donnie 28 W

Taylor, Sergeant John 361 SHP

Taylor, Steve 291, 322 E

Teague, Keith 231 E

Tee, Ricky 93 W

Thomas, Bob & Mary Ann 323 E

Thomas, Mike 229 E

Thomas, Sgt. John 220, 223 SHP

Thompson, Flight Lieutenant Ken 237 SHP

Tilley, Honorable Todd 232, 278 E

Tobacco Trail Motel 1, 16, 17, 80, 83, 212 W

Tolson, Tommy 264 SHP

Toppin, Sheriff Troy 111, 229, 233, 249, 262 CSO

Tripp, John Henry 370 WRC

Twine, Sergeant Donnie 63 DARE

Tynch, Captain Murray, Murray, Milton 248 E

Tynch, Murray 164 E

Tysor, Charles 228 E

U. S. F. & W. 344, 346 E

Underkofler, Bill 317 E

Underwood, Gil 224, 253, 267 E

Upright, Sergeant Walter 279 SHP

Vaughan, Harvey 76 W

Vaughan, Bill 75, 76 W

Vick Construction, Tommy, Billy, Jimmy 196, 203 R

Waff, Paul 262 E

Walls, Elmo 73, 293 WRC

Walston, Elsie, Jessie, Rudolph, Bernard 28, 29, 32, 33, 35, 41, 68 W

Walston, Rudolph 365 W

Ward, Ed 225 E

Waterman's Restaurant 222 E

Watts, Judge Thomas 135 E

Weathersbee, Captain Robert 360 SHP

Westover General Store 313, 343, 345, 346, Back Cover E

White, "Cowboy" 266, 325 E

White, "Jiggs" 278 E

White, Bobby 54 W

White, Tim 265 E

Whiteman's Store 138 E

Whitley, Trooper Butch 164, 272 SHP

Wiggins Mill 2, 28, 29, 83 W

Wiggins, Emmett 228, 326 E

Wildlife Magazine 288, 289, 290 R

Williams, Chief Harvey 132, 187, 189 EPD

Williams, Coach Roy 148 R

Williams, Donald 38 W

Williams, Steve 85, 86 W

Williams, Virgil 190 ALE

Williamson, Jimmy, Ronnie, Donnie, 8, 9, 13, 28, 31-33, 50 W

Wilson Hardware 8, 73 W

Wilson, Earl "Pink Pearl" 86 W

"Wolfman" Jack 221, 263, 274, 275 E

Woodard, Attorney David, Romaine 45, 55, 57, 85, 86 W

www.ingramcontent.com/pod-product-compliance
Lightning Source LLC
LaVergne TN
LVHW081536070526
838199LV00056B/3686